HOW TO SUCCEED IN
HOLLYWOOD

HOW TO SUCCEED IN
HOLLYWOOD
WITHOUT LOSING YOUR SOUL

TED BAEHR

WND Books

HOW TO SUCCEED IN HOLLYWOOD

Copyright © 2011 by Ted Baehr

Jacket design by Mark Karis. Interior design by Neuwirth & Associates, Inc.

WND Books are available at special discounts for bulk purchases. WND Books, Inc. also publishes books in electronic formats. For more information call (541-474-1776) or visit www.wndbooks.com.

ISBN: 978-1-936488-27-8

Library of Congress information available.

Printed in the United States of America
10 9 8 7 6 5 4 3 2

With love and great thanksgiving, this book is dedicated to:

Jesus Christ, my Lord and Savior,
My wonderful wife, Lili, and our faithful children, Peirce, Jim,
Robby, and Evy.

Also, I want to thank:

Sandra Bell, Joseph Farah, Tom Snyder, and all our contributors,
directors, supporters, and friends.

Do your best to present yourself to God as one approved, a workman who does not need to be ashamed and who correctly handles the word of truth.

—2 Timothy 2:1 NIV

Father in Heaven,

Thank you for giving us good news to proclaim—the news of new life available to each of us through your son, Jesus the Christ. Thank you for your Holy Spirit, our Teacher. Bless all who read this book. Grant us, as your people, the ability to communicate your truth more effectively to the world through all the media. Help us to reveal your Word to those in need. Help us to lift up your Holy Name, Jesus, through the power of your Holy Spirit.

Amen.

CONTENTS

Stories and Parables

Jesus told the crowds all these things in parables, and He would not speak anything to them without a parable, so that what was spoken through the prophet might be fulfilled:

> I will open My mouth in parables; I will declare things kept secret from the foundation of the world.
>
> —Matthew 13:34–35

One day more than 70 years ago, two literary giants in England stood talking about language, stories, and religion. In the middle of the conversation, the taller gentleman blurted to his slightly balding companion, "Here's my point: Just as a word is an invention about an object or an idea, so a story can be an invention about Truth."

"I've loved stories since I was a boy," the other man admitted. "Especially stories about heroism and sacrifice, death and resurrection. . . . But, when it comes to Christianity . . . well, that's another matter. I simply don't understand how the life and death of Someone Else (whoever he was) 2,000 years ago can help me here and now."

The first man earnestly replied, "But don't you see, Jack? The Christian story is the greatest story of them all. Because it's the *Real* Story. The *historical event* that fulfills the tales and shows us what they mean."

About a week later, Jack—also known as C. S. Lewis, the author of the classic books *Mere Christianity* and *The Chronicles of Narnia* (among many other works)—announced his conversion to Christianity to a friend. Lewis attributed much of his decision to his conversation with J. R. R. Tolkien.[1] Of course, Tolkien is the author of one of the greatest books of the twentieth century, *The Lord of the Rings*, which has been transformed into a magnificent movie trilogy by director Peter Jackson. Although Tolkien, a Roman Catholic, didn't always see eye to eye with Lewis, who was more inclined toward Protestantism, they both understood the truth of the ultimate story.

STORYTELLING AND MYTHMAKING

As Tolkien and Lewis said so long ago, stories matter deeply. They connect us to our personal history and to the history of all time and culture. Human beings are meaning seekers and meaning makers. We strive to connect ourselves to our experiences and the experiences of others. We are addicted to those "aha!" moments in our lives when we see meaning, purpose, and significance.

Stories help us do this. They bring us laughter, tears, and joy. They stimulate our minds and stir our imaginations. Stories help us escape our daily lives to visit different times, places, and people. They can arouse our compassion and empathy, spur us toward truth and love, or sometimes even incite us toward hatred or violence.

Different kinds of stories satisfy different needs. For example, a comedy evokes a different response from us than a tragedy. A hard news story on the front page affects us differently than a human interest story in the magazine section, or a celebrity profile next to the movie and television listings. While different kinds of stories satisfy different needs, many stories share common themes, settings, character types, situations, and other recurrent archetypal patterns.

Many stories focus on one individual; often a heroic figure who overcomes many trials and tribulations to defeat evil or attain a valuable goal. We identify with such heroes because we recognize that we are each on our own journey or quest. How a hero's journey informs and illuminates our own journey is significant. We look for answers in stories.

Every story has a worldview: a way of viewing reality, truth, the universe, the human condition, and the supernatural world. Looking carefully at a story, we can examine the motifs, meanings, values, and principles it suggests. For example, a story with a redemptive Christian worldview shows people their need for salvation through a personal faith in the gospel of Jesus Christ. Conversely, a story with a secular humanist worldview explicitly or implicitly attacks Christianity. By examining a story's worldview, we identify the cultural ideals the story presents and the emotions it evokes. We also determine the moral, philosophical, social, psychological, spiritual, and aesthetic messages the story conveys.

Introduction

Whether you want to be in pictures, just enjoy watching them, or even just want to complain about them, it seems almost everyone is interested in the mass media and entertainment industry. Movies and television programs are certainly the storytelling media of our age. *How to Succeed in Hollywood* will tell you what you need to know about: telling stories through the mass media of entertainment; how to use your faith to change the culture of Hollywood; and how to make a creative contribution to the whole world. This book will show you how to develop your screenwriting, acting, directing, producing, and behind-the-scenes interests, to make Hollywood and the world better places for our children and grandchildren.

Many chapters in this book contain tips from the best and brightest minds in the entertainment industry, sharing behind-the-scenes secrets on producing great blockbuster movies and hit television programs. The list of contributors is an impressive and highly successful one: series creators, writers, directors, producers, animators, studio executives, actors, and even a television network owner. Each contributor addresses an important aspect of the entertainment industry, spanning from development to agency representation, writing, financing, production, and distribution. Each contributor shares his or her personal keys and secrets to success.

Some contributors also share their faith and spiritual insights on the entertainment industry from a Christian perspective. Each chapter includes succinct and valuable information on the key principles necessary for effective communication through film and television from a Christian perspective.

Additional contributors include:

Donzaleigh Abernathy, actress in *Gods and Generals*, *Stranger In My House*, *Camp Nowhere*, and many other movies and television programs

Pat Boone, famous actor, singer, and songwriter

Morgan Brittany, star of many movies and television programs, including: *Dallas*, *The Saint*, and *Melrose Place*

Richard Cook, former chairman of Walt Disney Pictures

Peter Engel, producer of *Last Comic Standing*, *All About Us*, *Malibu, CA*, *City Guys*, *USA High*, *Hang Time*, and the famous *Saved by the Bell* series

Bill Ewing, former executive vice president of Columbia Pictures

Bill Fay, executive producer of many movies, including *Independence Day* and *The Patriot*

Penelope Foster, co-producer of many movies, including: *Operation Dumbo Drop*, *Free Willy*, and *Rosewood*

Don Hahn, producer of many movies, including: *The Lion King*, *Beauty and the Beast*, and *The Hunchback of Notre Dame*

Brenda Hampton, writer of many television programs, including: *Love Boat*, *Safe Harbor*, and *7th Heaven* (creator and executive producer)

Bruce Johnson, president of PorchLight Entertainment

Dave, Gary, and Joan Johnson, writers and producers of many television programs, including: *Against the Grain, Doc*, and, *Sue Thomas: F.B.Eye*

Al Kasha, Academy Award winning songwriter and composer for many movies and television programs, including: *The Poseiden Adventure, The Towering Inferno*, and *The Rugrats Go Wild!*

Paul Lauer, director of Icon Pictures Marketing for *The Passion of the Christ*

Ron Maxwell, writer and director of many movies, including: *Parent Trap II, Little Darlings, Gettysburg*, and *Gods and Generals*

Brad Moore, president of Hallmark Hall of Fame

Jim Muro, director of photography and cinematographer for many movies and television programs, including *Open Range* and *Crash*

Dan Nichols, producer of many movies, including *Raiders of the Lost Ark* and *Always*

Bud Paxson, former owner of PaxTV

John Ratzenberger, voice talent and star; played Cliff in the television show *Cheers*, and has voiced every Pixar movie

Barry Reardon, former president of Distribution for Warner Bros.

Phil Roman, executive producer of *Garfield, Tom and Jerry*, and *The Simpsons*

Jane Russell, Hollywood star

Linda Seger, script doctor and author of many books, including: *Making a Good Script Great, Creating Unforgettable Characters, The Art of Adaptation, From Script to Screen,* and *Advanced Screenwriting*

Clifton Taulbert, novelist, producer, and screenwriter for *Once Upon a Time When We Were Colored*

Andrew Stanton, the scriptwriter for *Toy Story, Toy Story 2, A Bug's Life, Monsters Inc.,* and *Finding Nemo* (which he also directed and produced)

Chuck Viane, president of Walt Disney Company's Buena Vista Film Distribution Group

Randall Wallace, the writer of many movies, including *Braveheart, Pearl Harbor,* and *We Were Soldiers* (which he also directed and produced)

Frank Yablans, former president of Paramount Pictures

These renowned entertainers have many Christian virtues in common:

Their incredible humility: They deflect praise, give God the glory, and their teammates the honor.

Their wisdom for sharing faith: Many contributors mentioned their dislike for heavily 'preachy' or judgmental messages in movies, but all valued stories, parables, and allegories as ways to inspire the heart.

They are very clear about being believers. They are not embarrassed of their faith.

They live by the Word. Several spoke about the "opposites" in the Bible: The last shall be first; You have to go down to go up (humbled to be exalted); make less of yourself and exalt Jesus, who will draw all men unto Himself.

They are Spirit filled, and inspired in their work. Many business-focused contributors spoke about the value of the team, while talent-focused were more dramatic and inspirational, often including quotes and parables.

Behind their successes, these noteworthy people are at all different levels of spiritual growth and development in their individual walks of faith. Some are very deep and poetic; some are very scriptural and matter-of-fact, while others are content in the shallow waters of the faith, contemplating salvation. It's important not to judge these leaders on their spirituality. We should not expect things of them that only the Holy Spirit can accomplish, which He often does over the course of time. It's also important not to aggrandize the more spiritual sounding ones, for that will be their certain doom. Only the Lord deserves a throne in our hearts and minds!

These are people . . . real people! Many were interviewed during everyday tasks like driving children to school in a carpool, talking to their mother on the other line, gardening, or even cleaning the house. Others, we found on the set of movie locations, doing very impressive things with expensive equipment. Despite their fame and industry success, they were mostly vulnerable, down-to-earth folks, willing to speak earnestly about their faith in the context of the culture of Hollywood.

This book will help you answer the following questions on your journey:

- How can I communicate through the entertainment business?

- What do I want to communicate?
- Why do I want to communicate?
- Who do I want to communicate with?
- What are my gifts and talents?
- Who is my audience?
- What am I communicating?
- What medium should I use?
- How do I develop an idea?
- How do I write a script?
- How do I find an agent?
- How do I find financing?
- How do I get distribution?
- What do I need to know about production?
- What about television?
- What about movies?
- What does God want me to communicate?

How to Succeed in Hollywood illustrates how to share God's Word and the gospel through the media of entertainment. This book deals with the opportunities as well as the trials and tribulations Christians face in the mass media, and how to develop your craft to be "more than conquerors" in the entertainment industry. This book will also help you *understand* the entertainment industry, and teach you (and others with stars in their eyes) how to succeed in the competitive film industry that is Hollywood, without "stooping to conquer."

On the topic of noble success, the following interview with Pat Boone provides some timely cautions. With his characteristic white buck shoes, his handsome features, and his soothing voice, Pat Boone spent decades showing not just his screaming fans—but the entire world of show business—that a star could be *both* completely entertaining and completely honorable. As an actor, singer, and songwriter, Pat spent much of the 50s, 60s, and 70s writing and performing pop-culture songs and starring in popular movies. He was successful in getting a number of objectionable lyrics removed from early rock and R&B songs, and today he continues to speak compellingly of his life message that "entertainers should be influencers." Pat shares his best advice for those considering a career in entertainment.

RUN AWAY! (BUT IF YOU MUST STAY . . .)
—PAT BOONE

PICK SOMETHING ELSE!

To people of faith, Pat Boone advises, "Don't even think about being involved in the entertainment business. It's too treacherous, unpredictable, fickle, and unfair. I especially discourage young girls from going into the business because there are some very unscrupulous and charming and even satanic people that will wheedle and cajole and dangle opportunity before them, putting all kinds of pressure on them just to take advantage of their virtue and leave them ruined."

Pat is clear about the moral bent of the industry: "Young men and women should understand going in that they are going into an immoral (not just amoral) business where most people will sacrifice morals and anybody else's career wishes just to climb up."

Beyond his scrupulous warnings, Pat has clear, tested advice for those who truly believe they are being called to Hollywood: "If you must stay in the industry, commit your career to the Lord. If God opens doors and nudges you through them, you can proceed with confidence, not feeling that if you mess up somehow, as on *American Idol* auditions, you are forever ruined. With God that's not the case. Young girls, especially, have to be particularly fortified with God's will and prayer, and the prayerful support of their families, before they even think about a career in entertainment. If somebody is going into the entertainment world, he or she needs to go in almost like Abraham would have gone into Sodom and Gomorrah—with truth and love, not as Lot went in, with an accommodation and compromise that almost destroyed him and his family."

FORGET THE BIG BUCKS

Pat always advises young people with stars in their eyes to take advantage of every honorable opportunity to showcase their talents, without regard to compensation. As a teenager, Pat participated in the East Nashville High Citywide Talent Contest and won first prize—a trip to New York to audition on Ted Mack's *Amateur Hour*. He was the show's winner three weeks in a row. Pat's appearance on the *Amateur Hour* finals led to a professional slot on Arthur Godfrey's *Talent Scout* show, where he sang four mornings in a row and won their contest as well. Pat did not know, at the time, that winning on a professional show had disqualified him from winning the $6,000 scholarship on the Arthur Godfrey amateur show. Though initially disappointed, Pat soon realized that his appearance on the professional show would open the doors for a recording contract with Dot Records. His first record was a hit!

MAKE GOD YOUR AGENT

Pat recommends committing God-given talents back to the Lord, and praying that God will reveal honorable avenues for the use of those talents. "God opens doors that no one else can, and God's anointing carries people to places that name never could."

As for securing a human agent, Pat suggests interviewing other respected, successful Christians for agent recommendations.

BE EVER AWARE OF YOUR INFLUENCE

Pat was keenly aware that as a young recording star he had tremendous influence on kids, many of whom tried to emulate him. He took some ribbing and even some outright hostility because people judged him as "too good to be true." Pat knew, though, that if he used salacious or suggestive language in a record or played a part in a movie that glamorized immorality, he would be setting a reprehensible example. This position cost him some movies and hit records, and his refusal to endorse cigarette- or alcohol-based sponsors nearly cost him his own TV show. Soon enough, Chevrolet offered him his own show, and Pat happily accepted—especially since he was driving a Chevy at the time. As Pat recalls, "All of these events made me confident that God had his hand on my career, and if I would try to do what my conscience and my knowledge of his Word dictated, I could be both successful and blessed of him."

Recalling the "clean" movies of yesteryear, Pat says. "In the heyday of the film business, families used to go together at least once a week to see a good movie in the neighborhood cinema. You could always count on it being a happy family experience. Today filmmakers, music makers—and even half-time shows at sporting events—purposely insert foul language and other offensive materials into their 'art,' not because these things are essential to their work, but because they think it makes them more cool. They would rather have a PG or R rating than a G rating, thinking that more people will want to go see it because of the slight hint of forbidden fruit. Actually, movies that don't offend a large portion of their audience tend to make more money . . . funny thing!"

TACKLING TEMPTATIONS

Pat believes that the failure to resist temptation is the catalyst for a season of tribulation. "As I look back, I don't remember too many trials and tribulations, though many temptations. And, some of the tribulations I wound up having to pray my way through were the result of not completely resisting the various temptations. The way you overcome trials and temptations is to continually involve the Lord, commit yourself and your opportunities and decisions to Him. He won't let you down."

MAKE GOD'S WORD THE PLUMB LINE

"Unless a person is praying, studying, and reading the Bible for himself, it will be impossible to know God's will," Pat says. He has seen that those who have committed their lives and abilities into God's hands are confident, even when they feel they may have missed out on something. Pat believes the "God confidence" that comes by staying in the Word will bring a contentment and steady knowledge that God is in charge and ordering the believer's steps—no matter what the circumstances. "It's a great way to relax and not feel so much pressure."

Pat remembers fondly his high school teacher in Latin and biblical Studies, John L. Rainey. "He influenced me to read the New Testament in the original Greek in college, so I came to know God's Word, his will, and his teachings. These have always been my guidelines, and I don't think there are any other reliable ones. Everything else is relativistic, humanistic, shifting like the sands and the weather. Now our country is being led in totally immoral directions in the name of tolerance and political correctness, and though it's well intentioned, God's will hasn't changed. We need to know his Word and take a stand."

BE SALTY, NOT A SELL OUT

On the subject of being "salt and light" in a dark industry, Pat has some definitive safeguards: "Jesus said we are to be light and salt in the world, but He also says if the salt loses its savor, how can it be restored? We must stay close to him and keep feeding ourselves on his Word and his spirit. My book, *A New Song,* goes into great detail about how I came to understand that more fully. I'm so thankful that I was raised in a Christian home with biblical training at both church and in school, and I realize that others without the benefit of Christian parents may have to work hard to anchor themselves biblically as adults. But regardless of our spiritual level, if we commit to being salt and light spiritually first, then utilizing our talents—whether writing, producing, performing, or directing—for worthwhile, productive, and beneficial endeavors, we will find that God will divinely order our steps. Don't sell out doing a lot of reprehensible stuff, thinking, 'This is the way I get to the good.' It may never happen."

LOOK FOR THE REDEMPTIVE FLOW

As for choosing the right projects, Pat encourages believers to limit their involvement to endeavors with a redemptive bent. He recalls the day when Twentieth Century Fox asked him to costar in a movie with Marilyn Monroe. "My mouth watered at the idea of making a film with Marilyn Monroe, but as I read the script, I saw that the whole story line—and particularly the part I was to play—was immoral and would have set a very unhealthy example for young people. It was tough, but I had to turn it down. At the same time, I said I would happily play Judas in a film if the overall tone of the film were to promote Jesus Christ and Christian values. So, the answer for me is that you choose projects by the subliminal content of the message and the story. Christians should try to always make sure that those are good and pointed toward Kingdom principles and purposes."

* * *

SO, WHAT'S IT ALL ABOUT?

The entertainment media have become the primary teachers of our children. The average child sees 40,000 hours of media by the time they are seventeen years old, compared to 11,000 hours in school, 2,000 hours with parents, and 800 hours in church (if they go for an hour every Sunday).

Figure 1: Today's TV Teachers

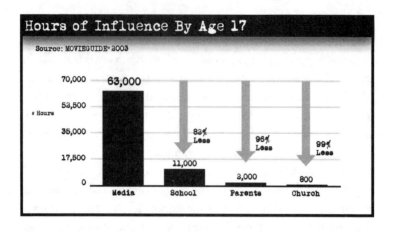

As a result, our children have lost contact with the values and faith of their forefathers. In fact, one study finds that 90 percent of our youth are abandoning the values of their parents. Shockingly, just 4 percent of children surveyed in 2001 were considered familiar with the Bible, compared to 70 percent in 1950. Without moral guidelines, children are facing growing physical and psychological problems, including outbreaks of sexually transmitted diseases—at increasingly younger ages—and in epidemic proportions.

It is a critical time for people of faith to communicate through the mass media of the entertainment industry. The New Testament uses five different Greek words that translate to "preaching" in English. The most common word is "kerysso", which Jesus uses sixty-three percent of the time. It means, "to go into the marketplace and proclaim or herald the good news of the gospel." This book intends to help you to do just what Jesus commanded: herald His good news in movies and television, the marketplace of entertainment.

FOUNDATIONS

There's No Business Like Show Business

A growing number of Christians these days have stars in their eyes—either because they spend too much time watching the current crop of celebrities on television and the silver screen, or because they have visions of receiving their own star on Hollywood Boulevard for producing some great movie or television program that will communicate "the Truth."

Forty years ago, there was a suspicion of the entertainment industry in the church. Now, there is a keen interest in the industry, and a surprising number of people in my audience approach me after my lectures or sermons to share their desire to make movies, or the story of a family member who has gone to Hollywood in search of fame and fortune.

The church has discovered Hollywood. Perhaps, more importantly, Hollywood has discovered the church. As a result, the major movie studios today hire Christian publicists to market movies to the 135 million to 165 million people who go to church every week. These same studios write Bible study materials to complement particular movies for church use. Considering that the average movie audience per week is only about 27 million people, the church-attending demographic comparatively forms the largest potential audience in the United States. Appealing to the Christian demographic has the potential to bring studios blockbuster earnings, (defined as box office sales over $100 million). Some examples include: *The Blind Side*; *The Chronicles of Narnia*; *The Lion, the Witch and the Wardrobe*; *Lord of the Rings*; and *The Passion of the Christ*. Of course, not all the movies being marketed to the church are theologically or morally sound—but at least the church is being pursued. There are many good movies that deserve the support of the Christian community, but it is up to the church to be discerning and make wise decisions by promoting the good and rejecting the bad.

THE CHURCH AND CULTURE

The purpose of this chapter is to explore how the church and culture, especially as reflected in the entertainment industry, have historically interacted with one another, and how we as Christians can use our gifts and talents to communicate effectively for God's glory through this powerful medium.

> Over the past 20 years we have seen the nation's theological views slowly become less aligned with the Bible. Americans still revere the Bible and like to think of themselves as Bible-believing people, but the evidence suggests otherwise. Christians have increasingly been adopting spiritual views that come from Islam, Wicca, secular humanism, the eastern religions and other sources. Because we remain a largely Bible-illiterate society, few are alarmed or even aware of the slide toward syncretism—a belief system that blindly combines beliefs from many different faith perspectives (George Barna, Barna Research Group . . . *Americans*

Draw Theological Beliefs from Diverse Points of View
[The Barna Update, 2002], Oct).

In the past, the church shaped Western Civilization, otherwise known as Christendom, with an aim to train children in the way they should go: heal the sick, feed the hungry, clothe the poor, and create art to worship a loving and just Creator who gave form and function to reality. Now, our culture is shaped by the entertainment industry. The results are confusion at best, and the vilest paganism at worst.

The Barna survey quoted above also shows that a shockingly large number of Americans believe that when Jesus Christ was on earth He committed sins, which would mean His death on the cross was not a sinless offering. Sadly, most of those who contend that Jesus sinned are under thirty-eight years of age, which places them in the very generation impacted by the Supreme Court's biased and un-Constitutional decision to remove prayer and faith from the public classroom.

If Jesus is no longer a sufficient sacrifice for our sins, then it is no wonder that almost half the population believes that deliverance from eternal condemnation for one's sins is earned rather than received as a free gift from God through Jesus' death and resurrection. Thus, half of all adults argue that anyone who "is generally good or does enough good things for others during their life will earn a place in heaven."[2]

In reality, everyday human relationships illustrate the biblical truth that no one is righteous. Therefore, it is not terribly surprising (though it is heartbreaking) that 40 percent of all adults, and young adults in particular, hold the confused belief that "the Bible, the Koran, and the Book of Mormon are all different expressions of the same spiritual truths."[3] In reality, each book of faith claims a unique way of life and a specific path to salvation that excludes every other way. To add to the confusion, a large majority of both adults and teenagers contend that there is no absolute moral truth, and that truth is always relative to the individual and the circumstances.

This relativism provides a self-contradicting, egregious argument for those who believe nothing is morally wrong in appropriate context, including abortion, suicide, or euthanasia. The common rubric seems to be, "It's just a matter of opinion."

Nice Is Not Good Enough

This moral relativism may be the reason the antihero in movies has become so prominent that audiences are now considering the antihero to be somehow "good." For instance, the protagonists in *Ocean's 11*, starring George Clooney, Brad Pitt, and the rest of the new rat pack are nice, but they are clearly not good. They lie, they cheat, and of course, they steal. They are the heroes, and we are apparently supposed to root for them.

This theology of relativism is also creeping into the church. In the United States, we are experiencing an unprecedented 22 percent decline in Christianity among children and teenagers (a personal observation by George Barna). Good News Publishers has noted that fifty years ago, 70 percent of children had heard the gospel and were familiar with the Bible. Today that number is just 4 percent. As in other countries where the church has collapsed, there are many in the believing evangelical church grasping at straws and forming alliances with strange, non-Christian bedfellows to try to slow the fall.

These non-believers are nice people who often preach a legalistic theology of works and may even seem conservative. In a way, these non-Christian, conservative leaders are unconsciously guarding the adversary's right flank, just as the anti-Christian liberal leaders were guarding the left flank in the era of the social gospel, which, sadly, seems to have returned. Neither lawlessness nor legalism will cure our culture's ills.

As Paul writes in Ephesians 4:1–32, God does not want us to live as the godless pagans do, in the futility and darkness of their thinking. Instead, we must live a worthy life and gently, humbly, patiently, lovingly make every effort to keep the unity of the Holy

Spirit through peace. There is to be only one faith, one Lord, and one God, who has given each person his measure of divine grace as Jesus the Christ has apportioned it. Jesus prepares God's people for works of service:

> To build up the body of Christ, until we all reach unity in the faith and in the knowledge of God's Son, [growing] into a mature man with a stature measured by Christ's fullness. Then we will no longer be little children, tossed by the waves and blown around by every wind of teaching, by human cunning with cleverness in the techniques of deceit. But speaking the truth in love, let us grow in every way into Him who is the head—Christ. From Him the whole body, fitted and knit together by every supporting ligament, promotes the growth of the body for building up itself in love by the proper working of each individual part (Ephesians 4:12–16).

It is not possible to do any of this if we listen to people who do not know Jesus Christ or who practice a theology of Christian relativism, no matter how well intentioned or smart they are. "Since you put away lying," Paul writes in Ephesians 4:25 and 5:1–2, "Speak the truth, each one to his neighbor, because we are members of one another . . . Therefore, be imitators of God, as dearly loved children. And walk in love, as the Messiah also loved us and gave Himself for us, a sacrificial and fragrant offering to God." Paul continues in Ephesians 5:6–10, "Let no one deceive you with empty arguments, for because of these things God's wrath is coming on the disobedient. Therefore, do not become their partners. For you were once in darkness, but now [you are] light in the Lord. Walk as children of light—for the fruit of the light [results] in all goodness, righteousness, and truth—discerning what is pleasing to the Lord."

Are There Limits to Tolerance?

It is understandable why the mass media places a premium on tolerance, given the increasingly diverse culture in which we live. While some of this tolerance is aimed at diluting the influence of Christians in our culture, most is born out of an attempt to reach the entire demographic range in the United States.

In stark contrast to the media's obeisance for tolerance, the late intellectual and humorist Steve Allen spoke on this important topic at the National Religious Broadcasters at my invitation. Since his wife was a very committed Christian, Steve decided to tackle this difficult topic, even though he himself claimed to be an atheist who read the Bible every day.

Steve waxed eloquent on the subject of tolerance and explained why intolerance was sometimes the only option. He asked the audience, "if you were a Jew and came upon a burning bush where it was clear that God Himself was speaking to you, and the event was so frightening that you fell on your face before Him, and God told you He is a jealous God who would have no other Gods before Him and told you exactly what judgment you faced if you refused to obey him, what would you do?" Steve concluded that you would obey the awesome Almighty, Creator God whom you just met in person, and you would forever after be intolerant of other gods. In other words, the divine distinctive of Judaism, as well as that of Christianity, often compels intolerance, if you believe that your faith comes directly from the Almighty.

Yes, intolerance to relativism is appropriate. It is not "just a matter of opinion." There is an absolute Truth that sets us free. The Holy Creator God does not tolerate evil and neither should His people.

Seek Wisdom, Knowledge, and Understanding

The church needs to be discerning in order to prevent Hollywood's manipulation. In this regard, the church has always had five different perspectives toward culture, with one or another perspective in the ascendancy. Each of these perspectives can be supported with Bible verses, but none of them can be identified as the "correct" reading to the extent that they justify exclusion of the others. Since no single correct reading can be identified, none of the five perspectives are considered credal or a measure of orthodoxy.

Yale theologian H. Richard Niebuhr first distinguished between the five approaches Christians have historically taken with regard to their world in his book *Christ and Culture*.[4] His distinctions have been modified and clarified for the purposes of this book.

The first position could be called "retreat from culture," though Niebuhr calls it "Christ Against Culture." He cites the Mennonite and Amish communities as the obvious examples of this tradition, though he could have also referred to the monastic tradition in the early church. While there are rich traditions of service within these groups, the world is viewed as a place from which to escape into communities of "separated brethren." The Schleitheim Confession of the Anabaptists (1527) argued: "Since all who do not walk in the obedience of faith are a great abomination before God, it is not possible for anything to grow or issue from them except abominable things. God further admonishes us to withdraw from Babylon and the earthly Egypt that we may not be partakers of the pain and suffering which the Lord will bring upon them."

The second perspective, which Niebuhr calls "The Christ of Culture," tends to equate creation and redemption and can be seen in those groups that identify Christ with utopian socialism as well as those who identify Christ with American culture. Those who follow this tradition hail Jesus as the Messiah of their society, the fulfiller of its hopes and aspirations, the perfecter of its true faith, the source of its holiest spirit. For these people, there is hardly any difference between Christ and the culture. These adherents view Christ as the moral example who points us to a perfect society.

Adopting the third approach, which Niebuhr calls "Christ Above Culture," are the centrists who live within the world, though they are not of the world. Centrists refuse to take either the position of the anti-cultural radicals or of the accommodators of Christ to culture.

The fourth tradition is "Christ and Culture in Paradox," which refuses either to reject culture or to confuse culture with Christianity. They see these as two different realms, not two antagonistic realms. In creation, God gives us work, service, pleasure, government, and family. In redemption, He gives us the church, the Word, and the holy sacraments. The Christian who follows the "Christ and Culture in Paradox" tradition participates in culture, but not as a means of grace. Rather, it is an aspect of being human, not merely of being a Christian.

The final category is "Christ the Transformer of Culture," which emphasizes God's lordship over all of creation and all aspects of life. Niebuhr appeals to John's gospel as an example of this approach. Here Christ is "the Word made flesh"—not only the priest of redemption, but the king of creation. This tradition, which is represented by Augustine and Calvin, takes the world seriously and contends that Christians have the potential not only to exercise leadership in the culture but to present the gospel as well. God loves the world, not just individuals in it (Romans 8:20–23). Those of the "Christ Transforming Culture" tradition would view culture as a distinct, though related, part of Christ's universal reign. While creating a movie, building a house, or raising a family may not be the redemptive activities of the Kingdom of God, they are important activities to which Christians realize a call, because they are commanded by the universal Lord in the "cultural mandate" of the early chapters of Genesis. Though human activity can never bring salvation, the activity of Christian men and women does bring a certain transforming element as they live out their callings in distinction and honor, serving both to attract non-Christians to the gospel and also bringing civil righteousness, justice, and compassion to bear on human relationships.

The church has historically moved through a cycle from one point of view to the other. During the middle of the twentieth century the church retreated from culture. Then, the church took up the battle cry of cultural warfare to resist the moral decay occurring in our society. Today, the church is beginning to move out as ambassadors for Jesus Christ to redeem the culture. Whatever cultural position you, your local church, or your denomination adopt, we are called to develop the discernment to know right from wrong; the wisdom to choose what is right, the knowledge to pursue what is right, and the understanding to persevere.

> For God has not given us a spirit of fearfulness, but one of power, love, and sound judgment.
> —2 Timothy 1:7

CAN ENTERTAINMENT BE HOLY?

The church has had a love/hate relationship with art, music, and drama for centuries. Modern drama as we know it was invented by the church in the Middle Ages to help the illiterate population understand the gospel. These Christian dramas—known as *Mystery Plays* or *Miracle Plays*—quickly became suspect in the eyes of clergy, who felt that the dramas were overshadowing their sermons. As a result, Pope Innocent III outlawed drama, and the dramatists whose creative abilities and desires were a gift from God went into the alleys and the beer halls to exercise their God given gifts in not-so-God-ordained ways. A similar scenario has happened many times throughout history.

Respected Roman Catholic theologian and scholar, Michael Jones, blames the growth of Protestantism on the willingness of the Protestants to use the newfangled printing press to print Bibles, while the Catholic Church rejected the new technology of communication in the fifteenth Century. Centuries later, in the early stages of moving pictures, a Cardinal in Paris was shocked by movies on the life and passion of Jesus Christ being shown in the Cathedral of Notre Dame. The Cardinal banned film from the church, thus turning the new medium over to the very people who were most opposed to the church. Edison tried to give the rights to the motion picture technology to his Christian denomination, but they rejected it. The first broadcast radio station was located in a church in Pittsburgh, but the rector of the church demanded that his younger associate have nothing to do with it and shut it down.

Terry Lindvall, former distinguished chair of visual communication and professor of film at Regent University, chronicles the other side of this love/hate relationship between the entertainment industry and the church in his book *The Silents of God*. The book begins with the historic Chautauqua Tabernacle's showing of a motion picture on June 22, 1900, and then moves on to discuss how many theatrical movies were shown in churches up until 1920. This practice stopped when theater owners told the movie companies that they would not play their movies if they were also shown in churches. Covering the historical period from 1908 to 1925, this study showcases pamphlets, magazine articles (from both religious and film periodicals), sermons, and other discourse that chronicle an early vision of church/photoplay cooperation and its subsequent dissolution with the advent of growing suspicion, Hollywood scandals, Sabbatical reform movements, and alternative communication technologies. This collection of documents challenges the enduring fiction that the church was hostile to the moving picture at its inception; rather, the church sought to appropriate its potential for evangelism, education, social reform, and uplift.

Proclaiming Good News in the Marketplace
With regard to the love/hate relationship between the church and the new technologies of communication and art, there are five Greek words that translate to the English word "preaching" in the New Testament. As previously mentioned, much of the time, Jesus uses the Greek word "kerysso," related to kerygma, which means to proclaim or herald in the marketplace. The word "kerysso" was particularly relevant to the people Jesus was talking to because they were familiar with the Roman heralds who ran into the marketplace

every morning and shouted out the news of the Emperor to the buyers and sellers.

Jesus Christ has always commanded his people to go into the marketplace of ideas to herald the good news. When Christians do so, as in the Protestant Reformation and the evangelization of South Korea, the church grows and prospers. When Christians fail to go into the marketplace, the church shrinks in size and suffers.

The Christian View of Art and Communications

Several years ago, I co-chaired an Art and Communications Committee of several prominent theologians for the Coalition on Revival to set forth The Christian World View of Art and Communication.[5] Together, we felt a calling to help Christians influence the entertainment industry. Our dialogue produced the following principles, which help summarize what a relationship between the arts and a Christian worldview should look like:

1. "In the beginning God created" and "In the beginning was the Word." God is the Author of creation and communication. As the supreme Creator and communicator, He is the source of art and communication.
2. God has given all authority in heaven and on earth to His Son, Jesus Christ. Since Jesus Christ is entitled to have lordship over all areas of life, Christians must bring all art and communication under Christ's authority.
3. Art and communication are part of God's created order. They cannot be labeled Christian or un-Christian. However, they can be used for good or evil.
4. Art and communication are neither synonymous nor mutually exclusive functions in God's economy. Communication is the act of sharing thoughts, ideas, information, and needs. The arts, whether or not they communicate, are expressions of God's creativity manifested through man.

5. Man, created in the image of God, has the capacity to create and communicate. Therefore, all artistic endeavors and communications involve more than technical skills. Their intended purpose is to glorify God. To accomplish this, all art and communication must be brought into captivity to the mind of Christ.

6. Christ is the standard of excellence. "Whatever you do, work at it with all your heart, as working for the Lord, not for people" (Colossians 3:23 GNT). Within this framework of excellence, art and communication should reflect the highest quality of creative work possible, given the resources available. Since all abilities are God-given, we can achieve excellence only when we submit them to the lordship of Jesus Christ and the guidance of God. This guidance comes from communication with God through prayer, study of His Word, and other biblical disciplines vital to being a Christian.

7. Art and communication have a great influence on society in shaping man's view of reality. A career in these fields should be considered a worthy vocation. To achieve such a career, Christians should discern and develop their God-given talents.

8. It is legitimate for Christians to engage in art and communication without the need to include overt Christian symbolism or content. A Christian may participate in any area of art and communication as long as he submits himself to the lordship of Jesus Christ in accordance with His Word, and acts in the conviction of faith, for "without faith it is impossible to please [God]" (Hebrews 11:6).

Theology of Art

Until the Twentieth Century, there was an active theology of art and beauty placing the Holy Spirit as the guiding influence in the arts and communication media. However, the reaction to modern secularism produced a retreat from such culture within the church. The church is now emerging from this retreat, but has regrettably lost many of the common symbols and modes of art and communication in the process. To a large degree, sacramental and incarnational models of communication and art are misunderstood by the contemporary church. These ideas often simply proclaim the milk of the gospel (as noted in Hebrews 5) and stop before getting to the meat of Hebrews 6. Some Christian colleges and schools credit either/or theories of art and communication and neglect the gospel message that Jesus Christ was both God and man. These theories diminish the biblical view of art and communications.

Traditionally, there are four philosophies of art. Plato believed that art represented the ideal. In reaction to Plato, Aristotle defined art in a materialistic context as something that was "not useful, made by man, and contrary to nature." The Roman Horace tried to syncretize the two Greek philosophers and defined art as something to both delight and inform. The Bible emphasizes that art should concern the true, the good, and the beautiful.

As a result of the materialistic modern culture following the philosophies of Marx, Darwin, Dewey, and Freud, the last fifty years have become primarily Aristotelian in the culturally accepted view of art. "Art" has too often been defined as anything contrary to nature or pushing the envelope. In order to continue pushing the envelope, if one movie features female nudity from the waist up, the next has to feature full frontal female nudity, and so on.

Hollywood's Pagan "Theology" of Art

In the last half century, a new aristocracy has emerged. The entertainer—whether athlete, celebrity, or news announcer—has become the new upper class. These Hollywood idols and their compatriots earn ludicrous salaries—former Walt Disney Company Chairman Michael Eisner earned over $350 million in stock options one year; several celebrities and sports stars earn over $20 million; and major television news anchors earn over $5 million annually. In highly visible positions, these "stars" wield an incredible power to shape the thoughts, dreams, and concerns of our youth and culture. As actress Susan Sarandon so poignantly commented, movie stars are dangerous because "we are the keeper of the dreams."

This new aristocracy of entertainers stems from our indulgent American inheritance. We have become wealthy beyond our wildest expectations, and we have turned away from the true joy of residing in God's grace in order to seek amusement in the world, the flesh, and the devil. With our culture in a precipitous backslide, the entertainment industry has seized the opportunity to extort our addiction to pleasure and bamboozle a willing populace into interpreting the First Amendment to read that everything from pedophilia to pornography is "protected speech"—except, of course, Christian speech. The reason these entertainment companies spend millions of dollars to stretch the notion of "protected speech" beyond any reasonable intent of the framers of the Constitution is to protect their profits from the sale of salacious pornography and extreme violence to vulnerable adolescents, children, and adults.

This new media aristocracy has developed its own form of *noblesse oblige* by selling us on the idea that the government should cover the cost of all social largesse. They have reinterpreted sin to mean politically incorrect speech, and carefully removed any burden of guilt from the family destroying sins of adultery and sodomy. As U.S. linguist and political analyst Noam Chomsky has said, "The United States is unusual among the industrial democracies in the rigidity of the system of ideological control—'indoctrination,' we might say—exercised through the mass media."[6]

The importance of this new elite demands the attention of the church. Please pray for the men and women who hold responsible positions of extreme national and international importance within the entertainment industry.

Jesus in the Movies

There is widespread confusion about what constitutes a "Christian" movie. Since the beginning of the motion picture business, Christians have been making movies about Jesus Christ, as well as movies with a Christian worldview and theology. In addition, Christians have made movies to disciple, instruct, and inform the church, including many missionaries who use the media of film to share their mission stories with supporters. Both small-scale Christian movies for the church and the more polished movies for theatrical release are worthwhile, though some might insult the low-budget church films and bemoan the idea that Christians do not make Hollywood movies. The truth is, many Christians do make Hollywood movies—some of the most successful movies and television programs—and you will hear from some of the most noteworthy Christians in Hollywood within these pages.

The opinions outlined above within the church mirror the rest of the filmmaking community. Educational movies are not derided for falling short of Hollywood's big-budget glamour, nor are documentaries, medical films, and the like. Just as the educational community needs educational films, the church needs media for training, discipling, and worship, even though these movies and videos are not as expensive or slick as Hollywood movies.

Since the inception of the motion picture, well before Mel Gibson's blockbuster *The Passion of the Christ*, many movies featured the story of Jesus. Some outstanding movies about Jesus Christ include:

1897:
The Passion Play produced by American theatrical producers, Marc Klaw and Abraham Erlanger, in Horitz, Bohemia.

1898:
The Passion Play, produced by R.G. Hollaman and A.G. Eaves, was photographed on the roof of a New York sky-

scraper. The length of the film was 2,100 feet or about 20 minutes. A narrator took the place of captions.

Oberammergau Passion Play photographed by a Mr. Hurd, Lumiere's American representative.

French *Passion Play* produced for the Musee Eden.

1902–1906:
The Passion Play produced by Ferdinand Zecca was 2,000 feet in length. It made use of panning shots, which were an innovation at the time.

The Passion Play produced by V. Jasset and Alice Guy reproduced Golgotha at Fontainebleau and used a gramophone to help the actors with their emotions. This may be the earliest use of an artificial aid.

1908:
The Life of Christ was produced in color by Pathe. In 1914, it was expanded to seven reels. In 1921, a modern prologue was added.

Ben–Hur was directed by Sidney Olcott and starred William S. Hart. Kalem was the production company.

1909:
The Kiss of Judas, The Birth of Jesus, a French production, and *The Star of Bethlehem* were produced by Thomas A. Edison.

1911:
Though Your Sins Be as Scarlet was a Vitagraph production, starring Charles Kent as Jesus Christ and Julia Swayne Gordon as Mary Magdalene.

Satan: Or the Drama of Humanity was a four-part Italian spectacle from Ambrosio, directed by Luigi Maggi. The second episode featured the life of Jesus Christ.

From the Manger to the Cross is the first major life of Jesus from his infancy to his death on the Cross. It was directed by Sidney Olcott for Kalem, the production company. The film was shot on location in Egypt and Palestine. *The Way of the Cross* was filmed on the actual Via Dolorosa in Jerusalem.

1916:

In *Intolerance*, D.W. Griffith used four stories to define intolerance: the Judean story, which presented a small portion of the life of Jesus of Nazareth and avoided the resurrection; the medieval story, which was a dramatization of the war between Catholics and Huguenots in sixteenth-century France; the fall of Babylon, which was a memorable epic of the ancient world; and, the modern story, which was a dramatic conflict between capital and labor.

Christus is a large-scale production from the Italian Cines Company, directed by Guilo Antomoro. Giovanni Pasquali played Jesus.

Hollywood veteran Thomas Ince cast George Fisher in the role of Jesus Christ in *Civilization*. Ince employed allegory in this tale of the supernatural to show that all war is evil.

1923:

I.N.R.I. tells about a convicted murderer who hears the life of Christ as told by the chaplain. The recounted scenes are enacted in the form of a Passion play wherein Gregor Chmara plays Jesus Christ. As a result of hearing the story, the murderer repents.

1926:

Ben-Hur was directed by Fred Niblo for MGM (Metro-Goldwyn-Mayer).

1927:

The famous H.B. Warner played Jesus in Cecil B. DeMille's *King of Kings*—still the classic of all movies about Jesus Christ. Produced by Pathé Exchange, Inc., this was the most famous, the most discussed, and the costliest religious movie made up to that point and was used for many years by missionaries to evangelize.

1934:

Written and directed by Julien Duvivier for Film Union, *Golgotha* was the first Passion play to be made in sound. Robert le Vigan plays Jesus Christ, and the renowned Jean Gabin plays Pontius Pilate. Since it is a Passion play, the movie covers only the events of Holy Week.

Oberammergau Passion Play was filmed again as a silent movie.

1951:

Quo Vadis is one of those incredibly pro-Christian biblical epics that it is hard to imagine Hollywood producing. Directed by Mervyn Le Roy for MGM, this exquisite movie clearly shows the redemptive power of the gospel of Jesus Christ transforming the evil world system of man.

1952:

Robert S. Flaherty made the *St. Matthew Passion* based on the choral work by J. S. Bach.

1953:
Directed by Henry Koster for Twentieth Century Fox, *The Robe* is utterly inspirational. Starring Richard Burton, Jean Simmons, and Victor Mature, this Hollywood classic is the story of a slave under the rule of Rome, who turns to Christianity after embracing the robe of Christ. Burton plays Marcellus, a Roman centurion who won the robe of Christ on the roll of a dice after the crucifixion. Tormented by nightmares, he returns to Palestine to try and learn what he can of the man he killed. His slave Demetrius swoops up the robe and converts to Christianity. Mad emperor Caligula cannot abide Christians and demands that Burton secure the robe for him. When Burton does not give up the robe, he is sent to his death.

1959:
Ben-Hur ranks among the most honored of films, taking 11 of 12 Academy awards. The movie starts with the birth of Christ and the visit by the Magi. Judah Ben-Hur of Judea (Charlton Heston) reunites with his friend, Massala (Stephen Boyd) who becomes the Roman commander of Jerusalem. However, Massala asks Judah to betray his own people by informing on the dissenters. When Judah refuses, Massala finds a way to frame his friend and send Judah to the galleys of the Roman war ships. He also sends Judah's mother and sister to a dark, cold cell. In battle, Judah rescues the governor and becomes a Roman "favorite son." In time, Judah becomes a skilled charioteer and defeats Massala in a daring chariot race. Judah then rescues his mother and sister who have become lepers and takes them to Christ. Though it is too late for them to meet Jesus, his shed blood heals them and regenerates Judah.

The Big Fisherman was directed by Frank Borzage for Centurion. This is a vast religious epic from Lloyd Douglas' book about the life of St. Peter. Regrettably, Peter is trivialized and the gospel is distorted. There is no Crucifixion, and Jesus Christ is shown without an enemy in the world.

1961:

King of Kings should not to be confused with Cecil B. DeMille's impressive life of Jesus in the 1927 movie by the same title. Not only was the movie poorly edited, but also treats the gospel as a revolutionary underground movement, with Barabbas and Judas working together to destroy Roman oppression and Jesus caught in the upheaval. Aside from the introduction of irrelevant battles, the movie lacks a clear emphasis on Jesus' divinity, omits miracles, and changes significant facts. Furthermore, Jeffrey Hunter does a poor job as Christ. However, the movie does portray an actual resurrection.

1964:

Director Pier Paola Pasolini's *Gospel According to St. Matthew* adheres rigidly to the facts and the spirit of this one gospel. Only at the Crucifixion is the Virgin Mary allowed to be emotional, and the effect is shattering.

1965:

The Greatest Story Ever Told is slightly overlong and crammed with stars but not as bad a movie as many critics claim. In spite of the involvement of the Protestant Film Office, the movie has some theological inaccuracies, including attempts to exonerate Judas, Judas falling into the sacrificial fire instead of hanging himself as the Bible tells us, and a weak ending, with a conceptually resurrected Jesus appearing in the clouds in a vision that leans toward nominalism. These and other divergences from the Bible are so apparent that it is clear that director George Stevens should have stuck to the facts.

1973:

Jesus Christ, Superstar presents a Jesus figure, using the musical idiom of the 1960s. It is interesting to note that it now appears very dated.

Godspell is a 1960s rock opera re-telling of the story of Jesus in a New York setting. Directed by David Greene for Columbia Pictures, *Godspell* lost out at the box office to the overshadowing *Jesus Christ, Superstar*. Also based on a prior, successful theatrical musical, *Godspell* does not have the song recognition that *Jesus Christ, Superstar* does. Furthermore, the New York City setting provides a distracting backdrop to the movie's symbolic style. Even so, the cinematography is stunning.

1977:

Jesus of Nazareth (TV) was directed by the renowned Franco Zeffirelli and produced by our friend and former history professor Vincenzo Labella for Sir Lew Grade and Radiotelevisione Italiana (RAI). This excellent television movie attempts historical accuracy. Many passages of the Bible are quoted verbatim and the locations look authentic. Aside from Robert Powell as Jesus, Olivia Hussey as Mary, and Stacy Keach as Barabbas, many of the other characters are actually played by Semitic-looking actors. Of its six hours and twenty minutes, the first hour is devoted solely to the story of Jesus' birth, and twelve minutes is devoted to the Last Supper as well as twelve minutes to the Crucifixion.

1979:

The Jesus Film, released in 1979 by Warner Bros, has been viewed by 3.3 billion people as of this writing thanks to the efforts of Campus Crusade for Christ. At least 108 million people have indicated they have placed their faith in Jesus Christ after seeing the film. The movie has been translated into 566 languages with 232 in process. The audio/radio version is available in 54 languages, and another hundred languages will be added this year. Also, *The Jesus Film* has been re-configured to reach different audiences (niche strategies).

1988:

Last Temptation of Christ is the most blasphemous movie ever made. As if that was not bad enough, it is extremely boring and sometimes even downright silly.

1996:

Matthew, produced by Visual Entertainment, translates the Bible verbatim. The first in the Visual Bible series, *Matthew* is one of the best and clearest translations brought to life through the movie medium. Indeed, the very words of Christ and every word by every character is lifted completely from the New International Version.

2003:

The Gospel of John, a word-for-word movie taken from the gospel of the same name, was one of the best movies ever made about the life of Jesus Christ.

2004:

The Passion of the Christ was Mel Gibson's great masterpiece about the final hours of Jesus Christ.

2006:

The Nativity Story tells the story of the birth of Jesus Christ in a dramatic, authentic manner.

WHAT CONSTITUTES A "CHRISTIAN" MOVIE?

It would be a great breakthrough in contemporary communications if we could refrain from using the word "Christian" as an adjective, and limit its use as the early church and the Romans did, by defining "Christian," only as a noun.[7] In the book of *The Acts of the Apostles*, a Christian is a person who confesses and follows Jesus Christ. Paul is a Christian who makes tents; however, the tents that Paul makes are not "Christian" tents.

By restricting the use of "Christian," we would no longer be confused by "Christian" art and media. Instead, we would have Christians, who make a work of art, or who communicate through a specific medium, such as television. The artwork made by a Christian may or may not communicate the gospel of Jesus Christ. If we evaluated the art as art, the television program as a program, and the tent as a tent (including any gospel messages woven into the fabric), then we would be delivered from the temptation to worship a particular thing as a sacred object set apart by the use of "Christian" as an adjective.

Setting the art, music, book, or any media apart by the adjectival use of "Christian," often allows several destructive attitudes to undermine the quality of a specific work. Blinded by the word "Christian," we often indulge sloppy or bad workmanship, thereby perpetuating inferior communication and art. Some artists and communicators may assume that the "Christian" adjective pinned to their work will cover a multitude of imperfections; allowing them to undermine the overall quality of work under a blanket of protection through association. These assumptions are ultimately destructive to creating a culture of kingdom-oriented artists and communicators. When an individual fails to exercise their talents, learn their craft, or invest time and effort into the work God has given them, they are falling short of God's calling. The Lord will work in us, but we must not rely on Him to do all the work. We are not saved by works;[8] but, we are called to work with diligence and industry,[9] knowing God will work in us, providing us with the strength to do His will.[10]

It is unlikely that the adjectival use of the word "Christian" will be abandoned in the near future, either by pagans or Christians. However, as Christians, we must always do our best as God's ambassadors—evaluating our work honestly against the highest possible standards—because we love Him, trust Him, and want all that we do to glorify Him. We must hold one another to the highest standards, and refuse to settle for anything less.

> Those who do not remember the past are condemned to relive it.
>
> —George Santaya

Once Upon a Time . . .

Christians often forget that the Church exerted a great influence on the entertainment industry from 1933 to 1966. For thirty-three years, every single movie script was read by representatives of the Roman Catholic Church, the Southern Baptist Church, and the Protestant Film Office. Their job was to evaluate a movie in terms of the Motion Picture Code. If the film passed the Code, it received the Motion Picture Code Seal and was distributed. If it did not pass, the theaters would not screen it.

The Short Form of the Motion Picture Code provided the following guidelines:

1. The basic dignity and value of human life shall be respected and upheld. Restraint shall be exercised in portraying the taking of life.
2. Evil, sin, crime, and wrong-doing shall not be justified.

3. Detailed and protracted acts of brutality, cruelty, physical violence, torture, and abuse, shall not be presented.
4. Indecent or undue exposure of the human body shall not be presented.
5. Illicit sex relationships shall not be justified. Intimate sex scenes violating common standards of decency shall not be portrayed. Restraint and care shall be exercised in presentations dealing with sex aberrations.
6. Obscene speech, gestures, or movements shall not be presented. Undue profanity shall not be presented.
7. Religion shall not be demeaned.
8. Words or symbols contemptuous of racial, religious, or national groups, shall not be used so as to incite bigotry or hatred.
9. Excessive cruelty to animals shall not be portrayed and animals shall not be treated inhumanely.

During the period of the Motion Picture Code, there was no explicit sex, violence, profanity, or blasphemy in movies. Also, films were not permitted to mock a minister of religion or any person's faith (the religious persecution in Germany prompted this wise counsel). For the most part, movies and television programs aligned with the biblical principles of communicating the true, the good, and the beautiful.

Then, in 1966, the churches voluntarily withdrew from the entertainment industry. Many of the media elite bemoaned the retreat of the churches. One prophesied, "If the salt is removed from the meat, then the meat will rot." Many studio executives felt the church involvement helped them to reach the large Christian audience in the United States and believed that Christians would avoid movies not carrying the Motion Picture Code Seal.

Censorship or Patron Sovereignty?

Patron sovereignty has traditionally been commended by Hollywood as the right of movie patrons to determine what they want to see—or avoid—by their activity at the box office. When there was talk in the 1930s of government censorship, the movie industry requested patron sovereignty in the form of the Motion Picture Code. Throughout the life of the Code and its successor, the MPAA rating system, the entertainment industry has continued to express its preference for patron sovereignty (rather than government intervention) to curb industry tendencies toward obscenity and violence.

When the churches retreated, the Motion Picture Association of America (MPAA) instituted the rating system to take the place of the Code. This changing of the guard was like letting a fox guard the hen house—the results were predictable.

In our culture's constant quest for political correctness, many scripts today are read by feminist, Marxist, and homosexual groups, such as GLAAD (The Gay & Lesbian Alliance Against Defamation). Very few scripts are read by Christian groups, such as the not-for-profit Christian Film & Television Commission and Movieguide. These groups, Christian and otherwise, award pictures and television programs that communicate their point of view and condemn movies and television programs which disagree with their point of view. For instance, one television network had to spend hundreds of thousands of dollars to re-shoot and re-edit a television movie so that it would not offend the Alliance of Gay and Lesbian Artists.

WHOEVER CONTROLS THE MEDIA
CONTROLS THE CULTURE

At the influence of these anti-biblical groups seeking cultural approval and political correctness, movies and television programs have become purveyors of immorality, blasphemy, and rebellion. They have influenced far too many viewers to mimic the evil they see on the screen. Alan Alda noted in the movie *Sweet Liberty* that to capture an audience, a movie must include the destruction of property (i.e., the car chase), rebellion against authority, and immoral sex. Of course, the audience he had in mind was the teenagers and young adults who generally flock to popular movies. It is interesting to note how this mirrors Karl Marx's four goals in his *Communist Manifesto*: abolish property, abolish the family, abolish the nation, and abolish religion and morality.

The destructive power of mass media was highlighted by the 1988 television remake of the famous movie, *Inherit the Wind*, which dramatically retold the story of the famous trial of *The State of Tennessee vs. Scopes* (i.e., Scopes Monkey Trial). Although the Christian defense won the trial, they lost the battle in the media. William Jennings Bryan defeated Clarence Darrow in court, but then Bryan was defeated in the press by the venomous anti-Christian reporting of H. L. Mencken. As in many cases since then, the Christians have won the skirmish, but lost the battle to the manipulators of mass media.

Christians should never forget the lesson of the Scopes Trial: it is futile to win the trial, but lose the battle for media representation. We need to claim the Lord's victory and win the war by taking every thought captive for Him.

To paraphrase John Locke, "Whoever controls the media, controls the culture." In the Scopes Trial, the press controlled the language and communicated an anti-Christian bias. Society adopted that bias with a strongly rebellious attitude, even though the Christians had the law on their side. In the same manner, if those who control the language of communication emphasize rape, pillage, and plunder, the culture will reflect an emphasis on communicating those things.

Like the Christians involved in the Scopes Trial, we often forget that there is a war being waged all around us. This war is not taking place on a physical battlefield. It's being fought on the internal landscape of our minds. It is a spiritual war for the souls of those who constitute our civilization, and it uses the most effective weapon ever conceived: communications.

Jesus was the master of communications. His parables are as pertinent today as they were 2,000 years ago. He knew the great power of communicating and understood how ideas shape civilizations. His words toppled one of the most powerful civilizations in history—the Roman Empire. They continue to transform the world today.

Though the tools of communications have changed, the words remain the same. The warfare of ideas and thoughts has exploded through the use of movies and television, revolutionizing our way of thinking. We are fighting against an enemy using every possible tactic to shift our focus from God and control our thoughts: materialism, secularism, humanism, Marxism . . . a long list of all the other "isms" that conflict with Christianity.

Daily, we are besieged with an onslaught of messages that tear us apart. If it's not the morning newspaper, it's the nightly news, or cable television portraying a lifestyle of drugs, illicit sex, and violence.

Ugly Americans

Already, the United States is considered by many to be the most immoral country in the world. Movies are often re-edited to include more sex and violence when released in the U.S. market. For example, the Australian release of the movie *Return to Snowy River* shows the hero and heroine getting married, while the U.S. release, portrays the couple co-habiting without marriage.

In January, 2003, Boston University released a shocking study detailing the image of Americans held by teenagers around the world, entitled *The Next Generation's Image of Americans: Attitudes and Beliefs Held by Teen-Agers in Twelve Countries: A Preliminary Research Report*, by Margaret H. DeFleur, Ph.D. and Melvin L. DeFleur, Ph.D.

This Boston University study revealed that young people worldwide have a generally negative image of Americans. It also brought to light the belief that this negative image was—at least in part—

responsible for the anti-American uprising underlying the bombing of the World Trade Center on September 11, 2001. The study predicted that the negative image would continue to grow, and also linked the worldwide distaste for American culture specifically to the image being presented by Hollywood (not the attributes of real Americans). In other words, Hollywood is our ambassador to the whole world. The study assumed that: The collective condemnation expressed by a people when a negative incident occurs must come from somewhere. As a general principle, a negative incident can become a cause celebre, rallying widespread anger, only if a necessary condition is met. That condition is this: There must already be in place a foundation of shared negative beliefs and attitudes toward the United States upon which the feelings generated by the specific incident can be based.

According to the authors, "The results show that members of the next generation studied in nearly all countries appear to hold consistently negative attitudes toward Americans as people." The results also suggest that problems for Americans are likely to continue into the foreseeable future. Teens surveyed predicted that America would continue to suffer from the threat of terrorism, public health issues related to stress, and possible economic problems.

Though the United States has historically been considered a good world citizen and provided many forms of assistance to other struggling nations, the study showed no indication that a good track record would help the U.S. overcome current negative impressions among foreign teens.

This study focused on teenagers because, "they are the ones who are trained and equipped to conduct terrorist acts. When examining the nature of such threats, and who it is that carries out actual terrorist activities, either in the U.S. or in other countries, one fact becomes very obvious. They are the young. Many Americans have seen televised scenes of youngsters as young as 12 being trained in terrorists' camps to engage in aggression against the infidel [read: Americans]."

The study noted, "Those who actually flew the airliners on September 11 were young adults, to be sure, but it is clear that their beliefs were shaped earlier, during their teenage years. In the final analysis, then, it is the young who are recruited to do older men's bidding—to deliver their bombs and weapons to the point of impact, even if it means their own death."

Among other beliefs, the study found that teenagers in these countries believe the following: Americans are generally quite violent; many American women are sexually immoral; Americans are very materialistic; Americans like to dominate other people; and, many Americans engage in criminal activities.

Few of those surveyed had any direct contact with Americans; only twelve percent had visited the United States. Many of the teens surveyed had access to American television programs, movies, and pop music, and therefore based their conclusions (like those listed above) on the culture portrayed in American media.

"These results suggest that pop culture, rather than foreign policy, is the true culprit of anti-Americanism," Melvin DeFleur says. "Hollywood should at least be asked by our public leaders to accept responsibility for the damage it is doing."

Figure 2: Foreign Teen Attitudes Toward Americans

Overall Attitudes Toward Americans

Source: BOSTON UNIVERSITY, 2003	Very Negative -5	-4	-3	Generally Negative -2	-1	Neutral -0	+1	Generally Positive +2
		NEGATIVE				POSITIVE		
Saudi Arabia	-3.13							
Bahrain		-1.95						
South Korea		-1.76						
Mexico		-1.50						
China			-1.05					
Spain			-0.89					
Taiwan			-0.79					
Dominican Rep				-0.50				
Pakistan				-0.45				
Nigeria				-0.05				
Italy						+0.03		
Argentina							+0.69	
Overall	-3.13							

Figure 3: Foreign Teen Beliefs about American Culture

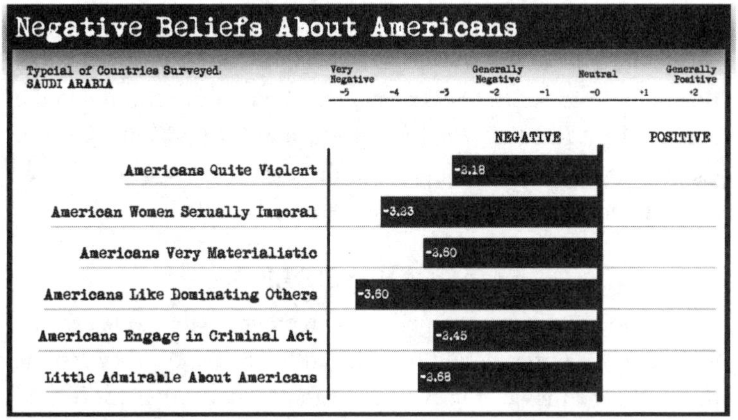

Negative Beliefs About Americans

Typical of Countries Surveyed: SAUDI ARABIA	Very Negative		Generally Negative		Neutral		Generally Positive
	-5	-4	-3	-2	-1	-0	+1	+2

	NEGATIVE	POSITIVE
Americans Quite Violent	-3.18	
American Women Sexually Immoral	-3.33	
Americans Very Materialistic	-3.60	
Americans Like Dominating Others	-3.60	
Americans Engage in Criminal Act.	-3.45	
Little Admirable About Americans	-3.58	

Movies Are a Tool

It is important to understand that each media medium has unique advantages and disadvantages. To communicate how something looks, an oft quoted Chinese proverb tells us, "A picture is worth a thousand words." If, however, we want to communicate the true nature of some person, event, or thing, then a few words, such as "the Word was made flesh and dwelt among us,"[11] say more than a thousand pictures.

Each media medium can be seen primarily as a communication tool,[12] capable of accomplishing one or more functions of communicating. A tool itself is neither good nor bad; it develops association appropriate to its use. When we use a tool to perform the function it was created to perform, it performs well.

A screwdriver, for instance, is very useful for driving screws. It is of some value in scraping paint off the side of our house; but it would not perform well used to hammer a nail—and it would be no use at all in gripping a nut. Using a screwdriver to repair a church artifact does not make it "good," just as using it to stab someone does not make the same screwdriver "bad." Rather, the person using the screwdriver is the one morally responsible. The same principle applies to the various media of communications.

Movies and television programs can be used to build up the Body of Christ (i.e., *The Passion of the Christ*), or to tear down the church (i.e., *The Last Temptation of Christ*). Any filmmaker can use the movie medium for good or ill. It is up to the filmmaker to develop sensibility and good judgment.

ASK AN INSIDER

Since people watch movies and television programs that seem exciting and last only a brief period of time (an hour or two), they assume that making a movie or television program is not very hard. In fact, most people are shocked to find that it costs Hollywood over $100 million to produce and release a movie ($106 million, on average, as of this book's publication date). Therefore, it is imperative to a basic understanding of the entertainment industry that we consult an insider; an expert who will help us start asking the right questions.

Dan Nichols does just that in the following article. Dan has produced and has been involved in many movies, including *Raiders of the Lost Ark* and *Always*. Recently, he was executive producer of Movieguide's award-winning movie, *Luther*. He has taken movies with real story problems and turned them into successful films. In the article below, Dan shares some wonderful insight on getting involved in the entertainment industry.

SO, WHAT'S YOUR STORY?

—J. DANIEL NICHOLS

It was 5:20 a.m. on a typically beautiful day in Hawaii. On location with a short-lived TV series I was producing for Universal Studios, I stood by the "bottomless" black stone swimming pool of a hilltop estate, watching my cast and crew rehearse a scene at the far edge of the yard. The camera angle included a spectacular panoramic view of Honolulu, framed by the inevitable morning procession of rainbows floating through Manoa Valley toward the glistening beach of Waikiki.

I was abruptly pulled from the beauty of the view when I heard the A.D. shouting insistently for silence from the rest of the company, gathered in the distance around the many trailers and trucks in the estate's expansive parking cove. He closed his colorful exhortation with the statement, "*This* is what it's about ladies and gentlemen," using his entire arm to point toward the two lone actors standing in front of the lens, struggling to make the moment work for the sake of the story they had been hired to tell. His words made it very clear to everyone that the story was the sole reason for our presence at that place, on that day, at that time, with all of that gear and our 102 people.

To my relief, the people who were being exhorted did not respond with resentment or indifference. Instead, they responded with evident agreement that they had been wrong and deserved the correction. Veteran drivers, greenspersons, make-up artists, day players, grips, electricians, and others redirected their focus and attention to the common good. They may have been connected to their work through their expertise in their chosen crafts, but they were connected to the industry and its unwritten rules of purpose in an even deeper, more reverent way.

As for me, I'll never forget the meaning in those words. That simple moment helped define for me what business I was in. There are many industries in which I could apply the same skills used to produce a weekly series for primetime TV and make a decent living, as could any of the other craftspeople on the set that day, but that one incident made it very clear what our business was. It was not about the beautiful view, or the camaraderie among the talented cast and crew, or the smell of fresh coffee in the early morning, or the laughter, or money, or all of the other feelings of personal enjoyment and belonging experienced on a set or location shoot. The measure in this business that most typically assures another day of employment is, was, and always will be, the story. The question at the end of every day is, "Did we get our day's worth of story?"

Since that incident, I have met with hundreds of young people who have wanted to get into the business of film and television production. I have not met with many who came looking for information about how to get into media marketing or distribution or sales. That fact has always intrigued me. The crafting of film or television product distribution, the marketing of those products, and the development of ancillary markets for film and television program products comprise the components of the industry most directly related to earnings. Yet, the industry's appeal to many energetic, purpose-driven people seems to be the process we see and hear so much about on "behind-the-scenes" programs and DVD extras: the creation, development, and production process and the celebrity relationships that result from that business of creativity.

So, the first question I ask the rookies is, "Do you know what business *you're* wanting to be in?" They look puzzled for a moment, and then provide an answer as if wondering why I am asking. They usually just say, "The film business," or "Television," or "Interactive media," or "Theater." It's as if they expect me to know which of the many, many occupations within any of those businesses they are talking about. If they respond by answering, "The entertainment business," the number of potential professions they must ultimately choose from has increased exponentially. If they do respond with one of those generic answers, then I know that the person has not yet answered the important questions about their involvement in the industry that will bring focus to their life's journey.

To live without focus and purpose by working in any area of the industry that provides employment for the moment provides nothing more than an extended internship in producing and builds no future. Not everyone should be a producer. Not everyone *could* be a producer. Yet, producing is the primary skill-set within the industry that is best served by knowing at least a little bit about every aspect of the industry—from development to exhibition.

I'm not saying that it is unbeneficial for anyone interested in the industry to work as a production assistant on a few large productions to decide which aspect of the industry one finds most appealing, but I suggest that a few are sufficient. Thereafter, a person needs to determine what they truly want to do in the industry and then focus on working in that area of expertise so the appropriate preparation and relationships can be defined and initiated. Choose carefully, then waste no time.

Typically, anyone who has recently entered, or is thinking of entering, the production industry will fall into one of two categories. The first category is the person, or group, who comes as an owner of products. The second category is the person who comes as a craftsperson, looking to use their trade to make a living in the production business.

Although the people in either of these groups could probably make a more secure and better work/family–balanced living in the outside world, I will not try to explain the internal drives that make a person want to be associated with the screen arts industry. For each person, it is a different set of reasons. However, all should at least ask themselves why they are wanting in. Is it for fulfillment? Freedom? Adventure? Self-validation? Money? Control? Power to make future creative choices? What? Perhaps, it cannot be explained anymore than why man creates anything, but the more a person understands one's personal reasons for wanting to be a part of the business, the easier it is to formulate the next questions that must be answered to intensify one's focus even further. With each new set of questions a person can answer related to motive and intention of oneself, the more constructively controlling one is of the industry's impact on one's life.

The first of the two groups I mentioned is producers who believe they have one or more wonderful projects that will succeed in the marketplace if those projects can make it to a screen. These people may also be the writers of their projects, but writers fall into the second category. This producers group almost always comes in search of money or an established person in the industry who can move their project forward. To this producer group I say be serious about your work. Examine your motives carefully so you understand what the point of reference will be for all of the decisions you will need to make with little time to think about them. What is your true motive? Not the cause-centered one, but your personal one . . . the one in your heart. It is your heart that will be put to the test as you move forward as a producer. The first two questions you will have to answer are, "Who am I willing to hurt?" and "Who am I willing to lose as relationships?" Is your motive truly your desire to tell a story? Perhaps you are as altruistic as you believe you are. Will you be willing to give it to someone else to produce just to see it done? Or, do you need to control how the story is told? Then your motive may be self-expression. Could nobody do the story as well as you could? Perhaps, you seek self-validation or just a break. Perhaps, you lack humility. Could you have the same impact writing articles? Teaching? What are you using as your benchmark for success? Exceeding Bible sales for the year or exceeding box office receipts for *The Passion of the Christ*? Or, just getting your project distributed?

Those in this first group need to well understand that the role of producer is one of the most emotionally demanding positions anyone can fill because the development process can be destructive to relationships. It is common for friends to enter this world together because they have rallied around a particular project they feel is worthy of their collective efforts only to find that the decision-making process required in creative collaboration results in good friends and allies becoming opponents, at least for the duration of development and possibly throughout production. Often, relationships are never restored. If you desire to lead the production, will you be willing to hurt your friends for the sake of the production and the quality you deem greater than the quality they define? You may hurt them simply by rejecting their ideas or thinking. But, what if you're wrong? Creativity, even in its most collaborative form, is ultimately about control. Who gets to decide what "good" means? Who gets to make the final choices in each of the processes and facets of production? You may find yourself in a position in which everything is at stake because the project has to find distribution if it is going to impact the culture the way you promised your investors it would, or if money is to be earned. So, whose viewpoint will be used as the point of reference for decisions of taste and quality and, inevitably, conflict resolution? All of this is done everyday by many people, but if one has not yet addressed the questions while it is still possible to do so in a mind-rehearsal state, one may not be ready to move forward into an arena in which these questions must be answered through actions that have irreversible consequences.

The second group of entrants is the people who are dependent upon finding an employer who trusts their abilities and believes in their talent. These people range from writers to actors to drivers to wardrobe designers to every other craft that contributes to the success of the industry.

The entertainment industry is comprised of an array of occupations that have little or nothing to do with entertainment as it is talked about in the media, but has everything to do with storytelling. Each of these master craftspersons contribute subtly and sometimes not so subtly to what the audience perceives as story. However, it is only because the products created by the craftspeople of these occupations is captured on a visual medium and sold as a product itself that an audience ever sees their work. I recommend that anyone interested in becoming a craftsperson in the industry clearly define the occupation they are interested in and master that skill for use within the industry or in the outside world. The major difference between the production industry and the outside world is that most often production requires faster work, more of it, with greater dependencies, and therefore a greater chance for failure, in a more condensed period of time. It can be a rush for those who thrive on self-satisfaction in their accomplishments.

Writers and actors of film and television are very specialized craftpersons, so those specific skills are not as easy to apply in the outside world. However, the basics of the skills can find markets other than film and television. Sadly, one of the misconceptions of our society is that anything other than the public arena of screen arts is a lower measure of success than "making it" in the production business. My response is that I have met many multimillionaires and happy people who have nothing to do with the entertainment business. It's all about focus and purpose and the right fit for an individual. No one should perceive the industry as a measure of success, only a measure of personal fulfillment if the industry is one's goal.

I well understand that the *perception* of the industry is appealing to any creative person, whether that person has trade skills in writing, acting, carpentry, interior design, transportation, botany, laboratory sciences, computer sciences, or any other industry that is used in the production industry. It is appealing to people to be part of something that the media exposure can make larger than life: That gives an added value to the work and contribution of an individual, but that credibility-by-association should never be the measure by which a craftsperson determines one's professional value or retirement plan.

Whichever path a person chooses, it's important that one has a very clear understanding of one's motives, expectations, and reasons for working in the industry to survive it. When people who love the industry are getting to work in it, there is no better feeling. When we are in pursuit of work that often seems so close yet so far away, it is agonizing. We become like children eating our favorite candy: We relish the flavor and emotional gratification, but when it is gone and the supply is out of reach, we flop ourselves on the floor in wailing misery. When we grow up, most of us know how to balance our desires with the reality of life. If you cannot do that regarding this industry, then it will devour you. Only give it the value it is worthy of, as it relates to the whole of your life. Admire the power and influence of the industry as such, and desire to be an influence in it, but guard your heart from the pain and frustration your personal participation or lack of participation can cause.

As a side note, I often encounter people who love watching television and films so much that they believe they want to be a part of the industry. Many start writing screenplays or looking for opportunities to get into the industry in any way possible, doing whatever they can do, just to get in the door. I try to explain to them that there is a big difference between being a person who appreciates the industry and the emotions the finished products bring into one's life, and making a living—or just working—in the industry. Many people who are attempting to break into the industry are much better off continuing to simply enjoy the industry as viewers. Sometimes, the biggest contribution a person can make to the industry is to simply appreciate it as a consumer. Ask yourself the question and face the answer even if it is hard to accept.

So how does all of the above relate to the incident in Hawaii and the value of story?

Let me ask you what *your* story is. Are you getting into a business to see how it treats you? Are you getting into an industry because you like how other people's work in that industry makes you feel? I suggest you approach it more seriously than that. Know what the business of entertainment really is. More importantly, know who you are outside of the industry and what your relationship to the industry of entertainment should be. If you desire to make a living as a craftsperson within the industry, focus on that craft and master it. Do not relate to it solely as part of the entertainment industry. If you want to be a producer, understand who you want to tell stories to and be serious about telling those stories in whatever form best affords you that opportunity. Don't always think "big time" if there is no need for a particular story to be big time. Some stories should only be told to small audiences. Never get caught up in the fascination of the production processes to the point you lose sight of why all of the equipment, people, techniques, technology, and money are being used. Make a development plan and work hard to stay on track. Understand what you want out of the industry to a greater degree than you understand what you'll be willing to allow the industry to take out of you.

Don't become engaged in all of the meaningless and endless pursuits that the fringe of this industry disguises as relevant. You will stay very busy, but you will not be productive. The cafés of Hollywood and every other media capital in the world are filled with busy people discussing deals and believing their time is being well spent, but the vast majority of those people will never see their projects come to fruition because each step of their process is defined by the previous step and who makes it. They will never see a person's life changed because of their meetings.

To anyone with a biblical worldview interested in pursuing a career within the production industry, I ask you to especially consider what occupation you truly wish to pursue. What is your primary reason for that answer as it relates to the business of telling stories? Is your interest in the viewpoint or the view? In the values or the value? In the result or the process? In the impact to our culture or the personal gain? If your answers are not the first option of each question just asked, then I suggest that you consider a broader market for your talents in which normal hours, good base pay without overtime, and consistency of employment are standard fare.

If you have read all of these words and still have a burning desire to be part of this incredible business, perhaps you should be.

* * *

Watch the Credits

As Dan mentions above, there are many people who work on a Hollywood television program or movie—just read the credits. There are the actors, the producers, the director, the writers, the cinematographer, the director of photography, the editors, the art directors, the soundmen, and the list seems to go endlessly on.

Just operating the camera requires a director of photography, a cameraman, a person who moves the camera, a person who clears the way for the camera, and so forth. Also, there are coaches, coordinators, gaffers (electricians), gofers, costume designers, etc. And this is a small sampling of people who might work on a $106 million Hollywood movie.

With so many specific roles available, you need to decide which area of the entertainment industry is best suited for your gifts and talents. Keep reading. This book will help you to do just that!

ASK THE RIGHT QUESTIONS

Dan has helped us focus in on the idea that the movie and television industry is all about telling stories, and has prompted you to think about your story. He has also pointed us in the right direction by outlining the most relevant questions for any Christian seeking to find a career in the entertainment industry. Asking the right questions is absolutely the key to making a great movie or television program. Begin thinking about these questions:

What is your interest in the entertainment industry?
– Success?
– Fame?
– Good relationships?
– Obedience to God and His Great Commission?

Whatever your goal, you must be able to communicate effectively in your chosen medium to achieve it.

THE POWER

In the summer of 1981, I was invited to Knoxville, Tennessee, by nine local churches representing different denominations, to consult on the design of an exhibit that would represent those churches to attendees of the 1982 World's Fair. A crowd of nearly thirty consultants, media experts, and theologians from all over the U.S. came to this consultation to advise the Knoxville churches on their exhibit. The theme of the World's Fair was energy, so the prevailing opinion of those present was that the exhibit should contain posters illustrating energy (e.g., a power plant, an engine, an atomic bomb), with biblical scriptures (e.g., "Blessed are the peacemakers,"[13] "Blessed are you who are poor,"[14] and "the land is mine and you are but aliens and my tenants"[15]).

I thought this approach sounded very dull. As the meeting continued, I recalled the 1964 World's Fair in New York City, where almost all the exhibits had long waiting lines—except the Protestant Exhibit—which was decorated with posters with biblical subscriptions.[16] I reasoned that people came to a World's Fair to be entertained by visionary exhibits that would capture their imagination. If the churches wanted to attract people to their exhibit, I suggested that they use the latest technology and the best creative talent available to build the most exciting exhibit at the World's Fair.

The churches asked me to be the executive producer of the exhibit, which we named *The Power*. In prayer, God gave me a vision for an exciting Disneyland-type exhibit that presented God as the Author of all energy—*The Power*. A month of meetings with creative talent focused this vision into an interactive exhibit where the audience would step inside a time-rocket and blast-off back to the beginning of time. They would find themselves plunged into total darkness, watch God create the heavens and the earth, land in paradise, and then get kicked out for disobedience. They would enter into man's world, become overwhelmed by the cacophony of voices competing for attention, and cry out for help. They would meet Jesus, and follow Him though the cross into His Body (The Church), where they could be filled with His Spirit, and empowered to do His work. The exhibit would finish with everyone singing "The Lord's Prayer" together.

After months of hard work by some of the top electronic media and show business talent[17] in the country, *The Power* became a reality—the most technologically sophisticated exhibit at the 1983 World's Fair, visited by over one million people, and representing the combined statement of fifteen denominations. Newspapers from all over the United States called *The Power* the most exciting exhibit at the World's Fair, and children of all ages enjoyed this trip through time and space.

I thank God for all the miracles, and the tremendous contributions of all the talented individuals who created, built, and maintained the exhibit. But truly, it was the churches, working and communicating together that made *The Power* possible. They adhered to the basic principles of good communication, and through God's vision and these principles, a great idea took flight.

The churches asked similar questions to those we've outlined before in this book:

1. What do we want to communicate (what story do we want to tell)?
2. What is the forum and marketplace for communicating our message?
3. Who is our audience?
4. What is the appropriate genre (or format) for communicating our message?
5. What is the appropriate medium for our communication?
6. What is the appropriate grammar and language to use in sharing our message?

The churches wanted to communicate their presence and biblical views to the World's Fair visitors—that was their goal. They succeeded. In addition, *The Power* was purchased after the World's Fair closed by the Media Ministry of the Missionary Oblates for permanent display at the National Shrine of Our Lady of the Snows in Belleville, Illinois (just outside of St. Louis, Missouri). Through this permanent display of *The Power*, the churches involved in the exhibit will continue to communicate their message to people for years to come.

The story of *The Power* has a happy ending, but some of our communications are also likely to fall short of what we want them to do. Sometimes our communications fail because of circumstances beyond our control. As one of Murphy's Laws reminds us, "If you explain something so clearly that no one can misunderstand, someone will." Often, our communications fail because we have failed to ask the right questions—either because we are lazy, impatient, solipsistic,[18] or fearful.

LEARNING THE LANGUAGE

To communicate through the mass media of entertainment, we must learn the language and the grammar of our medium. A broadcaster once told the story of a baby mouse and a mother mouse. The mother told the baby she was going to look for food and that the baby should not leave his mouse home. While the mother was gone, the baby noticed a delicious piece of cheese on top of a table not far from its home. The baby scurried to get the cheese, and the cat caught the baby. The mother saw what happened, ran up behind the cat and screamed, "Bow, wow!" The cat dropped the baby mouse and ran. The moral of the mother mouse's story is this: "You must learn how to speak two languages."

For Christians, effective communication means much more than achieving one's goals, desires, and needs because communication is at the heart of the story of Jesus Christ, and we have been called to communicate that story.[19] His story begins with communication: "In the beginning was the Word" (John 1:1).

That Word of God is Jesus the Christ, the Son of God, the great communicator, indeed the very Author of creation, who made all things. Since the fall, His story continues; the Word of God is in the business of rescuing people. We are created in His Image, and He has called us to help Him.[20] As Jesus says, "You will receive power when the Holy Spirit has come upon you; and you will be my witnesses . . ." (Acts 1:8 ESV).

We want to proclaim His gospel because we love Him, and because we love our neighbor so much that we want to save our neighbor from death. Our witnessing is a direct, natural, inevitable consequence of our becoming and being Christians, according to Jesus in Acts 1:8. Filled with power, we will witness. The good news is that "we are God's fellow workers,"[21] called to witness, yet it is He who witnesses through us.[22] Unlike Islam, where the Muslim must convert the non-Muslim any way possible—through argument, persuasion, bribery, or torture—we do not have to worry about converting anyone, for God's Holy Spirit converts.[23] Our great commission is to communicate Jesus and His salvation.

In preaching Jesus Christ, we must not compromise with the world system, or forsake our zeal for Him.[24] Yet, since we love Him and our audience, we need to translate our communication into the appropriate language and place it in the appropriate context so that our audience is able to hear and understand what we have to say. We should make ourselves "a slave to all, in order to win more people" (1 Corinthians 9:19).

Community

A psychiatrist, who was at the time advising me on the production of a PBS television program on divorce prevention, noted during our conversation that he had recently been on a U.S. government commission to discover the reasons for chronic poverty in Appalachia. Before going into the field, the commission assumed that the state of poverty was closely tied to environment or lack of education. In the field, the committee found a disparity among Appalachian residents, even those living in very close proximity to one another. The team found that just a few miles from "civilization" they might discover a house and family in ruins, and then just down the creek, come upon a well-kept home and an industrious family. The difference was not isolation or lack of education. The commission found that the more successful family nearly always had a relative nearby, or a close neighbor, who cared enough to be demanding and interested in the welfare of that family.

We must be interested in the welfare of the family of believers.[25]

"I don't care" and "Don't get involved" are negative and destructive adages. Healthy criticism—which is loving, not judgmental—and sincere concern help all of us.[26]

Provision

Frequently in today's busy lifestyle, we feel like we do not have time to love our neighbor. We are too busy worrying about money, because we really do not trust God to provide. The good news is that He will provide when we take the time to love Him and our neighbor.[27] Trusting God to provide takes time, and trusting Him to the degree that we can be available for—and responsive to—our neighbor (which includes our families, our friends, and even our enemies) takes time and the power of His Spirit.

Sometimes, we are just too concerned with our business to pay attention to others; but Jesus, the Communicator, is always available, and calls us to be available.[28] If we focus on Him and His grace, we will be freed from fear and available to communicate His gospel. For instance, four days before *The Power* exhibit was to open at the 1982 World's Fair, we were $150,000 short of funds. We were paid up to date (more than $1 million in goods and services, plus $600,000 in cash expenditures), but the crew was anticipating that we would not have the final $150,000 to pay them on Friday morning, the day before the grand opening.

The crew was comprised of the best talent in the country, chosen for of their skills, not their religious beliefs. Many crewmembers were more committed to receiving their wages than proclaiming the gospel message. The churches had spent all the money they could, and had no idea where they could find funding to cover the deficit. One of my associates suggested I give up, stay in Atlanta, and not bother going to Knoxville. I countered that this was God's exhibit and He would finance it.

I flew to Knoxville late Tuesday afternoon. My director took me aside to inform me that the crew was planning to walk off the job. I prayed. Around 9:00 p.m., a man stopped by the exhibit and asked me how things were going. I quickly told him that we needed $150,000 in the bank in Atlanta by Thursday. He did not have a lot of money, but he felt that the exhibit was the responsibility of the people of Knoxville, and invited me to a prayer meeting that the sponsoring churches were holding early the next morning. Thanks to God's grace, we had $175,000 in the bank by Thursday. The extra $25,000 was just enough to pay for maintenance of *The Power* for the first few months of operation.

We should never worry about finances, time, or any of the other obstacles that seem to stand in the way of our fulfilling God's calling for us. "Now this is the confidence we have before Him: whenever we ask anything according to His will, He hears us. And if we know that He hears whatever we ask, we know that we have what we have asked Him for" (1 John 5:14–15). Instead, we should concern ourselves with doing His will, so that we can trust in His provision.

We learn God's will by studying His Word, the Bible, and by allowing His Spirit to live in us. The good news is that He gives each of us our own unique combination of motivations, talents, and gifts which, when discerned, will help us discover how we can do our best to communicate the message of our calling. All too often, we become frustrated trying to communicate in a particular way or through a particular medium that does not suit our unique motivational talents. Some of us are chosen to be writers, some executive producers, some directors, some art directors, etc.

When you discover your unique motivational talent and learn the language of the medium through which you will communicate your calling, then you will be able to access any channel of communication (television, radio, newspaper, etc.), capture and motivate an audience, and communicate the gospel in all its glory.

Years ago, as president of the Episcopal Radio TV Foundation, Inc., (commissioned by the Protestant Radio TV Center—a consortium of four denominations) I initiated and produced a television series for PBS television satellite distribution called *Perspectives*.

After one year on the PBS satellite, *Perspectives* was carried on one hundred and twenty PBS stations and cable systems. Several programs in the series won important national awards.[29] Every program I produced and hosted had a biblical perspective.

One evening, at a benefit dinner, a renowned church organist opened a conversation with me by complaining that Christians could not place programs on PBS television because PBS would not carry programs containing a religious message.[30] A friend of the organist—a Christian who produced television programs—had complained to my new friend that he could not convince PBS to carry his latest program. I mentioned *Perspectives*, and suggested that the problem could be the quality of the program in question, or the program format, rather than a problem with PBS. In fact, I was aware of the program in question. Though it had a great message, it was not directed, or edited, very well.

Of course, the problem could have been with one of the PBS member stations, or with personnel. However, all too often the problem is not with the gatekeeper,[31] or "the other guy," but instead with the design and quality of our communication. This book will help you overcome those problems and will specifically examine the medium of television and how to place your program on the channel of your choice.

W.C. Fields proclaimed one of the most practical rules of effective communications when he said, "Tell them what you are going to say; say it; and, tell them what you said." With that principle in mind, let's look at the structure of this book.

To communicate effectively, you must learn the basic principles of good communication, as well as the language and grammar of the genre and the medium through which you will be communicating. Asking the right questions is the key to both the basic principles of good communication and the principles of the genre and the medium of your choice.

This book is your manual and guide to communicating effectively through movies and television programs. I pray that this book will be a blessing to you!

· 2 ·

In the Beginning

The key to winning a war, whether physical or spiritual, is intelligence. Not the native intelligence that gets a student into the college of their choice, but rather the information about the enemy which can help you understand the strategy of battle. The Bible emphasizes what is required to tackle any task successfully (including movie and television production) in another way, ". . . desire that ye may be filled with the knowledge of his will in all wisdom and spiritual understanding . . ." (Colossians 1:9 KJV).

Most people outside the entertainment industry who want to make movies or television programs have no idea what is involved in either process. As an analogy, they resemble people who watch brain surgery on the Discovery Channel, and then attempt to perform brain surgery on their friend. Wisdom and life experience tell us immediately that one needs to study medicine before attempting such a surgery!

It should be understood that movies and television programs are firstly entertainment, and secondly, vehicles to communicate and contain artistic elements. Since the beginning, movie production was called the "movie business," not the movie art. Writers and other guilds wanted the legal benefits of a business designation, but they also understood that they were supplying a product to an audience for the express purpose of making money. In this book, we will focus on the communication aspects of the mass media of entertainment because Christians are called to preach—communicate—the Word (see 2 Timothy 4:2). Most Christians who seek advice about getting into the entertainment industry do so because they want to share the gospel through their work, or because they want to help clean up the entertainment industry.

Dan Nichols' reflections in the previous chapter opened the door toward understanding the complexity of movie and television production. His article, "So, What's Your Story," also suggested many of the questions you should ask before getting into the entertainment industry. Let's consider three of these ascertainment questions.

1. What do you want to communicate through movies and television?
2. Why do you want to communicate through movies and television?
3. To whom do you want to communicate?

NO MAN IS AN ISLAND[32]

Communication is essential to being human. It joins people together by giving us the ability to exchange thoughts, ideas, needs, and desires; and even hold such things in common. Communication also gives us a pathway toward communion with God. The Lord our God is one who communicates—who speaks forth creation and who is Himself the Word, as John so eloquently proclaims: "In the beginning was the Word, and the Word was with God, and the Word was God" (John 1:1).

Babies come into the world trying to communicate their desires, needs, and feelings. They become frustrated when they are not understood. They are happy about learning to talk, but in the interest of preserving their identity, they want their audience to understand their approach to language. All too often "the child is father of the man" with regard to the way we approach communication as adults, although not in the sense that Wordsworth intended.[33] The alternative to poor communication is for us to pause before we begin to communicate and survey the situation. We should take time to ascertain the nature of our audience, inventory our own talents, and investigate the communicative medium we have chosen to use. With pertinent questioning and preparation, our efforts will achieve the intended result(s). Effective communication enables us to share our thoughts, achieve our goals, fulfill our desires, and survive as adults (or babies) in a fallen world teetering on the brink of destruction.

The task that confronts us is to continue to strive for more effective communication that proclaims the gospel through every medium. In the first forty years of television, mainline churches produced excellent religious television programs, such as, *The Lion, The Witch, and the Wardrobe, Insight,* and *Davey and Goliath.* These days, it's not just mainline churches producing quality Christian media. Parachurch organizations, such as the Billy Graham Organization (which produced the *Climb*); churches such as Sherwood Baptist (which produced *Fireproof*); and concerned individuals like the irascible Mel Gibson, who produced *The Passion of the Christ,* are all spreading the Word. It is important that all Christian communicators band together to push toward the goal, and avoid time-consuming rivalries or competitions.

Christians often assume that movies and television programs with strong Christian content must be produced by Christians. Several renowned Christian speakers have told me about the influence the movie *Chariots of Fire* had on their lives. In particular, these speakers note that Eric Liddell's statement in the movie that his running "gave God pleasure," and encouraged each of them to exercise their God given talents, rather than limit their engagements to predetermined "Christian" endeavors. I always point out that the actor who played Liddell and the scriptwriter had collaborated on the dialogue which proclaimed the gospel so clearly, yet neither of them was a Christian. In fact, self-designated agnostic Colin Welland, the scriptwriter, says to this day that the plot of *Chariots of Fire* is about a "couple of young fellows who put their fingers up to the world."[34] Clearly, he has a very different perspective toward what *Chariots of Fire* is saying than most Christians. Most of the money for *Chariots of Fire* was put up by a Muslim, Mohammed El Dodi Fayed (who died in the car crash with Princess Diana), and the producer was Jewish. In fact, the only committed Christian who was prominent in *Chariots of Fire* was the actor who played Abrahams, the Jewish runner. *Chariots of Fire* shows that God can and will "raise up stones" to witness for Him through the entertainment media, if Christians fail to do so.

A RELIGION OF COMMUNICATION

In the words of Johannes Heinrichs "Theologically speaking, Christianity can be wholly and completely interpreted as a religion of communication, both divine-human and inter-human."[35] Therefore, as Christians, our ability to communicate effectively and successfully through movies, television programs, and other media is extremely important, so we can witness the great news of new life available in Christ, and minister to the needs of our neighbors.

Our most basic communication ascertainment question is: How do I communicate exactly what I want/need to communicate to the person I want/need to reach, using the appropriate genre and medium properly so that my audience will understand and be convinced, motivated, educated, and/or informed?

Effective communication always takes work. Communication is a conscious process, involving two or more unique individuals. Communication is a bridge for thoughts, ideas, and information between those individuals. Before any bridge is built, it has to be properly designed, or it will collapse. Every detail is important.

As we have heard all our lives, the process of writing (for most of us) is 10 percent inspiration and 90 percent perspiration. The same is true for communication through movies and television: learn and apply the right questions, the right language, and the right grammar, and the communication bridge will be 90 percent built.

Of course, no matter what the media of communication, like a baby learning to talk, there comes a time when the right questions, the words, and the syntax are second nature to us. Once we become adept at talking or communicating, we should not regress into baby talk unless we have just suffered physical or psychological damage, or the baby talk is a necessary, conscious, and effective part of a specific communication.

Producer Bruce Johnson helps us understand the slow, sometimes painful steps of learning a craft and developing talent. Bruce is recognized as one of Hollywood's most prolific creative talents, having amassed over five hundred producing credits including feature films, television movies, TV series, specials, educational films, and documentaries. A three time Emmy Award winner, Johnson co-founded PorchLight Entertainment in 1995 with the entire family as its target audience. Since the company was formed, Johnson has been the executive producer of several television series and movies, establishing PorchLight as a leading independent supplier of family friendly content, both as a producer and as a distributor.

But that's getting ahead of "the story behind the story."

It's Not Just About Your Faith; It's About Your Talent!

An interview with Bruce Johnson

Logline: An unknown Midwesterner makes his way through the Hollywood bazaar.

The Backstory

"There were no expectations from anyone, including me, that I would carve out a career in Hollywood," says Johnson. "My parents back in Minneapolis certainly expected me to pursue a more practical career!" *Not* growing up in Beverly Hills, *not* rubbing shoulders with kids whose parents were powerful agents, producers or directors, and *not* knowing how daunting Hollywood could be, gave Johnson the freedom to follow his own instincts—to pursue what he says "seemed right" to him. Consumed by what he describes as "an overwhelming desire to communicate," television and film "opened up" as places where his passion for storytelling could be exercised.

"I am doing what I believe I was meant to be doing with my life. I followed my instincts, and learned what I could and could not do." Johnson also adds that it was critical to get good training, to go through the slow, sometimes painful steps of learning a craft, taking every opportunity to develop your talent. "Everyone's journey to Hollywood is different," says Johnson. His began with a degree in English from the University of Minnesota, Morris, and continued with graduate school at Northwestern University, where he studied film and television, along with English and education. "I took every writing and production course I could find," says Johnson, and the more encouragement he received from his professors, the more confident he became in his sensibilities for commercial entertainment.

Johnson "followed his instincts," which led him from Northwestern to Films, a small film company in Chicago, where he helped package and sell educational films including a classroom version of *Roots*, the acclaimed TV mini-series. Then in 1979, he came out to Los Angeles "to see what would happen." Thankfully, he's still there, twenty-five years later. "It has become my world," says Johnson.

Going Hollywood

Johnson got his start in Hollywood making educational films for Dave Bell Associates. "We were right in the middle of Hollywood, within a stone's throw of the major studios, but the day-to-day work was a long way from mythological Hollywood." His focus was on producing films that would be used in classrooms, but it gave him first-hand experience as a writer, producer, and director, with many opportunities to learn and grow. "During that period of time, I watched lots of movies, read lots of scripts, and began hanging out with editors, cameramen, and other filmmakers and producers. I learned the craft frame by frame, film by film, series by series." He says he also learned a valuable lesson from Dave Bell. "On the day I was given my first producing assignment, Dave pointed to a TV screen in his office and said 'If your show is not working there (on the screen) then you'll be out there (pointing to the street). It was 'sink or swim.' I've never forgotten those words." Bruce learned that ultimately, it always comes down to "the material"—the story waiting to be told.

It Starts with the Story

"I have always had a voracious appetite for books. I'm usually hauling two or three along with me wherever I go, in addition to two or three scripts. Good writing feeds my mind—it's like health food for me. I have always enjoyed reading good stories and scripts, and it may sound ironic, but Hollywood is a natural extension for someone who cares about what's on the page," Johnson says. He never knows when the next series or film will emerge, or where it will come from. "The business of producing is all about finding and nurturing new material, whether the material is found in books, art, scripts, or somebody's off-the-cuff brainstorm. The point is to recognize it, embrace it, shape it, and communicate the essence to someone who is capable of financially supporting it."

The Pitch

Johnson attributes his ability to develop and "pitch" new programs as the thing that enabled him to survive and grow in such a demanding, unpredictable industry. He says he learned the "art of the pitch" from one of Hollywood's legendary creative talents, Joe Barbera. Following "the next step" on his journey, Johnson began working for Hanna-Barbera Productions, the large animation studio best known for creating *The Flintstones, The Jetsons, Scooby Doo, Yogi Bear,* and other renowned cartoons. "The pitch" is all about telling a story in the most entertaining, engaging way possible—making it fast and funny, or short and sweet, and Johnson is quick to acknowledge how much he learned by watching Joe Barbera in action.

The Story Continues

"I hadn't really set out to work in animation," says Johnson. "Ironically, my sister is a very good artist, but even though I can barely draw stick figures I enjoy working with artists, and there's nothing more wonderful than seeing fresh, unique designs for a new series. The other key to animation is writing, and since I had written so much myself by then, I found that I enjoyed working with writers, helping shape the scripts and stories. I became what—in Hollywood—is called *a creative executive.*"

During his Hanna-Barbera years, he supervised countless animation episodes. "It was a huge operation," remembers Johnson, "producing a lot of programs. There was a constant flow and my job was to help move programs through the channels of writers, artists, animators and voice-actors. I've always liked teamwork, and that's what a lot of Hollywood production is all about, along with delivering entertaining, high quality work." Looking back, he cites various *Yogi Bear* spin-offs, remakes of *The Jetsons* TV series, *Jonny Quest* remakes, several original cartoons and long-form TV movies as projects he helped produce. He also helped bring to life one of Joe Barbera's favorite projects: *The Greatest Adventure—Stories from the Bible.* Story editing and co-producing these animated episodes brought Johnson closer to his own faith. "All of these stories were of course familiar to me, but re-writing them and making biblical language accessible to today's kids was a great experience for me."

The series became one of the most successful original video series of all time.

The Plot Twist

Working his way up the studio ladder, Johnson's career at Hanna-Barbera appeared to be moving at a steady, uneventful pace. Then one day he received a call informing him that Ted Turner had just purchased Hanna-Barbera, including its vast library of over 5,000 cartoons. This library would form the basis of the Cartoon Network. Everything changed at Hanna-Barbera. Johnson was named Executive Vice President and General Manager, with responsibility for integrating Hanna-Barbera's vast library into Turner's worldwide distribution system (which later became part of Time Warner). In 1994, Johnson left Hanna-Barbera and was instrumental in starting PorchLight Entertainment, along with entertainment executive William Baumann.

PorchLight: Inspire, Entertain, Inform

"We wanted a name that reflected family values and would also communicate a certain warmth and sincerity in the midst of a fairly cynical era and industry. I had grown up across the street from an outdoor hockey rink, and in the winter I would play hockey after school until my mom would turn the porch light on—which meant it was time to come home. The image of a warm, glowing home and a strong family stayed with me—that's where the name originated, and the goal at PorchLight is to produce programs that reinforce positive family values, programs that will resonate with viewers, challenge them to think and learn, or simply entertain them."

PorchLight has maintained its focus on family and children's entertainment, producing animated series and specials, along with "live action" movies. *Adventures from the Book of Virtues* was the company's first animated series. Based on a best-selling anthology by William Bennett, the series offers classic children's stories from around the world, each one illustrating a virtue such as friendship, honesty, loyalty, and courage. Another PorchLight series, *Jay Jay the Jet Plane*, is a preschool series introducing "life lessons" to young kids, while also offering an introduction to the world of science and nature.

The company has also produced a number of movies for networks such as Disney Channel, Family Channel, Animal Planet, Pax TV, and others. "What we're doing in our movie production business is producing films that can be watched by the whole family. Usually this means putting characters in jeopardy, and letting them use their ingenuity to get out of trouble. We look for unique, interesting stories that will appeal to audiences here and throughout the world. With all of our films and TV series we are empowering the audience, giving them something that they can keep. I like to think we are entertaining viewers, and we are also providing some "inner-tainment."

As Johnson looks back, he can clearly see how the skills he acquired through his education and career paths now fit together like a puzzle to provide him with the knowledge and experience that is crucial to managing a successful entertainment company. He also acknowledges the importance of faith in day-to-day life.

Let Faith Be Your Anchor

"My faith in God is the anchor of my life—both at work and at home," nods Johnson. "It's an integral part of who I am. It's not that I wave banners, but I have an inner faith that has been part of who I am for a long time, it's where I get my core values, and every decision I make that is of any consequence is done prayerfully and with the hope and trust that this is the right next step on the path I'm walking." Johnson relates his faith to *character development*. "In the same way that good stories are about interesting, well developed characters, working in Hollywood can actually be a good place for your own 'character development,' testing your faith, giving you the chance to make right or wrong decisions."

Find a Fabulous Spouse

According to Johnson, all of his major decisions are made with prayer, but also in close consultation with his wife. "I've been fortunate to be married to someone who provides incredible insight into creativity. We take long walks, talk about everything, and we've become a partnership in decision-making," smiles Johnson. "I wouldn't have it any other way."

Toughen Up

People who want to get involved in the entertainment industry must have thick skin, believes Johnson. "Understand that rejection is much more common than acceptance. And while it's not an industry that necessarily embraces people of faith, there are no roadblocks, either. It's really not about your faith; it's about your talent. It's about delivering what you are asked to deliver. Hollywood was once described to me as being cold, tough, and impersonal, and I think it is. But this town has a voracious appetite for talent, and when talent surfaces, this can be a warm, embracing, and magical place."

Johnson says that getting started is the most challenging part. "I came out here with no job and no prospects. But my wife could teach, so I spent six or seven months writing unsold scripts and looking for a job that didn't exist. This was a very difficult time for me, because I'm such a work-focused person. But I kept making cold calls and finally got some interviews. I learned that you don't just go out and apply for a producer job. You have to work your way into a company any way you can—being a temp, assistant, mail room clerk, runner, go-fer—anything to get inside a company and become acquainted with people and their projects. From there, it's just a matter of demonstrating your competence, focusing on your goals, and seeing if your abilities match up with the situation in which you find yourself working."

Talent Helps—But Agents Close Deals

On the talent side of the industry (writers, directors, actors, producers), as opposed to the business side (agents, lawyers, accountants, business affairs), agents often play a critical role in opening doors and selling the services of talented people and their ideas, according to Johnson. "The economics in this business are daunting because the risks are huge. Agents serve a valuable role in screening projects and moving people and scripts through the system. They represent all of the actors we use, and I'm glad about that fact. It makes it easier on everybody. But of course, getting an agent is not always easy. If you're a writer, send them your best script. If you're a director, show them your film. If you're an actor, show them a reel of your work—even if it's just scenes from a student film. Put your best foot forward at all times. Ultimately, an agent can open the right doors for you, but it's up to you to deliver the goods."

Hollywood—an "Open-air Bazaar"

In the final analysis, Johnson is optimistic about new opportunities in the entertainment industry for anyone willing to truly dedicate himself to the process. "It's not easy, but it's not impossible, either. I sometimes think of Hollywood as this giant bazaar, where everyone has set up a table and is selling their wares. Ideas, scripts, skills, songs, talents—it's all for sale in the Open-air Bazaar of Hollywood. Everyone is selling or pitching or trying to move from the mailroom to the editing room. Your friends can help you; you can help your friends—networking is vital! But it's a place where anyone can sell anything—it's that simple. And if you like the excitement of 'anything can happen today,' and you place a high value on entertaining people, telling stories, and communicating ideas, then this business just might be for you."

* * *

With Bruce's wise reflections in mind, let's look briefly at some of the right ascertainment questions for us to ask to improve our communications. These questions are grouped in categories chosen to clarify their purpose. In reality, these categories and questions are closely inter-related; however, to help focus our communications they have been separated and distinguished from one another. Some of these questions will be treated in depth in the chapters that follow. Additional questions, which relate to a specific medium or topic, will also be treated throughout the book. You should adapt, add to and subtract from these questions to suit your own particular needs. Ask these questions before you begin to communicate.

POWER

Yours, Lord, is the greatness and the power and the glory and the splendor and the majesty, for everything in the heavens and on earth belongs to You.

—1 Chronicles 29:11

Are my communications powerful?

What empowers my communications?

"Life and death are in the power of the tongue . . ." (Proverbs 18:21). Power is by definition the ability, the capacity, the strength, the authority, the energy, the force, and the right to do or accomplish something. As believers, we know that God is omnipotent; God the Father is the source of all power (see 1 Chronicles 29:12); Jesus has all authority in heaven and on earth (see Matthew 28:18); and, the Holy Spirit gives us power to communicate His gospel (see Acts 1:8 and 10:44). Therefore, in the final analysis, every power question begins and ends with God.

However, there are many levels of power in communicating. To understand what empowers a specific communication, the first question that each of us should ask ourselves is, "Why do I want to communicate?" The book of Romans gives a good response: "For this reason I raised you up: so that I may display My power in you, and that My name may be proclaimed in all the earth" (9:17).

The essence of powerful and effective communication is *passion*, and passion comes from self-knowledge, vulnerability, openness, and a clear understanding of "Why I want to communicate." Whether you want to reach, teach, serve, proclaim, respond, sell, or ask, knowing the ultimate reason why you are motivated to communicate (Self? Others? God?) will help you to evaluate the driving power of your communication.

The question, "Why do I want to communicate?" also refers to the motivational level of power that prompts your desire to communicate in the first place. This motivation is the "vehicle" that drives the message of your communication to its destination—the audience, and the conclusion. The motivational level of communication is comparable to the motivation of the driver who causes the car to drive somewhere. If the driver is in a hurry and thoughtless of others—the power at his fingertips may be dangerous, or at least annoying, to others on the road. If the driver is concerned not only about reaching his destination but also about others, he or she can be a rare blessing to others.

Furthermore, the motivation of the driver will help empower him to reach his destination, rather than give up when the thrill of the journey starts to wear thin. Quality communications require perseverance, just as most long hauls require stamina, to reach the ultimate goal.

The other critical power question we should ask before beginning to communicate is: "What is the premise of my communication?"

Although this question is the next 'power' question and is included for discussion at that point, you should ask, "What is the premise of my communication?" only after you fully understand the topic you are communicating. The premise of communication is the engine that powers the entire process. The premise hypothesizes the logical, inevitable outcome of the communication through the process of proving the argument put forth through the ascertainment questions. The premise dramatically and logically powers the communication. The premise is the essence of the story that we will consider later in this book.

Your premise, your motivation, your genre or format, your medium of choice, your gifts, your talents, and your audience will determine what you are communicating, regardless of what you want to communicate. Therefore, it is critical that you state your premise correctly and precisely, and that you distinguish between what you want to communicate (that is, your *idea*), and what you are communicating (that is, your *reality*), which both depend to a large degree upon your premise.

WISDOM

The fear of the Lord is the beginning of wisdom . . .

—Psalms 111:10

Just as there are many levels of power in communication, wisdom should be exercised throughout the process of communicating. Wisdom is the ability to make sound judgments and to deal sagaciously with the facts and with every aspect of communication so that you can make the right choice. With respect to our automotive metaphor, "wisdom" enables us to stay on the road by helping us make the many decisions involved in steering our car to our destination.

Now if any of you lacks wisdom, he should ask God, who gives to all generously and without criticizing, and it will be given to him.

—James 1:5

Our wisdom ascertainment question is: "Who am I?"

As Christians, we know that each of us is created by God, in his image, for a special purpose. Each of us has been given the gifts, talents and desires to fulfill His purpose for us. Proverbs 28:26 answers well, "The one who trusts in himself is a fool, but one who walks in wisdom will be safe."

Too many of us do not feel like we know what God's purpose is for our lives, or even what our unique gifts and talents are. We are often ineffective in our communications because the genre or the medium we have chosen is not suited to our talents, or the role we have chosen is not appropriate for us (i.e., we are trying to communicate as an evangelist when we have been called to be a prophet).

This does not mean that some of us are exempt from testifying to the gospel of Jesus Christ. We are all commanded to proclaim the gospel (see Matthew 28:19; Romans 10:14–15). However, the way we present the gospel will depend on the gifts and talents God has given us. Remember that the question, "Who am I?" should be asked in conjunction with our other questions and should not be treated as ontological speculation.

CALLING

> Then I heard the voice of the Lord saying: 'Who should I send? Who will go for Us?' I said: 'Here I am. Send me.' And He replied: 'Go! Say to these people . . .'
>
> —Isaiah 6:8–9

God has called us out of darkness, into the eternal glory of His kingdom (see 1 Peter 2:9, 5:10), to take our place in his Body (see 1 Corinthians 12:27–30), be his witnesses "in Jerusalem, in all Judea and Samaria, and to the ends of the earth" (Acts 1:8). Responding to God's call requires power, wisdom, and understanding. We have asked the power and wisdom questions; shortly, we will consider understanding. Here we will begin to look at the aspect of our call that relates to the people we have been called to communicate with—our audience. The calling ascertainment question is: "Who is my audience?"

The question, "Who is my audience?" is in fact a set of questions, including:

1. What are the physical, psychological, emotional, spiritual, racial, political, sexual, and other characteristics of the audience whom I am trying to reach?
2. What do they want to hear?
3. Will they respond to the genre I have chosen?
4. Where do they live?
5. Will the medium I have chosen reach them?
6. Who will, and who does, the medium I have chosen reach?
7. Is there a more appropriate, more effective, or a less expensive medium I can use to reach my intended audience?

Our audience must be clearly defined and understood if we want to reach the audience we intended with our communication, and if we want our communication to have maximum impact.

If our intended audience is small, then it would be foolish to buy prime time on broadcast television to reach them; however, satellite-casting might be advisable if that small audience is spread out over a large, sparsely populated area, such as Alaska or Minnesota.

> After he had seen the vision, we immediately made efforts to set out for Macedonia, concluding that God had called us to evangelize them.
>
> —Acts 16:10

Once we have chosen the appropriate medium to reach our intended audience, then we have to determine how we can best adapt, translate, and contextualize our communication without compromising our message so that our audience will not only understand—but also relate to what we are communicating. Just as Paul talked to the Epicurean and Stoic philosophers about the "unknown God" whom he proceeded to make known, so we should tailor our communications to our unknown audience, being extremely careful not to lose our message in the process. Part of this process is choosing and conforming our communication to the appropriate genre or format: a story, parable, interview, instruction, sermon, or something else.

It is not uncommon for Christians to fall into the "make believe mission" trap either by choosing the wrong medium to reach their intended audience, by failing to speak to their audience in a language which the audience can understand, by failing to adapt their communication to address the audience's cultural perspective, or by all of the above. To say that we are reaching Afghanistan for Christ, because we are sending an English language television program over a satellite whose footprint covers that area of Asia, is a "make believe mission" if almost no one in Afghanistan has a satellite dish and very few speak English, or cannot otherwise relate to the cultural context of our communication.

Whoever we are called to reach, we have to know who they are and where they are to reach them with our message. In terms of our automobile metaphor, knowing who our audience is and where they live gives us our destination, where we are going, and the knowledge of where we have been called.

UNDERSTANDING

> Look! The fear of the Lord—that is wisdom, and to turn from evil is understanding.
>
> —Job 28:28

Frequently in Scripture, power, wisdom, knowledge, and understanding are mentioned together in discussing the attributes of God (Isaiah 11:2) and of those individuals who seek, follow, and love God (Proverbs 2). By definition, understanding means to comprehend, or apprehend, the meaning of something. Understanding is the power to comprehend, judge, and render, an experience intelligible.

God considers understanding so important that He tells us to get it "though it cost all you have" (Proverbs 4:7 NIV). We must understand our motivation, our premise, our medium of choice, our gifts, our talents, our resources, the truth, and our audience, to communicate effectively. This may sound difficult but, by asking the right questions and trusting in His grace, we can communicate powerfully, effectively and in love. Although understanding applies to all aspects of our communications, the question that directly involves understanding is: "What am I communicating?"

> Understanding is a fountain of life to those who have it.
> —Proverbs 16:22 NIV

The first step toward understanding what you are communicating is to set forth exactly what you want to communicate. It would be nice to say that you know exactly what you want to communicate, so do so. However, it is clear that many people have the desire to communicate, the means to do so, the ability, but no clear idea of what they want to communicate. Every year movies, television programs, and other big budget communications fail because the author did not know what he or she wanted to communicate. Anyone who has stared at a blank piece of paper or at an empty computer monitor in the throes of writer's block understands well that we do not always know what we want to communicate.

However, for your communication to be intelligible to your audience, you must know precisely what you want to communicate. Asking the questions in this book will help you to formulate what you want to communicate. Also, recording your thoughts and ideas as briefly and succinctly as possible is an excellent way to get started.

Once you are clear about what you want to communicate, you must determine what format or genre you will use to convey your message. You will need to understand the genre you have chosen, and how that genre affects your communication style. Also, you must understand the medium through which you will be communicating and how that particular medium affects your communication. You must adapt what you want to communicate to your genre and medium of choice.

Furthermore, you must know your audience and how they will receive your communication. As noted above, you must adapt your communication to your audience. You must also understand what God wants you to communicate and how that affects what you want to communicate. Finally, after you have communicated, you should seek feedback from your audience so that you can improve and perfect your communication.

In terms of our automotive metaphor, understanding what we are communicating is comparable to being able to deliver our message in an intelligible fashion when we arrive at our destination—the audience.

TRUTH

Speak the truth to one another.

—Zechariah 8:16

We all know what truth is: veracity, sincerity, genuineness, conformity to rule, exactness, and correctness. Truth is the opposite of falsehood. Truth is often defined as that which conforms to reality. As Christians, we know that truth conforms ultimately to the Word of God. Truth is also necessary, even in the most imaginative fiction, for such fiction must be true to the rules established by its author, otherwise it will seem shallow, empty, and false to its audience. Christians can and should create imaginative communications in every stream of media; realizing, like C.S. Lewis and Bach, that truth does not demand strict neo-realism, rather it demands an attention to detail so that our message is true to its own rules. Truth, like all the other categories we have considered, affects the various levels—both internal and external—of our communication.

The key truth question is: "What does God want me to communicate?"

> Do not be hasty to speak, and do not be impulsive to make
> a speech before God.
>
> —Ecclesiastes 5:2

God wants us to "make disciples . . . teaching them to observe everything I have commanded you" (Matthew 28:19–20). God wants us to witness in word and deed to his Word, his salvation and his good news (Colossians 3:17). This is both a simple and a complex task, for though the gospel can be stated very briefly (John 3:16), the whole gospel contains eternal and infinite truth which bursts forth from Scripture to fill every aspect of life and death, touching the very threshold of eternity.

In the Word, we are told, "Samson went to Gaza, where he saw a prostitute and went to bed with her" (Judges 16:1). The Word of God is true to life—the good and the bad—because God wants to save us from death. Often, we create false visions of life because we deny the realities of evil and death. On the other hand, pagans often deny the realities of good, and very seldom touch upon the possibility of real life; eternal life. Even so, there are instances of non-believers clearly communicating God's truth, as in paintings of the crucifixion, or movies such as *Chariots of Fire, Jesus of Nazareth* and Pier Paolo Pasolini's *Gospel According to St. Matthew*,[36] produced and written by non-believers (God can raise up stones).

Truth is the gasoline in our automobile analogy. Water it down and our car will run very poorly—eventually, it will break down completely.

STEWARDSHIP

> Each one should use whatever gift he has received to serve
> others.
>
> —1 Peter 4:10 NIV

We have been appointed by God as stewards over everything he created on earth, in the sea, and in the air (see Genesis 1:27).

As stewards, we are to manage, supervise, harvest, protect, nourish, and care for the magnificent creation he has been entrusted to us. Fulfilling our role as stewards requires effective communication, and to communicate effectively we must be aware of the resources that are available to us.

Everything said about "asking the right questions" could be seen as a function of stewardship, since the key to good stewardship is accurate ascertainment. In terms of our automobile metaphor, stewardship not only involves determining whether or not we have enough money, gas, oil, food, water, and other supplies; but also, whether we have the motivation, the ability, the skill, the right car, and a predetermined destination, all of which are necessary for our communications trip. However, to help focus and clarify our ascertainment of questions, our stewardship question does not include other of questions that we cover elsewhere.

Our stewardship question is: "What are my resources?"

> For which of you, wanting to build a tower, doesn't first sit down and calculate the cost to see if he has enough to complete it? Otherwise, after he has laid the foundation and cannot finish it, all the onlookers will begin to make fun of him, saying, 'This man started to build and wasn't able to finish.'
>
> —Luke 14:28–30

At some point in our lives, most of us have fallen into the predicament of not being able to finish a project either because we did not have enough resources (money, time, supplies, energy, and/or assistance), we mismanaged our resources, we failed to recognize our resources, or all of the above. As Jesus notes, this is an embarrassing and usually unnecessary situation, although there are those occasions where unpredictable circumstances sabotage a project. Before we start to communicate, we should count the cost, ascertain what our resources are, choose our medium of communication, and target our audience based on the resources available to us.

Counting the cost and ascertaining our resources does not mean that we forsake our call to communicate to a specific audience. Rather it means that we take the time to prepare our communications properly by ascertaining what resources are available to us and what resources we will have to secure through fundraising and prayer, or what steps we will have to take to adapt our communication to our limited resources.

It is very important to remind ourselves when we ask this question that, sometimes, trying to do everything ourselves ("hands on" production) is the most expensive approach in the long run. The excess cost of "hands on" production can show up either in the time that it takes for us to learn how to communicate through the medium of choice, or in the lack of quality of our final communication which prevents it from reaching our audience and communicating what we intended.

Once, while I was teaching a Communicate Workshop, a student told me that his church had been talked into purchasing a large amount of video equipment to communicate their presence to the community. The church proceeded to use the equipment to produce a desired communication. To their great surprise, the finished product looked like a home movie. In their disappointment, they put their new video equipment in a closet and forgot it. This is a classic case of "video burnout."

They would not have burned out on the equipment if they had taken the time to learn about the equipment, their available resources (including talent), and how it would all measure up to their production goals before purchasing the equipment. After ascertaining what the equipment could do and what their resources were, then they should have decided whether or not to buy the equipment. Whether or not the church made the purchase, they should have considered hiring the right talent to produce their communication for them ("hands off" production). Note the mistakes inherent in their approach: they put their faith in the new technology to solve their communications problems (this state of mind could be called "videolatry"); they did not ask the right questions to determine how to communicate what they wanted to communicate, and they did not ascertain their resources.

"Hands off" production should not become a shibboleth. There are many instances where "hands on" production is appropriate, especially where the talent is available to communicate effectively in the medium of choice or learning the medium of choice is an important part of the communication. At a church in New York City, we involved a group of teenagers in producing their own television program that aired on the local access cable television channel. Producing their own television program helped them to think about the nature of the medium, the nature of the gospel, and how they could communicate the gospel through that medium. Many of the teenagers discovered their motivational talents. Several of them came to know Jesus as Lord and Savior while producing that program.

In counting the cost of equipment, remember that the more sophisticated the equipment, the more it usually costs to maintain. When I was the director of the television center at the Brooklyn College Campus of the City University of New York, the chief engineer estimated that the maintenance cost of new equipment per year was equivalent to one-third the purchase price.

Advances in technology have reduced these maintenance costs. Less sophisticated equipment and consumer grade (rather than professional) equipment cost much less to maintain. Even so, it is important that you count the cost of maintaining your equipment, and that you are prepared to meet those maintenance costs before you do purchase equipment, or you may find yourself with broken down, expensive equipment taking up precious space and reminding you of your folly.

You may have more resources available to you than you realize. In many cases, ascertaining what your resources are means becoming aware of what your talents and assets are. Local television or radio stations might be able to help you, if the medium is appropriate. In determining your access to the local cable system, television station, or radio station, you should find out who runs it, why they run it, and why they might be interested in your communication project. Most often, they run their station or system to make a profit, and they will be interested in what you want to communicate if it will help them to make a profit by gaining more viewers or listeners. Your project may give them more viewers directly, or it may improve their image with the community, and indirectly attract more viewers.

A few years ago, representatives of the Chinese community in New York City approached their local cable system about access to program time on the system's premier channel. At first, the cable system said that no time was available. The Chinese representatives pointed out that many new subscribers from their community would be added to the customer roles of the cable system and that the New York City licensing board would be more likely to renew the cable system's license if the system gave them the time that they wanted. The cable system changed its corporate mind and gave the Chinese community three hours per week on the premier cable channel.

Locating talent may be the most important aspect of ascertaining your resources. Gifted individuals, working together in love and motivated by God can do wonders with second-rate equipment. There have been many Emmy Award winning television programs produced on non-professional equipment by dedicated individuals. The talent questions in a later chapter will help you to find the right talent for your particular project and message.

Try to be a good steward of the talent available. Good talent must be given the freedom to be professional while they are guided toward the communication project goal. If you do not have the ability to shepherd the talent necessary for your project, find a producer who can. Respect is the key to working with talent.

As stated in the Introduction, God provides the resources for us to do what he has called us to do. If you count the cost and find yourself short of resources, pray. God answers.

IMPACT

No one should seek his own good, but the good of the other person.

—1 Corinthians 10:24

Impact is the other side of power. It is the force behind our communication that collides with the audience. The impact of our communication depends on our ability to address our audience where they need to be addressed. To ascertain how to communicate in a way that will provide the maximum impact on our audience, we should ask this multi-layered question:

"What needs to be communicated to my audience? My church? My community? My nation? My world?"

The poor and the needy seek water, but there is none; their tongues are parched with thirst. I, the Lord, will answer them; I, the God of Israel, do not forsake them.

—Isaiah 41:17

The advertising industry is built on addressing people's needs, so that people will buy a product to meet the addressed need. Often, the advertised product will not meet the need that the advertiser used to motivate the people to buy the product in the first place. For instance, to sell a product, a television advertiser may address the audience's social need for love, claiming that the product, such as toothpaste, will give the audience more friends of the opposite sex, even though that product will not meet the audience's need for love, nor will it give the audience more friends of the opposite sex. Listening to the audience through market research tells an advertiser what "needs" must be addressed for their communication to have maximum impact.

In determining needs, advertisers often rely on the research of psychologist Abraham Maslow, Ph.D., who attempted to synthesize a large body of research related to human motivation.[37] Maslow proposed a hierarchy of human needs:

1. Physiological: hunger, thirst, bodily comforts
2. Safety/security: out of danger
3. Belongingness and Love: affiliate with others, be accepted
4. Esteem: to achieve, be competent, gain approval and recognition
5. Cognitive: to know, to understand, and explore
6. Aesthetic: symmetry, order, and beauty
7. Self-actualization: to find self-fulfillment and realize one's potential
8. Self-transcendence: to connect to something beyond the ego or to help others find self-fulfillment and realize their potential

This self-transcendence is, in fact our spiritual need, which can manifest itself as the desire for any or all of the above mentioned needs, but it is truly a desire for communion with God, Father, Son, and Holy Spirit—for "man must not live on bread alone" (Matthew 4:4).

Needs are expressed by desires, but desires can be fanned by temptation into all-consuming concupiscence. Hunger is an essential desire that expresses the natural, physical need for food, but gluttony is hunger run amuck.

We are all sinners, but as communicators who are also Christians, we should not fan natural desires into sins just so we can motivate our audience to buy our products, or our ideas. The natural desires to procreate, to love, and to be loved have often been fanned and forged into lust so that an advertiser can sell a product such as blue jeans. More often than not, the desire (which has been blown out of proportion) will not be satisfied by the product in question—the product can't deliver on the promises made for it in the advertisement.

Communicators all too often resort to aggravating desires to give impact to their communication because they are too lazy, or rushed, to ask and answer all the other questions which would help make their communication effective. Addressing and aggravating desires becomes a quick fix—an easy way to impact an audience, rather than building a truly powerful, effective communication.

For our communications to have a powerful impact on our audience, we must ascertain and address the needs, wants, and feelings of our audience by listening to them. To do that, we must engage in the appropriate market research. Our communications will always deliver on God's promises if we are communicating his Truth. If we discipline ourselves to ask and apply the right questions, and learn the language and grammar of our medium, we will communicate powerfully and effectively.

PROPHESY

> The men of Nineveh believed in God. They proclaimed a fast and dressed in sackcloth—from the greatest of them to the least.
>
> —Jonah 3:5

Jonah did not want to go to Nineveh to proclaim God's judgment because he knew that God would relent from sending destruction on Nineveh if the Ninevites repented (see Jonah 4:1–3). Jonah wanted sinful Nineveh destroyed. He wanted the prophecy God gave him to preach to be fulfilled. He preached destruction, and he wanted that destruction to occur to prove his status as a prophet of the one true

God. He was concerned with his image and his righteousness. He was not concerned about the people of Nineveh. He did not want his prophesying to result in active repentance by the Ninevites, but it did.

By definition, to prophesy means to foretell or forthtell under divine inspiration. As Christians, all our communications should be divinely inspired because the Holy Spirit dwells in us. Our communications should forthtell, and/or foretell, in that they proclaim the truth.

As was the case with our other categories, to prophesy relates to and effects all aspects of communication. To distinguish our ascertainment questions, our prophesy question will focus on the consequences of prophesying.

The key question for our call to prophesy is: "Will my communication result in action?"

> John came baptizing in the wilderness and preaching a baptism of repentance for the forgiveness of sins. The whole Judean countryside and all the people of Jerusalem were flocking to him, and they were baptized by him in the Jordan River as they confessed their sins.
>
> —Mark 1:4–5

Unlike Jonah, most of us want our communications to result in action. In one sense, every communication results in action, even if that action is only the internal decision to perceive the communication and reject or ignore it. However, we are not concerned here with an internal decision to ignore a communication, nor are we concerned with communications that are received and then forgotten. Rather to prophesy is to demand a reaction: a movement of the heart, a conscious decision, or motivation to accept or reject the necessary consequences of the communication. If you have clearly stated your premise, which you will learn how to do if you don't already know, and you have answered all the pertinent ascertainment questions prior to this one, then your communication will result in action.

To prophesy is to proclaim our communication with such inherent power that our audience climbs into our car and drives with us into the kingdom of God.

REVELATION

For now we see through a glass darkly; but then face to face: now I know in part; but then shall I know even as I am known.
—1 Corinthians 13:12 KJV

From the first chapter of Paul's letter to the Romans, we know that all of creation reveals God's eternal power and divine nature. God communicates Himself and His will to us through revelation, and we share His revelation with others. Communication should make the unknown known. Therefore, our revelation question is: "Did my communication succeed?"

The Spirit searches everything, even the deep things of God.
—1 Corinthians 2:10

"Did my communication succeed?" may be restated in several ways to help us evaluate the effectiveness of our communication:

1. Did my communication shed light on the unknown, by pulling back the curtain and revealing the Truth?
2. Did my communication relay what I intended?
3. How did my audience react to my communication?

To reveal the effectiveness of your communication, you must have feedback. Feedback simply means taking the time to listen to your audience after your communication, whether or not they have joined us on our drive in the eternal Kingdom of God.

There are many methods and devices for obtaining feedback from your audience, but regardless of what listening technique you use, the important point is that you seek feedback—both from your audience and God—and that you heed that feedback. Feedback helps us to continually reevaluate our communications and improve them.

This does not mean that we compromise or dilute our message because we receive negative feedback. Instead, this means that the feedback allows us the opportunity to improve our presentation of the revelation that we have received from God so that we can help bring more people into the kingdom. Feedback should bring us closer to God and to the joy (and cost) of communicating His good news. As Jesus said, "For I gave them the words that you gave me and they accepted them. They knew with certainty that I came from you, and they believed that you sent me" (John 17:8 NIV).

At the beginning of this chapter, we asked the most basic communication question:

How do you communicate exactly what you want/need to communicate to the person you want/need to reach, using the appropriate medium properly so that the audience will understand, and be convinced, motivated, educated, and/or informed?

The answer we have seen is threefold:

1. Ask and answer the right ascertainment questions to *form your communication premise:*
   - What idea do I want to communicate?
   - Why do I want to communicate that particular idea?
   - Who do I want to communicate with as my audience?
   - How do I want to communicate my message?
   - What genre and medium are appropriate, considering motivational talents?
   - What impact or consequence do I want my communication to have?
2. Learn the language and grammar of your chosen genre and medium.

3. Apply the ideas and lessons outlined above, and you will communicate effectively.

To simplify our task in the future, let's review the ascertainment questions posed in this chapter, keeping in mind that there are other questions which we may add to this list depending on the nature of a particular communication and that a specific communication may not demand that we ask all these questions. The chapters that follow will treat some of these questions in depth and pose other ascertainment questions:

- Why do I want to communicate?
- Who am I?
- Who is my audience?
- What are the physical, psychological, emotional, spiritual, racial, political, sexual, and other characteristics of the audience whom I am trying to reach?
- Is there a more appropriate, more effective, or less expensive medium I can use to reach my intended audience?
- What needs to be communicated to my audience, my church, my community, my nation, and my world?
- What do they want to hear?
- Will they respond to the genre I have chosen?
- Where do they live?
- Will the medium I have chosen reach them?
- Who will the medium I have chosen reach?
- Who does the medium I have chosen already reach?
- What am I communicating?
- What is the premise of my communication?
- What does God want me to communicate?
- What are my resources?
- Will my communication result in action?
- Did my communication succeed?

· 3 ·

Places, Please

This above all: to thine own self be true, and it must follow,
as the night the day, thou canst not then be false to any man.

—Polonius, *Hamlet*[38]

WHO ARE YOU?
WHAT IS GOD'S PLAN FOR YOUR LIFE?

When he was four years old, our oldest son wanted to be a government official (the president) and a baseball player. At the time of the first draft of this writing, he was translating the Bible in Papua New Guinea for Wycliffe Bible Translators. Now, he is married with children in Tasmania, Australia, building a retreat center.

Most of the students in my Communicate Workshops, no matter what their age, come into the workshop wanting to be the star, the director, or the producer of their own television program. Philip Carey in Somerset Maugham's *Of Human Bondage* wanted to be an Anglican priest in his youth, then he decided to become an artist, then an accountant, and, finally, he finds out that he is called to be a doctor. The question arises, does it matter what profession Philip chooses? Or, what my son becomes (aside from his father's pride)? Or, what roles the students take in the Communicate Workshops?

With regard to Philip, the answer is a resounding "Yes, it matters!" because Maugham has so drawn Philip's character that he has no alternative other than to eventually become a doctor. In drama, novels, and other storytelling genre, the dynamics inherent in a character's bone structure determine the character's development and actions as that character reacts to the other characters within the context of the premise. If an author has done an adequate job of getting to know a character—by determining every aspect of the character's physiology, (such as, sex, age, posture, appearance, defects, and heredity), sociology (such as, class, occupation, education, race, and home life), psychology (such as temperament, attitude, complexes, motivations and abilities), and spirituality, then that character will develop in the story as the author intended because the character's make-up is such that the character cannot do otherwise. If any other alternative is available to the character then the author has not done his or her job, and the bone structure of the character has to be rethought.

As Henrik Ibsen emphasized:

> When I am writing I must be alone; if I have eight characters of drama to do with I have society enough; they keep me busy; I must learn to know them. And this process of making their acquaintance is slow and painful. I make as a rule, three casts of my dramas, which differ considerably from each other. I mean in characteristics, not in the course of the treatment. When I first settle down to work out my material, I feel as if I have to get to know my characters on a railway journey; the first acquaintance is struck up, and we have chatted about this and that. When I write it down again, I already see everything much more clearly, and I know the people as if I had stayed

with them for a month at a watering place. I have grasped the leading points of their characters and their little peculiarities.[39]

Philip has to become a doctor because Maugham has constructed Philip so that he will become a doctor. However, what about our eldest son? Or, second son, third son, or youngest daughter for that matter? Or, the Communicate Workshop students?

Unlike a character in a story, a human being can persist in pursuing a job or role that is not suited for him or her. According to some studies, three or four out of five people are in the wrong jobs. Though we may persist in the wrong job, we are all designed for—and called to—excellence in a job that suits our very specific motivational talents and gifts.

According to many career counselors, every individual has a unique combination of characteristics that give him or her the ability to excel in a particular career. Of course, different people perform the same job differently. In fact, saying that a person creates a job is probably a more accurate point of view than saying that a person adapts to a job.

As Christians, we realize that these findings by scientists and career counselors are nothing more than an affirmation of the fact that God has designed each of us for a particular purpose. God created and is interested in the real world. Just as He became a carpenter; so He chooses some of us to be rulers, some to be bankers, some to be craftsmen, some to be scientists, and each of us to be what He has created us to be.[40] He tells us: "I create the blacksmith, who builds a fire and forges weapons. I also create the soldier, who uses the weapons to kill" (Isaiah 54:16 GNT).

He gives each of us those talents and desires to excel in a particular role. He also gives us the free will to choose to flourish by fulfilling His plan for our lives, or to choose to be frustrated by rebelling against Him and ourselves.

Even before the fall, work was a part of God's plan for man's life:

The Lord God took the man and placed him in the garden of Eden to work it and watch over it.

—Genesis 2:15

After the fall, work became difficult and exhausting. But, in spite of our fall, God wants to bless and prosper us and wants us to rejoice in all that we do because He created us for His pleasure. He rejoices over us, and He loves us. This is great news: God wants us to be joyous and enjoy our work; however, to do so, we must submit to His glorious plan for our lives, give thanks and be content in all circumstances.

In the Church, we sometimes assume that God's plan for us is limited to prayer, praise, worship, social action, evangelism, Bible reading, and the other aspects of spirituality we discern in the New Testament. Living a holy life is a worthy goal (even if it is only fully attainable in heaven); however, since work is part of God's plan for our lives, our sanctification takes place in our living out His plan, not in our escaping the secular work world to adopt a religious role for which He has not created us nor called us.

God may call us to be apostles or clergy, but too many Christians upon conversion drop out of the so-called secular world to pursue so-called "Christian" careers. The institutional churches have recently come to the realization that they are partially responsible for this rush to change from a secular to a sacred career by sometimes adopting a low view of the laity and an exalted view of the clergy. (The opposite perspective is also wrong.) Churches must learn to recognize, bless, and ordain non-clerical jobs, as Jesus did. As Martin Luther said, "Be the monk never so holy, his work is no more holy than the farmer in the field, or the housewife at home."

Another influence causing this leap into the clothe or into so-called Christian professions is the prevailing, unbiblical view that wealth and profits are bad, when, in fact, God protects property

("Thou shall not steal"), wants us to prosper, and praises the man who makes a profit. It is not money that is bad, but the love of it.

Several times a year, I meet a successful communicator who has come to know Jesus as Lord and Savior and who wants to know how to get into "Christian" communications. Many of these influential individuals leave prominent positions at network television stations, advertising agencies, or on the editorial board of major newspapers where they can impact the mass communications industry. They enter the Christian communications industry where they are never heard from again, or their voice is limited to the Christian communications enclave.

When we come to know Him, God frees us from bondage to sin not so that we can escape from the world, but so that we can witness to Him in word and deed in the marketplace where He called us, unless He indicates otherwise. God calls us to "Occupy till I come" (Luke 19:13 KJV) by working in and taking charge of the mass media and all areas of life. His plan is for us to be co-workers with Him in redeeming the world by doing that which He has designed us to do best in His name.

Every individual has a specific contribution to make to society and civilization. Every job that each person performs within our society is important to our society whether that person is working as a doctor, a corporate executive, a shoemaker, a homemaker, or a janitor—though in our fallenness—we tend to glamorize some jobs, belittle others, and discount the remainder. We should, however, respect every job, even though some jobs demand, deserve, and receive more compensation and/or authority than others. In the biblical model of the world, there is a very definite hierarchy, but that chain of authority is qualitatively different from any social hierarchy we experience because each person is dedicated to loving, respecting, and serving God, and each other.

This brings us back to the question, "What is God's plan for your life?" In other words—what has God designed you to do? And, how do you find out what God has designed you to do?

Each of us has many talents and motivations, which come together to determine who we are and in what job we will flourish. We can be defined by the meeting point of our motivations, talents, physiology, sociology, psychology, and spirituality, almost like a character in His story. Just as Philip Carey's future occupation was clear from his bone structure as revealed in the beginning *Of Human Bondage*, God's plan for us is revealed in the talents and motivations we exhibit throughout our personal history. Even our weaknesses are instruments of God's grace. By discerning and analyzing our characteristics as they reveal themselves in our own history, we can discover the jobs and roles God has designed for us.

At age seventeen, Joseph, although he was the youngest brother, clearly exhibited talents and motivations that would make him the leader of his family, his people, and the Egyptians. Joseph was respectful of authority, responsible, obedient, intelligent, wise, and a man of vision. Joseph was motivated by his dream of leadership.

As a youth confronted by a messenger of God, Gideon exhibited the fearlessness, cunning, and drive to save Israel. Later in his life, these same characteristics would propel him to become a mighty warrior judge of his people, even when God put him in impossible positions so that He would receive the glory. Daniel, as a youth, exhibited characteristics that eventually made him a leader and a prophet:

> The king ordered Ashpenaz, the chief of his court officials, to bring some of the Israelites from the royal family and from the nobility—young men without any physical defect, good-looking, suitable for instruction in all wisdom, knowledgeable, perceptive, and capable of serving in the king's palace, "Daniel determined that he would not defile himself with the king's food or with the wine he drank. So he asked permission from the chief official not to defile himself . . ." God gave these four young men

knowledge and understanding in every kind of literature and wisdom. Daniel also understood visions and
dreams of every kind.

—Daniel 1:3–4, 8, 17

From Noah through Abraham, David, and Solomon to John the
Baptist, Peter, and Paul, those characteristic talents and motivations which determine each one's role in history can be discerned
at the very beginning of their lives, including the weaknesses which
caused any victories to be attributed to God rather than to a man.
God has his plan for each of us. All we need to do is to discern
it. Two interview articles from our contributors will help us learn
more about discerning God's plans. The first is from Donzaleigh
Abernathy, a wonderful actress.

INTEGRITY, RELATIONSHIPS, AND FAITH

—AN INTERVIEW WITH DONZALEIGH ABERNATHY

In the movie *Gods and Generals,* there is a beautiful young woman
who quotes from the book of Esther when she asks for her freedom.
She says, just as Mordecai said to Esther, "Think not that because
you are in the king's house you will escape more than all the others.
For if you remain silent at this time, relief and deliverance will
arise for thy people from another place, but thou and thy father's
house shall perish. And who knows whether thou art come to the
kingdom for such a time as this?" (Esther 4:13–14 rephrased by
the scriptwriter for dialogue benefit from KJV and NKJV). Donzaleigh Abernathy plays Martha in *Gods and Generals*; her character
is a beautiful and impassioned slave. Donzaleigh, herself a gentle
and centered actress, shares with us a glimpse of her journey thus
far. She has traveled many miles: from seeking to enlightenment,
through the desert and finally, to her dream.

DON'T LET GO OF CHILDHOOD DREAMS

As a young girl of six or seven in Atlanta, Georgia, Donzaleigh used to leave her ballet class and go to the Robert's house—Julia Robert's house, that is. Julia's parents conducted acting classes, and perhaps to their surprise, Donzaleigh was the daughter of the famous civil rights leader Ralph David Abernathy. Donzaleigh stood on the side, longing to act and taking it all in, though she was not old enough to participate. It was from such a wallflower position that she decided she truly wanted to be an actress. "I loved it and wanted so much to participate. I hated that I was too young. I watched the others learning the craft, though, and I promised myself I'd make it one day . . . that I'd be acting for the rest of my life."

LEARN, LEARN, LEARN!

Donzaleigh did get her opportunity a few years later as she was accepted into The George School, a Quaker preparatory academy in Pennsylvania, which boasts such graduates as George Segal, Blythe Danner, and the children of Mary Martin (most renowned for her role as Peter Pan). Here, Donzaleigh honed her craft and met many other children whose parents were in the industry. After The George School, she attended Emerson College in Boston. The opportunity was presented for her to attend an Ivy League college that she couldn't accept, mostly because she couldn't pursue her acting there. "My parents were devastated, but I was determined to study acting." During college, Donzaleigh got her Screen Actor's Guild (SAG) card, went to New York, and auditioned for her first play. Much to her surprise, she got the female lead in a play called *Akhnaton, the Light* written by the famous Bruce Mulholland. "He was a wonderful, distinguished old man, a gifted playwright, and I wanted to soak up his presence. I wanted him to teach me all he knew about the golden days of Hollywood since he had written *On The Twentieth Century* with Gloria Swanson."

Bruce would turn out to be just one of many crucial mentors in Donzaleigh's life.

SEEK LIFE AND SAFETY

Through the years, Donzaleigh could see the hand of God protecting her, while at the same time exposing her to limited amounts of show biz reality. While still in college, she worked for the production designers of *Saturday Night Live*. "The show was at its height, and its comedy was brilliant. I loved it because I got to see life in the New York fast lane, while still being somewhat protected." Donzaleigh spent time with the production designer's children, doing homework with them, bonding with the family, and learning about the business from the safe haven of their home. It was a place and time she considers very personally enriching.

DISCOURAGEMENT CAN KILL THE VISION

From there, Donzaleigh graduated, and moved back to Atlanta. Then she began working as an actress at the Alliance Theatre, in *Antony and Cleopatra* and the southeastern tour of *For Colored Girls*. "I auditioned for *Julius Caesar*, but I was told I was the wrong color to play Lady Portia, that the theatre didn't want their leading lady to be black. The director wanted to hire me, but the theatre said no. It was good to hear the director's perspective, very motivating, but I was discouraged and went to work behind the camera to learn the business."

Just as Jacob in the Bible had to work for Laban for seven years before he could fulfill his desire to marry Rachel, so Donzaleigh was to spend seven years working behind the camera, dead to her earlier dreams of acting, before hope would soon resurface.

TAKE THE HAND EXTENDED

Often, other people recognize talent unfulfilled, and help point out the right paths. One day, while she was working behind the camera on a movie with Christian Slater, Sidney Poitier's daughter, Beverly, called. "Beverly worked at the SAG office in Atlanta. She told me that they were casting for the television drama *In the Heat of the Night*, which was being filmed in Georgia. She said, 'I need you to audition for this to show that there's talent in Atlanta, or they'll pull the plug.' She wanted the job to stay in Atlanta, so I agreed to audition, just this one time." Donzaleigh had a wonderful audition, but though the director and producer raved about her audition performance, they didn't hire her, but sadly relayed that the head of the show said she didn't look like the character: a hooker. The director called her personally to say that though he couldn't hire her now, he'd help her with her career. Again, Donzaleigh's thoughts turned to an acting career, but was it really meant to be?

SOMETIMES ONLY THE LEFT COAST WILL DO

During this time of soul-searching, Donzaleigh had gotten married, and her husband said to her one day, "We're going to move to California." Donzaleigh refused, believing that it was best to stay close to her family, taking care of her parents, cooking for them and her brother, and retaining the close-knit roots of the family's heritage. "I loved my father so much and wanted to do any and everything I could for him and with him. I never thought I'd ever leave and go all the way across America. Her father told her, "When you give up your dream, you die a little inside. Follow your dream, Donzaleigh. I've lived my life; now go live yours."

FOLLOW YOUR PEACE

Finally, after listening to her parent's blessings and encouragement, Donzaleigh agreed to leave "safety" and pursue "life" in California. Little did she know that life is exactly what heaven had planned for her trip out west. "Somewhere in the desert between Arizona and New Mexico, I had a spiritual awakening. My whole life changed. I cried all the way to Los Angeles, but I had such peace. I knew I was supposed to be an actress, and that it would work. I was not destined to perish in my career or in an earthquake, but rather God would take care of me and guide my course."

Despite her spiritual high, Donzaleigh felt extremely shy and lost in the vastness of Los Angeles until her first audition. "The sister of a casting director in Atlanta was casting *The Long Walk Home*, so I auditioned and was immediately introduced to the director, who put me on tape. I waited to hear, and then waited some more. I wanted to play a part opposite Whoopie Goldberg, but I didn't get it. I then auditioned for another movie, *Ghost Dad*, directed by Sidney Poitier. Again, I didn't get it. The part I wanted was written for a man." Sidney Poitier did encourage Donzaleigh, but openly expressed his disapproval of her working behind the camera. "What are you doing? You're an actress! You don't work behind the camera!"

YOU'VE GOT TO LEAVE THE NEST!

Donzaleigh knew he was right, but she needed to work to earn a living. While she was working on Poitier's *Ghost Dad*, she got a phone call. The director of *The Long Walk Home* offered her a part in the movie, which was already in production. They asked if she could fly to Montgomery, Alabama, right away. "I said to Sidney Poitier, 'I got lucky, and you got your wish.' He hugged me, and was proud to see me follow my dream. But before I returned to L.A., Sidney's people called me and offered me the role of a nurse in *Ghost Dad*. I got to shoot four weeks filming on that movie."

Soon thereafter, Donzaleigh auditioned for *Murder in Mississippi*, a movie about the death of three civil rights workers. "I read for one of the leads, despite the fact that my agent said I couldn't get it. "They'll want a name actress," she said. "I did my best, though, and they liked me better than anyone in L.A. My agent worried because they continued to audition in New York, but for the first time I was amazingly confident. Sure enough, I had stuck out in the director's mind. He said, 'I want that little girl in the white dress,' and he came back and offered me the part. I was ecstatic. I got to work with Blair Underwood, Josh Charles, and Tom Hulce. It was wonderful. It got my whole career started."

CREATE A CLEAR NICHE

After her work on *Murder in Mississippi*, Donzaleigh developed a reputation for doing great, socially minded projects. "They knew

I wouldn't do any schlock. I only work on honorable movies with redeeming values. Soon the ball started rolling, and my career picked up momentum and steam. I was moving faster and faster uphill toward my dream."

Donzaleigh did continue to work on memorable, uplifting projects, and recently she played the part of Martha, the only slave depicted in the movie *Gods and Generals*. In this film, Director Ron Maxwell wanted to portray a black woman with religious beliefs and dignity, not the stereotypical southern "mammie" that other films often depict. "I didn't have a rag on my head, or weigh 300 pounds like the slaves in *Gone with the Wind*. Those portrayals aren't accurate anyway because no one was well off enough to eat that much, least of all nearly starved black people. The slaves went through a war, just like the whites. Men and women are emaciated, especially the blacks. This movie needed a lean woman. My character was noble, dignified, and graceful, not a caricature of a pagan savage." Donzaleigh says she's forever grateful to Ron Maxwell for his brilliance and direction on the project.

Another project Donzaleigh worked on was the Lifetime television series *Any Day Now*, playing the dual role of Sarah Jackson, Renee's mom, young and old. As senior citizen Sarah, I wore a fat pad, a gray wig, and had lines drawn on my face. The makeup man was good." As the young mom, Donzaleigh wore a short wig and acted like a school-marm, offering children cookies and milk, full of religious strength, wanting to work, but not allowed to by her husband. "I love that the American female audience is so taken with the show, still watching reruns. It was one of Lifetime's most popular shows." The show ran four years, completing about eighty-eight episodes in all.

TELL YOUR STORY

In addition to acting, Donzaleigh wrote *Partners to History*, a large-scale overview of black history since the 1600s. In the book, Donzaleigh draws on the wisdom of her father, the late Ralph David

Abernathy, as well as Martin Luther King Jr. and others. The book provides a visual and textual portrait of the influences of men such as Booker T. Washington and Presidents Lincoln, Kennedy, and L.B. Johnson, whose words help make up the foundation of the book. "I did extensive reading on the subject. For one year, seven days a week, I did nothing else. I was grateful to be afforded that time and opportunity to work on my book." After the first draft, she wrote two additional drafts, continuing to perfect and improve the manuscript until her publisher finally protested and forced her to put her pen down. The book was published in October, 2003 and nominated by American Library Association as one of the best books of the year.

"This was an extremely prestigious nomination. The librarians thoroughly read each book and decide. It's quite an honor; I had no idea I'd get this acclaim." Donzaleigh sees now, in hindsight, that the timing of the book was perfect. "Dr. Ted Baehr said it was good my book didn't come out during the filming of *Gods and Generals* because the time commitment would have been too great to do both. It really worked out well."

In addition to promoting the book, Donzaleigh is focusing on her personal life, and also auditioning for the next big movie, wherever it may be. Recently she did a comedy, *Red Riding Hood*, from the director of *Grease*. "It was so much fun, and it's a musical."

FIND GREAT MENTORS

Donzaleigh has worked in the entertainment industry since 1989, often behind the camera as an Assistant Director or a production assistant. "My first job on a movie was as a wardrobe assistant to dress Ruth Gordon. I really enjoyed her. She wrote me a Christmas card, then died shortly thereafter. She gave me advice and also told me: don't work behind the camera, and be an actress. She was so incredibly supportive, giving me techniques and wisdom on how a lady conducts herself on the set. She really stressed one's commitment to the job—to show up on time, know your lines, and be ready to work. That's my mantra. I'm always early to the set, I know my lines, I hit my mark, and I'm fun and easy to get along with. Mrs. Gordon ("Ruthie") gave me that foundation."

Donzaleigh worked with Gregory Peck on *Other People's Money*, and really received some great mentoring in technique. "He taught me how to break down my script and taught me about each scene and its dynamic within the overview of the story. And that's really what every actor needs to know. Mr. Peck is from the old school of acting, which I like. I'd visit Gregory and his wife, Veronique, at the house. They extended friendship to me during the filming. I actually spent at least two days per week with them during the filming. Veronique and I would have lunch and just talk about life and writing. They had a tremendous impact on my life, teaching me the craft and just giving me broader life perspective."

One of Donzaleigh's favorite mentors, though, will always be Sidney Poitier. "Susan will call for Sidney every so often and ask, 'How is Hollywood treating you?' I hear from a few of his daughters, who have been supportive and involved in my life. Another mentor is Bill Wittliff, screenwriter on *Lonsome Dove*, *The Perfect Strom*, and *Black Stallion*. Bill told me he didn't know how to put the boy on the horse until it came to him in a dream. He dreamed about the swimming in the water. Bill's a very talented man."

Bill also wrote *Ned Blessing*, a TV western about spirituality, in which Donzaleigh played a black woman on the range in Texas. "My husband is mute, so my character runs the show. There's a man, Sticks (Tim Smith of *Lonesome Dove*), who works for me, when a bad guy, Bill McKinney, comes to fight and run us off our land. The hero, Brad Johnson, saves the day, " Bill and I talk about writing all the time. I asked Bill how he wrote, and he said 'Longhand, on a yellow pad.' So that's how I write." I wrote my entire book longhand. I listen to my father's speeches, and I write books and screenplays longhand. Then, I type it into the computer. I got that from Bill."

BE A MENTOR YOURSELF

Not only does Donzaleigh look to her mentors for life's wisdom, she also values her involvement in the lives of others coming along the path. "In my acting class, I made friends with a young actor, Scott Foley, who has become a sensational actor. I convinced him to quit his waiting job and become a serious actor. He bought a suit, got his first agent, and auditioned for the lead in *Felicity*. Then, he met Jennifer Garner on the show. I dreamt he married her, and they did. I must say that I helped support their career and their love. I love supporting my friends."

ENJOY THE FULFILLMENT

Donzaleigh had a spiritual awakening in the desert that changed the course of her life and drew her into acting. Despite all her visions, though, she experienced a momentary delay when she let go of her dream. "After being in the desert, my faith in God became stronger, and I knew that everything would be OK. Everybody's got a dream. Follow your dreams. Then work hard to achieve success because it's God-ordained. I knew everything would be OK, and . . . it has been, just like in my dream. Sure, I've had difficult times, many uncertain hours, because it's not easy, but I pray at the top of Mulholland Drive, one of the highest points in the Santa Monica Range. I go there at least one day a week."

Since the beginning, Donzaleigh has asked the Lord to guide her through the process. She likes to keep her soul in a positive faith-mode, and not listen to or focus on negative reports that would steal her peace. "When I was writing my book, my friend Dar Bijarchi supported me in making this dream a reality. It's important to have loving friends, and I'm forever grateful for that love and friendship. I heard they were making *Gods and Generals*, I said, 'I have to be there.' Later Ron Maxwell tried to tell me who I was up against for the role of Martha, but I didn't want to know. All that mattered was that I got the part. I knew I was supposed to do it, so I just set my course."

Donzaleigh prays every day. "I've prayed this morning already, and I'll go back to Mulholland later and pray again. It's a place of worship without walls, like the Mount of Olives where Jesus went. People bring their burdens there and lay them down, as well as lovers come to find joy. That's how I live my life. I like to smile a lot. Laughter is good medicine."

When asked about her advice for people of faith exploring the industry, Donzaleigh replies, "They need to know they can fulfill their dreams without losing their soul. If they maintain their honor, integrity, and faith, they'll be blessed with abundance. It will be much more fulfilling than if they compromise." Donzaleigh's faith draws people to her, she believes. "There's like a magnet that draws people to me, and it's God. That's why I've been blessed to be with people of honor and integrity, and work on great projects. I like to present myself as a lady with integrity spirituality, and humility. People have no doubt that they're in the presence of a woman with the greatest respect and love for God. It leads me and gives life force to me. I'm grateful. God's greatest gift to us is life; our greatest gift to God is what we do with that life."

"Through laughter and tears I entertain and teach others how to live. I show people how to find a better way and people smile . . ." Donzaleigh's peace and life are infectious, and her career path should continue to soar as she seeks out great, inspirational, honorable movies and lives her life in a prayerful spirit of loving and giving.

* * *

An interview with Randall Wallace offers some other important insights into God's plan for your life, and certainly much more. In certain corporate circles, it's not uncommon to hear newly fired employees raising their arms and yelling out a thunderous "Freeeeeeedommmmm!" in the hearing of startled co-workers. Such outbursts can be traced to the famous movie *Braveheart*, where Mel

Gibson, as Scotland's William Wallace, screams this utterance as an impassioned encouragement to his countrymen. The writer of this compelling movie, as well as other memorable epics including *Man In The Iron Mask*, *Pearl Harbor*, and *We Were Soldiers*, is Randall Wallace—writer, producer, director, musician, and father. Below, he shares some of his personal background and life wisdom with those daring enough to make Hollywood a career choice.

HUMILIATION BRINGS EXALTATION

—AN INTERVIEW WITH RANDALL WALLACE

EXAMINE YOUR CALLING

Randall majored in religion at Duke University as an undergrad and then attended seminary there for one year. During this time, he sincerely wrestled with his vocational calling. "I had sensed that I really wanted—and was led to be—a writer, but didn't know how to reconcile that with a 'real' career. I didn't know anyone who had made a living as a writer, and I really wasn't sure what kinds of things I wanted to write. To me, writing wasn't a recognized profession. My friends from Duke were going to be pastors, and I fully believed they had a higher calling than I did. However, Thomas Langford, Dean of Duke's Divinity School and my faculty advisor, told me he thought that there was no such thing as one calling being higher than another. He counseled me that we were not to judge God's callings, just to follow them."

In addition, Randall's hometown pastor confirmed the fallacy in Randall's earlier thinking. His pastor told him that the highest calling was not to be a minister—it was to do only and exactly the calling God had for him to do. On the heels of such encouragement from two trusted mentors, Randall left seminary and moved to Nashville. Randall felt that what was happening in New York and Los Angeles at the time was not what he wanted to do, and though he didn't identify himself with country music, he decided to work in Opryland USA as a talent coordinator. During that first year he got a songwriting contract with the largest BMI publisher, Tree Music.

GO WEST, YOUNG MAN!

Soon, he was waking up at five, practicing his writing, and studying music, voice, and piano, but still not getting any vocational clarity. Deep inside, he still had the gnawing suspicion that there must be more. Was it time for a leap of faith? "I was unhappy in Tennessee, though I was from there. I was doing a lot of soul-searching and realizing that what was happening in Nashville wasn't what I was doing in terms of songwriting. Also, I viewed California like the Wild West, wide open with opportunity. I kind of made a non-specific, instinctive choice. I thought that California might offer possibilities I could discover only by going there."

DISCERN THE NEED

Randall packed his belongings into his Toyota and drove off to L.A. without any sense of how he'd get a job, though he assumed it might be in the music industry. Gradually, though, he found himself in the company of actors, many of whom were complaining about the quality of scripts they were getting. Randall began reading the scripts, and though he agreed that the content and inspiration were often lacking, he found that the format was conducive to his kind of writing. "Screenplays are straightforward and direct, which was my style. I had not come to L.A. with any sense whatsoever that I'd ever be in the film business, but I decided to try my hand at screenwriting. It seemed to be a really good thing for me."

Randall just sat down and started writing, though he admits he didn't know anything about screenwriting. He reasoned he'd better take some courses. "But then I thought, 'I really want to find my own approach first. I want to see what's in me before I'm told by someone else what ought to be. I'll blunder my way through a screenplay, and then I'll take a course and hear the rules and know which ones I believe." After his first screenplay landed him an agent, he realized he didn't actually want to take a course after all.

ALIGN THE NEED WITH YOUR PASSION AND GIFTS

Randall never imagined during this season that he was going to be a director or producer; it wasn't his particular dream. "But, the more I learned about the way movies are made, the more I thought that directing films would be a fabulous job. Directing the actors, shaping the music, shaping the visuals, and putting it all together is the movie experience." But, how did one find his way to becoming a writer/director?

FORGE YOUR OWN PATH IN THE WOODS

At the time of Randall's greatest search, there seemed to be no career advice available. "If I wanted to be a lawyer, doctor, or minister, I could see the path. It's clearly laid out, the entrance to these paths is clear, and the milestones along the way are common. But, there is no handbook or map for being a writer/director. Even people who had succeeded in this field couldn't help me. What had worked for them was not likely to work for others." When Randall discussed his dreams with his mentor, Dr. Langford advised, "When you enter the deep, dark woods, you become a woodsman. You begin to discern the pathways and make your own way." Randall believes this was one of the wisest things ever said to him, and it certainly proved to be true of his journey.

MAKE FRUSTRATION A CATALYST FOR CHANGE

Though Randall's first screenplay never sold, he still viewed the process as a great encouragement. "In life, encouragement itself is a great victory," says Randall with a smile. He did get work in television from that first unsold script, but it was frustrating, as he recalls. "It was good in that it paid me money, but it was projects I couldn't relate to, couldn't put my heart in . . . There was no heart to be had. People were looking for inexpensive, new writing, and in some circles the creative process seemed to be a bunch of people shouting at each other. It was I who was supposed to make it all matter somehow. This was exasperating, but it taught me a great lesson. Unless my heart was in something, it would never work well."

SHIFT YOUR FOCUS AND CLEAR YOUR MIND

During this period of mostly heartless TV writing, Randall made some money, but he remained frustrated with the creative process. To revive his imagination, he spent a year writing a novel based on the screenplay that hadn't sold but had generated interest. "I didn't have an agent at the time, so I went to the library and copied the addresses of publishers from novels on the shelf. I sent seventeen letters of inquiry, describing my book. One publisher wrote back asking to see the first few chapters. On Thanksgiving week, he called me saying they wanted the rest. I was elated. G.P. Putnam published that novel, entitled *The Russian Rose*. The funny thing is that then I started getting rejection letters from some of the other publishers—some coming a year after the book was already published in hardcover!"

HAVE CLARITY OF FAITH

Throughout his ups and downs, successes and rejections, Randall Wallace tried to remember that grace is not measured by the yard-stick of fame or fortune. "I'd remind myself that the Bible says, 'Wide is the way that leads to destruction, and narrow is the road that leads to life . . . Few be there that find it.' My religion says that the poor in spirit are blessed, that the discouraged and humble are the ones that will be lifted up, that you have to go down to go up. Ironically, when the way is hard, and people are against you, it may, in fact, show that you're on the right road."

Having grown up Southern Baptist in the heart of the Bible belt's Tennessee, Randall had a stubborn notion that if everyone agreed with him, he could be pretty sure he was wrong!

USE DISAPPOINTMENTS AS SPRINGBOARDS

Randall went on to write his second novel, *So Late into the Night*. It got terrific reviews. One reviewer gushed, "It is elegant prose, reminiscent of the best of Robert Penn Warren." Another, Edwin Yoder, compared Wallace's work to that of Charles Dickens. "Yes, it got great reviews but no sales," says Randall. "A book's life is largely determined before it ever comes out, all based on the marketing and the pre-publication buzz."

Around this time, Randall had gotten married, and he really began wanting children. "My wife said that if I got her pregnant, I had to take her to Europe. I said, 'absolutely.' We did, and I did. I became conscious of something in California I hadn't experienced in the south. There is a huge consciousness about someone's ethnic background—whether they are Jewish-American, Italian-American, Hispanic-American, or African-American. As a southerner, I saw myself as only an American. My son's mother was Irish-American, and I wanted to tell him all about my background too. I knew I was Scottish and that Wallace was a Scottish name, but I didn't know many other details. My wife and I went to Scotland together, and we walked around Edinburgh Castle. There I was amazed to see a statue of William Wallace, though I'd never heard of him and didn't know of his existence. On the other side was Robert the Bruce."

Randall asked a member of the Black Watch, "a tough guy in a kilt," who William Wallace was. The man replied that he was Scotland's greatest hero. "I wondered, 'How is it possible that I, an American keenly interested in history, have never heard of this man—my own namesake?'" I asked the castle guard if this William Wallace, whose life dates overlap Robert the Bruce's, was an ally of Scotland's greatest king. The man leaned forward and said, as if to share a secret, 'Our legends say that Robert the Bruce may have betrayed William Wallace in order to clear the way for Bruce to be king.' In those few words, I heard a great story. It was as if I'd been told that St. Paul and Judas were the same person."

Randall's mind was racing. What if Robert the Bruce had actually betrayed William Wallace? What if something about the way William Wallace lived and died taught Robert the Bruce what it truly meant to be noble? But, Randall was not in a place where he could write such a story. He had just written *Love And Honor*, a story of integrity, sacrifice, and courage—set in the Russia of Catherine the Great, but he hadn't sold it yet. "I had a baby on the way and no prospects for money. I was not prepared to sit down and commit to writing a story no one would think at the time was commercial."

PREPARE FOR THE DEATH-OF-THE-VISION STAGE

Instead of writing what was burning in his heart to write, Randall went back and worked in TV for four more years. He then had a falling out with his mentor in television. 'I wanted to do projects with more spiritual substance. We disagreed, and ultimately, I left his company . . . and then spent some cold, dark times not able to get a job. I was not even able to pitch a story. Word was out that I was no good as writer. I couldn't get a single opportunity in the world of TV, so I was forced to turn to movies."

Randall had seen his father lose a job when he was a young boy. "He'd never lost at anything, but his company was sold, and the new MBAs cut costs by cutting the 'old' guys. My dad, at age thirty-seven, with two kids, was let go. It crushed him. He totally collapsed . . . And then he rebuilt his life."

Randall Wallace's father died on September 11, 2001, from complications with heart surgery. "Because all planes were grounded after the terrorist attack, I didn't make it to his bedside, but he knew I was there. My father was a great man—the greatest I ever knew. He showed me that the darkest day of your life might be your greatest opportunity. Here, I was in my darkest hour. I couldn't sell anything. I had a beautiful home, German cars, and kids in private schools, but I really believed I was going to go under financially. I decided that if I did, I'd do it with my own flags flying. I was going to write what I wanted to see. I was going to finish *Love and Honor* and then write *Braveheart.*"

Randall Wallace did just that, and *Braveheart* became his first produced film, which won the Academy Award for Best Picture and captivated the souls of audiences worldwide. The man so willing to go down in glory found that, indeed, you go down to go up.

ENJOY THE MOUNTAINTOPS

After *Braveheart,* Randall had the opportunity to write, produce, and direct *Man in the Iron Mask,* the inspiring, haunting movie about the days of the famous musketeers. "I loved this time when those who had been famous and widely praised as young men were now floundering and asking themselves if they're relevant anymore. My own heart was in this story, and that's a prescription for success. I was writing what moved me, trusting that if it moved me, it would move others." Then, he wrote and executive produced *Pearl Harbor* and wrote, produced, and directed *We Were Soldiers.*"

WAIT FOR THE INSPIRATION

Many movie analysts have studied the Christian themes and parallels of *Braveheart*'s William Wallace and Jesus Christ. For instance, both men lived under the oppression of a foreign government, both realized their purpose was to do their father's will, both came into their calling through trials, criticism, and betrayal, and both had followers to rally for freedom. In both cases there was an enemy who sought to "marry" the bride, or the elect, as a slap in the face to the true deliverer . . . the allegorical parallels go on and on. "Whenever you feel in the grip of inspiration, you never feel you're doing it yourself," Randall says.

WRITE WHAT YOU KNOW

Randall wrote many drafts of *Braveheart,* but the essential things in that story came out on the first pass through. Many of the sub-themes revolved around true scenarios from Randall's childhood. "When I was in Tennessee, my uncle had a neighbor whose wife died, and he had a lot of young children. The only way to feed them was to be a farmer, and there was no one to take care of the kids. Neighbors pitched in to help out, and various families took some of the children into their homes until the farmer could find a sister or aunt who could help. My uncle and aunt took the farmer's daughter into their home for a few weeks. When it was time to take her back, my uncle stopped the car without speaking, without moving. His wife said, 'Alton, we've got to take her back.' My uncle said, 'I can't.' My aunt and uncle approached the farmer and expressed their desire to raise the girl and love her as their own . . . She's one of my cousins now."

In the same way, in *Braveheart,* there's the boy no one wants to take in. He's another mouth to feed, and besides, he's a wild boy. Randall says, "I wrote about a child at a grave with no one to comfort him . . . Someone has to do something. Another child understands and gives him a flower. When he comes back into town, he takes (the grownup version of) the girl on a ride. He can barely speak to her. This was always like me when I really liked a girl . . . I could hardly look at her . . . When they stop, he doesn't kiss her; he gives her the flower. This took my breath away. I hadn't done that on purpose."

IF IT GRIPS YOUR HEART, IT'LL GRIP THEIRS

When asked about the sources of his inspiration, Randall is quick to say that the primary source is the New Testament, mainly the gospels. "It's Gethsemane, when Jesus was abandoned by his friends. William Wallace goes into Edinburgh like Jesus goes into Jerusalem." As for his choice in stars, Randall tells us that he didn't know then that Mel Gibson was a person of faith. "He was known for *Lethal Weapon* at the time, but we thought he could pull this off. Mel read the script and saw the Wallace character praying, dreaming, and struggling to live a life answering his call, much like Mel's own story. He saw the divine sacrifice . . . I don't know another actor who could have embraced it like he did."

Randall says that it wasn't like he set out to tell story of Jesus, disguised, but it was more that the story of Jesus is so present to him. "I'm not a model Christian, but I've read the Bible every day for most of my life. I've read the gospels—those four little books, and they spoke to me more than anything. I still read the gospels all the time. That's the way I see the world. It's just in me."

It was actually later that Randall realized his work contained so many biblical parallels. He quotes a phrase he came across in seminary, from Reinhold Niebuhr: "The genius of Jesus of Nazareth is that he found holiness, not among the monastic, but among the profane." Indeed, all of Randall's stories show that it's in the gritty realness of life that the greatest valor and character can be displayed.

Randall was raised in what he calls a Puritanical environment. "No one used alcohol. I didn't know anyone who did. We had family gatherings of hundreds of people, but there'd be no beer and no profanity. It was how we lived. But, I realized how profane the world could be. It rang true that Jesus did not seek to separate himself from life, instead he was criticized by the self-righteous for associating with sinners."

Randall wanted to create a Scotsman that was rough, raw, and earthly. "Years later a friend told me I had to read John Eldridge's book, *Wild At Heart*, which quoted *Braveheart*. I read it, and it talked about how in church you'll find bored men sitting there and women saying, 'Where did all the men go?' Women don't want to marry Mother Teresa; they want William Wallace. I met John Eldridge, a brilliant writer, a real man, and we had some great discussions about that."

TELL A GREAT STORY AND DON'T WORRY ABOUT TARGET MARKETS

At the time of the release of *Braveheart*, studios were saying that its major audience would be 17-year-old males . . . that women won't like it. "That was such fallacy. Once (the love interest's) throat is cut, the women in the audience react more violently than the men.

At that point, there's nothing you can do to the bad guys that's bad enough," laughs Randall.

HAVE FUN!

Randall loves capturing the funny, poetic, and ironic moments in his filmmaking career. He shared about how Leonardo DeCaprio played the dual role of the brothers in *Man in the Iron Mask*. "When we were casting, someone told me that Leo loved *Braveheart* and wanted to meet me to discuss the new film. I went to the set of *Titanic* and heard that Leo would irritate Jim Cameron by standing on Titanic's deck and yelling 'freedom!'"

SUBMIT TO GOD'S PLAN

Randall encourages people to remember that God has a plan for everyone. "The things that drive—even things like ego and pride—God can use. He'll use all the good, and he'll burn away all the bad. Many people say, 'If you will lift me up, God, I'll draw all people to you. It's a bargain we try to make with God. But, Jesus said, 'If I be lifted up, I'll draw all men unto me.' It's not about lifting yourself up. It's bad enough to try to make a deal with a Hollywood movie studio, but don't try to negotiate with God."

A lesson Randall is constantly relearning and sharing with his sons and loved ones is that you have to be true to your heart. "Your heart has to be healthy and whole, no matter the cost. You're not profited if you gain the whole world and lose you soul. People will come up and say, 'How do you sell your first screenplay, or get an agent?' They should really say, 'How do I find my voice as a writer? What's the movie I want to see?' If you learn that, the other things will happen. If you don't have that, you can sell all the screenplays you want, but your work won't have heart; it won't matter."

MAKE IT ORGANIC; NOT DOGMATIC

Randall is keen to make the point that artists should not cloak their work in the dogma of their faith. "I believe that one stumbling block for spiritually concerned people is the tendency to be preachy and dogmatic. But, if something is specifically about dogma, it isn't really about faith. For instance, in *Braveheart* and *We Were Soldiers*, the characters weren't saying, 'I'm doing what I do because I'm a Christian.' They were being who God led them to be, but not cloaking themselves in dogma. People don't want to be preached at. You can make profoundly captivating spiritual movies without religious garments. That's important for Christians to remember."

Randall Wallace lives out his faith. The writings of the Bible, the encouragement of his mentors, and lessons learned in his valley of tribulation are all woven into each of his books and movies. Audiences eagerly await the next stream of Randall Wallace novels and movies and their captivating stories full of heart, valor, and passion.

* * *

As indicated by Donzaleigh and Randall's experiences, there are as many ways to discern God's plan for our lives as there are people, careers, and career counselors. Most systems boil down to designating several distinct periods in your life, recalling four or five of your achievements during each period and then analyzing what motivations and talents went into those achievements. From this analysis, your motivational talents, drive, characteristics, and unique pattern may be discerned and applied toward jobs where that combination of motivations and talents is a prerequisite.

Research indicates that companies structured according to motivational talents are much more productive and successful than companies who hire and organize people solely on the basis of a job description. The classic example is hiring a secretary because she can type one hundred words a minute without a mistake, only to find that she doesn't fit into the position because she is motivated to lead and organize the office, not type. If her history had been reviewed with an eye toward discovering her motivational talents, it would have been clear, for example, that she was a leader throughout her childhood and she was best suited to be an office administrator.

Of course, this is a very simplistic example. All of us have many talents, many motivations, and many gifts. Someone, for instance, might be motivated to race cars, read books, compile statistics, and design houses; however, they may be talented at learning languages, playing chess, and persuading audiences of logical imperatives. Furthermore, they may have the gifts of helping and teaching. It is clear that our hypothetical person should not run off and become a racecar driver without considering the total picture defined by their motivational talents and gifts. As noted in the last chapter, motivation is often more important than talent, although both talents and motivations should be considered in choosing a profession.

If you want to communicate effectively, it is very important that you understand how your motivations, talents, and personal characteristics relate to the art of communicating. Communication impacts all aspects of life and there are many different methods of communicating effectively involving many different motivational talents. As a medium, television involves a constellation of motivational talents from financial wizardry through electronic genius to a highly developed sense of time, space, and rhythm, to the motivated ability to project an image through time and space to a faceless audience.

To know which method and which medium of communication you should utilize, you should know what your motivational design is. Not knowing your motivational design, you can find yourself frustrated: communicating ineffectively, through a medium alien to you, and in a style that works for others but not for you.

Pick out a few of the better preachers in your community and analyze their preaching. You will no doubt find that some of them are good storytellers, some are good exegetes, some are good teachers, and some are powerful prophets. For you to choose to be a storytelling preacher when neither the method of storytelling nor the medium of preaching is appropriate for your motivational talents would be extremely frustrating and perhaps even self-destructive.

In the Communicate Workshops, the students work through a few exercises trying on different roles, as star or director, in accordance with their fantasies. They quickly discover whether or not they have the aptitude for that role and whether or not they really like being in their fantasy role. More often than not, the student finds that they really do not want to be the star or the director, but that they do enjoy participating in another role and skill set; whether it is lighting, set design, engineering, or another important television task. The students often find—sometimes to their own surprise—that they excel at jobs for which they have the propensity and the right motivational abilities.

This is not a career-counseling book, but each of us needs to be aware of our motivational talents if we want to communicate effectively. This chapter will acquaint you with the process of discovering your motivational talents through a series of practical exercises that demonstrate the methods used by several career counselors. After you have discovered your motivational talents, there is an exercise for determining your role in movie and television production.

View the system herein as an illustrative guide, though not a definitive one, to help you communicate more effectively. Many excellent communicators recommend such exercises as a valuable tool to help define and discover your path within the entertainment industry. If you are seriously interested in discovering your motivational talents—and you should be—consider consulting a career counselor, or invest in a good book devoted to the subject.[41]

MOTIVATIONAL TALENTS AND PATTERN EXERCISES

Step 1—Past Achievements
This is the first step in discerning your inherent, God-given motivational talents and the picture they form—a sort of outline to His

plan for your life. Divide your life into three periods, such as age 1 to 18, age 18 to 25, and age 25 to the present. Review each period in your mind, and pick out three or four achievements from each period you are the most proud of.

Transfer the following form to three pieces of paper (or more if you need it) and use each new form to write down your achievements for each of the three periods in your life. Do not get bogged down in too much detail. Pick things that you are proud of, or that gave you a feeling of accomplishment, not achievements you think someone else would choose for you.

The key word here is joy. What did you enjoy doing? What are you happy to recall? What do you remember doing with great pride and pleasure? These achievements may be things that no one else knows about you, or which no one else would admire. Richard Bolles has this advice:

> Keep your eye constantly on that 'divine radar' enjoy-able. It's by no means always a guide to what you should be doing, but it sure is more reliable than any other key that people have come up with. Sift later. For now, put down anything that helped you to enjoy a particular moment or period of your life.[42]

Please note that you are participating in this exercise for *yourself*. This is not a test. It is only a guide. There are no right or wrong answers. Enjoy yourself, and let your characteristic patterns and unique motivational talents emerge. You might even be surprised at the results! Keep a few additional sheets of paper handy to write down each of the questions listed in the book and answer them at length.

Some examples of achievements others have listed:

"Crocheting pot-holders and exchanging stories with my grandmother at age nine."

"Writing with an ink pen before anyone else in my class,

although no one knew it."

"Diplomatically bringing my father and mother back together after they had an argument, when I was four or five years old."

"Putting on plays for my brothers and sisters."

"Cornering the market in raccoon coats at my college before they became a fad."

"Discovering how to enjoy and relate to my children after years of being preoccupied with business."

My Achievements - Age _____:

1._____

_____

_____

_____

2._____

_____

_____

_____

3._____

_____

_____

_____

4._____

_____

_____

_____

Step 2—Rank Past Achievements

Look over your list of achievements and choose the five that you feel are the most important to you. Rank these five in order of importance.

1._____

_____

_____

_____

2._____

_____

_____

_____

3._____

_____

_____

_____

4._____

_____

_____

5._____

_____

_____

_____

Step 3—Dissect Achievements

Analyze each of your five most important achievements in terms of the classic questions: who, what, where, why, when, and how. Look at those five achievements and determine: How and why you were involved; What you actually did; How you did it; Who else was involved, and how or why did you relate to them; and, most important of all, what made each achievement important and enjoyable to you?

Achievement # ___:

Brief summary of achievement: _____

_____

_____

How you were involved: _____

_____

_____

Why you were involved: _____

_____

_____

What you actually did: _____

_____

_____

How you did it: _____

_____

_____

Who else was involved: _____

_____

_____

How you related to them: _____

_____

_____

Why did you relate to them in the manner you did? _____

_____

_____

What made this achievement important for you? _____

_____

_____

Step 4—Present Likes and Dislikes

To help discern the pattern of your motivational talents, it is important to take into consideration where you are now. Look at your present job or jobs, and analyze what you like, what you dislike, and why.

Present job: _____

_____

_____

Brief statement of job: _____

_____

_____

How you got the job: _____

_____

_____

Why you took the job: _____

_____

_____

What you do: _____

_____

_____

What you like doing: _____

_____

_____

Why you like those aspects of your work: _____

_____

_____

What you dislike doing: _____

_____

_____

Why you dislike those aspects of your work: _____

_____

_____

Step 5—My Vision

List and analyze a vision of what you would like to achieve before you leave this earth.

Future Achievement # ___:

Brief statement of vision: _____

_____

_____

What you hope to accomplish: _____

_____

_____

Why you hope to accomplish it: _____

_____

_____

What you will do: _____

_____

_____

How will you plan it: _____

_____

_____

Who will be involved: _____

_____

_____

Step 6—Discerning Your Motivational Talents

As noted above, a person can have many motivations (such as the motivation to become a pianist), many of which may not correspond to that person's talents (such as no finger dexterity).

Motivational talents are those natural, God-given abilities that you are motivated to use and develop. For example, if our above mentioned hypothetical person did have finger dexterity, tonal memory, pitch discrimination, rhythmic ability, timbre discrimination, and a love of music, then that person would become a great pianist, if he or she allowed those motivational talents to control a career choice.

Of course, a person may also have talents he or she is not motivated to use. Those talents may be subservient to another talent, or set of talents, due to an overriding motivation. Our hypothetical person may not become a great pianist because he or she hates to perform in public; or, he or she may be motivated to go into audio engineering because of an overriding interest in the practical solutions for improving the audio portion of television transmission. Therefore, instead of concentrating on motivations first and then on talents, as many career counselors do, the following exercises will focus on the talents you are already motivated to use.

The first step in discerning your motivational talents is to compare what you have discovered about yourself in steps 1 through 5 with the following lists, so that you can define your motivational talents. These lists are organized according to categories that will help you discern your unique motivational pattern. The lists are not complete or inclusive; rather they are partial and suggestive. How to proceed:

1. From the following lists, pick out the five talents you are motivated to use.
2. Verify your motivation by analyzing the evidence as revealed in steps 1 through 5, earlier.
3. Rank your motivational talents to discern your basic motivational direction.
4. Discern your motivated faculty, object, relations, and situation using the outlined steps.
5. Bring all of the information together to discern your motivational picture.

Motivational Talents Lists

Your basic motivational talents and the picture they form are present in all your achievements, uniting and empowering everything that you do well and enjoy doing. Compare your achievements, your likes and dislikes, and your vision, as set forth in steps 1 through 5, with the following lists of motivational talents. Pick out five talents you have been motivated to use, like to use, and look forward to using.

Administrative Motivations:

Execute—the motivated ability to get things done by following a project or task through to completion.

Expedite—the motivated ability to facilitate and accelerate the process or progress of a project or task.

Govern—the motivated ability to exercise authority in controlling the activities and personnel of an organization so as to keep a straight course and smooth operation for the good of the whole as well as the individuals who make up the whole.

Manage—the motivated ability to carry on business or affairs.

Navigate—the motivated ability to chart and direct a course through the unknown waters of the future.

Organize—the motivated ability to arrange interdependent parts into a whole.

Oversee—the motivated ability to inspect, superintend, and supervise.

Plan—the motivated ability to develop a method, program, schedule, or scheme of action, procedure, or arrangement.

Prioritize—the motivated ability to rank and prescribe the order in which assignments are to be attended.

Athletic Motivations:

Athletic motivations are self-defining; therefore, the following list leaves out some definitions. Add to this list any other abilities which belong here and which apply to you.

Catch, Climb, Dive, Fight, Hit, Hike, Jump, Ride, Run, Skate, Ski, Swim, Throw, Walk, etc.

Cognitive Motivations:

Analyze—the motivated ability to study a problem or situation in detail in order to determine the solution or outcome.

Appraise—the motivated ability to evaluate or judge quality.

Experiment—the motivated ability to test, to discover some unknown principle or effect, or to demonstrate some known truth, principle, or effect.

Foresee—the motivated ability to anticipate and apprehend events so that prudent action may be taken.

Intuit—the motivated ability to instinctively obtain knowledge.

Investigate—the motivated ability to research by patient inquiry, observation, and examination of the facts.

Learn—the motivated ability to acquire knowledge or skill by study, instruction, or investigation.

Memorize—the motivated ability to retain what has been learned or experienced.

Perceive—the motivated ability to be acutely aware and discerning.

Reason—the motivated ability to think out systematically and logically.

Synthesize—the motivated ability to combine separate elements into a whole.

Communicative Motivations:

Argue—the motivated ability to confront and debate others.

Critique—the motivated ability to correct and perfect communications.

Discuss—the motivated ability to dialogue, interview, share, and listen to others.

Entertain—the motivated ability to amuse and involve others in flights of fancy through storytelling, drama, performing, telling jokes, music, and so forth.

Express—the motivated ability to express feelings, desires, needs, thoughts, ideas, or memories.

Perform—the motivated ability to act, speak, and perform in front of others.

Persuade—the motivated ability to influence and convince others.

Praise—the motivated ability to encourage and commend others.

Preach—the motivated ability to proclaim the gospel of Jesus Christ or a religious belief system.

Promote—the motivated ability to advertise and enhance the reputation of someone or something.

Prophesy—the motivated ability to confront others with a critical message.

Sell—the motivated ability to communicate about something or some idea in such a manner that the audience purchases the object of the communication.

Teach—the motivated ability to lecture, inform, and instruct others by demonstrating, explaining, summarizing, discussing, and/or defining. [*also a service motivation]

Translate—the motivated ability to interpret something or some message that has been said to others.

Creative Motivations:

Build—the motivated ability to create and fashion permanent structures, organizations, and things.

Compose—the motivated ability to conceive and create works of art, music, and literature.

Design—the motivated ability to imagine, visualize, and create designs.

Innovate—the motivated ability to introduce something new and make changes in anything established.

Invent—the motivated ability to create physical, chemical, mechanical, and other innovations.

Produce—the motivated ability to create, multiply, and manufacture animals, plants, and things, including widgets, gadgets, movies, clones, and so forth.

Solve—the motivated ability to creatively solve problems and improve things.

Leadership Motivations:

Command—the motivated ability to take charge over people and things.

Decide—the motivated ability to make decisions and to guide and lead others.

Direct—the motivated ability to orchestrate and conduct the activities of people and things.

Encourage—the motivated ability to empower and motivate others to achieve something.

Guide—the motivated ability to show the way to others.

Influence—the motivated ability to use character and status to exert authority over the minds and actions of others.

Initiate—the motivated ability to start an activity or action.

Prevail—the motivated ability to lead a crusade to defeat adversary ideologies, people, and things.

Recruit—the motivated ability to enlist resources and others in a common task.

Physical/Manual Motivations:

Acquire—the motivated ability to accumulate property and things.

Construct—the motivated ability to put together, make, or build something.

Develop—the motivated ability to promote the growth of something.

Exploit—the motivated ability to make use of all aspects of something for profit.

Handle—the motivated ability to hold, move, balance, and manage something using the hands.

Improve—the motivated ability to make something better.

Maintain—the motivated ability to keep something in good condition.

Manipulate—the motivated ability to treat or operate something with the hands.

Mold/Adapt—the motivated ability to shape something with the hands.

Possess—the motivated ability to keep and control things.

Repair—the motivated ability to restore something to good condition after it is broken or decayed.

Playful Motivations:

Amuse—the motivated ability to divert, occupy pleasurably, or entertain.

Challenge—the motivated ability to invite someone to engage in a contest.

Compete—the motivated ability to contend in rivalry, as for a prize.

Contest—the motivated ability to struggle for victory.

Enjoy—the motivated ability to have satisfaction in experiencing.

Frolic—the motivated ability to make merry or to play.

Gamble—the motivated ability to play a game for money or another stake.

Master—the motivated ability to become adept in or subdue something.

Outwit—the motivated ability to surpass in ingenuity or cunning.

Recreate—the motivated ability to change occupation or indulge in diversions for the sake of relaxation and refreshment.

Strategize—the motivated ability to use artifice, science, and intrigue to win a game.

Toy—the motivated ability to trifle, play, or dally with something.

Service Motivations:

Coach—the motivated ability to assist, instruct, tutor, or prepare someone for a task, game, or examination.

Conciliate—the motivated ability to resolve disputes by causing the various parties to agree and become friends by gaining their good will, drawing them together, and winning them over to a compatible point of view.

Counsel—the motivated ability to exercise prudence in advising someone based on mutual deliberation.

Facilitate—the motivated ability to make something easy or less difficult for someone.

Feed—the motivated ability to provide food or furnish something essential for the growth, sustenance, or maintenance of someone or something (such as feeding coal to a furnace).

Heal—the motivated ability to help cure or restore someone to health.

Help—the motivated ability to assist, wait on, lend aid to, improve, protect, rescue, relieve, or aid someone.

Mediate—the motivated ability to act as an intermediate between two or more parties.

Nurse—the motivated ability to take care of someone or something.

Nurture—the motivated ability to bring up or train.

Teach—the motivated ability to impart knowledge to someone. [*also a communicative motivation]

Tend—the motivated ability to watch over and take care of someone or something.

Spiritual Motivations:

Adorn—the motivated ability to add to the beauty, splendor, or attractiveness of something.

Believe—the motivated ability to have faith or religious convictions.

Bless—the motivated ability to praise, glorify, consecrate, or hallow.

Commune—the motivated ability to confer together and have fellowship with God as well as other people.

Dream—the motivated ability to have vision or to perceive the reality of the supernatural.

Explore—the motivated ability to seek for or after a discovery so that the unknown may be made known.

Love—the motivated ability to strongly care for and give selflessly to another.

Meditate—the motivated ability to contemplate and reflect on something.

Obey—the motivated ability to respond in love by executing the commands of someone.

Overcome—the motivated ability to conquer or to succeed.

Perfect—the motivated ability to strive for maturity, or to help improve and complete.

Persevere—the motivated ability to persist in any enterprise undertaken in spite of opposition.

Preach—the motivated ability to proclaim the gospel of Jesus Christ or a religious belief system. [*also a communicative motivation.]

Prophesy—the motivated ability to confront others with a critical message. [*also a communicative motivation.]

Rebuke—the motivated ability to reject and renounce evil.

Rejoice—the motivated ability to feel and give great joy and delight.

Rescue—the motivated ability to redeem or deliver from bondage.

Restore—the motivated ability to heal and make relationships whole.

Symbolic Motivations:

Account—the motivated ability to value, estimate, or balance a collection of items.

Budget—the motivated ability to prepare a financial statement of estimated income and expenses.

Calculate—the motivated ability to compute.

Equate—the motivated ability to express as equal, reduce to a common standard, or derive an equation which expresses the process of equating by means of symbols.

Estimate—the motivated ability to approximate.

Formulate—the motivated ability to express in a systematized symbolic statement.

Graph—the motivated ability to symbolize through a chart, plot, or tracing.

Measure—the motivated ability to ascertain the dimensions, quantity, or limits of a thing.

Solve—the motivated ability to creatively solve problems and improve things. [*also a creative motivation.]

Tabulate—the motivated ability to reduce information to a table of figures.

From the previous lists, identify the five motivational talents that most likely apply to you. On a separate sheet of paper for each of the five motivational talents, write down the name of each motivational talent and the list category to which it belongs. Then, review steps 1 through 5 from the beginning of this section, and check to see if each of these motivational talents is present in your achievements, likes, and vision. You may want to use the following form for each of your five motivational talents.

MOTIVATIONAL TALENT FORM

Motivational talent: _____

_____

_____

Category: _____

_____

_____

Demonstration of presence in steps 1 through 5:_____

_____

_____

Step 7—Discerning Your Motivational Direction

Your basic motivational direction is the internal guidance system that drives you in a specific direction. This guidance system is formed by your unique combination of motivational talents, and it is the backbone of your God-given bone structure. Your basic motivational direction is determined by considering your primary motivational talent and the ranking order of your secondary motivational talents. To discern your basic motivational direction, simply list your five discerned motivational talents in order of importance by referring to the frequency of occurrence and importance of each in steps 1 through 5.

Motivational direction:

_____

_____

Primary motivational talent:

1._____

_____

_____

_____

Secondary motivational talents:

2._____

_____

3._____

_____

_____

_____

4._____

_____

_____

_____

Step 8—Discerning Other Motivated Characteristics

You have other God-given motivated characteristics that fill out your bone structure. From each of the following lists, pick out the particular motivated characteristic that you feel applies to you, and then compare that motivated characteristic with what you learned in steps 1 through 5. This comparison will demonstrate your primary motivated characteristic in each category.

Motivated Faculty:

Your motivated faculty refers to the physical or mental power (or function) you have been most motivated to use, enjoy using, and look forward to using. It is your most fully developed faculty.

Allure—the physical power to attract people.

Balance—the power to be poised and to balance things.

Charisma—the quality of extraordinary spiritual power, usually manifested in the ability to elicit popular support.

Coordination—the physical power to function harmoniously and effectively.

Dexterity—the faculty of being able to use your hands with quickness, skill, and ease.

Emotional—the power to feel emotion, empathy, sympathy, and love.

Energy—the inherent power to perform a great deal of work or do many things without becoming tired.

Hearing—the faculty of perceiving, discriminating, and remembering sounds, tones, pitch, timbre.

Intellect—the faculty of using your mind to know, reason, judge, and comprehend.

Memory—the power to remember and recall.

Perception—the faculty of being aware and intuitive.

Rhythm—the faculty of being able to perceive, remember, or emulate cadence, motion, beats, accents, or time.

Sight—the faculty of seeing, perceiving, discerning, visualizing, and remembering images, designs, colors, proportions, objects, and all of the real world.

Smell—the power to detect and perceive smells, odors, and aromas.

Strength—the faculty of power, endurance, force, and toughness.

Taste—the power to perceive, recognize, and remember the flavor of something.

Touch—the faculty of perceiving by contact.

Motivated Object:

Your motivated object is the particular object you have felt most motivated to use, enjoy using, and look forward to using. This list is not inclusive; please add any objects that apply to you.

- Animals
- Art
- Books
- Budgets
- Building Materials
- Cameras
- Electronics
- Fabrics
- Hardware/Tools
- Ideas
- Images
- Land
- Mechanical Equipment
- Money
- Musical Instruments
- Numbers
- Organizations
- Paints
- Plants
- Projects
- Symbols
- Systems
- Wood
- Words

Motivated Relations:

Your motivated relations are the relations with another person, or with multiple other people, in which you have felt most motivated to be involved, enjoyed being involved, and look forward to being involved again.

- Coach
- Healer/Doctor
- Helper
- Individualist
- Leader
- Manager/Governor
- Mediator
- Nurse
- Partner/Friend
- Server
- Team Member

Motivated Situation:

Your motivated situation is where you have been most motivated to achieve, enjoy achieving, and look forward to achieving.

- Alone
- At ease
- Free
- In a classroom/lecture/crowd
- In competition
- Isolated
- In a structured environment
- Solving problems
- Under stress

From each of the preceding lists in this section, pick out one motivated characteristic that most likely applies to you. Just as you did in the case of the motivational talents, on a separate sheet of paper for each motivated characteristic, write down the name of the motivated characteristic and the list category to which it belongs. Then, review steps 1 through 5 and show that each of the motivated characteristics that you picked out are present in your achievements, likes, and vision. If you find it helpful, use the following form.

MOTIVATED CHARACTERISTIC FORM

Motivational talent: _____

_____

_____

Category: _____

_____

Demonstration of presence in steps 1 through 5:_____

_____

_____

Step 9—Discerning Your Motivational Picture

Your motivational picture is a portrait of who you are, produced by bringing together all the information you have compiled about yourself in steps 1 through 8, where you discerned your motivational talents, thrust, and characteristics. Your motivational picture defines who God created you to be and His plan for your life. To discern your motivational picture simply review steps 1 through 8 and fill in the following form.

Motivational picture: _____

_____

_____

Motivational Direction

[Primary motivational talent]:

_____

_____

_____

Secondary Motivational Talents

_____

_____

Motivated Faculty   Motivated Object

_____   _____

Motivated Relations   Motivated Situation

_____   _____

You may have noticed that this form contains extra space for you to add other motivated characteristics you have learned about yourself from steps 1 through 5, or you may increase the details you record about yourself in steps 1 through 5, to fill in this information. You may also record further information in similar exercises developed on your own.

For instance, you might like to add your motivated geographic location, or your motivated working environment. The more detail you develop, the clearer you will be about God's will for your life. Keep in mind that these exercises are illustrative, not definitive. To accurately discover your motivational talents, consult a career counselor, or an authoritative book on the subject. Of course, whatever your unique motivational picture turns out to be, it is not a one-way ticket to your destiny. It is still necessary for you to work at fulfilling God's plan for your life!

Motivational Summary:

Knowing your motivational picture will enable you to communicate more effectively by helping you determine the answers to our ascertainment questions:

1. What do I want to communicate?
2. Why do I want to communicate?
3. Who do I want to communicate with?
4. What genre and medium do I want to communicate through?

Your motivational direction and motivational talents will tell you what matters most to you and why you want to communicate. Your motivated characteristics and talents will indicate the circumstances and setting you are most comfortable and effective communicating within. Your motivational picture will guide you toward using an appropriate medium for your gifts and talents (which will be best applied once you have learned more about the nature of each available media).

Of course, God and unique circumstances can also make you a very effective communicator in subjects and media that do not seem predictable by your motivational pattern. Remember that God does frequently use our weaknesses to accomplish his purpose—Moses, with his speech problem, is a good case in point. Exceptions like this aside, knowing your motivational picture gives you increased self-awareness, and a clearer picture of your goals and talents with respect to God's calling in your life. Each of these things will make you a better communicator; both in the way you are able to present yourself, and the way you are able to relate to others.

For example, an acquaintance of mine is an excellent lecturer/teacher of memory techniques. Reviewing his personal history, it is clear that: he has been driven by the desire to memorize (his motivational drive is to memorize); his secondary motivational talents are to promote, solve problems, teach, and overcome, in that order; his motivated faculty is charisma; his motivated object is image; his motivated relationship is leadership; and, his motivated circumstance is in a lecture hall in front of an audience. He knows what he wants to communicate—memory techniques; why he wants to communicate—to help others by teaching them; who his audience is (a live audience where he can exercise his leadership) and, what his appropriate medium is: lecturing. He is an effective communicator because he is true to his motivational pattern.

Years ago in 1984, the Continental Basketball Association (CBA), the minor league of professional basketball, held an amateur contest to find the official CBA television "color" commentator. About three hundred lawyers, accountants, doctors, salesmen, and even an FBI agent showed up to try out for the CBA sportscaster position. Having to keep up with a four-minute segment of fast action on a television monitor, one Connecticut man blurted out in frustration, "the players are running around everywhere!" A New York equipment operator sat through the four-minute segment in embarrassed silence. Hal Lancaster reporting on this in *The Wall Street Journal* captured these comments: "'It's a lot tougher than you think,' says Rick Hansen, a computer researcher for International Business Machines Corp. 'It looks so easy sitting at home.' Adds Robb Larson, the CBA's vice president of entertainment services: 'One guy said it was worse than his first date.'"[43]

Most of the contestants did not take into consideration their motivational talents before they tried out to be a sportscaster.

As you learn more about the various media, you will be able to discern how you can communicate most effectively through each particular medium. Here is an exercise that illustrates, through talent questions, the different major roles involved in a simplified movie production. Ask these questions of yourself with reference to your motivational pattern to see where you would fit in a television production environment.

SIMPLIFIED TV AND FILM TALENT EXERCISE

For each role or job, a series of questions follow, briefly sketching the major motivational talent required for that role. These questions are also useful for recruiting talent to produce a television program or a film.

Executive Producer:
- Can you raise money and secure resources and talent?
- Are you good at getting?
- Can you wheel and deal?

Producer:
- Can you get a group of creative individuals to work together and finish a project?

Line Producer:
- Can you take orders and execute them?
- Can you keep track of resources?
- Are you careful with your bank balance?

Director:
- Can you bring out the best in people?
- Can you visualize a book or a script as a movie?

Author:
- Can you articulate your ideas dramatically?

Scriptwriter:
- Can you take ideas and develop them into a story?
- Can you write dialogue?

Production Manager (TV):
- Can you keep people working on time?
- Can you organize people?

Director of Photography:
- Can you visualize stories?
- Do you recognize authenticity?

Cameraperson:
- Can you frame a picture?
- Can you focus a camera?
- Can you compose a picture?

Audio Engineer (TV) and Post Production Sound Mixer (film):
- Do you like music?
- Do you dislike a bad recording?

Soundperson:
- Do you enjoy sounds?
- Can you tell the difference in the quality of a recording?

Art Director (TV) and Production Designer (film):
- Can you capture a period? A look? A moment-in-time?

Video Engineer (TV):
- Can you make sure that the video equipment is functioning properly?
- Can you think and act immediately?
- Are you a whiz?

Technical Director (TV):
- Are you good at running a model railroad?

Location Manager:
- Do you know your way around?
- Do you have a good sense of direction?
- Can you get the cooperation of the people affected by the production?

Prop Manager:
- Do you enjoy rummaging through thrift shops?
- Are you good at treasure hunting?
- Can you find just the right thing?

Grip:
- Do you like to help?
- Are you strong?

Gaffer/Chief Lighting Technician (film) or Lighting Director/ Engineer (TV):
- Do you see things in dark (black) and light?
- Are you good with electrical wiring?
- Can you fix an electrical appliance?

Secretary/Continuity:
- Can you keep track of details?
- Do you follow through?

Editor:
- Can you make sense out of chaos and throw away surplusage?

Makeup:
- Can you see the best in people?
- Can you see the character in people?
- Can you paint?

Wardrobe:
- Do you like designing clothes?
- Can you capture a look?

Special Effects:
- Did you have a chemistry set as a child?
- Can you make the impossible possible?

Sound Effects:
- Can you mimic sounds?
- Are you aware of noises?

OTHER NATURAL TALENTS

It should be noted that each one of these production roles is important in producing a movie. Without a continuity person, scenes shot on different days will not match and the movie will fall apart. Every production person is important and worthy of respect.

Having discerned your motivational talents and related them to production roles, you can do the same with any other medium by simply analyzing the talents required by each role involved in that medium and compare those talent questions with your motivational picture. Furthermore, since every career, job, or activity requires communication, you can analyze the communication talents required in that career, job, or activity and compare those required talents with your motivational picture, keeping in mind that almost all careers, jobs, or activities can be modified to some degree to fit with your motivational talents.

One area of God-given talents that we have not yet considered in depth is the spiritual gift or gifts that God gives us when we become a member of His Body. These gifts are set forth in 1 Corinthians 12, Romans 12, and Ephesians 4. They are an integral part of "who you are" if you are a Christian. Many of these God-given spiritual gifts relate directly to communications, and you should take the time to review them as set forth in the above mentioned chapters of the Bible.

Using the same method that you used to discern your motivational talents, you can discern your spiritual gift or gifts by focusing in on those achievements that relate to your Christian walk.

It has been said that only a fool would distrust his Creator. God has created us, giving each of us a unique combination of motivations and talents so that we can glorify Him and enjoy His creation. Furthermore, as Christians, we are His children and heirs to His kingdom, anointed with spiritual gifts. We should know who we are so that we can fulfill His plan for our lives and so that we can communicate effectively in the position or role for which He has designed us.

He calls us into his Body so that we can occupy every area of life for Him. We should praise Him not only with our lips, but also by loving ourselves—who He has created us to be.

> But each person should examine his own work, and then he will have a reason for boasting in himself alone, and not in respect to someone else.
>
> —Galatians 6:4

However, knowing "who you are" and acting accordingly is only part of the process. To communicate effectively we must ask, answer, and apply each of the ascertainment questions. Furthermore, each of us must persevere in being that person who He has called us to be in spite of the opposition inherent in our fallen world. Trust God and follow Him.

> For it was You who created my inward parts; You knit me together in my mother's womb. I will praise You, because I have been remarkably and wonderfully made. Your works are wonderful, and I know [this] very well. My bones were not hidden from You when I was made in secret, when I was formed in the depths of the earth. Your eyes saw me when I was formless; all [my] days were written in Your book and planned before a single one of the began.
>
> —Psalms 139:13–16

· 4 ·

If It's Not on the Page . . .

The first sign that a baby is going to be human comes when he begins naming the world, demanding stories that connect its parts.

—Kathryn Morton[44]

Babies are human because God created us in His image—not because they cry, demand, or tell, stories. Communication, however, is an important part of the uniqueness of humankind. The human drive to communicate through a variety of forms, formats, and media is remarkable. In the garden of Eden, God tasked Adam with naming all the animals. That desire to name, to create, and to communicate is still one of the most essential human traits, lasting from infancy through adulthood.

Christians and Jews have long been known as people of "The Book." Since the Bible is full of stories and Christians are called by Jesus to communicate the Good news, which He did through Parables, Christians are a storytelling people. In faithful obedience to this call, they tell the Good news through every conceivable medium and genre. Thus, the church invented modern drama with the Mediaeval Mystery Plays. And, since the beginning of the motion picture industry, Christians have used movies to communicate the gospel because movies and television programs are the most powerful, audio-visual storytelling media.

POWERFUL EMOTIONAL IMAGES

Around the world, viewers seek out, see and hear the stories told on television and in movie theaters every day. Not only are movies and television pervasive in our society, they also are the most powerful tools of communication. They plant powerful emotional images in our minds, direct our purchases, influence our lifestyles, and redirect our hopes and dreams.

Gary Smalley, president of Today's Family, has pointed out that altering people's actions or attitudes has always been difficult, but in 1942 Walt Disney demonstrated the power of movies to blast through the defensive barriers people erect to change their lives and the world around them. Disney's animated movie *Bambi* painted a picture that went straight to the heart. Almost overnight this Walt Disney film nearly bankrupted the deer hunting industry. As Gary notes:

> The year before the film was released, deer hunting in the United States was a $9.5 million business. But when one particularly touching scene was shown— that of a yearling who sees his mother gunned down by a hunter—there was a dramatic change in men's attitudes. The following season, hunters spent only $4.1 million on tags, permits, and hunting trips![45]

We may applaud this use of the emotive power of film to save wildlife, but we cannot overlook the power of film to negatively affect people and our civilization. The heinous power of the emotive, emotional pictures was dramatically brought to the world's attention by Dr. James Dobson's television interview with Ted Bundy just hours before Bundy was executed in Florida's electric chair.

To the dismay of newscasters across the nation and to the shock of many Americans, Bundy acknowledged that pornography had played a critical role in leading him to murder as many as twenty-eight young women and children. In a poignant excerpt, a tearful Bundy noted that in the many years he had spent in prison with violent criminals:

> Without exception, every one of them was deeply involved with pornography—without question, without exception—deeply influenced and consumed by an addiction to pornography. The FBI's own study on serial homicide shows that the most common interest among serial killers is pornography.

Exclusion

Because every communication excludes what it does not include, its omissions create powerful secondary messages in the mind of the audience. In an Annenberg School of Communications study on "Television and Viewer Attitudes About Work,"[46] it was found that in the television environment blacks and other minorities were generally excluded from prestigious professions. These omissions had a profound affect on specific demographic groups; some groups were demoralized by the exclusion, and others affirmed.

In a similar study, a young African-American girl is recorded saying that she wants to be a doctor so that she can travel a lot, and have a big house, a pool, a plane, and a yacht. Her perception of the medical profession had been totally distorted by television's portrayal of the medical environment. Instead of being attracted to medicine as an opportunity to heal, serve, and help, she was drawn to medicine as a way to acquire things.

Selling Murder

For another poignant illustration of the power of movies, consider the work of Dr. Joseph Goebbels, who was the National Socialist

(Nazi) propaganda minister from 1933 to 1945. He exploited radio, press, cinema, and theater in Germany to destroy the Jews, evangelical Christians, handicapped Germans, and other groups of people. In 1994, the Discovery Channel aired *Selling Murder*, an important documentary investigating how Goebbels used mass media to influence the German people to accept the mass murder of human beings. The documentary shows that a majority of German people rejected mercy killings (a euphemism for murder), even though the ministry of propaganda had released several clinical documentaries trying to convince the German people to accept the inhuman practice. Finally, Goebbels produced a dramatic movie called *I Accuse*, an emotive feature film about a beautiful, intelligent woman who is dying of an incurable disease and begs to be allowed to commit suicide. After the movie was released, a majority of German people said they had changed their minds and now supported mercy killings. After a few more of Goebbels's films about invalids and handicapped people, the German people voted for mass mercy killings. As an insight into the power of the mass media, historian Paul Johnson writes in his book *Modern Times*,[47]

> Hitler appears always to have approached politics in terms of visual images. Like Lenin and still more like Stalin, he was an outstanding practitioner of the Century's most radical vice: social engineering—the notion that human beings can be shoveled around like concrete. But, in Hitler's case, there was always an artistic dimension to these Satanic schemes. Hitler's artistic approach was absolutely central to his success. [Historians all agree] the Germans were the best-educated nation in the world. To conquer their minds was very difficult. Their hearts, their sensibilities, were easy targets.

Indoctrination, with specific use of newsreel and films, was vital to Hitler's control of the new generation. Gerhard Rempel, in his book, *Hitler's Children: The Hitler Youth and the SS*[48] wrote, "Each day began with a newsreel, followed by the various types of training. On Sunday mornings, an ideological program was substituted for church services, and Sunday nights were set aside for motion pictures."

On the Other Hand

On the positive side of the influence of the mass media of entertainment equation: the movie *The Passion of the Christ* convinced millions to repent; the epic television program *Jesus of Nazareth* introduced millions of people throughout the world to Jesus Christ; *A Man Called Peter*, about the preacher Peter Marshall, brought a flood of many young men into the pulpit; and, *Chariots of Fire* brought many to Jesus and gave many more a sense of God's purpose in their life.

Story, Image, and Effect

There are three elements of a movie or television program that help capture the attention of the audience: story, image, and effect.

When I was the Director of the TV Center at City University of New York (CUNY), Brooklyn College, one of the professors, Jim Day, had been a founder of Children's Television Workshop (CTW) that produced *Sesame Street*. CTW would test every program. In one segment, they wanted to show the difference between an internal skeleton and an external skeleton. The animation showed an ant while a voice over said that the ant had an external skeleton so it could not grow as big as an elephant, which had an internal skeleton. As the narrator spoke, the animated illustration showed the ant growing as big as an elephant and then exploding. When CTW tested the segment and asked the audience whether an ant could grow as big as an elephant, 90 percent of the audience said "yes, an ant can grow as big as an elephant," because they had just seen it in the animated sequence, and the visual was much more powerful than the audio.

CTW also tested the extent to which each *Sesame Street* program would capture and hold the attention of the audience. CTW would show a program segment and have a distracter machine next to the TV set. (The distracter machine was merely some blinking lights.) Observers would watch the eyes of the audience to see when they looked away from the TV program and at the distracter machine. At that point, CTW would put in another effect, such as a cut, dissolves, pan, wipe, or animated sequence, that would hold the audience's attention.

For Better or for Worse

Communicating effectively requires learning and applying the basic principles of language, grammar, rhetoric, technique, and general rules that govern each genre and medium. There are three levels of such principles: general principles (which apply to most communications), genre specific principles, and media specific principles. There are also several steps involved in producing powerful communications, including movies and television programs. Here is a brief outline of the most important foundational steps in preparing your communication. Each genre and medium will modify this outline by adding or subtracting steps or substeps. However, this outline is your basic guide to the steps required to communicate effectively.

12 Basic Foundational Steps to Communicating Effectively:

1. In light of who you are, why you want to communicate, and well thought-out research and ascertainment, make a brief note of what you want to say, your idea, conviction, or your key thought. This idea, thought, or statement must be something that you believe and want to communicate through a movie or television program.

2. Ask and answer the appropriate ascertainment questions to target your audience, determine your genre

and medium, and plan the execution of your communication.

3. Rephrase your idea or key thought into an active premise that you can prove in your communication, taking into consideration your answers to the pertinent ascertainment questions.

4. Identify the elements needed to prove your premise, most of which are inherent within your premise. In drama, these elements are your characters, conflict, climax, and resolution.

5. Structure these elements taking into consideration your audience, genre, medium of choice, and your answers to the ascertainment questions which are appropriate for your communication.

6. Write out, plan, or script your communication, punctuating it with technical, dramatic, or literary effects to capture and retain audience interest.

7. Prepare, storyboard, and/or rehearse your communication.

8. Produce, polish, or otherwise finish your communication.

9. Edit, review, and revise your communication.

10. Deliver, distribute, or broadcast your communication.

11. Survey your audience to find out how effective your communication was and how it can be improved.

12. Review and revise your communication to improve it if possible.

Half of this process is preparation. Many people fail to prepare or dash off a script and believe that they will perfect it when the right person buys it. However, you never have a second chance to make a first impression, so you need to perfect your script right from the beginning, even if you need to change it later.

Remember that the average movie takes nine years from start to finish. *The Passion of the Christ* took ten years. *Evita* took twenty-three years. *Batman* took seventeen years.

There are several reasons why it takes so long. First, there are 300,000 scripts submitted every year to the Writers Guild of America and many more are written that are never submitted, aside from the flood of novels every year, but less than three hundred movies open in theaters every year. Thus, most scripts never make it into production. Second, Hollywood movies cost over $104 million to produce and distribute in 2010, and it takes a long, long time to get all the elements together so that some distributor or investor will want to put up this kind of money. Third, most people take years to get the script right. The *Los Angeles Times* interviewed a woman who was trying for twenty years to sell her script. She said that in all those years she had not had the time to take a scriptwriting course or read a book on scriptwriting. *The Los Angeles Times* and all of us should be perplexed: What was she doing all that time that she could not take a moment to learn her chosen craft?

Before examining how to write a good script, let's listen to the words of a novelist who wrote the powerful book, *Once Upon a Time When We Were Colored*, Clifton L. Taulbert.

* * *

THE GIFT OF WRITING—GOD'S GIFT OF CREATIVITY
BY CLIFTON L. TAULBERT

Even as a little boy, I was always intrigued by books and the fact that big people could pick up a book to read and within a short period of time, I was closing my eyes and imagining myself in the place and among the people in the story being read. Reading and writing is powerful—an amazing gift to humankind. And now, I find myself among those who write to inform and entertain others. However, over the years, my "faith" helped me to realize the importance of handling this important gift of influence with care and responsibility. If properly handled, this gift of creativity—writing can be a healing balm, a wonderful passage of escape to worlds of fun and adventure, or a journey into our past so that we can better plan for our future. And as a Christian, I feel that this gift must be handled with care and responsibility—reflecting the heart of God.

As a Christian, I have the choice of how I will use this incredible and powerful gift. Apart from professional standards, there are many influencing factors with which we as writers must contend. Hollywood has its own set of standards—determined by box office draw. The publishing world lets you know what set of circumstances will most likely sell your book: sex, murder, racial conflict, and more sex. If, we then have the power of will, how will we allow our gift to be influenced?

Embarking upon my first literary work, I experienced this conversation within my soul. My first book, *Once Upon a Time When We Were Colored*, was a journey into the days of the segregated south. How would I approach this story of racism and personal pain? I must admit, I was tempted to make sure that I captured the hurt and humiliation of the period for the world to remember and never to forget. However, as I began the writing process, my faith kicked in, and I was now faced with a decision. Would I write to redeem and transform? Or, would I write solely to expose the evil of the system at whatever the cost? As I weighed my options, I now know that it was God who took me back to my youth with these questions. Was anything "good" happening during that period? Did I ever smile? Did I have memories of others who came to my rescue? Did I encounter unselfishness within my community? How was my learning experience? And, how did the church impact daily life? As I began to ponder these questions in my mind, I was left with the reality that in spite of the harshness of the season, God was there and I had been a beneficiary of his presence. So rather than heading down the path solely to show the world the wickedness of such an oppressive system, my Faith reminded me of the strength of those who trusted in God and in so doing salvaged generations of others, like myself from the full reach of legal segregation. In the context of this approach, Human Resiliency and Sustaining Faith were recognized in the midst of this dehumanizing system. And this wisdom, far beyond my young years, since publication has allowed the readers to ask the questions and ponder circumstances I wanted to lay bare. From leaders of governments to middle school children around the world to ordinary citizens of all races, this small volume has become an opened door to the full world that I encountered. I wrote without anger and bitterness and listened closely to God's heart as I used his gift of creativity/writing, to leave an emotional and spiritual path to a better tomorrow.

At this writing (Spring of 2004), my first book has been circulating around the world since 1989 and it still has within it, the ability to captivate readers to the both the good and the bad of those times, while leaving them with a sense of hope for tomorrow. I now believe wholeheartedly that one's faith when allowed to impact and influence the use of our God-given creativity, will always leave within the midst of the story, reflection, redemption and transformation. The story of our faith is one of redemption and transformation, a loving God in the midst of chaos and sin writing with his life that in spite of what you see, and what you currently experience, we have a way out. Writing is an incredible gift, one that God will use to allow us to remind ourselves as well as show others a way out. For Christians, our agenda has been set and all our efforts, even those that involve the use and disposition of our creative gifts should always reflect God's higher purpose. . . reflection, redemption, and transformation.

Not everyone understood my approach to writing my first book. Some felt I was being too easy on the time-period; thus letting some of the hook for their roles and continued participation in various forms of racism. At one point, I began to question my format and my earlier commitment to writing a "door" left ajar to a path that would ultimately make us better. Did this mean that other writers who had painstakingly pointed out the sins of the era were wrong and out of God's plan? Certainly not! I had to understand that I, me personally was being challenged to listened for my specific voice for my time, one that had said "yes" to Christ. In so doing, I was left with the understanding that many of the earlier works were akin to the "law" and were absolutely necessary and needed to prick hearts and change minds, but He laid upon my heart, the writing of "grace." In the midst of the law, Jesus came and so it was for me as a southern writer. In the midst of great writings of human bondage and cruel sufferings, another voice, my small voice came along and said, "In the midst of the travesty, God was there, and He was experienced by thousands as they found themselves surrounded by a people who through their unselfishness built and sustained their lives—an unselfishness firmly linked to their faith."

The book became incredibly successful and remains so today. However, when the success caught the ears of Hollywood, they came calling. Hollywood had read the review in the *Boston Globe* and the *New York Times* and quickly started the wheels turning. I was on cloud nine or higher. However, my joy was short-lived as they read the book and felt as if it was too soft. Where were the hangings? They were not impressed with the strength of family. Where were the rape scenes? They were not impressed with the commitment of the "Colored" field workers to educate their children. Where was the cotton field sex? They were not impressed with a church-going community, who in spite of legal segregation built a strong community for their children. They were not in search of redemption and transformation. And one-by-one, the conversations ceased, and the prospects of going to Hollywood looked rather dim. They had their picture of the "Colored" family, and it didn't look like the one I had written about.

I was determined to leave the book as it was written, even if it meant, no movie. However, God had different plans, and, after I had given up and turned it over to Him, out of the blue, an answer came as a young white writer in Hollywood decided to write the screenplay as a "spec" project. It worked and eventually, Hollywood Producer Tim Reid became a champion for this story of family and faith. Even so, the financing was very difficult as various sponsors wanted to add or take away certain aspects, but Mr. Reid promised me that he would stay true to the story, and he did. *Once Upon a Time When We Were Colored* eventually hit the big screens, though limited in release, but achieved the impact intended and continues to challenge men and women to reflect for redemption and transformation. Even today, the movie, in spite of its success and reception has not made any of the financial returns anticipated. The powers-to-be had little faith in such a family oriented film. But, I sleep well knowing that long after, I'm gone, this story will still be read and the movie will always be watched and those reading and watching will have this image of faith—lived out in the midst of a challenging time.

Many years have passed since the book and the movie, and I continue to write books and along with young Luke Gheen, my screen-writing partner, also write screenplays. We both laugh, because we know what sells in Hollywood, but our faith guides our creativity. We often find ourselves laughing and discussing whether God could handle a scene. For me, it's real important to factor in all that I believe. How can I face my judgment if I have allowed my gift to be used in a way that does not bring glory to His purpose? I do believe that good films can be made and be successful without compromising our faith and commitment to God. It isn't easy, but I am convinced that it can be done, if the God-given talent is there.

In writing the new screenplay based upon my second book, *The Last Train North*, Luke and I were determined to make it a good movie, without the sex and the unnecessary violence, and yet keep it true to the story and the times. We keep asking each other questions and stepping back to see if what we have written makes sense or if we are trying to bring in unnecessary sensationalism to appease the buyers. Because we both come from similar church backgrounds, we both want to make sure that we glorify God in the use of our gift of screen writing. Quality of writing is not to be compromised in the name of Christ. We are both committed to getting it right, even if it means doing it over scores and scores of times. We just want to make sure that we have gotten it right with Christ first. We ask ourselves hard questions, and we look for the door that leads to the path of redemption and personal transformation in some form. We are both well aware of just how much impact the media has upon our culture, and likewise, the culture upon the media. In the midst of our writing and talking, we always know that "prayer" is the essential third writing partner keeping us focused and faithful.

Far before the writing days of Luke and Cliff, an earlier script version of *The Last Train North* was rejected, and we were asked to create a world of drugs, sex, and violence that would have been light years from the truth. I had no choice but to walk away. I would never have been able to live with that version, nor would my faith. It could have been financially successful, but not the type of film that parents and schools and even churches would show again and again to challenge our thinking about relationships. If it had been made as discussed, I feel that it would have drawn a crowd, but not lives to faith. *Once Upon a Time . . .* accomplished that, but it almost didn't make it to the screen.

I know that "writing" is a great gift to the human family and to me specifically. As I continue to write books, essays, and screenplays, God will be in the midst of my decisions helping me to see His hands and heart in the story. It's not always easy to follow His blueprint, but it's best to do so, because He guides our lives for a much greater purpose and for a much longer time period—eternity. In a small way, I have witnessed His staying power with the book, *Once Upon a Time . . .* and I am convinced that He can do it again as I use His gift to me to achieve His purpose and plan for us while temporarily living on planet Earth.

* * *

Screenwriting is a difficult task, full of rejection. As Clifton points out, you need to be rooted in God's loving grace. Some valuable insights into the process of scriptwriting will help, however.

In this regard, most screenwriting books specialize in some particular aspect of screenwriting. For instance, if we looked at the whole process as a car, then these must-read books focus on components of the vehicle: Lajos Egri's *The Art of Dramatic Writing* would be the engine of the car; Robert McKee's *Story* would be as the transmission taking the power from the engine to the wheels; Linda Seger's *Making a Good Script Great* would be the body of the car; Syd Field's *Screenplay* would be the paint job; and, Linda Seger's *Creating Unforgettable Characters* would be the driver and the passengers.

Once Upon a Time

A story is a connected narration of real or imagined events. There are many types of story, including science fiction, romance, myth, fairy tale, tragedy, and adventure. The full range of storytelling is limited only by the human imagination, yet there are key principles that apply to all stories, and all stories can be classified in different categories or subgenre.

Stories have an internal logic driven by a premise acting through characters and conflict to move the plot from a beginning point of attack, through one or more crises, to a climax that resolves into a resolution. There is a wide range of variation within this approach, but the key principles apply to almost all of them. The classic story formula goes something like this: (1) The hero wants something enough to do anything to get it. (2) The hero faces a difficult adventure or problem in trying to get what he wants. (3) The hero faces serious obstacles. (4) The hero overcomes the obstacles. (5) The hero reaches his goal and gets what he wants (i.e., the princess, the money, revenge, etc).

STEPS FOR CONSTRUCTING YOUR STORY

1. Start Your Engines: Formulate Your Premise

The engine of your communication is the premise that your communication must prove in a logical, impressive way (given your genre and medium of choice) in order for your audience to be affected by your story and message in exactly the way you desired. In most cases, an impressive proof of your premise will require lots of interesting illustrations—verbal or pictorial—and plenty of technical, dramatic, or literary effects.

For another perspective: the premise is where you are going (let's say Hollywood); the plot is how you get there (let's say you miss your plane and decide to take a car, but the car breaks down, etc.); the people who travel with you are the characters (let's say that each one is a friend of yours who does not get along with anyone else); and, the themes are the continuing interactions between different sets of characters (let's say your friend Joe wants to lead your friend June to Jesus Christ).

The audience will want to know where you are going up front. In *The Lord of the Rings* trilogy, the audience knows right from the first act that Frodo has to take the ring to the mountain where it was originally forged and destroy it. From the beginning of *Finding Nemo*, the audience wants the father, Marlin, to find Nemo. How the hero achieves his goal in spite of all the obstacles the writer throws at him produces the excitement in the story.

The key element is your premise. The premise is the motivating power that drives your communication. Your premise is an active, dynamic statement of the argument that you will prove in your communication. It is the essence of your communication. The premise holds the key elements of the message within your story, in a neat and compact package. Quite simply, the premise is a sentence with an active verb, a subject, and an object that summarizes your story, and tells you where you are going—your goal. In discussing the role of a premise and elements that emerge from the premise in a dramatic play, Lajos Egri has noted:

> A play [or movie] can be judged before it reaches actual production. First, the premise must be discernible from the beginning. We have a right to know in

what direction the author is leading us. The characters, growing out of the premise, necessarily identify themselves with the aim of the play. They will prove the premise through conflict. The play must start with conflict, which rises steadily until it reaches the climax. The characters must be so well drawn that, whether or not the author has declared their individual backgrounds, we can make out accurate case histories for each of them.[49]

A writer has many ways to arrive at the premise. You may have an idea, or a conviction, which you will convert into premise. You may be intrigued by an obligatory scene, event, or situation and want to develop that scene, event, or situation into a premise. To convert your scene or idea into a premise: look for the drama, the meaning, the conflict and the purpose inherent in that idea/ scene. State the purpose, meaning, and conflict in a simple, active sentence. This sentence becomes your premise.

Suppose your idea is to communicate that God is love. Ask yourself what your purpose is—why you want to communicate this particular message. Your answer may be that your purpose is to show your audience that God loves them, us, mankind, and/or the world. Be as specific as possible by refining your purpose in light of the answers you have found to your ascertainment questions. In this example, you would also want to ask the question, "How does God love them, you, or us?" Your answer will depend on the way you answered your ascertainment questions, but may be that He loves us by comforting us in sorrow, by delivering us from fear, forgiving us our transgressions, or by rescuing us from drug addiction.

For our example, let's say your purpose is to demonstrate the forgiveness inherent in God's love. In light of your answers to the ascertainment questions, state your premise in a simple but specific sentence such as, "God's love forgives the transgressor."

What does that mean? What is the conflict inherent in that

statement? Forgiveness must mean that a wrong was committed which has alienated the wrongdoer, perhaps because of his/her feeling of guilt, or knowledge that a just judgment is awaiting him or her. God's love conflicts with and triumphs over that alienation by forgiving the individual from judgment and healing him/her from guilt.

Your premise gives you the direction, the basic elements, and the conclusion of your communication. In our example, the direction and the conclusion of your communication is inherent in the active verb, "forgives." Since you are going to demonstrate how God's love forgives the wrongdoer, you will conclude your communication at that point where the forgiveness is a reality for the transgressor. The initiating force in your communication is God, and the object of your communication is the forgiven transgressor. The conflict is the negation of the verb/object combination, which, in terms of your premise, is the transgressor's alienation that resists forgiveness. By resisting the direction and conclusion of your premise, the conflict forces your proof and propels your communication along.

Let's assume that you decide, because of the audience and medium that you have chosen, to demonstrate your premise through a story. You could choose to make the wrongdoer a young woman who decides to run away from home to live the good life. After several adventures, she ends up destitute. She feels guilty for running away and for ending up destitute. You might decide because of your audience to represent the subject of your premise as the father who manifests God's love. His love for his daughter causes him to go search for her. She sees him, but avoids him because of her guilt and fear of judgment. In the process of avoiding him, she is thrown in jail. The father finds his daughter, spends all he has to pay her fine and takes her home. When the father finds the daughter and forgives her, and she accepts his love and forgiveness, your premise is proved and the story is resolved, although you may want to top and tail your story to highlight the message of your premise.

Because of the nature of your audience, you may want to prove your premise in another genre. Whatever method you choose to prove your premise, by condensing your idea into a premise statement, you have given yourself a clear direction to follow in your communication plan.

Remember that any idea, scene, thought, or conviction may be converted into a premise that will drive your communication to a powerful conclusion.

Analyzing the Premise

In every story, the premise can be found by analyzing the story. In the *Star Wars* trilogy, the evil empire is taking over the universe. A young man who is full of goodness, perseverance, and integrity is forced to fight the empire. He wins. "Good triumphs over evil" is clearly the premise. Every film or television program with that clear-cut premise, "Good triumphs over evil," tells a different story by proving that premise in a different way. However, it is the process of proving the premise that satisfies the expectations of the audience.

Every parable Jesus told through the Bible has a premise. Plays, books, short stories, and even TV commercials all contain a premise. As an exercise, you may want to try to discover the premises in some of the parables. Pay close attention to the next commercial or movie preview you watch, try to find and state the premise.

Many well-produced films, television programs, and other media communications fail, not because of the quality of the production, but because of a defective premise. Such defects include a double premise, or just an unclear premise. Each of Shakespeare's plays offer good examples of clear-cut premises, as do the parables of Jesus. Without a clear-cut premise no idea, thought, or conviction is strong enough to carry you through to a logical conclusion (Lajos Egri, Ibid).[50]

The movie *2010* was beautifully produced, but failed because three-fourths of the way through the premise changed, and the second premise was never proved through the medium of the story to the audience's satisfaction. The first part of *2010* told the story of how "cooperation triumphs over adversity." Then, after proving the first premise, a second premise, "supernatural being(s) bring peace," was introduced which took the movie in another direction.

A badly worded or false premise will force you to fill space with pointless and irrelevant material. A communication with more than one premise is confused because it is trying to go in more than one direction at once. Note, however, that an anthology, variety, or series of separate and distinct communications will have separate premises for each communication, but no one distinct communication should have more than one premise. A premise that says too much is ambiguous and says nothing. A premise that does not take a position is ambivalent and says nothing. Don't write what you don't believe!

In storytelling genre, if there is no clear-cut premise your characters will not live, because without a clearly defined premise, it is impossible to know your characters. No single premise expresses the totality of universal truth. Every premise is limiting. For example, poverty does not always lead to crime, but if you have chosen the premise that poverty leads to crime, then it does in your case, and you must prove it. The elements of a premise are a subject, an active, transitive verb, and an object. The verb must be active—present tense—not future or past tense, to give direction to your communication. If the verb is past tense, the goal of your communication has been achieved historically, and there is nothing to prove. If your verb is future tense, then your premise is purely speculative. The verb must be transitive to motivate your communication. An intransitive verb states a fact and portrays a static picture, giving you no basis for proving your premise and reaching a conclusion. To say "Jesus is love" is a static portrait of a fact. To say "Jesus loves you" sets up a dynamic situation where starting with Jesus, there must be a demonstration of his love for whoever "you" is, and the questions: How? Why? Where? When? and What? become relevant and necessary to answer.

Here are some sample premises:

- *Hope triumphs over despair.*
- *Greed consumes itself.*
- *Great love conquers death.*
- *Ruthless ambition destroys itself.*
- *Jealousy destroys love.*
- *Love conquers jealousy.*
- *Poverty encourages faith.*
- *Faith conquers fear.*
- *Honesty defeats duplicity.*
- *Pride leads to a fall.*
- *Good triumphs over evil.*

If you pay close attention, you can find premises everywhere. Look at an interesting situation and ask what motivates that situation. The best premises and characters come out of genuine experience. Look at a strong, even militant character and examine their motivations. Look at an idea and ask what that idea means translated into action. Your premise expresses the motivation, action and reaction, through a subject, active verb, and object, which in turn, drive your story to its conclusion.

If you are starting with a novel, before you write the script, write your premise. In this regard, the great director Alfred Hitchcock said that the worst books make the best movies. The corollary that good books often make bad movies can be seen with movies such as *Bonfire of the Vanities*, *The Name of the Rose*, and *Midnight in the Garden of Good and Evil*. Often, a good book is too complex with too many goals and too many characters. So, the first step must be to choose the storyline you want to follow in the book and express that storyline as a premise.

Conflict: For Every Action, There Is a Reaction

In every premise, it is conflict that drives the communication forward. To prove your premise you must disprove the negation of your premise. The disproving of the negation of your premise is what actually propels your communication. If there is no negation and no conflict possible in your premise, then your communication will be stillborn, with no direction or goal. Many Christian movies fail from a lack of conflict. They should keep in mind that the world is caught in a spiritual battle; thus, conflict is both necessary and inevitable.

Drama means, "to do" or "to perform." In performance, for every action, there must be a reaction. To illustrate this, have two friends stand five feet apart, facing each other, and ask them to tell each other in as many ways as they so desire, "I love you" for no less than two minutes. After a very short period of time, this dialogue without conflict will become very boring. However, if you ask *one* to convince *the other* of his or her love for *the other*, and you ask *the other* to resist this advance, the dialogue will be very entertaining, and *one*, or *the other*, will have to relent, thereby establishing the premise for that brief scene as either "love triumphs over rejection" or "resistance destroys love."

Some Christian radio and television interview programs are boring to all but a few loyal supporters, because the host avoids conflict or loses sight of the value of loving conflict. In these boring programs, the host and the guest spend all their time affirming each other so that the program remains static and uninteresting. If the host defines what he wants to discover in the interview, which is his premise, in such a way as to probe who his guest is and why the guest is there by asking the tough questions which the audience needs and wants to know, then there will be real dialogue. The interview will be interesting because there is conflict built into the program, even if only on the level of a premise such as "curiosity discovers important information."

This conflict does not have to be mean, petty, or angry, as so much conflict is on non-religious television. The conflict can and will be loving if the tough questions which prove the host's premise are asked in love. A thoughtful, loving host can ask tough questions in a loving way to reveal the interesting story that every guest has to tell. The conflict in the interview is merely the vehicle by which the guest proves his or her story to the host and the audience. Without a clear -cut premise, there will be no conflict, and neither the host nor the audience will have any idea what the host is trying to communicate.

There are four basic plots that categorize the primary types of conflict inherent dramatic stories: 1) Man against man, 2) Man against nature, 3) Man against himself, and 4) Man against the supernatural or sub-natural, including aliens.

These categories help us to evaluate the premise or main proposition in a story, but they may not help us determine whether the story fits the Christian worldview. Another traditional literary approach proposed by Northrop Frye[51] divides stories into five different kinds:

Mythic: The triumph of the hero/protagonist(s) by an act of God or god(s).

Heroic: The triumph of the hero/protagonist(s) by his or her own means.

High Ironic: The triumph of the hero/protagonist(s) by a quirk of fate.

Low Ironic: The failure of the hero/protagonist(s) by a quirk of fate.

Demonic: The defeat of the hero/protagonist(s) by evil, demons, et cetera.

A story that fits the Christian version of the traditional mythic story, where the God of the Bible or Jesus Christ helps the hero or protagonist overcome his or her antagonist, is a story that fits the Christian worldview. A story, however, where the hero or protagonist—especially a Christian one—is defeated by demons is probably not a story that Christians should want to see because it contradicts the biblical worldview.

Beyond the basic story types, there are various themes. The eight basic themes are: Survival, Redemption, Revenge, Betrayal, Coming of Age, Love and Romance, Mistaken Identity, and "Fish Out of Water."

THE NOTION OF GENRE

The notion of genre is a simple way of talking about the different kinds, types, or formats of communications. George Gerbner has reduced human communication to three genres: stories that tell about how things work; stories that tell about what things are; and, stories of action.[52] Aristotle was most likely aware of the three ultimate categories of drama, epic, and lyric, which have evolved into drama, fiction, and poetry according to some contemporary literary critics.[53]

Other philosophers and pundits have proposed other generic classifications, such as comedy, epigram, satire, epic, and tragedy. Often, movie reviewers classify movies in genres such as these (this list is suggestive, not exhaustive): Romance, Action Adventure, Drama, Tragedy, Comedy, Children's, Religious, Fantasy, Detective/Police, Thriller, Horror, or Sports.

> Write the way an architect builds, who first drafts his plan and designs every detail.
>
> —Schopenhauer[54]

2. In a Galaxy Far, Far away: Define Your Environment, Subgenre, Style, and Point of View.

Your environment must be real, even if it is far, far away in time and space. Before you start constructing your story, you must define in detail the environment in which your story takes place. The environment and the laws that govern that environment create the illusion of reality in your story. The more detail you know about when and where your story takes place, the more real your story will be to your audience.

The novel *Time and Again* by Jack Finney works in spite of an implausible plot where the hero wills himself back in history, because Mr. Finney has defined the setting of the novel with such meticulous care. Many movies, especially science fiction, fail because the setting of the movie is only partially realized. *Battleship Earth* has many scenes where the sets look like sets—unreal with no sign of having been inhabited. *The Lord of the Rings*, on the other hand, has outlandish sets that look real because time was taken to make them real through detailed definition.

YOU MUST LEARN, DEFINE, AND OBEY THE RULES OF THE SUBGENRE YOU CHOOSE.

Whether you choose to construct your story as a romance, a science fiction, a comedy, a contemporary stream of consciousness, a history, or a detective story, you must obey the rules that the subgenre imposes on your story.

Note that the principles of the genre to which the subgenre belongs apply to the subgenre as well as the particular principles or variations on major principles that define the subgenre.

Select your style to fit your premise, your environment, your characters, and your subgenre. The style, rhythm, and tone you establish are as important as your plot. A satiric or low ironic style may be appropriate for a detective story, but not for a historic portrayal of Jesus' ministry, unless you are attacking the gospel, or you have chosen Judas Iscariot's point of view.

Within a style:

> To shock, you must make the incredible credible.

> To create irony, the audience's assumptions must be contrary to the outcome.

> To create a paradox, logic must be contradicted by fact.

> To create satire, the normal is exaggerated.

> To create suspense, withheld information must confront the desire to know.

YOUR POINT OF VIEW AFFECTS YOUR CHARACTERS.

The first person point of view involves the audience in the thoughts of one of the characters. The first person "I" is not necessarily the protagonist, or the antagonist. The "I" can be any character in the story.

The first person point of view may be pure stream of consciousness, but the rules of storytelling still apply. The first person may be established in a neutral style, which overcomes the limitations imposed by the "I" speaking in dialect. If you choose a first person point of view, you must define that person in the same detail as you would define any other character.

The third person is the most common and flexible point of view. The third person allows for different perspectives, involving the audience with different characters, or establishing an omniscient perspective.

3. Why the Hero Isn't Always the Protagonist: Define Your Protagonist.

In a dramatic communication, the subject of your premise is the protagonist. He or she initiates the action of the verb and carries that action through to the conclusion. The protagonist takes the lead in the movement of the story, creates the conflict, and makes the story move forward. The protagonist knows what he or she wants and is determined to get it. The protagonist can be the hero, the villain, or any other character in the story. The protagonist may not be the central character in the story, but without the protagonist the story flounders.

Your protagonist is the driven, driving subject inherent in your premise who forces the conflict that moves your story to its conclusion. Your protagonist takes the lead in your story. He or she knows what he or she wants and will act to get it.

Your protagonist must have something very important at stake. He or she acts out of necessity and is forced (by character and by circumstances) to do what he or she does and become what he or she becomes. Your protagonist has one highly developed motivation, such as love, hate, revenge, greed, envy, caring, faith, or hope, which becomes the driving force toward either success or defeat. Even if the motivating characteristic of your protagonist seems passive, it must be active in terms of your premise and his or her situation. For instance, if your protagonist is motivated to patiently endure, then he or she must be willing to act on that motivation even if it brings him or her to martyrdom, as is the case with many Christian martyrs.

If your premise is "love conquers death," your protagonist must love his or her beloved enough to do everything possible including die to save the beloved from death. Your protagonist could be: a loving father who risks his own life to save his son, who has fallen through the ice; a loving mother who will give up everything to save her family from destruction; or, Jesus who gave his life so that death would be defeated.

As a guide to the impact a hero—who may or may not be the protagonist—has on a story, the following restating of the archetypal story styles are helpful:

> *In the mythic story,* such as *The Lord of the Rings,* God triumphs, or Frodo the hero triumphs because of an act

of God and the help of supernatural forces.

In the heroic story, such as *Harry Potter*, the hero triumphs because he or she is superior.

In the high ironic story, such as *Forrest Gump*, the hero triumphs because of a quirk of fate or circumstances.

In the low ironic story, such as *Death of a Salesman*, the hero fails because of a quirk of fate or circumstances.

In the demonic story, which includes not only many horror films but also psychological movies and political films such as *The Diary of Anne Frank*, the hero is hopelessly overwhelmed by evil or wields evil to fight evil.

4. Make Beautiful Music Together: Define and Orchestrate Your Characters.

All these elements are embodied in your premise and are important to understand and define clearly so that your audience will know exactly what you are trying to communicate. If you have decided to communicate dramatically through a story, then you must define your characters carefully and get to know them inside-out. Get inside your characters, live with them, find out and define what makes each character a unique individual.

Well-orchestrated characters are one of the primary reasons for rising conflict in any story. It is the differences which distinguish each of your characters and moves your story from start to finish through conflict. You may have two apostles, two tax collectors, or two thieves in your story but they must be different, they must contrast with each other so that they will move the story along. The contrast between them must be inherent in their character as you define them.

Orchestration is simply creating well-defined, strong characters who are in conflict and therefore move your story along. Through this conflict your characters will grow and your story will develop, proving your premise.

If you want to really define your characters, use the process for motivational talent set forth in Chapter 3. At a minimum, define each of the character elements listed in the form below. Continue to take notes on further character development, as you think through other concepts throughout the book.

This form will help you to define and orchestrate your characters:

Character Definition Form

Name of Character:

Physical Characteristics:

Sex:_____

Age:_____

Height:_____

Weight:_____

Hair:_____

Eyes:_____

Skin:_____

Race:_____

Ethnic Group:_____

Appearance:_____

Posture:_____

Deformities: _____

Abnormalities: _____

Background:

Class: _____

Education: _____

Home: _____

Occupation: _____

Nationality: _____

Politics: _____

Relationships: _____

Marital status: _____

Hobbies: _____

Parents: _____

Relatives: _____

Children: _____

Psychological Characteristics:

Ambition: _____

Preferences:_____

Motivations:_____

Temperament:_____

Attitude:_____

Fears:_____

Wants:_____

Likes:_____

Relationship patterns:_____

Talents:_____

Qualities:_____

Intelligence:_____

Emotional state:_____

Religious Characteristics:

Beliefs:_____

Hopes:_____

Faith:_____

World view:_____

Cares:_____

Religious background:_____

Religious environment:_____

Use this form, or modify it, to define each of your characters. Your story is built by your characters, so be as thorough as you can. The difference between a simple and a sophisticated story is primarily determined by the complexity of the characters. Visualize your characters as if they were people you have known all your life.

5. Good vs. Evil: Define Your Antagonist in Opposition to Your Protagonist.

The antagonist is the conflicting force inherent in the premise who opposes the protagonist. The antagonist can be the hero, the villain, or any other character in the story. The antagonist has to be as strong as the protagonist so that the conflict between the two will carry the story forward to its natural conclusion. If the antagonist gives up at any time, then the story will die. There must be a unity of opposites between the protagonist and the antagonist.

Your antagonist opposes your protagonist. He or she wants to prevent your protagonist from acting—from doing what your protagonist is driven to do. The will of your protagonist must clash with the will of your antagonist, and your antagonist must be as strong and as driven as your protagonist.

Your antagonist and your protagonist must be locked in opposition. There must be a unity of opposites, only be broken by the death of the motivating characteristic in either one or the other of these two characters. Either your antagonist or your protagonist must be completely defeated for your story to reach its natural conclusion. Because of the strength of will of these two characters, the initial conflict between them must lead to a crisis, which must in turn lead to a climax, and ultimately, to a resolution.

If one or the other of these two characters gives up early, your story will stop. If one or the other of these two characters is a push-over, if they are unequally matched, then you have no story because there will be no conflict to drive the plot. Compromise is out of the question unless it is the result of a completely realized conflict that has proved your premise. If one character is determined to win and the other doesn't care, there is no challenge, no battle, and no story. A strong person pitted against a weak one is a farce, unless the weaker has the courage, will, and hidden ability to put up a real fight and perhaps win.

Every character will fight back under the right circumstances. It is up to you to catch your character at that point where he or she will carry the premise through conflict.

Your antagonist is inherent in your premise. He or she is what your subject/protagonist must oppose to fulfill his or her goals. He or she reacts against the action of the subject. Depending on the outcome determined by your premise, he or she must change for your protagonist to reach his or her goal, or your protagonist must change in the face of his or her opposition.

6. En Garde: Define the Crisis of Your Starting Point.

Your starting point in story development must be a crisis, which must lead your story to a climax, and ultimately, a conclusion or resolution. Your movie or television program should not start at the beginning of someone's life (he was born in a log cabin), but at a critical *point of attack*—where something worth living or dying for is at stake (as he was being born, the villain attacked), thus creating jeopardy (or something at stake) which propels the plot to its destination and fulfills the premise. Every Hollywood movie should start with a "bang" (as opposed to European movies that often take some time to develop the situations involved in the story).

If you want your story to move and to capture your audience, you must choose the right point of attack. The right point of attack is that moment in time and space when your protagonist is at a critical turning point where he or she must act to achieve his or her goal, thereby initiating the action of the premise. This turning point is a crisis point where a decisive change—one way or another—must occur. No story starts at the beginning; there is always something that occurred prior to the beginning of the story. Genesis starts with God acting to create our universe, but it does not tell us what was going on in eternity before God decided to create. In the beginning of Genesis, God (as the protagonist) is at a turning point where He acts to create the heavens and the earth.

In your moment of crisis, the protagonist acts out of necessity because something extremely important is at stake: love, survival, health, honor, or any combination. This point could be where your protagonist has made a decision, has reached a turning point, or where something important suddenly arises. Remember, whatever precipitated this moment of crisis has already occurred when your story begins. Your story grows out of to the events that are causing your protagonist to act—and that action forces the climax that proves your premise in its resolution.

7. Avalanche: Develop Rising Conflict.

Your story builds through a rising series of conflicts, each one building in intensity on the previous conflict until the climax is reached and the premise is proved. Each conflict moves your story forward through action and reaction; attack and counterattack, which causes change, growth, and new conflict until you have reached the proof of your premise. The first conflict in your story comes from your protagonist consciously trying to achieve the goal that you determined in your premise.

CONFLICT EXPOSES YOUR STORY AND YOUR CHARACTERS.

Conflict will grow out of the characters in opposition. The more evenly matched your characters are, the more real rising conflict will move your story toward its resolution. Through conflict, your characters and your story are revealed and exposed. Each dialogue and every interaction between characters reveals who they are, what their background is, what the environment is, what the plot is, and where the plot is headed.

CONFLICT CAUSES CHANGE AND GROWTH.

Every conflict causes change. Constant change ensures that your characters, and the situations they are in, will not be the same at any two points in your story. As a result of conflict, each character will change emotionally, psychologically and spiritually. Growth occurs continually until the story proves your premise.

In your story, if your premise is "love conquers hate," the conquered character must grow from hate to love. To do so, he or she must go through every step of change which leads from hate to love: hate—dislike—annoyance—understanding—interest—attraction—caring—love. Each small conflict and change will move your character along the road from hate to love, where his or her growth will be complete.

AVOID STATIC CONFLICT.

Static conflict occurs because:

1. One or more of your characters can't make a decision. Each of your characters has to grow from one emotional, psychological, or spiritual point to another in your story. If he or she stops at one of the intermediate steps along the way because he or she can't make a decision, then you will have static conflict and your story will stop.
2. Your story lacks the motivating force of a premise.
3. Your characters share exactly the same point of view because you have not orchestrated them by carefully defining them as unique individuals.

Static conflict will bring your story to a halt. No dialogue, effects, descriptions, or rhetoric will move your story if the conflict is static. The exercise suggested earlier where you ask two friends to try to "express their love" for two minutes is an example of static conflict. Since they are both starting at the same point of view, there is no inherent conflict to generate a story.

Here is an example of an indecisive character:

JANE: "Do you want to go out, my darling?"

JACK: "Maybe."

JANE: "When will you decide?"

JACK: "Sometime."

JANE: "Do you care?"

Jack: "I don't know."

Jane: "When will you know?"

Jack: "Soon."

Jane: "Will you tell me?"

Jack: "Sure."

These characters and this story are going nowhere because Jack is indecisive.

AVOID JUMPING CONFLICT

Jumping conflict occurs because:

1. One or more of your characters has skipped one or more of the important stages of growth through which he or she must go to reach the conclusion inherent in your premise.
2. You are forcing one or more of your characters to do something that is not within his, her, or their uniquely defined characters.
3. You have not given one or more of your characters a chance to grow steadily and realistically through rising conflict.
4. You have not thought through the process of proving your premise.
5. You have not defined your premise clearly.

Here is an example of jumping conflict:

Jane: "Do you want to go out, my darling?"

JACK: "Maybe."

JANE: "Well, if you don't know for sure, I'm walking out on our marriage."

JACK: "But, I'll make up my mind."

JANE: "It's too late you inconsiderate slob." [She leaves, slamming the door.]

To avoid jumping conflict, determine the stages of growth through which each character will progress from where they are emotionally, psychologically, and spiritually when your audience first meets them, to where they must end up as dictated by your premise. As your characters grow through conflict, they are only allowed to choose those solutions to each conflict that will help prove the point of your premise.

For instance, if your character has to go from rebellion to submission in your story, make sure that you have predetermined each one of the stages that he or she must pass through in the process: rebellion, alienation, loneliness, insecurity, fear, need, longing, desire for help and protection, and submission.

CONFLICT FORESHADOWS ITSELF

Each minor conflict in your story leads to the next conflict, because none of the intermediate solutions will resolve your story until your premise is proved. Each conflict foreshadows the next conflict because it contains the seeds of the next conflict by the very nature of how you have defined and orchestrated your characters in light of your premise.

Conflict is the product of the tension that is inherent in your characters. Every conflict contains all the elements of a story in brief.

8. Talking Pictures: Dialogue Quotes a Character's Words or Thoughts.

You have defined each of your characters; each character defines the dialogue he or she speaks. Dialogue that does not flow clearly and validly from the character who uses it is unnatural and defeats your story (unless it is a science fiction effect). If dialogue is an effect, it still must be true to the character of its real source.

Dialogue reveals who a character is and hints at who he or she will become. Each character should speak in his or her own language and dialect, but too much dialect will usually sound phony and should be avoided. Informal, natural dialogue is most effective.

Rising conflict produces healthy dialogue that foreshadows the direction in which the premise is leading. Dialogue should be concise and succinct. In most cases, surplus dialogue vitiates. Sacrifice brilliance for character. Do not preach through dialogue unless that preaching reflects who a character is and occurs naturally in context. Never overemphasize dialogue. Don't be didactic.

9. Reel vs. Real: Creating the Illusion of Reality.

Observe, experience, be unique, and create the illusion of reality in your story, even if that reality is set in a cosmos far, far away.

It must be noted that television series do not follow the typical movie script—they are character driven. The audience tunes in to follow their favorite or most hated characters. Our friend Gary Johnson has some interesting insights into becoming a television writer. Given our nation's often trashy, MTV, R-rated mentality of the past decade or two, who would have believed that PAX TV's wholesome, charming, family-values oriented programs, *Doc* and *Sue Thomas: F.B.Eye* would be top-rated television fare in the 2000s? And, who writes such popularly unconventional shows? The answer is people like Gary R. Johnson—along with his wife, Joan, and his brother, Dave.

* * *

Use Your Connections

—an interview with Gary R. Johnson

When Gary's brother Dave came out to Hollywood as an actor after college, he soon found his way into a writing TV shows with a partner. In the meantime, Gary, a traveling musician, was entertaining live audiences with his interactive, pick-on-someone-in-the-audience humor shticks. One night Dave called Gary, urging him to pick his favorite show and write some sample scripts for it. "Some day I'll have my own show, and I want to hire you as a writer," said Dave. "So you've got to build a resume starting now. I can't tell my friends out here, 'No, he's never written anything, but, trust me, he'd be good!'"

The Game's Not Always Fair

So, Gary got busy and started refining his writing craft. Soon, he and his brother got the privilege of writing for a 1993–94 television sitcom called *Against the Grain*, about a former football star who takes on the coaching job at his son's school and, after a brush with death, learns some poignant lessons about life, relationships, and priorities. A young Ben Affleck played the son in the show. Much to everyone's disappointment, even though the show got high ratings, NBC cancelled it after only eight episodes. Though the cancellation was a deep disappointment, Gary knew he must move on and seek his next open door.

There's Life After Loss

Gary and Dave worked on projects together and individually, and really enjoyed tackling the creative process as a team. Jeff Sagansky, the former president of CBS, worked at PAX-TV (now defunct), with Dave at the time, and he saw that the brothers had a heart for family programming. The three met to brainstorm about different ideas for family-friendly shows. One of the brothers' favorite shows had been *The Andy Griffith Show*, so the team started discussing the possibility of creating a modern-day version of the old classic. The men thought it would be fun to have a show about a doctor from Montana who addresses hospital-related issues with a rugged, honorable, often humorous and light-hearted tone. Thus, *Doc* was conceived, and PAX-TV was delighted to broadcast it.

There's Life After Life!

After seeing how successful *Doc* was, PAX approached the brothers about creating another show. Gary and Dave declined, insisting that there was not enough time in each day to even write for *Doc*, much less to add a whole new show to their crowded plate. Finally, a persuasive producer begged and bribed, and the brothers relented. They had met the beautiful, hearing-impaired Deanne Bray and had been hired to write a feature film about her—which hadn't been made yet. A show about her would bring warmth and uniqueness to a mystery/action theme, the producers agreed. Gary was skeptical, though, that he wouldn't have enough control over the program to ensure that the TV character would remain true to the wonderful, real person Deanne was. However, after people in high PAX places rallied to ensure the writers that they'd have all the control they could want, the team created *Sue Thomas: F.B.Eye.* Thankfully, it was an instant hit.

Let Your Past Serve Your Present

When asked about the factors that made him a successful writer, Gary is quick to point to his past—seemingly unrelated—training as a musician. When he would travel with his band to state and county fairs, conventions, nightclubs, and resorts, he'd engage in live, ad-lib banter with crowds. He'd stand on stage and try to find funny things about people to point out and comment on. His job forced him to constantly think, "What's the funniest way to present this?" It taught him to think on his feet and phrase things for the most entertaining impact, and soon good, clever, sharp dialogue started flowing. Gary now sees that God trained him for television writing by having him hone his timing and comedic bantering skills with hundreds of live audiences.

Writers Write

According to Gary, writing is really hard. You have to learn structure, timing, humor, drama, characterization, and fast editing skills. "Write," says Gary, "whether you're getting paid or not." Gary's wife, Joan, wrote fifteen spec scripts before she finally got paid for her first. "If you want to be a writer, you have to write," Gary insists. "Don't say, 'I'm going to be a writer, but not until someone pays me.' Practice your craft right now!"

It's a Platform for Your Message

In the past, Dave and Gary both turned down jobs because of their immoral content. With *Doc* and *Sue Thomas*, though, writing became a great experience. "The PAX Network wanted faith-based and values-based programming. If this had been another network, it'd be a weekly battle about content and would affect my life in not-so-pleasant ways. Working with PAX was a dream. The network basically let me spend two hours of their time every Sunday night to send my messages to viewers. And, I was trying to affect lives in a positive way through every show."

Teamwork and Patience Do the Trick

Dave, Joan, and Gary co-wrote and/or wrote both *Doc* and *Sue Thomas* episodes. They had to create twenty-two episodes of each show every season. The trio worked from a story room and had a staff of writers who helped come up with a story, broke it into four acts, and created different moves and twists in the story. The writers did a thorough outline of every piece of every show, and then finally, someone wrote the script. Within two weeks, the producers had to have the first draft. If the writers were working together as pairs, they would have only one week. After the first draft was finished, the group did a read, wrote another pass, made notes, and did a final polish.

Make Yourself a Character

To do his best creative writing, Gary imagined himself to be part of *Sue Thomas* or *Doc's* world, perhaps an observer into their lives. He pondered what every point of view and every reaction of every character would be in the story. "Coming up with the idea is easiest," says Gary, "turning it into a story is hardest." He adds, "Anybody's first script will not be that good, but you keep going. Just as eventually a novice will become a good piano player, so will a writer polish his craft through diligent practice."

Real Stories Win Hearts

Doc won a Movieguide award for the episode entitled, "Nobody," about homelessness. Billy Ray Cyrus, who plays Doc, had written a song about a homeless girl, and the writers formulated a script around it that included an edgy message about a teenage girl with baby out of wedlock. Gary, Dave, and Joan were especially excited to use this theme as a pro-life message. The producers actually hired real homeless people who really lived in the church where the TV crew was filming.

Learn the Technical Craft

According to Gary Johnson, writing is not just coming up with big-picture ideas. One must have a real handle on the technical aspects of the industry. For instance, each episode of *Doc* and *Sue Thomas* had to be broken into four acts, each exactly eleven minutes of edited programming. The end of each act must have a cliffhanger, and at the end of act three, they had to reveal the destruction of the plan. For instance, the girl might think she's fixed the problem, but everything blows up.

At the end of the show, very meticulous editing had to be done. If the program was to be forty-four minutes, it could not be forty-three minutes and fifty-nine seconds. The editors literally take out four frames here and add five frames there, equating to fractions of seconds.

"Writers must be funny, creative, and emotion provoking, all under strict technical guidelines," Gary says. "They must have discipline, as well as inspiration. If burnout happens, you can't stop—because every seven days, the network needed a new *Doc* and a new *Sue Thomas*. It's like running in front of a steamroller . . . You've gotta stay ahead."

Burn the Midnight Oil

When the show is in production, Gary says, it's not unusual for the writers to work twelve to fourteen-hour days, and part of their weekends. In the summer, it's not as bad, though the writers continue writing on a "less horrible" schedule. Though Gary and Joan have no children, his brother Dave has children, and really tries to balance work and family so as to not miss important fathering opportunities.

Think Budget

Gary encourages his writers to think in production terms as they write. "We're not going to have a train run into car on a TV budget. If we're doing a restaurant scene, we'll try to put two scenes into the same location. Saves a ton of time and money on setups." Writers must also write with a consideration for how many days the episode will shoot in studio vs. an outside location. In *Doc*, it was usually three outside locations versus four indoor.

"We shot one episode at a time and finishing shooting the entire script in seven days. Then it went to post-production, which included editing, music, sound effects, and final edits. At any given time, there were typically four or five episodes in post-production, one in production, one in prep, and three or four being written," says Gary. "We've had to be efficient with time and money."

Stay Connected

PAX filmed both *Doc* and *Sue Thomas: F.B.Eye* in Toronto, whereas the writers were in Los Angeles. "We always had a writer on the set—to make sure the director shot the show we wrote. Directors are not employees of the studio; they're usually independents. So if a director started blocking or shooting something, and it's not within the story's intention, our writer would say, for example, 'This is supposed to be light and funny here, not poignant.' Also, sometimes actors would want to change lines in order for the verbiage to ring more true to what they would naturally say. In these cases, the writer would call me or Dave, and we would work it out long-distance."

Let Your Light Shine

Working with PAX was wonderful, according to Gary, in that Bud Paxson and the whole PAX network were really intentional about airing faith-based, family-based, even overtly Christian programs. On other shows, though, it has been clear that Gary was the only Christian on a project, and the only conservative. "You can't wave a flag and say, 'you're all sinners and you're going to die.' You must pick your moments, or you'll be offending a lot of people out there. Most people know I'm a believer, but it's not the first thing they know about me. I like to establish credibility first, apart from my faith. Once there's a place of trust, I can gently influence the project. For instance, if someone wants a minister to marry a gay couple on a show, I can present my dissenting view as a business decision. I might say, 'That'll totally upset your audience and alienate hundreds of thousands of viewers. Why don't we do this other, equally compelling idea?' It's just wisdom."

You're a Little Fish in a Big Pond

Writing is extremely competitive, says Gary, just like being an actor or a singer. "Well-meaning people often encourage young artists to come to L.A., saying, 'you should be an actor, you're so good-looking.' Well, little does she know that fifty others look just like her—just as beautiful and talented. Now, what will she do to rise above that? For writing, it's the same. You just have to write as much as possible, keep improving, give your work to people with an unbiased, critical eye. Your family will always think it's good," laughs Gary.

To Agent or Not?

Agents can be a "Catch 22," says Gary. "If you need one, you can't get one. When you don't need an agent, you can get anyone in town." Gary explains that there are times when something is so extremely good that an agent will take on a new writer, but the percentage is quite low. "An agent isn't necessarily an end-all, either. You still have to promote yourself." On one job before *Doc*, Gary saw whole walls of scripts, three or four hundred in a studio. "You beat all those out," the producer told him. Nowadays, Gary gets scripts sent to him, but he has no time to read them. When he does, he immediately asks, "Does this person have ability to voice characters, dialogue, story, and structure?" According to Gary, a thorough, critical reading of a script could take three to six hours, so those pre-screened or sent by a good agent will keep him from wasting precious time.

Attend Seminars and Workshops

Gary encourages, "If a writer is wanting to meet people of like-mind, find the place to be with . . . very credible people."

Credible people, Gary? We say, "Takes one to know one." Keep on entertaining and influencing!

* * *

Once you have determined who you are, why you are communicating, and what the idea, scene, or conviction is that you want to communicate, every other element, including your premise, should be fashioned, structured, and constructed in light of your answers to the ascertainment questions. Use the information that you have discovered by answering the ascertainment questions to shape your communication. If your audience likes to ski, frame the elements of your story or your proof in terms of skiing. If your audience is preoccupied with the human condition, design your premise and your proof thereof with the human condition in mind. Designing your premise and its proof in light of the answers to the pertinent ascertainment questions does not mean that you need to dilute the gospel; rather, it simply means that you need to consider what is the most effective way in which you can communicate the gospel.

Throughout the process of constructing your communication, use your imagination and allow your message to be emotional. Powerful emotions and images will give life to any communication whose premise is well defined and proved. Whether you are communicating through movies or television, concrete, emotional images created in words, pictures, and/or sounds, each will cause your communication to have a powerful impact on your audience. Allow yourself the privilege of imagining your audience and their reaction to your idea—that process will actually help you to make your communication more interesting.

THE MECHANICS OF TRANSFORMING YOUR STORY INTO A SCRIPT AND BEYOND

We have considered the script process from the foundational dynamics necessary to create a screenplay that will capture the audience. Now, let's consider some of the mechanics you need to turn your story into a script, unless you hire a scriptwriter to do so, and assuming that you did not start out with a script.

In many cases, a producer will start with a script which he or she will boil down to a one- or two-page treatment to sell the story idea to networks. If you start with a story or a book, usually you will want to turn it into a script and a treatment before you can make the sale to a network, or interest prominent talent in your production.

The author of a book is not always the best person to transform their own work into a script. An author often has trouble sacrificing scenes, devices, or characters to meet the time and space limitations of movies or television. In a book, for instance, you can carry on several complex subplots with many minor characters who come and go. Also, the author of a book can describe characters, feelings, situations, and motivations in great detail, where a scriptwriter cannot. Movies and television force you to simplify and condense most books, discarding characters, scenes, and situations, if necessary.

A play is easier to adapt in terms of condensation, but creates other issues in the translation process. It can be difficult for the playwright to shift their thinking from the stage to the big screen (or small screen) environment. With regard to TV, a television audience is not captive, as is an audience in a theater, so you must find unique ways to capture your television audience.

Bringing in a scriptwriter to reformulate a book, play, or short story, can save time and money—and often improve the final teleplay or film. If you bring in a scriptwriter, you must be diligent to keep the author's intent, since that is the reason you bought the story in the first place.

Finally, you should involve a "script doctor" like Linda Seger, who invented the profession of the same name. A script doctor will help you take your script from "good" to "great" and help you market your script to major movie studios. Please note that the script doctor will not pitch or sell your script for you, but their coverage of your script will help the studio take your script seriously. Over three hundred thousand scripts are written every year; less than three hundred movies reach the theaters. Studios are constantly trying to defend against a flood of scripts. Your job is to get your script moved beyond their defenses. A script doctor can help to do just that.

The script, rights, financing, access, and talents steps of a movie or television production often occur simultaneously, with each affecting the other. If you have a script, in most cases, the major movie studio/distributor or television network who picks up your story will want to review and revise it, as will the big name talent you bring on board. On the other hand, the talent and the network will often defer making a final decision on your story until they know how good your script is, because many great stories defy scripting.

The Treatment

Whether you have a script or a story, the first step in selling either is often a short treatment. Entertainment industry executives do not have the time to read every story or script submitted, so they will give them to a reader. The reader will boil it down to a one or two page summary, and give an opinion of the story idea. To avoid reader bias, it is very important to prepare your own treatment, and present it along with your script.

A treatment should include: (1) your log line, which is the basis of your pitch, (2) the premise of your story, (3) your main characters, and (4) a very brief synopsis of the story itself. The more concise your treatment is, the better. Many movies and television programs have been sold to the networks solely on the basis of a one sentence, *TV Guide* type log line/synopsis/premise. One producer, after failing to sell a complex story idea, said, "How about a Grand Hotel on the water? A Love Boat?" That brief statement of the story sold the television network on the program *Love Boat*.

Sometimes, you will be required to expand your story into a full-length synopsis of thirty to fifty pages. Develop your synopsis succinctly, keeping in mind the principles you have learned.

Formatting

If you have not hired a scriptwriter and you are adapting your story into a script, you will find that there are many formats for scripts. Most books on scriptwriting will give you these formats, or a quick search of the Internet will find the many computer programs that will help you format your script for the appropriate medium. The computer program *Final Draft* is one of the best at the time of this writing, but newer and better programs are released all the time, so a little research on the internet will be invaluable. These programs, by the way, will not help you with the foundational dynamics of story that has been covered above in brief. For a commercial and public service announcement (PSA), the script[55] may look like this:

30-SECOND PSA[56]

LOVE IN ACTION

VIDEO	AUDIO
1. SOUP BEING SERVED TO A	
	V.O.[57]: For I was hungry,
STREET PERSON IN A	
	and you fed me . . .
SHELTER.	
2. A YOUNG BOY HANDING A	
	V.O.: Thirsty, and you gave me
HOUSE PAINTER A DRINK.	
	to drink . . .
3. A COUPLE WHOSE CAR	
	V.O.: I was a stranger and you
BROKE DOWN IN A STORM ARE	
	invited me in . . .
BEING WELCOMED INTO A HOME.	

News programs, variety programs, game shows, documentaries, teleplays, live-taped teleplays, and Hollywood movies have different script formats and layouts. Before you start writing, research these different formats because you want your script to be professional so that you can sell it to a movie studio or network.[58]

The degree of detail in a script will vary depending on the scriptwriter, the director and the producer, as well as on the use of the script within a production. A master script will not have the detail of a shooting script prepared with the director, nor will it include the camera shots and angles that are found in the camera script. The master script is the beginning of a long process. The scriptwriter who prepares the master script may have nothing to do with the final shooting script.

In a traditional script, you write in terms of scenes. The reason for this is that film is shot by location, so that once you set up your equipment in a location, you film all scenes associated with that location to save money, time, and energy.

Master Script

What follows is an example of a master, or "master scene," Hollywood style script for an excellent television movie. Note that there are very few directions, such as "wipe to," "dissolve to," "close shot," or "high angle shot." The keys to a good script are in depth character analysis, having the action spelled out and the dialogue completely realized. Quite often the visual and the action move the story along as much as the dialogue.

As noted, once you have written your script, you should hire a script doctor to analyze your screenplay. The amount of money you spend on a script doctor will be more than made up in the money, time, and energy you save trying to sell a script which is good, but not great. As lyricists Alan and Marilyn Bergman note, "Whether it be a lyric, a novel or a screenplay, what separates the professional from the amateur is not so much the ability to write, as the ability to rewrite."[59]

Stage directions, shots, video and audio directions, and other details will be added by the producer, the director, the director of photography, the editor, the actors, and even the scriptwriter as the production planning process refines the script. A movie or television program is rarely the product of one man or woman; and, if it is, it is rarely any good:

"MY PALIKARI"[60]

BY GEORGE KIRGO & LEON CAPETANOS

FADE IN

1. int. olympia restaurant—NIGHT—CLOSE ON PHOTO

A large framed panoramic view of Athens, featuring the Acropolis. HEAR recorded Greek music. PULL BACK slowly to REVEAL PETE PANAKOS, wine glass held high. Pete is handsome, powerful, vigorous, full of himself. The toast:

PETE

To the greatest country in the world—after the U.S.A., natch—my Greece! Yiassou!

2. FULL SHOT

His celebrants respond: "Yiassou, To Greece, L'Chayim, Salud, Bon Voyage Pete!" . . .

* * *

CUT TO:

9. EXT. SEA—DAY. (Stock or 2nd Unit or 1st Unit)

As the ship comes toward Piraeus. The Ionian. In the distance: a large ocean liner. Sound of ship whistle.

10. EXT. SHIP—DAY.

That's Pete on the forward deck, scanning the sea ahead. Passengers pass. Impatient, Pete lights a cigar, a chore in the wind. He paces a few steps. Stops. Peers out again.

11. POV and ZOOM IN TO ACROPOLIS.

Big rush of emotion.

* * *

PETE

Chris, Chris, come here!

CHRIS

What?

Pete

(exasperated)

What? I'll show you what. Come on!

The passengers sit up to stare at this crazy man. Pete glares as Chris slowly saunters over. Pete grabs him and LEADS him to the forward deck.

PETE

Look, look!

CHRIS

Where?

PETE

There, there—

14. POV.

Land. Acropolis, Port, Hills, etc.

15. PETE AND CHRIS

Pete grins at Chris as his son coolly studies the sight.

PETE

Huh? Huh?

CHRIS
It's nice.

16. ANOTHER ANGLE.

On Pete and Chris with land in b.g.[61]
PETE
(incredulous)
Nice?
CHRIS
Yeah. Kind of like . . . Brooklyn.
PETE
Brooklyn—! This is Greece! Alas!

He crosses himself and whispers, as the tears almost fall from his eyes—

* * *

This script is intended for film production, but it could be shot with video using electronic field production (EFP). You could also adapt this script to shoot it in a studio with inserted stock shots, as is the case with many programs, such as JAG.

Helpful Hints In Building Your Script:

Here are some hints for writing your script, teleplay, or screenplay:

1. **Organize flow**. Make sure your script flows smoothly and continuously, resulting in a unified, coherent, and entertaining program. If you prove your premise with rising conflict, your story will flow.
2. **Organize pacing**. Make sure that the length of your shots, scenes, and sequences develops the tempo which is required by the story and which enhances the story. Rapid sequences provide excitement and stimulation.

Slower cutting slows the pace and induces a feeling of serenity and ease.

3. **Organize rhythm**. There should be a definite rhythm to a series of cuts, dissolves, and devices, which will match the rhythm, mood, and action of your story.

4. **Organize interrelationships**. Establish motion through a continuous sequence of images. A sense of action is suggested at all times. Even when there is no physical motion during a particular scene, action can be suggested through contrast, or repetition.

5. **Organize visually**. Keep progression, opposition and repetition of image size consistent. Create variety through camera position, lighting, and shading.

6. **Organize effects**. Use any one effect sparingly; overuse will intrude on your story. Remember, your story is the heart of your production. Effects can enhance a good story, but they cannot make a bad story better. New effects and new devices for creating effects are continually being developed, but commonly used effects include:

   - *Dissolves*. One to five seconds in length and will establish a smooth transition between scenes.
   - *Fades in and out*. Open or close an independent segment and can be considered a curtain that opens on new material and closes at the end of an act.
   - *Lap dissolves*. One image is faded over another, and matched dissolved, where two items of similar or identical shape are matched in the dissolve, and are used to create effects, mood, and promote action.

- *Superimpositions.* Frame buffing and more contemporary technical effects should be studied before incorporating them into your script so that you are aware of the affect they have on the audience.

7. **Organize sound.** Sound should be established before (or during) the picture. Avoid sound on cue. If sound comes on at the same time as the picture, it will be unnatural and mechanical. If you are about to have a train come into view, introduce the distant sound of the train first. Or, if you have someone walking across the desert, show the person walking first, then bring up the sound of walking on sand. Avoid distracting music.

8. **Dialogue.** Speech should be natural, and generally short. Long speeches impede action and bore the audience. Clichés and colloquialisms should be used carefully and sparingly.

9. **Actions.** Movements should be described thoroughly, precisely, and as briefly as possible. Rather than have someone walk over to someone, have them walk fearfully or forcefully over. Use present tense directions. Be unique and inventive!

Tension in the Script

In all charts detailed next, the bottom line represents low tension. The top line represents high tension. Use the example charts as a guide to create your own. Chart each factor that contributes to the rising tension of your script, such as image, effects, sound, music, and scene lengths. Together these charts will add up to your master chart of the rising tension and rhythm of your script.

Figure 4: For overall tension, your (master) chart might be:

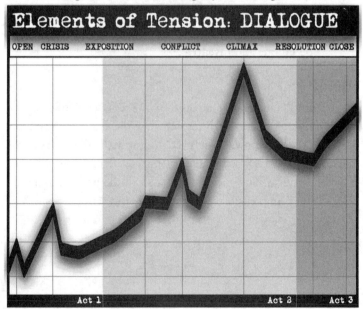

Figure 5: For tension in dialogue, your chart might be:

Figure 6: For tension in the action, your chart might be:

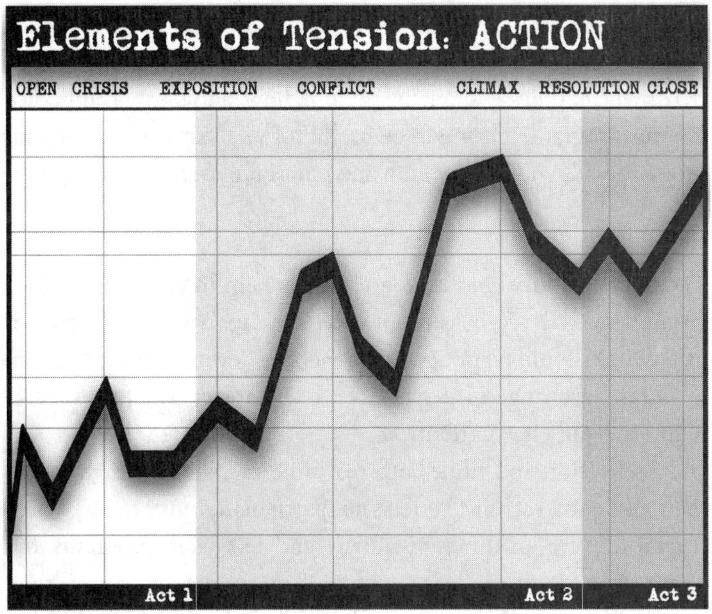

Elements of Tension: ACTION

| OPEN | CRISIS | EXPOSITION | CONFLICT | CLIMAX | RESOLUTION | CLOSE |

Act 1   Act 2   Act 3

Figure 7: For tension in plot turning points, your chart might be:

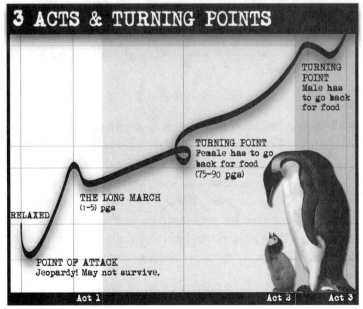

3 ACTS & TURNING POINTS

TURNING
POINT
Male has
to go back
for food

TURNING POINT
Female has to go
back for food
(75–90 pgs)

THE LONG MARCH
(1–5) pgs

RELAXED

POINT OF ATTACK
Jeopardy! May not survive.

Act 1   Act 2   Act 3

As the production of your program script progresses, you should add charts for factors that contribute to dramatic tension, and revise the original charts you prepared to keep them current. Eventually, these charts will graphically show the rhythm, flow, and tension embodied in your program. They will be useful for analyzing how well your program will emotionally grab and entertain your audience.

Effects

Technical, literary, and dramatic effects help to capture and hold an audience. Every communication message (program script or otherwise) should be punctuated by effects, even if it is only a turn of phrase, a change in perspective, or whatever is appropriate to retain the audience's attention.

In television and film, both real time media that reach out to their audience, technical effects are particularly important. Watch several minutes of different movies and television programs and count the technical effects, such as cuts, camera moves, action, and scene changes per minute. You will find that most television programs have between ten and fifty technical effects per minute to capture and hold your attention. It becomes a challenge to maintain audience captivation with fewer effects, unless the premise, its execution, and the emotive images within the program are unusually powerful.

Your Voice

Aside from the effects you use, where appropriate, keep your communication simple. As the famously laughable anagram KISS notes, "Keep It Simple Stupid." This does not mean you should force yourself to communicate in a manner that is alien to you. If your communication is unnatural, it will fail. Be true to yourself, your own voice, your premise, your medium, your audience, and your characters. Where appropriate, be brief. Where your communication demands, capture the tone, language, and grammar that will be most effective.

Be truthful in your communication; true to its demands on you and your demands on it, taking the time to edit, cut back, and/or elaborate as needed to be perfectly clear and coherent. Articles abound in literary magazines urging communicators to be ruthlessly plain and natural. Just as many articles appear urging writers to recapture the beauty of the romantic flights of fancy in the great Nineteenth Century novels. There is room for both—if you communicate effectively, clearly, and coherently. In an article in the *New York Times Book Review* entitled "Is Fiction The Art of Lying?" Mario Vargas Llosa notes,

> In fact, novels do lie—they can't help doing so—but that's only part of the story. The other is that, through lying, they express a curious truth, which can only be expressed in a veiled and concealed fashion, masquerading as what it is not . . . Every good novel tells the truth, and every bad novel lies. For a novel "to tell the truth" means to make the reader experience an illusion, and "to lie" means to be unable to accomplish that trickery.[62]

For a communication to be true, it must adhere to the rules you have set up as the communicator. After all, you have very good reasons for setting up those rules. If at one point in planning your movie or television script you feel that you want an objective reaction to it, do not have your friends review your communication because they will be prejudiced and will not give you an objective evaluation. For a truly objective review, have your most critical enemy look at it. However, if you must have your friends review your script, then ask them to stop when they feel bored. If they stop, it is at that point where your communication has failed.

If you state your premise clearly, define all of the elements contained therein with great precision, and carefully prove your premise, then your premise will powerfully drive your communication no matter what genre and medium you choose. If you follow the twelve steps, or your own variation, in light of your answers to the ascertainment questions, then you will communicate what you want to communicate to your audience. Finally, for your communication to be most effective and successful, "Commit your activities to the Lord and your plans will be achieved" (Proverbs 16:3).

· 5 ·

Lord of the Box Office:
Making Sure Your
Script Pays Off

E very once in a while, a movie like *The Passion of the Christ* or *The Blind Side* will come along and make the elite decision-makers in Hollywood scratch their heads. Then, someone in the press often will remark that it's impossible to know what movies will be successful and what movies will flop. Balderdash! The unique success of these particular movies is not a strange occurrence striking out of the blue. The tremendous success of these two movies, and many others like them, can be attributable to major factors that have always driven the movie industry, ever since D.W. Griffith, Charlie Chaplin, and Cecil B. DeMille started making movies.

Our annual analysis of movie content and the cinematic box office at Movieguide proves, beyond a shadow of a doubt, that writers, filmmakers, and studio executives have a much better chance of being financially successful if their scripts and movies contain positive Christian content, biblical principles, godly virtues, and traditional moral values. Contrary to popular thinking in today's "anything goes" culture, graphic violence, sexual immorality, nudity, foul language, and substance abuse usually don't sell all too well.

This is especially true if you look at the top box office champs of all time, whether you adjust for inflation or not. For example, if you adjust for inflation, the top two box office champs of all time, *Gone With The Wind* and *Star Wars*, beat their closest rivals by nearly $300 million or more. Also, there is only one R-rated movie in any of the box office top ten Movies at the Box Office of All Time, *The Exorcist*, whether you adjust for inflation or not, and that movie itself had a very strong Christian theme where the devil is clearly the villain! All the information you need to make informed decisions is noted in the charts and analyses in our Movieguide's annual report to the entertainment industry. Therefore, you need to get copies of our annual reports if you wanna be in pictures.

RETURN OF THE KING

The phenomenal success of Mel Gibson's *The Passion of the Christ* in 2004 sent a lot of tongues in tinsel town wagging, but the success of these strongly pro-Christian movies came as no surprise to our team at Movieguide and the Christian Film & Television Commission. There have been plenty of very successful pro-Christian movies in the last five to seven years. Even the popular comic book movies, such as most of the *Spider-Man*, *Superman*, and *Batman* movies, contained positive, strong references to New Testament passages and the Christian worldview. Many other extremely popular movies have contained positive Christian content, including such movies as *My Big Fat Greek Wedding*, *The Patriot*, the *Spy Kids* movies, *The Blind Side*, *Up*, *I Am Legend*, *The Lord of the Rings* trilogy, and *The Chronicles of Narnia* movies such as *The Lion, the Witch and the Wardrobe*.

Not only did the king return in *The Lord of the Rings* in 2003; but also, the King of Kings returned in *The Gospel of John* and in

The Passion of the Christ the very next year. What is even more incredible is that Jesus Christ will return in six or seven more faithful movies and television programs about His good news, including *Kingdom Come*, *The Lamb*, *The Gospel of Mark*, and *The Greatest King*.

BRINGING DOWN THE HOUSE!

The good news is that in our comprehensive analysis of the box office in Movieguide's report to the entertainment industry, we found that movies with very strong moral, biblical, and/or Christian content do much better at the box office than movies with excessive or graphic foul language, sex, nudity, violence, alcohol use, and substance abuse. Although some comedies with graphic or excessive violence, sex, and sexual nudity, such as the *American Pie* movies or *The Hangover*, do very well, they still cannot match the financial success of movies with very strong positive content, like the original *Iron Man*, *Spider-Man 3*, *Finding Nemo*, *The Return of the King*, or this year's *Toy Story 3*, according to Movieguide's Christian, biblical standards.

Also, movies with occult and anti-Christian content are not doing as well as they have been doing in recent years. In fact, when you combine all the negative worldview elements together, it is clear that movies with anti-Christian worldviews and strong immoral, unbiblical content don't do very well on average, especially when compared to movies that fit more in line with Movieguide's high biblical standards.

Movies with strong or very strong moral, redemptive, and Christian content are much more likely than movies with strong or very strong immoral, non-Christian or anti-Christian content to make it into the top grossing movies at the box office. As noted in Movieguide's report to the entertainment industry in recent years, seventy to one hundred percent of the top five and top ten movies have a Christian or moral worldview, and eighty to ninety percent of the top ten had at least some moral or Christian content in them.

In fact, one of the top three movies of the year in 2010, *Toy Story 3*, is one of the most Christian-friendly movies, thematically speaking, of the year. And, similar movies from the past like *The Blind Side*, the *Spider-Man* movies, *The Passion of the Christ*, *Finding Nemo*, and *The Return of the King*, (based on the most popular Christian novel ever written, J. R. R. Tolkien's *The Lord of the Rings)*, make to the top of the list and the top ten, year in and year out.

Figure 8: Strong Christian Content Wins

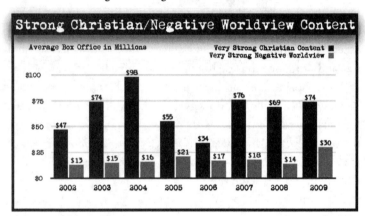

That's why each year my staff and I find that movies with "Very Strong Christian Content" and "Very Strong Moral/Biblical Content" earn four to six times more money per movie than movies with very strong negative content!

MASTER AND COMMANDER OF THE BOX OFFICE

One thing that separates Movieguide from its competitors is its analysis of the dominant philosophical, theological, and political worldviews of movies and television programs.

A worldview is a way of interpreting reality. Although political ideologies are not technically worldviews, they often display attributes or qualities similar to worldviews. For example, the communist writer Karl Marx said that his communism was the ultimate humanism and advocated that a humanist society should abolish religion, family, nation, and private property. That is one reason why Movieguide has a separate worldview content category for communism. Movieguide also shows readers when a movie merely has a moral or biblical worldview, as opposed to an explicit or implied Christian worldview.

Figure 9: Christian Worldview Tops the Chart

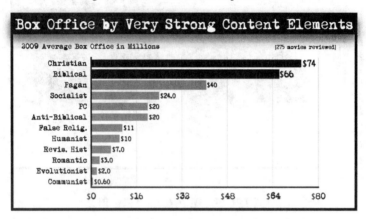

Since 1999, movies with a very strong Christian worldview (CCC) have steadily done better at the box office. In 1999, movies with a very strong Christian worldview earned an average of $30.1 million per movie, while in 2002, they earned $50.3 million per movie—a significant increase of 67 percent in only three years. In the last two years, the average earnings statement of such movies has zoomed past $75 million per movie, for a five-year average of $65.3 million!

In general, the more Christian a movie's worldview is, the better it tends to do at the box office. This is true at both the blockbuster level and the level of small independent releases like *Fireproof,* which earned the most money in that category over a whole three-year period.

Figure 10: CCC Rating Boosts Sales

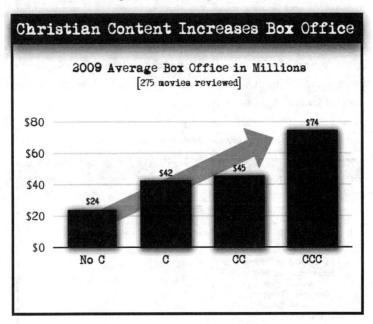

MOVIEGUIDE PICKS THE PIX

Movieguide's aesthetic standards match the aesthetic standards of the general movie-going public. Entertainment industry executives and readers can depend on Movieguide's quality ratings when they're deciding which movies to pay their hard-earned money to see. In fact, ever since we've been tracking our quality ratings, the movies with excellent quality (four stars) from Movieguide earned at least twice as much as movies which earn three stars, two stars, and especially one star from us.

LORD OF THE BOX OFFICE

Based on Movieguide's moral and spiritual acceptability ratings, movies that reflect Movieguide's Christian, biblical standards do better at the box office on average than movies that don't reflect these views. Thus, movies with positive acceptability ratings from Movieguide (+1 to +4) earn significantly more money than movies with negative ratings (-1 to -4), and especially more than movies with the two lowest ratings (-3 and -4). In other words, the most family-friendly movies tend to earn more than twice as much money as the least family-friendly movies.

The same results hold true for movies rated G and PG as opposed to PG-13 and R. When adjusting the all-time box office champs for inflation, the most successful movies, hands down, are movies with only G or PG ratings, like *Gone with the Wind*, *The Sound of Music*, *Star Wars*, and *The Ten Commandments*. All of these movies appear on my personal "best movies of all time" list.

Mr. Smith Goes to Washington

Movieguide's annual report also shows that moviegoers not only favor family-friendly, Christian-friendly movies with traditional moral values; they also favor family-friendly, Christian-friendly movies with patriotic, pro-American, pro-capitalist values that reject radical left-wing viewpoints. Every year, these movies make far more money at the box office than movies with anti-capitalist, anti-American, socialist, radical feminist, pro-homosexual, Communist, atheist, anti-Christian, and politically correct content.

For example, the most conservative movies of the year in 2009 averaged $83.11 million that year while the most liberal and most leftist movies averaged only $25.85 million per movie. That last figure is even worse, if you include all the leftist documentaries and overtly homosexual-themed movies that appeared in fewer than fifty movie theaters in the United States. Also contrary to the conventional wisdom in Hollywood right now, our analysis and box office statistics show that movies with pro-homosexual content do very poorly, on average. In fact, we have found repeatedly that the stronger the homosexual content in a movie, the less it will earn at the box office, in significant proportions.

Terminator

Obscenity, sexual immorality, and graphic violence hardly ever make the most money. That's the continual lesson that Movieguide discovers every year in its annual report.

In fact, our statistics generally show that the more foul language, sex, and nudity a movie contains, the worse it does at the box office. Also, movies with very strong moral, biblical, and/or Christian content do far better than movies with strong, very strong, and excessive foul language, violence, sex, and nudity!

Figure 11: Foul Language, Failed Sales

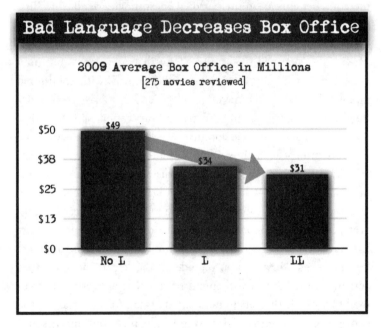

This continual finding proves that sex, violence, vulgarity, and immorality do not really sell as well as many people think—nor as well as the news media often reports. That's because God is still sovereign. His abiding love does not delight in evil, but rejoices with the truth.

If you want your movie to make a significant amount of money, you must drastically reduce, and preferably eliminate, all scenes of explicit sex, violence, nudity, and vulgarity from the script. People really want to see wholesome, quality movies like: *Finding Nemo*, the *Toy Story* series, *My Big Fat Greek Wedding*, Sam Raimi's *Spider-Man* movies, *The Blind Side*, *Despicable Me*, *Enchanted*, *The Princess Diaries*, *Elf*, the *Shrek* movies, *Spy Kids*, *The Lion, the Witch and the Wardrobe*, *Alvin and the Chipmunks*, and the *Ice Age* movies. They don't want to see—much less buy—movies with false, immoral, radical, or non-Christian worldviews that insult and violate the values and beliefs of the 184 million people who attend church (once a month or more) in the United States.

A MIGHTY WIND

Fueled by DVD mania, home video sales and rentals have been skyrocketing the past three to four years.

Among the top home video sales and rentals in these years, Movieguide has found that the top five, top ten and top twenty home video sales and rentals tend to be family movies like *The Blind Side*, *Finding Nemo*, the *Ice Age* movies, *Prince Caspian*, *Toy Story 3*, *Up*, *Alvin and the Chipmunks*, *Marley and Me*, *Enchanted*, and the *Shrek* movies, and movies for mature audiences with strong moral, biblical, or Christian elements in them, such as *Iron Man*, *Star Trek*, *I Am Legend*, *Alice in Wonderland*, *Gran Torino*, *Sherlock Holmes*, and *The Book of Eli*. Also, most of the top five and top ten home video sales—usually seventy to one hundred percent—contain no depicted sex scenes, little foul language, no sexual nudity, and no graphic or excessive violence.

AMERICAN SPLENDOR

Some Americans presume that moral, Christian movies might be successful in the United States, but not overseas. This is definitely not true. Year in and year out, most of the top five or ten movies overseas win top Movieguide Awards, including such movies as

Finding Nemo, Sam Raimi's *Spider-Man* movies, *Up*, the *Ice Age* movies, *The Lord of the Rings* trilogy, *Pirates of the Caribbean*, *Monsters, Inc.*, *X2*, *Live Free or Die Hard*, *Transformers*, *I Am Legend*, and the *Shrek* movies. Most of them also contain no foul language or only a few light obscenities or profanities, little or no sexual content, no explicit nudity, and no graphic violence with lots of blood.

Furthermore, most of the top movies overseas making $100 million or more have moral, biblical, and/or Christian content in them, typically earning eighty percent or more of the money among the top movies overseas every year.

THE CURSE OF THE BAD MOVIE

Finally, if you look at the all time box office champs and top movies at the box office in our annual reports, you will find that the most popular movies are science fiction adventure (*Star Wars*, *Jurassic Park*, *E.T.*, *Avatar*, *Transformers*, and *The Matrix* movies), comic book movies (*Spider-Man*, *The Dark Knight*, and *Spider-Man 2*), fantasy adventure movies (*Lord of the Rings*, *Alice in Wonderland*, and *Harry Potter*), big budget comedies (*My Big Fat Greek Wedding*, *The Proposal*, *Alvin and the Chipmunks*, *Enchanted*, and *Bruce Almighty*), supernatural horror movies (*The Exorcist*, *The Blair Witch Project*, and *Paranormal Activity*), computer animated comedies and comedy adventures (*Finding Nemo*, the *Toy Story* series, *Up*, the *Ice Age* series, *Cloudy with a Chance of Meatballs*, *Despicable Me*, *The Incredibles*, and the *Shrek* series), and hand-drawn animated movies with spiritual Christian themes (*Beauty and the Beast*, *The Lion King*, and *The Prince of Egypt*, which is the most successful hand-drawn animated movie, other than *Lilo & Stitch*, since *The Lion King*). Thus, if you combine positive moral, biblical, Christian, and conservative values with these kinds of movies, and if your script is well written, entertaining, and even exciting, you are well on your way to making a blockbuster hit.

Another safe conclusion looking at these numbers is that the world loves uplifting fairy tales and heroic adventure stories—movies that transport the audience to worlds they don't see in their normal daily lives. These, and popular biblical epics such as *The Ten Commandments*, *The Passion of the Christ*, *Ben-Hur*, *Raiders of the Lost Ark*, and *The Robe*, are truly the kinds of movies that delight and inspire.

Believable, honorable characters overcoming huge, difficult obstacles or finding a life-changing bit of God's grace will always be the kinds of stories that touch our lives, inspire the creative imagination God has given us, and help us endure and overcome tragedy and loss. That's the kind of story you should be writing if you wanna be in pictures!

The good news is that the entertainment industry is taking Movieguide's report to heart by producing fewer R-rated movies, and more movies with Christian Content:

Figure 12: CCC Content

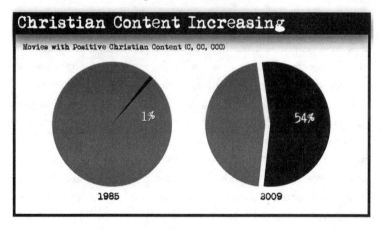

· 6 ·

Understanding Your Audience

> But if anyone causes one of these little ones who believe in
> me to sin, it would be better for him to have a large millstone
> hung around his neck and to be drowned in the depths of
> the sea.
>
> — Matthew 18:6 NIV

A few years back, the evening news broadcast a story about a
babysitter in Dallas, Texas who had molested the baby she was
supposed to protect. The parents, who had become suspicious of
the sitter, installed a hidden camera in their living room. The evening news showed what the parents saw: the babysitter starting to
undress in front of the baby and then cut away. The news anchors
were horrified and wondered how the parents had failed to check
this sitter's credentials. The news team closed by remarking that
this type of abuse probably occurred more often than anyone knew.

They were right. There are several babysitters who are constantly
abusing millions of our children. Those babysitters are the television set, the computer, and the other mass media of entertainment.
No one fires these babysitters, or brings criminal charges against
them, nor do many people try to rehabilitate them.

No matter how much we condemn the mass media for influencing the behavior of our children, we must admit that there are

several accomplices in this tragedy. Those accomplices include: (1) churches that don't teach parents how to teach their children discernment, (2) parents who allow their children to watch television, go to movies or surf the internet without adequate supervision or training in the necessary discernment skills, and (3) the creative people in the entertainment industry who do not care about protecting our children.

CHILD ABUSE VIA THE SILVER SCREEN

Even the secular press understands the problem of exposing children to violent and improper television and movies. In an article in the *Los Angeles Times,* James Scott Bell, a writer and novelist,[63] in Los Angeles, shares:

> The country was rightly repulsed at the videotape of Madelyne Toogood beating her 4-year-old child in an Indiana parking lot. We know such mistreatment can have a terrible effect on a child's mental health. But, how many Americans indulge in a worse form of abuse without a second thought? I'm talking about taking kids to the movies. The wrong movies. . . . The other night I saw *Red Dragon,* the third installment in the Hannibal Lecter series starring Anthony Hopkins. When the bad guy (Ralph Fiennes) bites off the tongue of a screaming reporter, then stands up, mouth bloody, and spits out the offending organ, I squirmed in my seat. What I couldn't stop thinking about, however, was the little girl in the seat in front of me. . . . She looked about 6-years-old . . . Two hours of mayhem ensued. People stabbed, set on fire, tortured. Your average day at the office for serial killers. Every now and then I'd lean over and see the little girl with her eyes fixed to the screen."

Seek Understanding

Understanding why and how the mass media affect children is an extremely important step in producing worthwhile movies and television programs.

Many scientists have argued that there is such a significant body of evidence on the connection between the content of the mass media and behavior, especially aggressive behavior, that researchers should move beyond accumulating further evidence and focus on the processes that are responsible for this relationship. It is claimed that there are over 500,000 studies. Certainly, every reputable university is studying the effects of the mass media of entertainment. From our studies at Movieguide, we can only find one legitimate study that indicates that the media does not have an influence, and it was conducted in 1980s in Canada by ABC television. It has never been replicated. Of course, if the mass media of entertainment did not have an influence, advertisers would stop spending millions of dollars to advertise.

According to Dr. Victor Strasburger, chief of The American Academy of Pediatrics section on adolescents, "We are basically saying the controversy is over. There is clearly a relationship between media violence and violence in society."[64]

A report on four decades of entertainment TV from the media research team of Robert Lichter, Linda Lichter, Stanley Rothman, and Daniel Amundson found about fifty crimes, including a dozen murders, in every hour of prime time television. This indicates that our children may see from 800,000 to 1.5 million acts of violence and witness 192,000 to 360,000 murders on television by the time they are seventeen-years-old.[65]

This contrasts radically with the generations of men and women who grew up *without* this flood of violent images from the entertainment media. Lichter and his fellow authors wrote, "Since 1955 TV characters have been murdered at a rate one thousand times higher than real-world victims."[66] If that same murder rate were applied to the general population, everyone in the United States would be killed in just fifty days.[67]

If you are over forty years old, statistics estimate that you probably watch only six movies a year in theaters, most of which are family films. In contrast, teenagers watch an average of fifty movies a year in theatres, eighty percent of which are R-rated or PG-13. They watch another fifty movies a year on video.[68]

Five Seasons

To understand why children are affected by the mass media, we need first to understand cognitive development. In this regard, it is important to note that psychology, including the field known as cognitive development, is descriptive in that it helps us to classify and understand human beings (after all, God gave man the job of naming what he saw in the world around him). For many Christians, psychology falls short of being prescriptive in the sense of curing a problem that it identifies, whereas the Bible has the cure for what ails us.

In the late 1970s, building on the research of the renowned child psychologist Jean Piaget,[69] television researcher Robert Morse adapted Piaget's stages of cognitive growth so that they could be more effectively applied to research in the mass media. Please note that current studies are refining and redefining these stages.

Every child seems to go through the stages listed below. Please also note that the use of masculine pronouns throughout the following sections is simply for ease of grammatical transition and is not intended as exclusionary language. These stages and principles apply to girls as well as boys.

> **The Sensation Stage**[70] (approximately ages 0–2 years old): The child's sole means of processing reality is his senses. These young children think that they are the center of the universe; something exists only if they can see it; and that everything around them serves them.

> **The Imagination Stage**[71] (approximately ages 2–7 years old): The child's cognition is dedicated to the

acquisition of representational skills such as language, mental imagery, drawing, and symbolic play and is limited by being serial and one dimensional. During this stage, the child has a very active imagination, often confusing fact and fiction, making him uniquely susceptible to what he sees in television and movies. It is not surprising that a four-year-old girl was critically injured when she apparently tried to fly after watching the *Harry Potter and the Sorcerer's Stone* movie. Authorities in Shelby, North Carolina, said that the girl watched the movie and then crawled onto a kitchen counter, straddled a broom and jumped off.

The Concrete Operational Stage (approximately ages 7–11 years old): The child acquires the ability of simultaneous perception from two points of view, enabling him to master quantities, relations, and classes of objects. At this stage, there is a strong correspondence between the child's thoughts and reality. He assumes his thoughts about reality are accurate and distorts the facts to fit what he thinks. Younger children in this range react to direct violence, but not to suspense. Children in the concrete stage of cognitive development are more upset by suspense than direct violence. Thus, young children will get bored by a movie like *Jaws*, which is mostly suspense, while older children may be traumatized by it.

The Reflection or Formal Operations Stage (approximately ages 12–15 years old): This is the time when abstract thought gains strength. In this stage, there is still incomplete differentiation as a result of the adolescent's inability to conceptualize the thoughts of others, as exemplified by the assumption that other people are as obsessed with his behavior and appearance as he is. For example, if he has a pimple and walks into a room filled with friends, he will usually think that everyone is looking at his pimple. In this stage, the adolescent will take risks because he still has difficulty conceptualizing the consequences of his actions. For instance, when the movie, *The Program*, was released, several teenagers mimicked the main characters by lying down in the middle of the road to prove their courage. Some of these teenagers were seriously injured and some were killed. One national radio personality said that these teenagers were really stupid. However, one of the teenagers who died was at the top of his class. What the radio personality did not understand was that these teenagers were in a stage of development where they were the most impulsive and the least able to consider the consequences of their actions. Like most adults, the radio personality didn't remember what it was like to be in a previous stage of cognitive development.

The Relationship Stage: The adolescent grows into a mature adult, and there is complete differentiation. As a result, the adult understands that others are different and accepts those differences by learning to relate to others. The adult is able to conceptualize the consequences of his actions and take the necessary steps to reduce his risks.

Babes in Toyland

Children experience fear reactions to horror entertainment. Exposure to large amounts of violence can produce either desensitization or imitation as a way for the child to cope with the emotions raised by the violence. Researchers Barbara J. Wilson, Daniel Lynn, and

Barbara Randall have examined the harmful effects of graphic horror on children and discovered some important distinctions:[72]

> **Visual Versus Non-Visual Threat:** The principle of perceptual dependence suggests that younger children are likely to be frightened by movies and television programs with visually frightening creatures like witches and monsters. Older children will focus more on conceptual qualities, such as the motives of a character,[73] and are likely to be more upset by an evil, normal-looking character or by an unseen threat than by a benign but grotesque character. Therefore, *The Wizard of Oz* is more frightening for younger children than for older children, while older children are more frightened by movies such as *Jaws*, which rely more on non-visual threats.

> **Reality Versus Fantasy:** Younger children are unable to fully distinguish between reality and fantasy.[74] Although the terms "real" and "make-believe" may be used in conversation, younger children do not understand the implications of these terms. The notion that a character or an event is "not real" has little impact on a younger child's emotions. Therefore, fantasy offerings involving events that could not possibly happen, such as *Harry Potter*, are more frightening to younger children, whereas fictional programs involving events that could happen, such as *Jaws*, were more frightening to older children and adults.[75]

> **Abstract Versus Concrete Events:** A concrete threat is explicit and tangible. For example, an evil character might attack a victim. In contrast, abstract threats

must be inferred from information in the plot. Examples might include movies about evil conspiracies, or disasters such as poisonous gases. Younger children have difficulty drawing inferences from entertainment and are more likely to focus on explicit rather than implicit cues in the plot,[76] and so they will be more frightened by a movie depicting a concrete threat than one involving an intangible or obscure hazard.

Threat Versus Victim Focus: Also, cognitive stages are distinguished by the degree to which the scenes concentrate on the actual threat versus the victim's emotional reactions to the threat. Movies that require viewer involvement and focus primarily on the victims' emotional reactions are less upsetting for younger than for older children. *Jaws* is a good example because the viewer often sees only the upper bodies of the victims as they are attacked by the unseen shark.

More important than the sheer amount of mass media horror and violence children watch is the way in which even small amounts of violence are portrayed.[77] Therefore, "a number of contextual features of violence are critical determinants of whether such depictions will facilitate aggressive behavior."[78] According to Wilson, Lynn, and Randall, these contextual features are:

Reward Versus Punishment Associated with Violence: Violent depictions for which the aggressor is rewarded are most likely to produce imitation effects or foster attitudes supportive of aggression.[79] In fact, characters need not be explicitly rewarded for such effects to occur. As long as there is no punishment associated with a violent act, young viewers will often imitate such depictions.[80] The lack of punishment is a reward for such behavior. Much media violence is portrayed without negative consequences; neither perpetrators nor victims suffer much, and the perpetrator is often rewarded for antisocial actions, as in *Harry Potter*.[81] The timing of the reward or punishment has important developmental implications.[82] In many movies, the perpetrator receives material rewards immediately after performing an aggressive act. Punishment, however, it is typically delivered toward the end of the movie. Since younger children are less able than older children to coherently link scenes together and to draw inferences from them,[83] younger children are more likely than older children to see the violence as acceptable and to imitate such behavior when rewards are immediate and punishment is delayed in a movie.

Degree of Reality of Violence: Violence perceived to be realistic is more likely to be imitated and used as a guide for behavior.[84] Older children are better able to distinguish reality from fantasy and are more emotionally responsive to programs that depict realistic events. Thus, older children are affected more by violent movies that feature events that are humanly possible, such as *Scream*. Younger children are responsive to both realistic and unrealistic violence as long as the acts are concrete and visual.

The Nature of the Perpetrator: Children are more likely to imitate models perceived as attractive or interesting.[85] Children who strongly identify with violent media characters are more likely to be aggressive themselves than are those who do not identify with such characters.[86] Younger children are more likely to focus on the consequences of a character's behavior in determining whether the character is "good" or "bad," whereas older children focus more on the character's motives.[87] Such age differences are presumably due to the fact that motives are typically presented early in a plot, so that the viewer must be able to draw inferences in order to link them to subsequent behaviors. Therefore, younger children will be more likely to emulate bad characters as long as they are rewarded, whereas older children presumably will be cognizant of the characters' motives in selecting role models.

Justified Violence: Violence that is portrayed as justified is more likely to be imitated.[88] A common theme in many movies is the portrayal of a hero who is forced to be violent because his job demands it (e.g., *Dirty Harry*) or because he must retaliate against an enemy (e.g., *Harry Potter*). Although the message may be ultimately prosocial (e.g., "don't be a criminal"), the moral is conveyed in a violent context. In one experiment examining "mixed messages,"[89] children viewed either a purely prosocial cartoon or a cartoon that contained a prosocial message delivered through justified violence. Kindergartners were more likely to hurt than to help a peer after watching the prosocial-aggressive cartoon. Moreover, both younger and older children showed less understanding of the moral lesson when it was conveyed in the context of violence versus no violence. Therefore, a hero who commits violence for some "good" cause is likely to be a confusing and negative role model for younger and older children.

Similarity of Movie Situations and Characters to Viewer: Viewers are more likely to imitate media violence if cues in the program are similar to those in real life.[90] Also, children are likely to imitate models who are similar to themselves.[91] Thus, movies depicting children as violent are more problematic than those involving violent adults. Preschool and early elementary school children focus on younger characters who are violent, whereas pre-teens and teenagers attend more to aggressive teenage characters.

Amount of Violence: Although the way in which violence is portrayed is more critical than the amount of violence in facilitating aggressive behavior, the sheer amount and explicitness of the violent content is important with regard to the viewer's emotions. Excessive exposure to violence may produce a "psychological blunting" of normal emotional responses to violent events. Children who are heavy viewers of television violence show less physiological arousal to a clip of filmed violence than light viewers. In one experiment, children who watched a violent film or television program were subsequently less likely to seek help when the other children became disruptive and violent. Thus, exposure to media violence leads to a lack of responsiveness to real-life aggression.[92]

Dangerous Minds

Part of the problem with television as well as movies is that they are so effective at propelling powerful, emotional images into the viewer's mind in real time with no time for the viewer to reflect, react, or review the information he or she is receiving—processes that are absolutely necessary for cognitive development.

Therefore, the very act of watching is harmful to the cognitive development of children and, as a consequence, adversely influences their moral, social, emotional and religious development. Videos and television also "debilitates an important cognitive function in adults, the one that permits abstract reasoning—and hence related capacities for moral decision making, learning, religious growth, and psychological individualization."[93]

Rush

Watching fighting or other violence can make the mind believe that it is about to engage in life-threatening activity, so the body will often respond by releasing adrenal epinephrine into the bloodstream, giving the viewer an adrenal rush without the threat of actual violence. Watching sexual activity and nudity makes the mind think that the person is about to mate so the body releases raging hormones that can often cause an addictive adrenal rush without the psychological burdens attendant to most human relationships. These *physiological phenomena* will engage and attract the viewer, often causing him or her to want more and more exposure to the stimuli that cause their artificial physical elation.

Scientists have discovered that mass media violence leads to aggressive behavior by overstimulating children. The more intense and realistic the violent scene, the more likely it is to be encoded, stored in the memory, and later retrieved as model behavior.

Another study showed that boys who watch a great deal of violent programming may exhibit less physiological arousal when shown new violent programs than do boys who regularly watch less violent fare.[94] This study seems to explain why consumers of mass media sex and violence desire more and more prurient fare or more and more violent fare. Of course, all of this can add up to addiction (best summed up by the phrase the "plug-in drug" as applied to television) because most of the offerings of the mass media are emotive, and not intellectual pursuits.

The impact of excessive movie and television sex and violence on teenagers is aggravated by the fact that their raging hormones give them a predisposition to seek arousal. They are subject to tremendous peer and media pressure at an age where fitting in with their peers is extremely important—even if that fitting in means rebelling against their parents. They have a predisposition to seek out movies and programs that arouse them. Some are so aroused they seek to replicate the emotive sexual or violent situations portrayed in the movie or television program in their own lives.

TRUTH OR CONSEQUENCES

Since 1966 (the year the church abandoned Hollywood): violent crime has increased in the United States of America by 560 percent; illegitimate births have increased 419 percent; divorce rates have quadrupled; the percentage of children living in single-parent homes has tripled; the teenage suicide rate has increased more than three hundred percent; and, SAT scores have dropped almost eighty points. Rapes, murders, and gang violence have become common occurrences. While there are many factors that have contributed to our cultural decline, it is clear that the mass media have had a significant influence on behavior.[95]

Researchers affiliated with the National Bureau of Economic Research and Stanford University wrote in the journal *Science*[96] that America's children are fatter, more suicidal, more murderous and scored lower on standardized tests in recent years than in the 1960s. After years of denial, even eighty-seven percent of the top media executives now admit that violence in the mass media contributes to the violence in society.[97] And children, too, are aware of the ability entertainment media has to influence their behavior.[98]

Yet, in spite of the clear correlation between violence in the mass media and violence on the street, very few people are yelling, "Stop!" The growing American tolerance for brutal sex and violence in the mass media suggests the proverbial frog who calmly dies as he is slowly brought to a boil. The following scriptures from Paul's Letter to the Romans describe the conditions in which we find ourselves today:

> And even as they did not like to retain God in their knowledge, God gave them over to a reprobate mind, to do those things which are not convenient; Being filled with all unrighteousness, fornication, wickedness, covetousness, maliciousness; full of envy, murder, debate, deceit, malignity; whisperers, backbiters, haters of God, despiteful, proud, boasters, inventors of evil things, disobedient to parents, Without understanding, covenant breakers, without natural affection, implacable, unmerciful: Who knowing the judgment of God, that they which commit such things are worthy of death, not only do the same, but have pleasure in them that do them.
>
> —Romans 1:28–32 KJV

A Sample of the Violence

The suggestion that the mass media of entertainment spawns violence is not anecdotal, it is real. Over the years, there have been innumerable reports of grisly crimes that were inspired by and mimicked the fictional product of the entertainment media. It is important to take note of these stories to realize the scope of the problem and the powerful influence of movies, television programs, music, and the other mass media. A small sampling of specific films and their violent outcomes is outlined below.

Child's Play?

It is clear to any parent that children learn to a large degree by mimicking the behavior of the adults around them, including those on television and in movies.

Figure 13:

One of the most famous examples was the connection that a judge in Liverpool, England, made between the horror movie *Child's Play 3* and the murder of 2-year-old James Bulger by two 11-year-old boys, Robert Thompson and Jon Venables.[99] According to the judge, the horror movie *Child's Play 3* presents some terrifying parallels to the actual murder of little James Bulger, and the movie was viewed repeatedly by one of the killers just before the murder took place. The judge noted: (1) The horror movie depicts a baby doll who comes to life and gets blue paint splashed in its face. There was blue paint on the dead child's face. (2) The movie depicts a kidnapping. James was abducted by the two older boys before they killed him, and (3) The climax of the movie comes as two young boys murder the doll on a train, mutilating the doll's face. James was first mutilated and bludgeoned by the two older boys and then left on a railroad track to be run over.

This story was widely publicized around the world, but the link to *Child's Play 3* seldom made the news. Why were these facts overlooked or withheld by the mainstream media?

SLASHER MOVIES AND STEPHEN KING NOVELS

In Houston, Texas, Scott Edward May, a 17-year-old obsessed with slasher movies, occult and heavy-metal music, attacked a girl during their first date, stabbing her when she closed her eyes for a good-night kiss.[100] They had just seen the movie *The Cutting Edge*. May told police he had urges to kill since childhood. "I love knives," May's statement reads. "I like to go to the movies a lot. A lot of people get stabbed in the movies. I really liked the *Texas Chainsaw Massacre*. A lot of people got stabbed in that."

Natural Born Killers?

The Oliver Stone movie *Natural Born Killers* has produced a slew of copycat murders.

Nathan K. Martinez, an unhappy 17-year-old obsessed with the movie *Natural Born Killers* murdered his stepmother and his half-sister in their suburban home fifteen miles southwest of Salt Lake City.

In Georgia, Jason Lewis, a 15-year-old, murdered his parents, firing multiple shotgun blasts into their heads. Letters found in his room indicated he worshipped Satan and, along with three friends, had formulated a plan to kill all their parents and to copy the cross-country swing of violence portrayed in *Natural Born Killers*.

Christopher Smith, an 18-year-old, shouted at television cameras, "I'm a natural born killer!" echoing the words of actor Woody Harrelson in the movie *Natural Born Killers* following his arrest for shooting to death an 82-year-old man.

One gruesome incident prompted novelist John Grisham to suggest that the survivors of these killing sprees should sue Stone.[101] The incidence that incensed Grisham occurred in March of 1995 when two teenagers saw *Natural Born Killers* in Oklahoma, then drove to Mississippi and killed Bill Savage in the same randomly violent way as the movie's protagonists do. They then went to Louisiana and nearly killed a woman in a convenience store (she is now a quadriplegic). One of the two said the movie led directly to their actions.

WHAT ELSE?

Increased violence in our society would be more than enough, but it is not the only effect of the mass media of entertainment on children. Four other consequences are discussed below: (1) decrease in creative imagination, concentration, and delayed gratification; (2) false memory syndrome; (3) movies/TV as religion; and, (4) spiritual warfare.

The Twilight Zone

Children who are heavy users of mass media demonstrate decreases in the capacity for creative imagination, concentration, and delayed gratification. With regard to imagination, they are less able to form "mental pictures," and they engage in less "imaginative play." With regard to concentration, children become "lazy readers" of "non-books" with greatly decreased attention spans (you have to exercise concentration or it atrophies). With regard to delayed gratification, the children have less tolerance for getting into a book or other activities.

The symbolic function, perception, and abstract reasoning are damaged in a manner that resembles dyslexia. The rapid increase in reading disabilities, or dyslexia, in the United States may be, in part, attributed to heavy television and movie viewing. Television in particular inhibits eye movement and, thereby, the acquisition of reading skills.

False Memory Syndrome

Another area of research studying the influence of the mass media on children and adults is *false memory syndrome*, unchained memories, memory therapy, and associated psychological insights that have captured the national imagination.

One area of life that most likely contributes to the false memory syndrome is the tremendous amount of movie and television sex, violence, and occultism that has filled the minds of youth over the years. Nefarious films and other mass media have planted images in the minds of our youth that they have processed in the same manner as the daily activities in which they engage. However, unlike the many daily activities which are repetitive and dull, most of these entertaining movies and television programs are a potent and often cognitively dissonant, if not traumatic, brew of emotive visual and audile messages which lodge in the nooks and crannies of the child's memory, waiting to pop into their dreams or consciousness.

Research indicates that the minds of our youth are overflowing with movies and television programs that they confuse with reality and history. Everyday examples abound, from the woman who saw the movie *Independence Day* and afterwards told a reporter that she believes the government is hiding a flying saucer, to those who saw the movie *The Wind and the Lion*, including a media literacy teacher, and assume that this historical incident involved a beautiful woman and a dashing desert chieftain, rather than the real characters—an old Greek immigrant and a Moroccan thief.

Memory therapists have been able to induce adults to fabricate a childhood history from disjointed memories. Regrettably, some of these adults have even acted upon these false memories.

GOD RE-WRITTEN, HOLLYWOOD-STYLE

The mass media influence not only our behavior, but also our beliefs. Therefore, it is important to realize that religion is alive and well in the mass media—though it is not the predominantly Christian faith of our founding fathers. It is, instead, a cacophony of ill-conceived religions such as materialism, consumerism, eroticism, hedonism, naturalism, humanism, cynicism, stoicism, the cult of violence, and a multitude of other modern variations on pagan practices that now vie for renewed homage in the mass media.

Dr. Kathleen Waller, Ph.D. and Dr. Michael E. O'Keeffe, Ph.D. team-teach the popular "Religion and Film" course at Saint Xavier University in Chicago, IL. They note that movies deeply influence how their students see God and theology. They wrote in Movieguide:

> We have come to two conclusions about our students that give us pause. The first is the relative insecurity many of our students feel when explaining their faith; and, the second is the undeniable influence that the mass media has on the religious ideas they do hold. . . . These students certainly consider themselves good Christians, but they lack the ability to discuss their faith with anything more than a surface understanding of who Jesus is and what Christianity is about. In short, they are unable to "explain" their views, particularly to classmates who come from religious traditions that do not use the same terms or speak from the starting point as they do. Thus even discussing something as seemingly straightforward as "the Bible is the Word of God" is difficult for them, particularly if they are called upon to explain the theological presuppositions that stand behind such a claim. . . . Perhaps because of this naïveté, many of our students also struggle with the second fact;

namely, their almost wholesale acceptance of the culture's understanding of religion. In other words, they are relatively uniformed about the faith given to them by their parents and their churches, and they are uninformed about the distinction between that faith and the "faith" packaged for them by the mass media, especially films and television. Hence our task is doubled: we not only have to help students sort out and explain the inherited faith of our fathers and mothers, but we have to distinguish true faith from the faith of Hollywood. In many cases, the faith of our students is more indebted to *The Simpsons* and movies such as *Stigmata* and *Dogma* than to traditional Christianity.

. . . Our experience confirms it is more difficult to dislodge Hollywood's version of Christianity, for Hollywood's version eventually becomes "real," becomes the way they see God, or heaven and hell, or sin and virtue, or the lives of believers vis-à-vis the lives of others. . . . The themes portrayed are consistent: malevolent supernatural forces are real, humans are powerless in the face of evil, Christian doctrine and religious training provide no recourse or significant spiritual guidance in the struggle with evil, and the Christian Church and its leaders are powerless before Satan and his minions. In addition, God is too distant, or uncaring, unable, or unwilling, to check Satan's power. These films, and others like them, borrow freely from Christian teachings and symbols, but usually subvert them beyond recognition or take such dramatic license that any sound theological insight is lost. They often purport to quote from the Bible or to interpret biblical eschatology, but these interpretations are horribly skewed at best. Several of the movies are visually stunning in their special effects so, even if one is able to recognize the faulty theology, the world they portray is so compelling that it is hard not to accept Hollywood's version as true. Thus it is not surprising that many of our students are unable to distinguish the unorthodox teaching in these films. Instead, they come away convinced they have learned something valuable about Christianity and its inability to deal with evil.

As theologian Paul Tillich explains, "your god is that reality which elicits from you your deepest feelings and ultimate concerns" and "religion is the state of being grasped by an ultimate concern, a concern which qualifies all other concerns as preliminary and which itself contains the answer to the question of a meaning of our life."[102] British playwright J. M. Barrie summarizes that "one's religion is whatever he is most interested in."[103] The internet, computer games, prime-time entertainment television, movies and popular music have become a religion for too many, especially some of those employed in the entertainment industry. Sadly, children have lost all memory of the Ten Commandments with the prohibitions against murder, theft, and adultery among the other absolute moral values, as illustrated by the following chart:

Figure 14

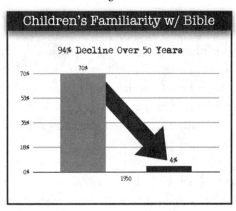

SPIRITUAL WARFARE

The cognitive/psychological and physiological influence of the mass media has a spiritual impact. The images of the mass media that tug at our desires, seduce our thoughts, and lodge in our memories are the demons of our age. They claw at our consciousness and entice us to do things we would not otherwise do; whether it is to buy a product we don't actually need, or something worse.

We often forget there is a war raging around us. It is a war being waged inside our minds, a spiritual war for our souls. The adversary is using every possible tactic to control our minds: materialism, secularism, humanism, and all the other "isms" that conflict with Christianity. He is using the most effective weapons of our time to win: the power of the mass media of entertainment. With the corrupted movies and television programs of our age, the adversary is fueling our sinful propensity to lust and hooking us on our desires. Once hooked, he drags us down to Hell.

> Do not be so deceived and misled! Evil companionships (communion, associations) corrupt and deprave good manners and morals and character.
>
> —1 Corinthians 15:33 AMP

The key in this battle is for Christians—and especially the church—to develop wisdom, knowledge, and understanding by rediscovering a biblical theology of art, entertainment, and communication. Thus, equipped, it becomes much easier to comprehend and produce great movies and television programs.

· SECTION II ·

STEP-BY-STEP

· 7 ·

The Producers

Motion picture and television technology is continually changing. By the time you read this, many changes will have occurred and most of the equipment used as I write may be obsolete. However, if you learn the basic principles and techniques of production you will be able to use whatever equipment comes along.

These techniques and principles will help you to communicate through other audio-visual media, teach you the unique principles you'll need to know, and help you use other audio-visual media to communicate more effectively.

To understand the techniques and principles that apply to movie and television movie production, let's examine the steps involved in producing a movie. A movie involves the most talent, the most equipment, the most resources, and the widest range of artistic and technical creativity and decisions. Reviewing the basic steps required to produce a movie will give you an overview of the medium and allow us to touch on most of the pertinent principles and techniques of production. In the process, specific aspects of television movie production will also be addressed.

With regard to television movies, Hallmark Hall of Fame has made some of the best. Hallmark is certainly a household word in America because of the company's outstanding greeting cards and other products. Hallmark Cards, Inc. is based in Kansas City, Missouri, and Hallmark Hall of Fame Productions is its television movie making subsidiary, with an additional office for production based in Studio City, California. The Hallmark Hall of Fame Series is now over fifty years old and is considered to be the most honored series in television history. The company has produced over two hundred movies, or about four two-hour programs per year. They have won a total of more than seventy-five Emmy's, plus numerous Peabody, Golden Globe, and other awards throughout the years.

Audience favorites include such recent movies such as John Grisham's *A Painted House*; *Sarah, Plain & Tall* starring Glenn Close; or *Fallen Angel* with Gary Sinise. Other popular titles, still available at Hallmark Card Shops, include such productions as *What the Deaf Man Heard*, and very recently, *The Blackwater Lightship*. Brad Moore is the president of Hallmark Hall of Fame Productions, which he claims is the best job in the movie business. Below, he shares a bit of his life experience and wisdom for people of faith pursuing filmmaking or television production.

* * *

"IT'S THE BEST JOB IN THE MOVIE BUSINESS!"

AN INTERVIEW WITH BRAD MOORE

GET A SOLID START

Brad grew up in Illinois, went to public schools, and then attended college at Southern Nazarene University in Oklahoma City, OK. He did his graduate work at Northwestern University in

Chicago, where he earned an MBA. After graduation, he worked in brand management and advertising at Procter & Gamble from 1972–1982. (Incidentally, Procter and Gamble, who founded the company in the early 1800s, were two men known to have strong religious faiths.) At this time, a headhunter reached him at P&G, also affectionately known as "the graduate school of marketing," and talked with him about a position with Hallmark Cards, Inc. as the Vice President of Advertising. He soon took over the responsibility of Hallmark Hall of Fame Series and became president of the Hallmark Hall of Fame Productions, Inc., its movie production subsidiary, when it was formed in 1993.

RESEARCH THE COMPANY'S HISTORY AND PURPOSE

In moving from P&G to Hallmark, it was again important to Brad Moore that he worked for a company with solid foundations. As he studied the company's history, he found that it was not a public company, but rather a family—the Hall family—owned it. A young man, J.C. Hall, founded Hallmark in 1910 at the age of eighteen. He had gotten off the train, stayed at a YMCA in Kansas City, and sold postcards from shoeboxes that he kept under his bed. He did well, and his little venture soon grew into a greeting card business. J.C. would reproduce the cards that sold the best, and within a few years, he was extremely successful, with his business having grown into the world's largest greeting card company. The company was called Hall Brothers until 1954, at which time it changed to Hallmark, the same name Mr. Hall had begun using on cards he sold.

The Hallmark Hall of Fame television series is based on three principles: quality, good taste, and enriching relationships. The objective was not to make money, or even to get the biggest audience. The Hallmark Hall of Fame series was coming at it from a completely different perspective than other television productions. "This company is highly successful, doesn't cut corners, and has ample resources to work with. As a matter of fact, our production costs are often double or triple what other TV shows have budgeted." Certainly audiences agree—the quality shows.

Hallmark's current chairman of the board is the son of J.C. Hall, and J.C. Hall's grandson is the current CEO of the company. Another grandson of J.C. Hall is the Senior Vice President of Human Resources. "The family has always maintained incredibly high standards," remarks Brad. "They're a wonderful, hardworking, caring family with great ethics and high moral standards. They're actually very unassuming, always looking out for the interests of their employees. Our movies reflect the values of the family that owns Hallmark. Fortunately, these values are completely consistent with my own moral values. That's one reason I think I have the best job in the movie business."

As Brad Moore speaks on college campuses, he advises young graduates to find an industry and a company where their values can be aligned. "It doesn't have to be a 'Christian company,' but it should be a company where you can embrace their values and they'll embrace yours, without you having to get on a soapbox and have an agenda. That may not even be ethical. You're there to meet the organization's objectives, not preach yours, but if you align your values, you can do what you feel is right, doing what you enjoy. It should be a natural fit. On the other hand, if you're always playing the role of a martyr, that's not really a Christian attitude."

Brad believes that people have to like what they're doing, or the relationship won't last. "Life is too short not to like it. Find an industry, a job, a company, or an organization where your values are compatible and the challenges fit your skill set."

MAKE A GREAT START

The Hallmark Hall of Fame series had a great beginning by rolling out its first production on Christmas Eve of 1951. It broadcast to national audiences the live production entitled, *Amahl and the*

Night Visitors, a story of a little boy in Palestine who meets the three wise men and offers his crutch to the Christ child. This production was the first opera to be broadcast on national television, and it captured the hearts of Americans. In fact, the company aired the live show five times, even once on Easter, and then actually made a movie of it in 1964, so it was eventually aired seven times, either live or recorded. Audiences were impressed with the story, but more importantly, they were inspired, and they trusted the company to be invited into their living rooms through more quality telecasts.

LOOK FOR NEW IDEAS AND OPPORTUNITIES

The Hallmark Hall of Fame series began successfully and has kept the wheels turning ever since with inspiring, quality productions. Hallmark Hall of Fame usually develops projects in-house, most often developing their movies based on a good book. "For instance, with *Sarah, Plain & Tall*, Glenn Close came to us with that idea," relates Brad. "She had read for the book-on-tape, which was authored by Patricia MacLachlin, and she handed us the book, saying, 'This is a wonderful book. I think you should consider it.' It's a very small book, fifty-eight pages long with big print, so we had our doubts."

Well, they read it anyway, and she was right. "Obviously, with such a small book, we needed more story elements to make a full two-hour movie, so we commissioned the book's author to write the screenplay. And, she did have much more story inside! It was so successful—the highest rated movie on television, on any network, during the entire decade of the 90s—that the company did a sequel, which MacLachlin also wrote, entitled *Skylark*. MacLachlin then wrote the book *Skylark* from her screenplay. Finally, we produced a third segment to the story, entitled *Winter's End*, again with Patricia writing the screenplay, then the book."

When asked more about Glenn Close, Brad smiles. "Glenn Close not only starred in all three movies, she was executive producer on all three as well. She became our partner on the series."

DOING IT THE HALLMARK WAY

In the early television years of the 1950s, explains Brad, most programs were sponsored in their entirety by a product, or corporate sponsor, but in the 1960s, most advertisers moved to a different process, in which they bought individual commercials on many different programs, rather than sponsoring or buying all the commercial time on a single program. Hallmark does the same thing, purchasing commercial time on many programs. However, unlike virtually every other company, Hallmark continues to fully sponsor its own programs. It even took the major step in 1993 of founding its own production company, Hallmark Hall of Fame Productions, Inc., to actually produce those programs itself.

One year the founder of Hallmark was asked why he sponsored programs based on such high standards, rather than more popular fare that might appeal to a bigger audience. He answered, "I'd rather make a few good impressions than a lot of bad ones." J.C. knew that you didn't just buy ads back then; you endorsed the content of a program. The company has retained Mr. Hall's philosophy of giving careful thought to its program content and sponsorship over the years.

SEEK QUALITY AND UNIVERSAL APPEAL

According to Brad, Hallmark's movies are not for children, yet children love the movies such as *Sarah, Plain & Tall*. "We're not family movies, per se. There are adult issues in that movie, and our programs are really geared to adult women. From time to time, though, we'll have something children will really love." Among its many awards, in fact, Hallmark has won Emmy award for Outstanding Achievement in Children's Programming.

Most of the Hallmark movies are geared toward adults, but they are always appropriate for all family members to watch. "We never include anything offensive in our movies," assures Brad. "It takes more creativity to keep an adult-oriented movie wholesome and entertaining, but we have great people who make that value a reality in all our films."

SEEK TO BUILD BRIDGES

One of Hallmark's values is enriching relationships, or bridge building. In *Blackwater Lightship*, a recent Hallmark movie, three generations of women—a grandmother, mother, and daughter—have been estranged for many years and are brought back into relationship through the crisis of a family member dying of AIDS. "I had a minister call me and say, 'This last movie is the best one you've ever done. It's all about grace, reconciliation, and understanding.'" The movie takes no position on the gay lifestyle, however, it does convey a strong message about the need to love and support one another, regardless of our differences.

Blackwater Lightship recently won the Ribbon of Hope award for HIV awareness. Angela Lansbury, who starred in the movie, introduced Brad to an audience of a thousand people last month, where he shared how the grace-filled nature of the movie had served to unite, rather than divide various factions. "These are the values our organization espouses," said Brad, "and our team works together to this end."

Step One: Get the Right Idea

At Hallmark Hall of Fame, about four or five creative and business-minded principals work together to develop each idea. Then they present it to the Hall Family, the chairman, president, and a couple of other decision-makers. "We review the idea first. If they agree it deserves to be part of the series—in other words, fulfilling the series' values of quality, taste, and enriching relationships—plus being very entertaining, then we'll hire somebody to write the script. We get the best writers in the business. We've accepted one already-written script in the past twenty years, and even then, we went through a number of rewrites. We've made the rest from scratch. For a while in the 1970s and early 1980s, the series struggled because we were taking things others had developed, and often had to settle for the least objectionable material out there. We realized we needed to step back and start baking from scratch. For the first twenty years, everything was baked from scratch, and we've returned to that for the past twenty years."

Step Two: Use Talented Writers

Hallmark hires the best writers for each genre. "You know who the good writers are," says Brad. "It's no secret. We look for the A-list writers. Sometimes, we also work with the writers of the source material—i.e., the original book or play, and get them to write the screenplay, even though they may have never written a screenplay before."

On one project, the company worked with the well-known playwright August Wilson, whose Pulitzer-prize-winning play, *The Piano Lesson,* Hallmark wanted to produce for the Hallmark Hall of Fame. "While the play itself included profanity and dramatized various situations we wouldn't put in our movies, we thought the underlying story was powerful, so we asked him if he would be willing to modify his work according to our needs. Three years later, after a lot of collaboration, we had a script that had eliminated large amounts of text from the original work—about an hour's worth. Obviously, a three-hour play must be cut down for a two-hour television program. After the production of the movie was completed, Brad asked August Wilson, "What's missing?" "Nothing's missing," the famous writer replied without hesitation . . . and there wasn't. All of the powerful elements had been retained.

The hardest part of movie making is getting a great idea and creating a great script, says Brad. "It often takes a number of rewrites. It can be a lengthy process to get it just right. One project actually took over twelve years to finish. The shortest has been twelve months from hearing the story idea, to getting the script written, to going on air."

Step Three: Get it Greenlighted

When they're happy with the script, Brad and his associates will take it to the Hallmark owners. "They read every script. We'll have a short meeting, and if they say yes, we'll move forward, and the next time the owners see it will be on national television. That's pretty amazing, by the way. It's probably the most straightforward, streamlined approval process in the movie and television business. When other people in the industry hear about it, well, they usually just don't believe it." If the Hallmark owners like a movie, they're decisive about green-lighting it. "There's no nit-picking," says Brad. "Like I say, I've got the best job in the business."

Step Four: Hire the Crew and Actors

The production company has a small number of employees in their Kansas City office, about six, plus about fifteen to twenty people who work full time on the West coast, but it's primarily a freelance business. "During the course of making each movie we'll hire a hundred to two hundred people. Some work only at the beginning, such as the casting director and location scouts, and others, such as a film editor and music composer, would work only at the end. Some work almost the entire time. Just like an actor is not our employee per se, so it is for the director, technicians, and all the cast and crew. Each is hired freelance for the specific movie being produced. It takes about six months of production time, from hiring the first people to wrapping it all up."

It begins with hiring an executive producer, producer, and director, who in turn oversee all the aspects including casting, location scouting, filming, editing, post-production, and music.

Hallmark tries to hire the best for every spot because they value excellence. "People will sometimes hold their time open for us. Even actors and crew people who wouldn't consider themselves conservative will come up and say, 'Thank you for letting me be a part of this. I can show my mother, or my wife and kids this movie. Some of the things I work on I'm just not proud of at all, but I can tell my friends and family I worked on this one.'" Brad finds that people value their relationship with the Hallmark Hall of Fame. Having talented people thank him is another reason he's got the best job in the business.

It's not unusual for a Hallmark movie production budget to be in the ballpark of six to ten million dollars. "Plus, we have to buy the airtime, produce the commercials, and pay for publicity efforts and advertising—to invite people to watch. The movie itself is just part of the process."

Step Five: Going to Air

Finding distribution is not a problem for the Hallmark Hall of Fame. In fact, Hallmark has an exclusive arrangement with CBS wherein the network will always take and air the Hallmark Hall of Fame movies. "We've promised them four movies a year, and they hold the time slots for us. It's really a good partnership," says Brad. "Les Moonves, Chairman and CEO of CBS, a big fan of the Hallmark Hall of Fame Series and one of the most successful executives in Hollywood, actually produced a movie for us earlier in his career. Les is clearly one of the most influential people in all of television. In 1992, he did a movie *Oh Pioneers* with Jessica Lang with us, producing it for us when he was running Lorimar, part of Warner Bros. When he joined CBS in 1995, we said, 'Why don't we bring you the Hallmark movie line, exclusive to CBS, and here's what we'd want in return.' Before he even showed up at CBS, originally as president of CBS Entertainment, he had a news conference and announced our partnership."

During most of the first thirty years of the series, the Hallmark Hall of Fame programs aired on NBC. "We aired one program at a time, but we didn't have an exclusive arrangement. For the next ten years, we were on all three major networks—CBS, NBC, and ABC, but predominantly on CBS." Then in 1995, the company made its first exclusive agreement with CBS. The movies almost always run on a Sunday night. Now, all Hallmark Hall of Fame movies also go to DVD and video, which are sold exclusively at

Hallmark stores.

Incidentally, Hallmark Card, Inc. also owns the majority of the Hallmark Channel, a national cable network available in about sixty million households. "It's a very successful channel." The Hallmark Channel airs the Hallmark Hall of Fame movies and other quality shows like *Mash, Little House on the Prairie, Touched by an Angel,* and *Perry Mason,* in addition to originally produced programs and series.

BE REALISTIC

Though Brad tells us with a smile that he has the best job in the world, it is clear that his feet are planted firmly on the ground of reality. "Though there are a few glamorous aspects, this is not a glamorous business," says Brad. "It's hard, and it's real work. As a matter of fact, I can't even drag my wife to the Emmys anymore," Brad laughs. "She'd rather watch at home, curled up in a comfortable chair. The business is filled with all kinds of people, just like other businesses. For the most part, though, I've had the privilege of working with hard-working, creative people and fundamentally nice people.

"I just want to be clear that movie making is hard, hard work, and there's a lot of rejection in the business. You have to know how to take it—of yourself or your ideas. A lot of times you don't get the job, or land the deal, or get your idea accepted, and you run into a lot of folks who sincerely have a different worldview than yours. It can be tough, but if you're drawn to it, it's also extremely rewarding. If you have purpose, resources, and support, you can make it, and I wish you well."

ALWAYS APPRECIATE A GOOD SITUATION

Brad's final thoughts centered on the company he so obviously appreciates. "Hallmark's avowed, stated purpose is "enriching lives." Our owners, our business purpose, the kinds of products we make, and the way those products help people share and connect with each other make me feel fortunate to be doing what I'm doing. Do I really have the best job in the movie business? I think it even goes beyond that. After all, there's no better company than Hallmark—in any business, and I have the best job at Hallmark."

Audiences look forward, now with much greater insight, to the next great series of Hallmark Hall of Fame movies.

* * *

SUCCESS, STEP 1:
PRODUCING YOUR MOVIE

The following steps will take us through the production process involved in producing a hypothetical movie from idea through follow up. The assumptions made throughout this process will guide you through the basic principles and techniques of a typical production. Each of the chapters that follow in Section II will focus on one or more steps starting with step two because the first step involves the foundational questions.

1. Reviewing Your Choice of Theatrical Movie.

To reach your decision to produce a movie, you had to work through the appropriate ascertainment questions, discern your talents, target your audience, formulate your communication, determine your genre, and choose your medium—motion picture for theatrical distribution. You decided that you are called to communicate the gospel to a mass audience, and that you have the motivation and talents to do so.

At first, you may have considered communicating through a television interview program, but realized that genre would limit your audience because television is best suited to communicating stories, whatever form they take: commercials, reality-TV, variety, contests, and sports. Lack of audience appeal has caused television executives to relegate most public affairs programs to poorly watched time periods, PBS, or certain cable television channels.

Producing your program for a secondary time period or PBS would limit the size of your targeted audience. (PBS offers advantages if you are targeting professionals.)

You may have considered producing a commercial, but you decided that genre did not give you the broad impact you wanted and ten, thirty, or sixty seconds was not enough time to logically present your communication. Sports, contests, and variety programs did not give you the logical, emotive power you wanted. Although your communication was good news, it did not lend itself to a current events format. Therefore, you decided to use a story genre, a movie.

2. Transform Your Story into a Script and a Treatment.

Once you have decided to produce a movie, you have to secure the rights to a good story and transform your story in a great script. Since the story and script is the foundation of your movie, the subject is covered in Chapter 4. Either you need to turn your story into a script or hire a scriptwriter to do so, assuming that you did not start out with a script.

3. "Rights," Financing and Your Access to Distribution.

Once you decide to produce a movie the question arises, how are you going to get your movie distributed? This question should be answered before you go to the trouble and expense of producing your movie. Your answer may change your mind about producing a movie, or will affect how you produce your movie.

Pre-Production
4. Breakdown, Budget, Schedule, and Timetable Your Production.

As soon as you have a story, you should have it broken down so you can start estimating the cost of producing your movie. The distributor, networks, and the financiers will ask you how much your movie will cost to produce. Before you go to a movie studio/ distributor, you turn your story into a script and prepare a budget based on that script, unless you are seeking development funds to prepare a script, in which case you need to budget the development funds you need.

5. Storyboard and Plan Your Production.

So that you can accurately plan your production, turn your script into a rough storyboard that you will want to revise and prefect as you proceed. A storyboard is a visual representation of the script as a series of sketches that can be very rough (using stick figures) or very detailed.

6. Bring Your Key Above-the-line Talent on Board.

Your above-the-line talent will be determined to a degree by whom you need to bring on board to make your production bankable. What big names, or talent with track records, will cause a major movie studio or private capital to finance your production? Sometimes all you need is one star. Sometimes a director will make your production bankable. Often, you will have to join forces with a co-producer, who may end up with the credit. Of course, getting mega-talents is close to impossible, but look for talent who appreciate the type of movie that you are producing and are available.

7. Finalize Your Script and Organize Inserts. (This Is Primarily for Television.)

With your key talent, finalize your script. Then working from your final script, obtain or arrange for graphics, photography, film, stock shots, film clips, properties, and everything that needs to be in your production.

8. Cast and Staff.

Casting is critical, and so is below-the-line staffing. Be selective. Be careful.

9. Organizing Artistic and Technical Services and Facilities.

Production

10. Rehearsals. (This Is Primarily for Television.)

At this point, you will start rehearsing your cast and crew.

11. Camera and Other Scripts.

Prepare breakdown sheets and other scripts.

12. Prepare Studio and Locations.

All too often, studios are rented and the personnel rushed in to produce the program, only for the producer and director to find that the studio is not prepared to do the type of production work which is required. You, your producer, and your director should meet with the studio to confirm the availability of everything that is essential to your production, i.e., space, equipment, back up facilities, crew, storage space, time to set up, technical equipment, dressing rooms, green room, etc.

13. Camera Blocking and Equipment Preparation.

Before your production starts, you need to know what you want your camera, sound, and other equipment to do, and when and how.

14. Run Through and Final Rehearsal. (This Is Primarily for television.)

Run through your script to remove any kinks and timing problems.

15. Location Production.

If you have planned carefully for shooting on location, things should go well.

16. Studio Production.

17. Cast Party.

Establish a good rapport with your cast. Plan to work together again. Be supportive.

Post-Production, Distribution, and Beyond

18. Music and Sound.

Music and sound effects will make or break a movie or television production.

19. Editing.

You will want to spend a great deal of time off-line reviewing your production.

20. Review.

Does your program work? Re-edit if necessary.

21. Distribution/Sales.

You are ready to distribute.

22. Follow Up.

Check the ratings, promotion, advertising, and any payments and billings that are due.

Having set forth most of the steps in a production, let's hear from one of the best what it is all about. In May 2003, everyone from toddlers to grandparents, and all those in between, lined up at the box office to purchase tickets for *Finding Nemo*. From the very first scene, audiences were captivated by the breathtakingly beautiful, realistic animation and the heart-warming story of the love of a worried fish-dad for his son. The movie was the first "perfect" family movie ever to be made according to one Movieguide reviewer—with no offensive elements in it, but rather an entertaining, captivating, hilarious story filled with memorable characters from the sea.

One of the most memorable characters was the turtle dad named Crush, with his hilarious "surfer-dude" accent. Little do some audiences know, however, that the man who voiced Crush was also the man who wrote and directed *Finding Nemo*. Below Andrew Stanton shares with us some of his wisdom and experience in his exciting industry of animated filmmaking.

FIND YOUR TRUE VOICE—WRITE IT, DRAW IT, AND LIVE IT!
—AN INTERVIEW WITH ANDREW STANTON

EDUCATE YOURSELF WITH THE BEST

Andrew went to school in Los Angeles at the California Institute for the Arts, or "Cal Arts," as they say. "It was kind of a *Fame* school, where you could take dance, film, theatre, and all the arts. I attended the Character Animation Department branch of the film school, founded by Walt Disney himself. Here, I learned to draw Mickey like everyone else with simple pencil drawings. I stayed very focused and lucked out to get some good employment after graduation."

Prior to his work with Pixar, Andrew did several years of moving around to various agencies, employers, and free-lance projects, learning the business in many varied hands-on forums. "I had made some short student films that did well in local festivals. As a matter of fact, in one of the festivals, John Lassiter was showing his *Tin Toy* short. I got to know him and soon ended up working for him at Pixar."

FIND A FABULOUS COMPANY

When asked about his company, Andrew Stanton says it's truly hard not to love Pixar. "This company is so unique. People don't believe me. It's like film school with all the teachers gone. We have the run of the place! It feels like you're still in film school making things you'd like to do for your own pleasure, or your own family." Andrew also appreciates the fact that Pixar is located outside of San Francisco, far removed from the rat race of Hollywood. "When we go home, there's no one we socialize with in the movie business. It keeps us grounded, and it keeps our creativity fresh. When we go back to work on Monday, it still feels like a privilege to make a movie. Nobody here is jaded."

FIND A CREATIVE, COHESIVE TEAM

Most of the employees at Pixar attended the same school, Cal Arts, and most find that working at Pixar is very much like going to art school. "It's a wild and expressive atmosphere, and we work as hard as we play. We know our people put in a lot of hours and that these guys don't need pushing to give two hundred percent. Everyone's basically an artsy 'Type A' personality—creative and driven." Andrew believes that on every project, it's all about the team.

MAKE THEM ALL YOUR FAVORITES!

Andrew and his associates at Pixar do seem to give two hundred percent on every project, and every movie has the look and feel of detailed professionalism. For that reason, it was tough for Andrew to decide which movie was his favorite.

"Oh, don't ask me that!" he moaned. "It's like picking your favorite child. My favorite movie is all five of the Pixar movies I've worked on." (Thanks, Andrew . . . that narrows it right down.) Andrew started out in animation and worked his way into the story sector. He was the screenwriter on *Toy Story 1 & 2, A Bug's Life, Monsters, Inc.* and *Finding Nemo*, the co-director of *A Bug's Life*, and the director of *Finding Nemo*, all of which bear his distinct mark in the areas of animation, humor, and style.

WWJD?

In the area of personal faith, Andrew has his own distinct style as well. "My personal view is that if you go into things on a pulpit or with an agenda in the creative world, it can easily get in the way of your creativity and quality. I'm more from the school of 'practice what you preach,' rather than 'preach what you practice." Be Christ-like in everything you do, not worrying about whether you're furthering the cause. I just have a lot of faith that this happens to be my spiritual gift: family entertainment. I put a lot of trust in what my heart is telling me to do, and I go with my instincts—not second-guessing what the industry or my audience wants or doesn't want."

RESIST PEOPLE-PLEASING

One of Andrew's top values is that the artist finds his true voice and doesn't pander to the pressures of the industry. "If you're out to people-please, to satisfy some imaginary public, its not your true voice, and people will sense that. Audiences want something of truth and value, something honest and personal, with a clear voice. It's easy to fall into a trap if you come out here with a spiritual agenda. Just give it up to God and say, 'OK, I'm going to go with something I'd like to see on the screen,' and it'll work." Clearly, real live audiences can attest to the fact that it's worked for Andrew and his team.

LET IT FLOW FROM WITHIN

Many movie clubs throughout the nation have analyzed Pixar's films, and some have pointed out that they use spiritual, allegorical truths and portrayals, such as the father in *Finding Nemo,* who seems to represent the pursing heart of God for his lost children, and the little forgetful fish, Dory, who seems to represent a guiding angel. When asked about how intentional these portrayals were, Andrew thinks for a moment. "In *Finding Nemo,* I was being as honest as I could be, and I just wrote. Some of the truths in the movie were intentional, and some were not. Definitely the protagonist's battle was to overcome fear by discovering faith, and certainly Dory represented the angel, or the helper who showed him how to let go and not be consumed by his worries. If you're truthful (and entertaining) with these elements, then they capture the audience. People can see their own personality quirks through an animated creature, and that makes a movie so universally relatable."

CHARACTER COUNTS

Throughout his experience in the industry, Andrew has found that honesty is the best policy, a character trait that's hard to stick to in filmmaking, it seems. "Many things are not constructed around real honesty in this industry, but you have to risk your job and your seemingly existing friendships to say what needs to be said sometimes. It's an art to know when to speak and when not to. I've never ever been in a situation at Pixar where I couldn't say what needs to be said. . . . After a while, people trust that you're always giving them the real answer."

Andrew also values the ability to stand alone, when necessary. "Most of this industry is run like a monarchy. There's a studio head, a boss, or a director with a big mandate. Someone's king, and everyone else is running around doing whatever it takes to make the king happy. Well, it's not about the king; it's about making the best movie possible. That should be the basis of all decisions, not politics. People should ask, 'Is this best for the movie?' not 'Is this best for me and my agenda?'"

Andrew is convinced that if people are always making decisions based on what's best for the movie, it will be hard to go wrong. "I'm fortunate to be surrounded by a ton of people who think like that. Nobody's going to get mad at you if you've made the movie better, no matter what you've done."

KEEP THE BAR HIGH

The people at Pixar work hard to keep their movies fun and entertaining—and question the use of offensive material. They even performed an experiment with *Finding Nemo*—which was trying to write a movie without a villain. "It's hard to come up with a villain that's not cliché or melodramatic. I'm much more fascinated with real conflicts, and I try to see if I can make an analogy in the fantasy world . . . There are very few "intentional villains" in life—maybe Hitler, but most bad guys think they're truly doing something good. It can be complex. In *Finding Nemo,* even the most feared thing in the ocean—the sharks—weren't truly villains. They were just being themselves and trying to better themselves."

BE REALISTIC IN DETERMINING TALENT

Talent is not fair, believes Andrew. "Everyone seems to understand this in sports," he says. "Just because you really, really want to play baseball, you don't get to go play for the Yankees. Some, with lots of dedication and time can overcome their amateur status and get into something professional, but that's a very small gene pool. Even if you do make it, someone will always do it better. You've gotta make peace with that fact before you get into the movie business. Talent is not fair."

Andrew does add that there's something that everybody is insanely good at; they just have to search it out. And, he believes that others will spot true talent; one just has to find trusted people who will be honest with them, perhaps a family member.

STAY TEACHABLE

"I'm a learn-aholic," Andrew confesses. "And, I got it from my dad. My father used to even correct the questions on my homework. I'm always listening, reading, getting advice, and learning—even when I think I've mastered it. Since I've been here, John Lasseter's been a real influence. He makes everyone feel they are an essential element to the success of the film. He finds the unique thumbprint of each artist and capitalizes on that, bringing it to the forefront on every project."

DON'T SHRINK BACK IN FEAR

Despite its challenges, and despite the fact that one must have recognized talent to make it, Andrew is clear that Hollywood is not the den of iniquity some people think it is. "You're going into the lion's den whenever you walk out of the house—no matter what the industry. Jesus spent much of His time with murderers, tax collectors, and even a prostitute. Living your life as a good example of integrity and compassion amongst people of other faiths and beliefs is a better service than shunning them or their ideas from a lofty moral platform. Remember that it's not a bad thing that you're around questionable people and weird situations. . . It'll keep you sharp. And actually, there's a lot more people of faith than you think in Hollywood."

And, how wonderful it was to interview such a man of faith, so skilled in the movie industry and so influential in the American family! We can't wait for the next Pixar movie!

* * *

To produce a movie or a television program, you have to be creative, self-disciplined, organized, unstructured, persistent, flexible, imaginative, and practical. As a rule of thumb, fifty percent of your energy will be expended doing the work of producing your program. Another fifty percent will be expended fighting for your production. If this seems overwhelming to you, just remember to trust God, and you will succeed in producing a powerful program telling the story He has given you to tell.

This overview of the techniques and principles that apply to producing a movie is applicable to your production no matter what size, but smaller productions will require less of everything. If you are embarking on producing a video on your church, review the steps necessary for a movie or television program and select those principles and techniques that are relevant to your production. By familiarizing yourself with the most complex form of production, you will excel in simpler productions, including productions in other audio-visual media.

An excellent exercise is to assemble a group from your church and produce a movie in miniature with amateur equipment. If you take care to follow all the appropriate steps, you will end up with a successful production. If not, you will know it because of the glaring flaws in your final product. Having trained many communicators, I have found that such an exercise is the most effective way to learn about the nature of the media of movies and television.

Try it. Have fun and apply yourself to achieving excellence, in His service.

· 8 ·

The Art of the Deal

SUCCESS, STEP 2:
RIGHTS, FINANCING, AND ACCESS TO
DISTRIBUTION

Once you decide to produce a movie, the next question you should ask is, "How are you going to get your movie distributed?" This question should be answered before you go to the trouble and expense of producing your movie. Your answer may change your mind about producing a movie or may affect how you produce your movie.

This question involves rights and financing, two of the basic building materials of movies.

Every year around nine hundred movies are rated by the Motion Picture Association of America (MPAA), but less than three hundred make it to your local theater. Furthermore, for over seventy-five years, seven major studios that own and control the MPAA have controlled theatrical distribution in spite of mega-anomalies like *The Passion of the Christ*, *My Big Fat Greek Wedding*, and *The*

Blair Witch Project. Although these studios have been releasing about 120 to 140 movies per year for several years, they often control around ninety-eight percent of the box office net or distributor's gross. That means that the sixty percent of the movies that are released by truly independent distributors usually earn less than two percent of the box office.

In the entertainment industry, there is a very tight concentration of power in the hands of a few executives, producers, and agents who make it very difficult for a producer, with no track record to break into the movie business.

With regard to television, the major networks have to fill twenty thousand hours of programming time every year and need new ideas to capture and hold their audience. On the other hand, there is also a tight concentration of power in the hands of a few producers, agents, and network executives who have very little contact with religion and make it very difficult for a producer with no track record to break into the network program schedule.

For forty years, a religious program producer had reasonable, though difficult, access to the networks because they scheduled a certain amount of religious programming as part of their obligation to operate "in the public interest, convenience and necessity."[104] Since the late 1970s, the Federal Communications Commission has been relaxing the public interest obligations of broadcasters. Therefore, to get on the air today you have to sell the networks on your concept, convince them that they should air material with religious content, and/or buy airtime.

At this point, you may decide to reconsider producing a movie for theatrical release or a major television network. You could retarget your audience and use a medium that is easier to access, such as cable television, PBS, independent television, or Christian television.

You should not aim for theatrical distribution unless that is the right medium for you and your communication. However, if your communication demands the most prestigious release in the entertainment industry, and you have the patience and stamina to go for it, you can get a distributor or even get your program on the air, with God's help. Movies like *The Passion of the Christ*, *The Chronicles of Narnia: The Lion, the Witch and the Wardrobe*, *Prince Caspian and The Voyage of the Dawn Treader*, *Fireproof*, *The Blind Side*, *Gods and Generals*, and *The Lord of the Rings* trilogy; and television programs like *Hallmark Hall of Fame*, *Doc*, *7th Heaven*, and *Sue Thomas: F.B.Eye*, are good examples of entertainment with strong Christian content.

The more you understand the entertainment industry, the more likely you will be to succeed. What follows are brief snapshots of aspects of the entertainment industry that will help you avoid some common mistakes or help you choose between your several options.

Movie Studios Are Financing, Production and Distribution Companies.

Once upon a time, once a month for several years, I brought together a group of wealthy investors who were united in their desire to make movies in order to help them understand the entertainment industry. Each month, they were introduced to a top executive or a top talent in the entertainment industry. During one of these meetings, one investor asked the president of a major movie studio if the investor brought the studio a great movie that would cost the studio $100 million to make, but only cost the investor and his team $10 million, would the president want to distribute his movie. The president asked, "Why would we want that?" The investor said, "To make more profit." The president asked, "Why would we want that?" Then the president added, "If you want to make movies, we will set you up with an office on the studio lot, which costs ten times more to rent per foot than it would across the street. And we will sell you supplies from the studio store for ten times more than you could buy them outside the studio store. Then we will assign you movies that we agree to produce and use your money to produce them." The investors were overjoyed at the opportunity. I told the investors that what they didn't understand is that a movie studio is in part a production company. As such, the studio writes off some of its tremendous overhead in the $100 million movie production budget. If the investor produces the movie outside of the studio, the studio cannot write off its sound stages, shops, personnel, utilities, etc. Therefore, the studio is interested in movies being made within the system, even if those movies are filmed in Hollywood, New Zealand or Canada, so that the costs of the production covers its un-fair share of the overhead of the studio.

Producers with Movie Studios Resemble Sharecroppers.

As the president noted to our investors group, if you come to work with the studio, you pay the studio for everything. After the Civil War, many plantations substituted sharecropping for slavery. Instead of providing food and lodging for the slaves, no matter how meager, the plantation rented the new sharecroppers their shacks and all the equipment the sharecroppers needed to farm the plantation. When the harvest was brought for sale to the plantation silo or warehouse, the price for the harvest was paid after deducting all that was owed for the shack, all the farming equipment, and the supplies that were leased to the sharecropper. Often, this meant that the sharecropper got practically nothing in return for his labor. Producers for the studios are often in the same position. The producer rents his office space, pays for the development of his movie or television program, and leases all his equipment from the studio. When the box office returns arrive, all these costs are deducted, often leaving the producer in debt.

Hollywood Doesn't Need Your Money.

The major studios not only produce movies—they also finance them and place the financing for them with banks and institutional investors. As of this writing, the average Hollywood movie costs $104 million to produce and distribute. When an outsider comes into Hollywood thinking that the studios need his money, he is usually treated as a dude from the east, a greenhorn or naïf who will soon be parted from his money by the studio that does not need it. The history of Hollywood is filled with brilliant, wealthy outsiders who lost a lot of money and left in disgrace. Joe Kennedy became infatuated with a starlet, was fleeced by Hollywood, made some rotten movies, and hightailed it back to Boston to rebuild his fortune so he could eventually bankroll his son J.F. Kennedy's run for U.S. President. The brilliant Howard Hughes lost bundles of money and acquired syphilis in exchange for all his efforts. Billionaire Kirk Kerkorian lost MGM twice and told the press that he never knew what went wrong. The list of others burned by Hollywood's manipulation goes on and on. On February 29, 2004, a *Los Angeles Times* article entitled "Chew. Spit. Repeat. The Movie Industry Consumes Carpetbagging Investors Like Prime-Cut Steak. What's the Appeal of Being Eaten Alive?" by Patrick J. Kiger, exposed the treatment of wealthy outsiders:

> 'We don't go for strangers,' spoke one of F. Scott Fitzgerald's characters in the writer's final, unfinished Hollywood novel. But he didn't get it completely right. The Industry likes interlopers just fine—as long as they empty their wallets and don't overstay their welcome. That scenario has been repeated in Hollywood almost as often as the two-unlikely-cops-become-wisecracking-crime-fightin'-buddies action thriller. An outsider, flush with success in some other industry or bankrolled by a family fortune, bursts onto the scene with dreams of becoming the next Louis B. Mayer, only to slink away a year or three later in ignominious defeat. The most recent, high-profile examples—Messier and Edgar Bronfman Jr., the Seagram heir whose Hollywood ambitions were intertwined with Vivendi's—are only the latest in a

series that goes back to the early days of Hollywood, when sharpies such as William Randolph Hearst and Joe Kennedy came West to get their pockets picked . . .

Since then, scores of other West Coast carpetbaggers have met with varying degrees of failure—old-line industrialists, Wall Street financiers, insurance conglomerates and corporate raiders, New Economy wunderkinds from this country, plus Dutch, Japanese, British, Italian, and Israeli hopefuls, But with few exceptions, such as Australian media baron Rupert Murdoch, the movie industry has chewed up and spit out newcomers like hunks of Morton's prime-cut steak . . .

Why do all these powerful, wealthy alpha males venture out of their comfy enclaves and plunge into an utterly unfamiliar, notoriously Byzantine business that they often approach with distain and condescension? What sort of mass-induced hypnotic state convinces a German investor, for example, that it's a sensible idea to sink millions into a film homage to L. Ron Hubbard's "Battlefield Earth"? . . . Is there some sort of semiotic explanation for why otherwise astute people from another culture—whether it's Amsterdam or Peoria—get hopelessly tangled up in movie industry lingo and end up mumbling about 'synergy' after that disastrous first-cut screening?

. . . 'Outsiders who've been very successful and made a lot of money rightly think they're smarter than the average person and perhaps even somewhat creative,' explains Roderick Kramer, a onetime Hollywood script reader who is a professor of organizational behavior at Stanford University's graduate business school, where he also teaches a course on the movie industry for MBA students. . . .

Unfortunately, the world's dream factory, by its very nature, doesn't quite work that way. And it could be that even the business world's richest and smartest minds are helpless to resist a fate that may be determined, in part, by our genes. . . .

Instead of locking horns like real bulls, the in-group may resort to trickery and exploitation. 'The in-group members may look at the outsider and think, "I'm not going to have reciprocal relations with this person in the future, because he's not going to be allowed to stay." So instead they go after whatever he's got that's of value.'

. . . 'The most important thing is [your] knowledge base, the contacts that give you "reputational capital,"' Kramer says. 'That's what gets you in. An outsider has a lot of trouble breaking into that kind of network, because outside money and power aren't going to trump those connections. They don't really have time for you. The ones who are willing to let you into a network are the ones who are less reliable, the ones who are out to take advantage. Because the only thing an outsider brings to the network is money—while he still has it.' . . .

'They don't do the same sort of traditional business analysis that they would if they were entering, say, the machine-tool business,' says Dartmouth College business school professor Sydney Finkelstein, author of the book, *Why Smart Executives Fail.* 'Then again, when you're making machine tools, you're not seduced by the idea of sitting in the audience with a bunch of movie stars at the Academy Awards. Instead, you get seduced by the glamour, and it screws you up'. . . .

From an empirical point of view, though, an outsider would have to be totally insane to try the movie industry in particular, because the economic model is bizarrely different from just about any other business. The movie industry actually earns only a 3% to 4% return on investment, which is lousy when compared with steel-making or book publishing . . .

To make it worse, the statistical curve for movie profits isn't much of a curve at all. If the movie industry followed a bell curve, the typical movie would make money, and it would be extremely rare for a movie to take in more than three times the standard deviation—the average amount that the films differ from the middle. Instead, it's shaped more like a playground slide—6% of the product earns 90% of the money, and 70% to 80% of the product sinks into oblivion. This results in what economist De Vany calls an industry of 'extreme uncertainty.' That is, successes are aberrantly rare and outlandishly enormous. The movie *Titanic*, for example, grossed $600 million domestically in 1997, in a year when the average film grossed $23 million. Results like that are impossible to predict. . . .

Another added complication: Most industries don't have Hollywood's peculiar distribution system, in which a would-be blockbuster suddenly covers most of the nation's movie screens like kudzu and competitors get what's left. That's the equivalent of one brand of microwave oven getting all the shelf space at . . . Target and Wal-Mart for a week, but then disappearing instantly if it doesn't sell. . . .

The carpetbagging mogul usually doesn't realize that until it's too late. Early in his Hollywood misadventure, William Randolph Hearst was so confident that he brushed off Adolph Zukor's offer of management help. 'Making pictures is fundamentally like making publications,' proclaimed Hearst, who orchestrated such flops as 1933's *Going Hollywood*, in which Marion Davies starred with Bing Crosby—an unfortunate bit of casting because the two shared an interest in alcohol and spent much of their time on the set intoxicated. The movie lost $250,000. Just a few years later, Hearst was ready to quit the movie business, despairing: 'I don't think I can make any money at it.'

. . . Stripped of his competence and confidence, the outsider is vulnerable. Stuart Fischoff, a sometime screenwriter and professor of media psychology at Cal State L.A., compares the process by which outsiders get sucked in by the Hollywood culture to cult recruiting or North Korean prison camp brainwashing. The would-be mogul is 'brutalized and humiliated, then infantilized and reduced to a helpless state, and then introduced to the new set of values,' Fischoff says. . . . Language also can be a problem for outsiders . . . 'The language of Hollywood is so filled with hyperbole that you have to be able to decode it,' behavior expert Kramer explains. 'Otherwise, you don't pick up that when a guy tells you that your project is fantastic and it'll be exciting to work with you, he really means that he's going to tell his assistant not to put through any more of your calls.'

In a follow up article entitled "Bitten by the Movie Bug" (Kiger), the Los Angeles Times listed the common delusional defenses of the investor seduced by Hollywood:

1. Denial: Keep telling yourself that you're the exception to the rule, the outsider who can swim with the sharks.
2. Anger: When you're in that inevitable meeting with backers who've lost faith in your leadership, go ahead and curse the unfairness of it all.

3. Bargaining: Find another naïf from the outside world and convince him that he's smarter than you. Remember that even after Coca-Cola paid more than half a billion dollars for Columbia, it still was able to sell it to Sony for many times that amount.
4. Depression: It's OK to feel a little down in the dumps. Indulge yourself. After Howard Hughes lost RKO, he retreated to a rented studio for four months and sat around naked, watching movies for days without sleep, gobbling junk food and befouling the floor like a caged animal.
5. Acceptance: Hire a ghostwriter to do a defensive memoir. Even if nobody is willing to pay $22.95 to read it, you'll feel much better.

If You Don't Have Money, You're Not a Player

Once upon a time, several of the investors whom I had assembled to learn about the entertainment industry decided to go to the Cannes Film Festival. I had lunch with some of them when they came back. They were derisive of the others who went to Cannes because they did not have a yacht and had to stay in hotels. Thus, the studios pay attention to your financial statues although they do not need your money.

Hollywood is a club.

If you have ever belonged to a club, you know that you can bring your friends and treat them to dinner, but they can't come back to eat the next day if they are not members. Whatever race or creed, they must be members of the club to use the club. Good clubs recognize their members. Hollywood is just such a place.

Hollywood is a poker game.

Literally, the top studio executives have weekly poker games where they share information and discuss the entertainment industry. If you are not in the game, well, . . . you are an outsider.

Hollywood is the lawless wild, wild West.

While a millionaire was buying a famous movie studio, his lawyer was selling the studio's assets to a competing studio that the lawyer in question also represented. The lawyer would be disbarred in any other area of the country for doing this, but no one tackles the ethics of Hollywood because the media shapes the culture and elects the politicians.

Hollywood is a family.

For years, Hollywood executives have hired their family and friends to fill the key roles at the studios. The non-family members are the exception rather than the rule.

Hollywood is the dream factory.

The entertainment industry gives us our dreams. America, in contrast, was founded on a vision of freedom, justice, and property ownership for each and every person. For the last hundred years, the Hollywood dream has been replacing the American Vision. Perhaps, we should wake up to Proverbs 29:18: "Where there is no vision, the people perish" (KJV).

Hollywood's Glass Ceilings

The entertainment industry has many different invisible barriers and glass ceilings. Minorities and women often complain that they may be hired as window dressing on the set (as actors or on-air anchors), but they have very little power in the boardroom. Other barriers are the implicit assumptions that: television producers, actors, and crew can't do movies; commercial talent can't do television or movies; and industrial talent can't do commercials, television or movies. Of course, there are exceptions, but built-in biases impose invisible barriers on the "lesser" genre of the mass media of entertainment.

Hollywood Development Hell Is "Yes, We Will Look at Your Project."

The entertainment industry does not produce widgets or gadgets such as mousetraps. If they did, then producing a better widget, gadget, or mousetrap would bring great success. Instead, the entertainment industry is the dream factory, and dreams are ephemeral. Who can evaluate which dream will sell this year? The major studios have spent billions trying to ascertain what dreams the moviegoer wants to buy, only to be frustrated when the requisite movie is produced and no one wants to see it. Therefore, the entertainment industry executives are always concerned that the next big dream will pass them by—or that they will back a dud. To avoid making a tough decision on a project that could go either way, the executive will often say that they will look at the project and then let it languish in "development hell." As long as they have the project, you cannot go anywhere else with it, so you are trapped unless you can figure out a way to push it forward.

Don't Try to Bluff a Hollywood Insider

One studio head said that they were seriously considering picking up for distribution an independent movie from a person of faith. The executive asked the young independent how much the movie cost to make. The independent inflated the budget. The executive walked, telling the independent that he made movies everyday and knew exactly what the independent's movie cost so who was the independent trying to fool?

Don't Stoop to Conquer Hollywood

The movies that do best at the box office are not those with sex and violence, but those with faith and values. One studio executive said that he was talking with a person who obviously came from the faith community who pitched a movie with sex and violence. Evidently the young producer thought that he needed to put in sex and violence to sell his project. The executive walked, telling the young person to be true to himself.

Tell Hollywood Your Story

Every story has its own logic. A movie about faith triumphing over adversity must show that faith triumphs. If it waters down the faith element, the story will be diluted. While many people will tell you not to preach, (which is good advice), the other side of that coin is that you must tell the story the way the premise demands. Otherwise, it will not make sense. Many movies by people of faith have been lackluster or mediocre not because the movie was preachy, but because the movie did not deliver on its premise. One movie about a missionary gave no indication why the missionary would give his life to save the pagan natives who killed him. Thus, the movie made no sense whatsoever. The neophyte Christian producer was trying to hide his light—and he succeed in hiding it—so well, in fact, that no one could make any sense of the movie.

Schadenfreude in Hollywood and the Church

Often in Hollywood, people are happier about someone else's misfortune than about their own success. Beware this demon of envy.

> The Germans have a word for it—schadenfreude the pleasure one takes from the misfortune of others— and in Hollywood it's a way of life. If show business were a religion, its first commandment would be: Instead of enjoying your own success, take pleasure in others' failure. One producer I know used to go around his office chanting "OPMF." Translation: Other people must fail. As Ned Tanen, a former studio chief at Paramount and Universal, once put it: 'The only words you need to know about Hollywood are "negativity" and "illusion." Especially "negativity."
> . . . Why do so many people in Hollywood root for everyone else to fail? You could chalk it up to jealousy and insecurity. You could say it's a telling example of Hollywood's spiritual emptiness. You could blame it on an insular culture that encourages cutthroat competition. Whatever the reason, schadenfreude is deeply imbedded in Hollywood culture. 'This is a town filled

with envy and jealousy,' says *Tomb Raider* producer Larry Gordon, who's been a high-profile force in Hollywood for years. 'You've got two kinds of people—the people who've made it who are angry that they're not more successful and the people who haven't made it who are angry because they think the other guy is a lucky [expletive].' The equation is simple: Power + Success = Envy (Patrick Goldstein, The Big Picture: Where They Root for Failure [*Los Angeles Times*, 2001] Aug 7).

Hollywood is still vulnerable. Even with all the negatives of the Hollywood culture, it must be noted that the entertainment industry is accessible. Mel Gibson proved this with *The Passion of the Christ*. Pixar proved this with great animation. Quality, perseverance, and faithfulness will overcome

More Than Conquerors

As Romans 8:37 KJV tells us, "In all these things we are more than conquerors through him that loved us." Therefore, we do not need to be afraid of going into Hollywood or the lion's den. In fact, the only phrase that is repeated in every book of the Bible is "Do not be afraid." So pursue the vision God has given you with confidence in His grace and do not be afraid. The key to theatrical release and to network television is your story. Not only movies, but according to George Heinemann, former Vice President of NBC, television is also "a once-upon-a-time, storytelling medium." A strong story will help you to convince strong talent with good track records, such as stars, a director, and perhaps a co-producer, to be part of your production. This talent in turn will help you to convince foreign distributors, and cable and independent television to pre-purchase your production, which, in turn, will help you to convince a major movie studio to distribute your movie.

Normally, a major movie studio can only be approached through an agent, such as International Creative Management and the William Morris Agency, although there are those are exceptions where the studios are successfully approached directly because the story is extraordinarily strong. Even an agent will want a strong story or your story will become a dust collector on the shelf. You must believe in your story for good reasons, which you can demonstrate to the agent in no uncertain terms. Agents push what's hot because it is an easier sale to the studios. If you are an unknown commodity, you may have to team up with a known commodity, such as a producer or director with a track record, to break through the psychological barrier at the agency. On the other hand, agents are on the lookout for new talent and saleable new ideas. The key is a saleable story since agents work for money.

With a Strong Story:

1. You can go directly to one of the seven major distributors and have that movie studio finance and distribute your movie. The studio will want to oversee your production at every stage and will want talent who are successful at attracting people to the box office involved in your production. Even so, many producers have found that ultimately it is easier to work with a major studio that will often allow you to insert your faith and values as long as the faith and values are woven into the fabric of the story.

2. If you are considering a television movie instead of approaching a network first, you can go to an advertiser like Hallmark and have that advertiser sponsor your program by buying the air time and by paying for program production. The advertiser will want hot, bankable talent involved in your production, and will want your story to enhance their image and/ or promote the sale of their product. There are more advertisers to approach than networks.

3. You can go to a cable movie channel, such as Home Box Office or Showtime, and have them prepay for the right to air your movie before, or after, it is released in theaters or airs on the network. You can use that prepayment to finance your production, which, once produced, you can try to secure with a distributor. Finished productions have the advantage of being known commodities; unfinished program concepts have the advantage of offering hope in a risk-oriented industry.

4. You can go to foreign television or film companies and have them pre-buy the right to air or distribute your movie in their countries. You can use that presale to finance your production which, once produced, you will try to secure a distributor.

5. You can involve a major, known producer in your production who will put the financing together, co-produce your movie with you, and try to secure a distributor.

6. You can go to a stockbroker, or investment banker, and have your production underwritten. However, stockbroker and investment bankers almost always want a major distributor attached.

7. You can go to friends or acquaintances for private financing to finance all or part of your production.

8. You can go to the church, or denomination, for underwriting to finance or part your production.

9. You can go to the body of believers for donations to finance your production.

10. Of course, you can involve any *combination* of the above sources of financing for part of the production moneys that will help you to secure a major distributor for the remainder of the production moneys. This is a common approach that gives you some bargaining power and control.

11. You can involve any combination of the above non-network sources of financing to such a degree that you can use their money to finance your production and distribute your movie yourself, just as Mel Gibson did with *The Passion of the Christ*.

The story is the key. You can obtain a good story by writing one, hiring someone to write one, or by buying the rights to a book, play, life story, or event (from those who were involved). Here we run into another key, "rights."

Network television, for instance, boils down to rights: the legal right to produce a good story as a television program; of which a known star, and/or director, and/or producer will want the right to a piece of future profits; which the networks will want the right to air to capture an audience to sell to advertisers; on which advertisers will want the right to advertise to sell their products; which foreign stations, cable systems, movie channels, and independents will want the right to play after network television; to which many companies will want the merchandising rights; and, which the public will pay for the right see by buying the advertiser's products.

Rights are the levels of ownership of the story, the pieces of the pie, or shares of future profits, which are bought and sold for money, time, energy, and commitment. Rights determine who owns what and what they can do with what they own.

The Episcopal Radio & Television Foundation[105] had C.S. Lewis record the Episcopal Series of the famous radio Protestant Hour that was broadcast on NBC radio in 1956. Lewis was delighted and gave the right to produce a television program and movie on all seven books of *The Chronicles of Narnia* to the ERTVF. *The Chronicles of Narnia*, which retold the story of the Bible from creation to Revelations in allegorical terms. *The Lion, the Witch and the Wardrobe* was the book in the series that retold the story of on the death and resurrection of Jesus as an allegory. After years of trying to make the movie, The Episcopal Radio & Television

Foundation contacted the president of Kraft foods through the church network of friends, who passed the idea of Kraft sponsoring a television program based on *The Lion, the Witch and the Wardrobe* on to Kraft's advertising agency. The agency suggested involving a co-producer with a track record, so the Episcopal Radio & Television Foundation joined forces with the Children's Television Workshop, who produced *Sesame Street*, by giving them a share of the television rights for producing the program. After a year went by, Kraft decided to sponsor the program by financing the production and buying the right to air the program on CBS. The Children's Television Workshop brought Bill Melendez, who animated "Peanuts" for television, on board as the producer of the animation, and the production was underway. When completed, *The Lion, the Witch and the Wardrobe* aired two years in a row during Easter week on CBS.

SUCCESS, STEP 3: RULES OF THUMB FOR DIVIDING MOVIE RIGHTS AND FUTURE PROFITS [106]

1. You may buy the movie rights from the author for a fee that should be around 2.5% of the production budget and no higher than 5% of the production budget. The author may share in 2.5% to 5% of your profits as producer. If you give the author a larger share, it will kill any deal in Hollywood.

2. You may secure private financing for your production by giving up 50% of your profits.

3. You may secure a big name screenwriter by giving up 2.5% to 5% of your profits plus a fee which should be no more than 2.5% to 5% of your production budget. Many screenwriters require no percentage of your profits. Whether a screenwriter will take a percentage, depends on how much you pay him or her and their reputation.

4. You may secure a big name star by giving up 2.5% to

5% of your profits plus a fee. If you pay enough, you may avoid the percentage.

5. You may secure a big name director by giving up 2.5% to 5% of your profits plus a fee. If you pay enough, you may avoid the percentage.

6. You may secure a big name co-producer by giving up 5% to 25% of your profits plus a fee.

7. You may pre-sell a foreign territory, such as Italy, Germany, or France, by giving up all rights and profits in that territory for a period of time, such as two years or two air plays, whichever comes first. The entertainment industry magazine *Variety* publishes one or more issues every year giving the prices that movies and television programs are getting in different territories. For instance, an A-level movie may get $1 million in Germany, while a B-level may get $500,000. These figures change every year so you should consult *Variety* to get the going prices.

8. You may pre-sell a cable movie channel at $.30 to $.50 per subscriber for a period of time, such as two years or two plays, whichever comes first. If you have a very hot property or "cover" which will be featured on the cover of the movie channel's magazine, then you may receive as much as $7 million if you give the movie channel the exclusive rights to play your television movie two or three times. If your story demands only a demy or half a page in the channel's magazine, then you might expect $4 million if you give the channel two or three exclusive plays. Of course, by the time you read this prices will change.

9. If your property will be a movie before airing on television, then you could secure financing from a major motion picture distributor, such as Paramount or Universal, by agreeing to receive 10% to 30% of

what that distributor receives from the theaters. The theaters often take 50% to 90% off the ticket price for their profit and overhead.

10. If you go to an advertiser, it will want the right to sponsor your program for two to five airplays on television, for the financing. After that, the program is yours.

11. If you go to a network directly, you may receive nothing but a fee and some subsidiary rights to foreign, cable, or merchandising profits.

Remember that though 100% of the producer's profits go to talent and financing, the theaters (or cable channels) take their percentage before the distributor (or movie channel) takes a percentage, with the producer's profits constituting the remainder. The box office receipts for a movie might end up being divided as follows:

$6.00 Box office gross or ticket price (this is a national average that changes every year, with most big cities charging $10)

- $3.00 or 50% for the theater.
= $3.00 Distributor's gross
- $1.50 Prints and advertising
= $1.50 Distributor's Net
- $1.20 or 80% for the distributor
= $0.30 Producer's Gross, which he or she has to divide with the financing, talent, and author.

You may end up giving up all your rights for a small fee that doesn't cover what you spend to buy and develop the property. In most cases, you will not make money on your property/program until it is in its third rerun, or second sale, to the networks, or to independents. To reach the third rerun, the movie must succeed at the box office and must capture a large audience in both of its previous airings.

If you are really dedicated to proclaiming the gospel of Jesus Christ, the amount of money you earn may not make a difference to you, although we are called to be good stewards of the resources He gives us. The most important thing to remember is to retain enough rights to control the production process, and make sure that the rerun is true to your story, despite the changes required by a different medium.

If you own the rights to a story you wrote or a story that is not in itself famous, watch out for similar storylines after you have shared your story with a producer. You cannot copyright an idea, only the particular way you wrote the idea. It is common to see the idea of a good but little known story copied in the entertainment industry with very few changes, and there is practically nothing you can do about it.

The best remedy to this problem is to own the rights to a famous story which would attract such a large audience that that title, property, and story is valuable as such. The other remedy is to register your story with the Writers Guild. This gives you some leverage, but not much. The best defense is a hot property. However, less than ten percent of movies are based on books and true stories—both are very hard to convert into viable dramatic scripts.

Accessing any other medium is easier than accessing the major movie studios and television networks, but you still have to understand the gatekeepers and persuade them that your communication will be a benefit to them and their audience. Research the medium, prepare your pitch, and then talk to them about your movie or television program.

Producer and former Columbia Pictures executive Bill Ewing provides us with important insights into the production process.

FAITH, FLEXIBILITY, AND FOCUS

—an interview with Bill Ewing

Mosquitoes hum eerily and tropical birds squawk their warnings to the cast and crew of a movie now in production on location in

Panama. Crew leads are shouting directions to their subordinates; props people are hammering, nailing, and drilling, and a motor whines as a crane lifts a cameraman high into the air to position him for his next shot. Producer Bill Ewing pauses to give some antibiotic cream to an actor who has cut his toe, the distraction creating an opportune moment for him to talk about his movie. Bill explains that he is making a film based on the feature length documentary he produced called *Beyond the Gates*, the story of an Indian tribe in 1956 that killed five missionaries—including Jim Elliott and Nate Saint. Most evangelical Christians in America have grown up hearing bits and pieces of the Elliott/Saint story, but now Bill Ewing and his cast and crew of hundreds are bringing it to life on the silver screen.

History Makes for Great Drama

Bill Ewing knows that making a movie based on illustrious historical figures is a formula for success. He explains how after Jim and Nate were killed, their wives—Elizabeth Elliott and Rachel Saint—went in and lived with the tribe, hoping to eventually convert them to Christianity. The documentary Bill produced highlights personal interviews from the tribe, the rescue party, and the missionary widows. It also gives Steve Saint's perspective as a young child who lost his father, and it carries the story through to Nate Saint's grandchildren. The feature film, on the other hand, communicates the story and missionary journey from the tribe's point of view. Filmmakers like Bill understand that audiences love watching true stories packed with drama, danger, and the empathy of various intriguing perspectives.

Start with a Great Script

Over the years, Bill has seen that a great script has great structure. "Screenwriter Bart Gavigan has done an amazing job in structuring this movie because the foundational pillar of good movie making is coming up with a solid, balanced, story structure with good conflict, turning points, and resolution. Couple that with a compelling character that the audience can identify with, learn with, and experience growth with during the journey of the film, and these are the key elements for a successful screenplay."

Hurry Up and Wait!

The production of a feature-length movie can take months, even years to film. Bill and his crew have been filming in Panama for about eight months. The modern Waodani tribe is playing the historical Indians of the story, and there are about two hundred others in the production altogether. Our interview happens during the last nine days of filming. "We started pre-production last year in October, we started shooting in January, and we're scheduled to finish the principle photography on April 5. Once we've captured it, we edit, put it together, and then go through creating the sound effects for film, dialog replacement, scoring, and composition of the music. We'll marry the sound and picture elements in the final dubbing of the picture. I hope to have a final answer print by November. It's been a long and wonderful process." Producers need to know a bit about every piece of a movie production, so it helps that Bill has worn many hats in his past.

Actors Become Writers Become Producers . . . Sometimes

Bill started in the industry as an actor, though there's no clear-cut road map for such a progression. The acting led the way to writing, and Bill became a screenwriter. His screenwriting experience led to his learning about production, and he became a writer/producer in 1980 when he co-wrote and produced *The Slayer*, a horror flick funded by Lloyd Adams' International Picture show Company in Atlanta, Georgia. He produced his second film in 1984 for Cannon Films called *Thunder Alley*. In 1986, he went to work for Sony/Columbia Pictures as a production executive, remaining there until 2002, at which time his newly energized faith served as the impetus for the formation of Bearing Fruit Entertainment. Incidentally,

Bearing Fruit Communications is the non-profit company that produced the Jim Elliott documentary, and Bearing Fruit Entertainment is the for-profit company that produced the movie.

Faith Is a Journey

Bill was raised in the Episcopal Church, but it was not until 1990 that he understood what a personal relationship with Jesus Christ is about. "I was baptized in 1990. I had always been a believer, but I became a follower at that point. Instead of knowing about Jesus, I got to know Jesus. It's been an incredible journey from that point to this."

Along the way, Bill hit up against resistance, trials, and testing, but there were many triumphs, and according to his testimony, many more blessings than hardships. "There were definitely trials and tests, roadblocks and temptations. But when your desire is to follow God's plan instead of your own, there's a strength and a peace you have that God both promises and delivers as you take the journey."

It's an Open Industry

Bill believes that the world of entertainment is as open a door as it is for any other industry. "There are no real rules in the entertainment industry. It's not like being a doctor, where you go to school, get a degree, do an internship, and get a residency. If someone gets the rights to a story that a major star is interested in and gets a good attorney, suddenly he becomes a movie producer. In other industries, you couldn't do this. You couldn't say 'I want to sell insurance now; it looks like fun.' But in Hollywood, there are lots of 'can do's' that are big 'can't do's' in other industries."

Obedience Follows Commissioning

The most important advice Bill can give to newcomers is to hear God's call to the industry. "If they're called, then obedience is their next step." When talking about the challenging area of knowing how to hear God, Bill advises, "First you have to pray. Then have a willingness to be led by the Holy Spirit. Some people for the majority of their careers are called to operate in the secular media. There are a number of Christians working in secular media. It's important to be sensitive to God's calling when determining what path to take, and don't just assume that it's going to be a standard, logical course."

Indeed, creative people often do find that their career and ministry course looks very unusual. Currently, Bill is reading Roy Nolan's book, *The Heart of the Artist*, and he is quick to recommend it for those in the entertainment industry. "It was written for the arts in terms of church ministry, but it's completely applicable to Christian artists working in the secular media as well."

Though artists should seek God's commissioning and commit to full obedience, Bill encourages those he mentors to rely on the grace of God and stand back in amazement at His provision. "The key to my success can be stated as 'God's provision of opportunities.' I didn't always realize that, but I can look back now and see where God was providing opportunity after opportunity after opportunity. Even when I wasn't paying attention to God, He was always paying attention to me. I can see that now."

Challenges Will Come

The making of the movie in Panama has been the most challenging and rewarding project that Bill has ever worked on. "The making of the film is an amazing story. And it's incredible that we're here in Panama, and we have an indigenous tribe working with us. We have one tribe portraying another. We have three languages spoken on our set—English, Spanish, and Embra. Some only speak their own language, but the common tongue is Spanish. We have to translate from English to Spanish to the other languages, so it can really slow down the communication some days."

Learn to Manage People

Because many days are wrought with inefficiency, delays, weather, and other obstacles, Bill has seen first hand that producers must be skilled at managing people. "Our normal crew is about 190, but with actors and extras we're up around 250. We have a little production office here, and we're all staying at the Sol Volea Panama Canal Hotel in Cologne, Panama. We went home for the holidays and have been back down here since the first week in January. It's a lot of folks to be concerned about, and a lot of schedules to manage."

In addition to the minor scrapes and cuts to which Bill attended, the crew has dealt with incredibly hot and humid weather, mosquitoes, chiggers, and actual mortal danger at times. "We are shooting in the former School of Americas, now a hotel, and the majority of jungle locations are five minutes from the hotel on Bunker Road. We soon saw that it was aptly named because we came across two land mines. We had to employ a bomb squad to do sweeps, and the munitions experts found the second mine halfway through the production. Formerly the bunkers housed munitions for the military, and there are munitions bunkers all over the place. It's a little unsettling sometimes."

Think Outside the Box

Instead of the usual filming in Los Angeles, Bill wanted the location to look as authentic as possible, so he contacted an old friend. "Bill Boling, one of our associate producers, was a location scout from Hollywood. He had scouted for a Tom Cruise movie that was never made—a picture we had dealt with at Sony Studio. I called Bill and asked him where we should make the movie, and he said, 'Panama, no question.'" Though the budgets can be much higher on foreign productions, producers believe that the pay-off is worth the extra financing effort.

There are Many Ways to Skin a Cat

When thinking about obtaining dollars for great productions, Bill explains that investors consider risks and results in their decision-making, but God is the ultimate provider. "There are many, many different avenues for financing a film. The important thing is that where God provides a vision, He also provides provision. In terms of a business model, in most cases, it's a very risky business. With all of the press with *The Passion*, everyone thought Mel was crazy putting his own money up. But that film was a calling on his life. Everyone thought that New Line Cinema was irresponsible for putting $300 million into *Lord of the Rings*. But again, it was a calling. Even *My Big Fat Greek Wedding*, which had no major stars, did really well because it was inspired . . . a calling for those that conceived it."

In Bill's current feature film, as well the corresponding documentary, both were funded on donation models. There are no profit participants, other than the five families of the slain missionaries, and the rest goes into ministry. In addition to maintaining good relationships with investors and financiers, Bill works to keep other valued relationships in their proper perspective—with agents, mentors, and family.

Keep Agent Relationship in Perspective

How important is having agent? According to Bill, it's important. "Artists should get a good agent, but it's important in the agent/client relationship to remember that the client is the employer, and the agent is the employee. The agent does not get paid unless the client pays them. A lot of times that relationship gets turned around . . . Many clients feel they're working for their agent. Understand the relationship and create a partnership that's mutually beneficial. Also, the agent should have an understanding of the artistic sensibilities of the client, and the client should have an understanding of the needs of the agent as an employee."

Mentors Help with Peace and Perspective

When the Lord called him out of studio, Bill was really at peace about the move. "You read scripture and see that God promises peace that surpasses understanding. I walked away from a good three-year contract, but I knew it was right. My friend, Larry

Poland, gave me a great word during this time. He said, 'Here's what you always have to keep in mind. God is your provider, and Sony your employer. God will always be your provider, but I think your employer's getting ready to change.' Bill has seen that mentors are extremely important to industry Christians. "Mentoring has been important to me and it's something that will continue to be a primary focus as we build the company . . . We want to bring people along in their faith and influence. You don't see it a lot because this industry likes to pigeonhole people, as opposed to developing and cultivating them in an organization, but mentoring is a big part of our plan for developing the new company."

Keep Family First

Despite the apparent glamour of filmmaking from an exotic location, producers like Bill Ewing understand that big parts of their hearts are missing them at home. Bill is married to his wife of twenty-two years, an actress, and together they have a son, Blake, now age nineteen. Blake is an actor, too, having played on *Full House* and acted the part of Waldo in *Little Rascals*. Now, he's a freshman in musical theatre at UCLA, and this week he's in New York, doing a workshop presentation entitled *The 5,000 Fingers of Doctor T*. Bill really misses his family right now. "We speak at least once a day, and eyeball chat with my new Internet camera so we can see each other. That has been the hardest thing—being away from my family." Thankfully, within two weeks of this writing, Bill will be enjoying a well-deserved time of refreshment back in the states with these so dear to his heart and ever-present in his thoughts.

* * *

As the on-set ruckus begins again, and the production engine demands his focus, Bill turns to give a final word of advice: "If you have stars in your eyes, remember who created the stars, and keep your focus there."

· 9 ·

From Soup to Nuts

STEPS TO SUCCESS:
4–9, PRE-PRODUCTION

The next three chapters give you a recipe for producing your movie or television program. In pre-production, your costs are limited to yourself and one or two others. In production, your costs will involve a large paid staff and lots of equipment. In planning your production, you will find ways to hold costs down by minimizing locations, using stock shots, cutting characters, and other devices. Time is money: if you have more time than money, invest it in cutting down your production and post-production costs. The time you spend budgeting and planning your production will save you a great deal of money in actual production.

Pre-production is the critical phase that is often rushed in a low to medium budget movie. Often, as soon as the money (or even some money) is secured, the pressure mounts to rush into production without the detailed planning necessary to help your movie become a success. Therefore, right from the beginning, determine that comprehensive planning will be the hallmark of your production.

One of the greatest directors of all time, Alfred Hitchcock, was a stickler for planning every detail. This often frustrated those around him, but the result was many of the best movies ever made. Peter Jackson, the producer and director of the *Lord of the Rings* trilogy, is another filmmaker who plans, plans, and plans again. If you take the time to pre-produce your movie properly, you will increase your odds of producing a hit.

As a rule of thumb, you will spend fifty percent of your time in pre-production, twenty percent in production and thirty percent of your time in post-production. As your skills improve, the time you spend in pre-production will decrease and the time you spend in post-production will increase until they are thirty percent pre-production, twenty percent in production, and fifty percent post-production.

Before we look at the steps, let's consider the insights of a major Hollywood producer, Bill Fay. It is very likely that we have all seen at least one Bill Fay movie in the last decade, though his projects cover a wide range of genres from science fiction to historical epics. Most will remember two of his biggest box office hits, *Independence Day* and *The Patriot*, but many of us have also seen *We Are Marshall*, *Godzilla*, and *10,000 B.C.* Here, Bill shares a bit of his adventure from film school to famous producer, and he imparts some heartfelt advice for those daring enough to join his fascinating, but demanding industry.

It's Only for the Passionate and Stalwart
—an interview with William Fay

Film School Is Helpful

One year, not so long ago, Bill Fay was attending Stanford University, trying to decide whether to go to law school or business school. Either would work, and yet he had a passion for neither. After much consideration, and remembering how he had done some screenwriting and had always been interested in the movie industry, Bill decided to apply to UCLA's film school, though they only accept twenty out of two thousand applicants. To his amazement, he was accepted and knew he couldn't pass up such a great opportunity. "I got a great education . . . very broad—both in film criticism, by watching things like classic Italian cinema, and in film production—by picking up a camera and shooting, and taking editing and post-production classes."

Indeed, one of the more memorable parts of Bill's film school education was his editing classes. "They gave us the dailies from *Gunsmoke*. I loved cutting together scenes of Marshall Dillon duking it out with the bad guys. Our class came up with twenty different ways to cut the show together. It was good exposure to the real world." When Bill got out into the real world, he knew how to do everything—from sound to camera, from lighting to directing, and producing. He even won an award for directing at UCLA. "It was a great, broad film background—especially for someone not connected in the industry."

Everyone Starts at the Bottom

Despite his noteworthy degree from UCLA, Bill found that he still had to prove himself in the industry after graduation. No one was handing him prestigious producing and directing jobs. As a matter of fact, Bill began with the relatively humble job of working as a production assistant for Roger Corman, the famous B-movie producer. He then worked for low budget producer Sandy Howard. "This turned out to be a great move. You do everything in low budget movie making. You're making a lot of pictures each year, and you can rise through the ranks very quickly. If you said you could do something, they'd take a risk on you and let you do it. Money was so low; they couldn't hire an experienced person."

In the low budget movie world, Bill learned a lot in a very short time. Within a couple years, he had risen to the level of production manager. From there, he found out that a friend in Seattle was raising money for a film he wanted to direct, so Bill decided to help him, and together they raised $500,000 for the movie. "I produced, and he directed a movie called *Bombs Away*, a comedy. I was twenty-six at the time . . . It's still out there, and though it didn't set the world on fire, it was a good film, and we got incredible amounts of real-world education and practice during the process."

More Success = Bigger Projects

After *Bombs Away*, Bill produced *Jake Speed*, a film for New World Productions, shot in Zimbabwe, Africa. From there, he worked his way up, producing bigger and bigger pictures, and finally started producing for the studios, producing the lower-budget movies at first. He worked on movies for both Universal and Fox, doing line producing. Bill is grateful that he got the studio jobs through a contact he'd made while filming *Jake Speed*.

Producer Hats Are Always Unique

When asked about the exact role of a producer, Bill is quick to explain that it varies, depending on the project. "You can come in when there's nothing done yet, or they'll bring the producer in after the director's on board. The producer works with the director to map out the entire plan of the film. We make decisions about how much money we'll need, where to shoot, whom to hire as actors, what script changes we'll need, and we put the entire plan together." For example, when Bill produced *Jake Speed*, he arrived in Zimbabwe to find that there was no infrastructure in the country—nothing related to the film business. He felt a great sense of accomplishment to come in and create an organization of hundreds of people working together to make the movie. "There were a million details to attend to—just the kind of challenge a good producer enjoys."

After the movie was finished in 1994, Roland Emmerich and

Dean Devlin came to Bill with an idea. It was the story of *Independence Day.* "That was a good break for me. I not only joined them for the making of that movie, but I also became president of their company, Centropolis Entertainment." Bill stayed at Centropolis for six years, and then the principals split the company and sold its assets in 2001. Other films made by Centropolis included *Godzilla* and *The Patriot*, among others.

As for the role of Executive Producer, it, too, can mean entirely different things on different pictures, reveals Bill. "The EP is sometimes the day-to-day producer; but on other movies he's the deal maker. The EP can be the creatively oriented producer, or the day-to-day online producer of film. For instance, Harvey Weinstein is billed as the Executive Producer on one movie, and the producer on another. As far as I know, he's doing the same job on both."

As for Bill, he considers himself more of a hands on, day-to-day producer than a deal making producer. "I've come up through business, and I like to stay attached to almost every aspect of the movie. Through Centropolis, our little team put *Independence Day* together. I was responsible for working with Roland and Dean, very creative people, to put the film together from start to finish. One of us touched almost every detail of the movie."

Never Underestimate the Media

According to Bill, the whole experience of producing *Independence Day*, and especially watching the snowball of media attention, was an amazing experience. "As we were making the film, every month or two something would happen on the set or I'd see something at our visual effects facility that would strengthen my feeling that it would be a great movie. They tested fire rolling down the street, and it was thrilling . . . When I saw Will Smith and Jeff Goldblum, and saw their camaraderie on-screen, I knew it would be a hit. "This was also a well marketed film. Tom Sherak at Fox (now at Revolution) is a genius at marketing pictures. He was able to create huge momentum for the film. He did the first motion picture Super Bowl ad."

Despite the memorable thrill of the *Independence Day* trailers, the movie had a relatively normal budget for marketing. As a matter of fact, a few weeks before the film opened, Twentieth Century Fox stopped running ads on it. An executive with Fox remarked, "The bubble is as big as it should get. We've got to stop advertising, or it will pop." According to Bill, the whole grassroots public fervor drove the publicity of the film. "It felt almost out of control, it was so big. We were on the cover of *Time* and *Newsweek*. People started having talk shows and nighttime programs covering the whole craze about whether there were aliens out there, and whether they were friendly or unfriendly. It was outrageous and exciting."

Kindle Your Imagination

The exciting, heavily marketed film, *Independence Day,* actually started as a single visual in the mind of Roland Emmerich, the director, known to be an incredibly visual person. He had gotten an image in his head—of a space ship seventeen miles wide, parked over a city. He asked Dean Devlin how he'd feel about waking up to a giant alien craft hovering over Los Angeles. The two tossed the idea around and began writing a script based on such a wild phenomenon. Little did they know at the time that this one scene from Roland's imagination would soon take off into all the media furor and speculation over aliens!

Never Stop Learning

Independence Day also ushered in a whole new level of special effects challenges with the spacecraft and aliens. "We had done visual effects, but nothing on this scale. It was an incredible learning experience. You really learn an amazing amount on each film, and it's something different on each one. On *ID4* we learned how to handle major effects sequences. We had huge facilities do the effects, and we were really pleased with the outcome."

On another one of his widely acclaimed films, *The Patriot*, Bill learned about the American Revolution, reading volumes of material on the famous conflict. "I now know more about that war than I could have possibly imagined in a lifetime. I just absorbed everything about it before making the movie."

Reading up on the script and subject matter is important, believes Bill. "It's part of getting the feel for your story . . . It's steeping yourself in the time and place. If you do, everything that comes out will be organic."

When Bill got a Movieguide "Faith and Values" award from Dr. Baehr, he said during his acceptance speech, "Making *The Patriot* was a life-changing experience. These people made so many sacrifices for freedom . . . We didn't just take the British out. Most of the men who signed the Declaration of Independence suffered, died, or were hung for their beliefs. They all suffered incredible trials and tribulations . . . So many died, penniless—their farms burned, and their homes destroyed. People really looked out for one another, and pulled for each other. Yet it was also a time of great divisiveness. There were many upstanding citizens loyal to the crown. It was one of the most difficult periods in history."

The knowledge that the production team had regarding the drama and angst of this period in history is clearly evident as this award-winning movie unfolds.

Be Careful What You Wish For

Bill's favorite part of his job has historically been the visiting of exotic locations for extended periods of time. "I loved traveling to Japan, to Africa, all over the world. I'm a very politically minded person. When I get to a country, I meet with the politicians, if possible, and try to really learn what goes on. It's been such a thrill to get an up-close perspective on so many places."

Such were the sentiments of the free and single Billy Fay. A whole new paradigm shift occurred when his name changed to "dad." "When I had children, the traveling became the least favorite part of my job. It was torture to film *The Patriot* for seven months and only see my three children (nine, seven, and five) for two weeks during that period."

Bill's greatest advice is that the only reason to be in the film industry is a search to satisfy an incredible passion for it that won't be satisfied in any other way. "If you want to be famous, cool, or think you'd get a kick out of the industry, these are bad reasons to come here. This business requires a great deal of sacrifice. It's great for the single person who enjoys hopping around world, but it gets tough when you're raising a family." Bill adds that he was grateful to have shot most of *Independence Day* in his hometown of Los Angeles.

In addition to his children, Bill has a very supportive wife, who also works in the business, and who knew what she was in for. "I was lucky enough to get married when I was first starting out." As a matter of fact, the couple met in college, when working on Bill's first film. "That makes it easier. As you get more successful, it's harder to make quality judgments about another's heart. You're always asking, 'Well, does she only like the excitement or the vibe, or does she really like me?' I didn't have to ask that."

Faith and Family Go Together

According to Bill, his faith has grown with him. "As a kid just coming out of college, I really didn't think about making decisions against the backdrop of my faith, and in terms of films I'd work on, I didn't think too deeply about what kinds of movies I was making. But having a family really reinforces your beliefs. It's hard to look at anything without thinking how you're impacting society—and your own kids. Now these decisions are very important to me."

For most of his life, Bill says he always felt like a fairly well grounded person. "My faith is important to me, and trying to live by a moral code out here is important to me and my family. Everything is a battle in this industry. My faith certainly informs everything I do."

And, Bill is not the only man of faith in Hollywood. "Despite what you hear, it is an open playing field here, and there's room for people of faith and values. As a matter of fact, most of the people I deal with are people of faith, who truly believe in what they're doing and make their decisions according to a clear moral compass."

Bill invites people of faith with stars in their eyes to venture out and try their hand in his industry. But he cautions them to first get an agent!

Agents Are a Must

Bill suggests that screenwriters only present their projects through agents—due to legal ramifications. "It was amazing to me some of the things that happened after *Independence Day*. People came out of nowhere, claiming they'd written a script like ours. Now our attorney tells us that we just can't read them . . . so we can say in court that we don't read any unsolicited material. If you send a script to a studio, know that no one will read it. There are too many lawsuits, and it becomes a sticky situation."

Anyone who has something great must find a reputable agent, says Bill. "People will be comfortable reading your script if there's an intermediary involved."

Final Advice

"My final caveat to the young person interested in film production is—Don't do it unless it's something you're passionate about. It can be such a struggle. It's wonderfully rewarding, but difficult, too. It's certainly been amazing for me due to the travel, the people I've met and worked with, and the constant education I've received. But it's only for the stalwart of heart who can endure the rugged journey to success."

* * *

SUCCESS, STEP 4: BREAKDOWN, BUDGET, SCHEDULE, AND TIMETABLE YOUR PRODUCTION

As soon as you have a story, you should have your script broken down and start estimating the cost of producing your film. The distributor, networks, and the financiers will ask you how much your motion picture or television program will cost to produce. Before you go to a movie studio/distributor, you should turn your story into a script and prepare a budget based on that script, unless you are seeking development funds to prepare a script, in which case you will have to budget the development funds you need.

A budget generated before a Breakdown and Schedule is nothing more than an educated guess at best. The Script Breakdown isolates all the elements necessary for the production from extras and wardrobe to set requirements and special effects (EFX). The Schedule then lays out the most efficient way of shooting all the scenes. Without a Schedule, you don't know how many days you will need a specific actor or, for that matter, how long it will take to realistically shoot the picture.

Therefore, prepare breakdown sheets showing the running orders of your filmings and/or videotapings:

FEATURE FILM BREAKDOWN SHEET
(SHOWING RUNNING ORDER)

Page Scene	Shots	Cameras/Audio	Day/Night	Csst
1 Painting 1	cam 1	sof	n	
5 Telly at table 6–9	1, 2, 3,	n	Telly & bits	
	recording_break			
10 Car	18	1 dub	n	Telly & bits
13 Street	23	1	n	Chris & girl

Feature Film Breakdown

Title: _____

Breakdown page no: _____

Int/ext: _____

Scene # _____

Set # _____ Day/night: _____ Page ct: _____

Loc: _____

_____

_____

Description:

_____

_____

_____

Notes

_____

_____

No. Cast	Extras	Animals/vehicles	Props

			Make-Up Hair
Special Equipment	Add'l personnel	Special effects	Costume

Also, prepare a Shooting Schedule showing when you are shooting what with what equipment, crew and cast:

TV Movie Shooting Schedule

Date_____ Sets-Scenes-Description_____ Cast_____Location _____
1st day Set: Restaurant   Telly   Studio
   Scene: Going away party   Chris
   Props: Painting of Athens   Bits
_____ Tables and chairs._____
2nd day Set:
   Scene:
   Props:

If you are producing a movie, prepare a more detailed shooting schedule. Below are examples of two different shooting schedules: (1) *It's a Wonderful Life*, a classic shooting schedule and (2) *Goldenrod*, a medium budget shooting schedule.

IT'S A WONDERFUL LIFE   Page 1

Shooting Schedule
Tue, May 25, 2004

SHOOT DAY #1—Mon, Jul 06, 1992

Scene #24   EXT—BAILEY BUILDINGS AND LOAN
                 SIGN OVER ENTRANCE—DAY   1/8 Pgs.

           Establishing Bldg. & Loan sign.
           Set Dressing
           Bldg. & Loan Sign

Scene #18   EXT—MAIN STREET—DAY   4/8 Pgs.
George takes a cab ride.

Cast Members   **Props**   **Vehicles**
1. George   Bert's Watch   Bert's Motorcycle
7. Ernie   Large suitcase   Ernie's cab
8. Bert   Stunt car
11. Violet

Extras
Elderly Man

Stunts
Car screeches to a stop
Stunt driver

Scene #22   EXT—FRONT PORCH OF HOUSE—
NIGHT   2/8 Pgs.
Grumpy old man watches George & Mary.

Cast Members   **Set Dressing**
37. Grumpy Old Man   Rocking Chair

END OF DAY #1—1 7/8 Total Pages

SHOOT DAY #2—Tue, Jul 07, 1992

Scene #23   **EXT—STREET—NIGHT**   3 5/8 Pgs.
George and Mary make a wish.

Cast Members   **Props**   **Vehicles**
1. George   Rocks   Bailey's car
2. Mary

	Special Effects	**Set Dressing**
3. Harry	Breaking glass	Rocking Chair
4. Uncle Billy		
37. Grumpy Old Man		
	Greenery	**Costumes**
	Hydrangea bush	Bathrobe
		Jersey
		Football pants
		Wet clothes

IT'S A WONDERFUL LIFE   Page 2

Shooting Schedule
Tue, May 25, 2004

END OF DAY #2—3 5/8 Total Pages

SHOOT DAY #3—Wed, Jul 08, 1992

Scene #21   EXT—TREE-LINED   RESIDENTIAL
STREET—NIGHT   3 5/8 Pgs.
George and Mary's moonlight walk.

Cast Members	**Props**	
1. George	Rocks	
2. Mary		
	Special Effects	**Costumes**
	Breaking glass	Bathrobe
		Jersey
		Football pants
		Wet clothes

END OF DAY #3—6 3/8 Total Pages

SHOOT DAY #4—Thu, Jul 09, 1992

Scene #25   INT—BAILEY BUILDING AND LOAN
               OFFICE—DAY   4 2/8 Pgs.
               B & L Directors meeting

Cast Members	**Props**	**Costumes**
1. George	Legal papers	George's coat
4. Uncle Billy	Wheelchair	
5. Mr. Potter		
21. Goon		
34. Dr. Campbell		
41. Lawyer		
42. Real Estate Salesman		
43. Insurance Agent		

END OF DAY #4—4 2/8 Total Pages

SHOOT DAY #5—Fri, Jul 10, 1992

Scene #19   INT—BAILEY DINING ROOM—NIGHT
               6 3/8 Pgs.
               Dinner at the Baileys'.

Cast Members	**Props**	
1. George	4 Pies	
3. Harry	Broom	**Set Dressing**
12. Ma Bailey	Dishes	Dining Room Set
16. Annie		
17. Peter Bailey		

Riding the Bullet

Thu. Nov 27, 2003
Script Dated: Nov 16/03 PINK Shooting
Based on: ****GOLDENROD One-Liner

****GOLDENROD Revised: Thu. Nov 27, 2003—7:53 PM

Script Dated -> Nov 16/03 PINK Shooting (Yet to be Issued)

Day 14 –> Call: 0800 Wrap: 2100 Sun: 0739/1619

DAY 14—Fri, Nov 28, 2003

---

121 INT HOSPITAL / 4TH FLOOR CORRIDOR Night—2
7/8 Pgs
LOCATION:
Alan finds his mom's room, enters.
St. Mary's, 4th Floor, 421

CAST MEMBERS	ART DEPT/ CONSTRUCTION	GRIPS	SPECIAL EQUIPMENT
1. Alan Parker	Curtains to block windows at end of hall 40 x T8-3200		Black south windows
30. Nurse Annie Wilkes	Rig light in stairwell	85' Lift	

EXTRAS	PROPS
Hospital Staff (2)	Alan's Wrist Bandage and Duffle Bag

HAIR/MAKEUP	ADDITIONAL LABOR
Spider Bite	Daily Elec xt @ Track Hairline Blood

122 INT HOSPITAL / MOM'S ROOM Night—2 2/8Pgs
LOCATION:
VISION. Mom points finger and screams.
St. Mary's, 4th Floor, 421

CAST	MEMBERS PROPS	HAIR/MAKEUP
1. Alan Parker	Alan's Wrist	Spider Bite
4. Jean Parker	Bandage & Duffle Bag	Track Hairline Blood
30. Nurse Annie Wilkes		

---

123 INT HOSPITAL / MOM'S ROOM Night—2 2 4/8 Pgs
LOCATION:
Mom's really alive.
St. Mary's, 4th Floor, 421

CAST	SET DRESSING	NOTES
1. Alan Parke	Alan's bleeding from prior	
4. Jean Parker	I.V.'s & Hospital Equipment	

30. Nurse Annie Wilkes	**PROPS** Alan's Wrist Bandage & Duffle Bag	**HAIR/MAKEUP** Head wound Alan subtle bleeding from behind ear Spider Bite

---

30 INT HOSPITAL HALL / MOM'S ROOM Night—2
4/8 Pgs
LOCATION:
VISION. POV moves down corridor into room . . . Mom
has no face!
St. Mary's, 4th Floor, 421

EXTRAS	SPECIAL MAKEUP FX	**COSTUMES**
Hospital Staff (2)	**SET DRESSING**	Jean Parker
Jean Parker Photo DBL	Heart Monitor	Photo DBL
Mom face removal		

PROPS
Hospital Bracelet

HAIR/MAKEUP

ADDITIONAL LABOR
Medicine Tray for BG
Jean Parker Photo DBL

KNB Makeup FX Supervisor
Push Trolley for BG w/sheets & pillows 7

NOTES

Video sync for heart monitor?

41   INT HOSPITAL / MOM'S ROOM Night—2 5/8 Pgs
      LOCATION:
      VISION—Mom just starts screaming.
      "Your mother needs you now."
      St. Mary's, 4th Floor, 421

CAST MEMBERS	**NOTES**	**ELECTRICS**
1. Alan Parker	**SET DRESSING**	Rain?
4. Jean Parker		Radio
		"Flashboard" Effect
21. Doctor in Mom's	**PROPS**	
Room	Dr.'s Stethoscope	

107–8   INT HOSPITAL / MOM'S ROOM   Night—2   1/8 Pgs
LOCATION:
MONTAGE. Mom near death.
St. Mary's, 4th Floor, 421

CAST MEMBERS   **NOTES**

4. Jean Parker   **SET DRESSING**
                        Shoot 8mm?

                        I.V.'s & Hospital Equipment

                        HAIR/MAKEUP
                        Jean Is Near Death

End of Day 14—Total Pages—4 7/8

Day 15 –> Call: 0900 Wrap: 2200 Sun: 0740/1619

DAY 15—Sat, Nov 29, 2003

Next to your script, your budget is the most important tool you have in a production and helps you determine where you are going and how to get there.

Most budgets are broken down into above-the-line costs and below-the-line costs. Above-the-line costs are the variable and nego-tiable costs that relate to writing, performing, and the production team—such as the scriptwriter, the star, and the director. These are generally the primary creative elements and the financing elements (i.e., executive producers). Below-the-line costs are the various fixed costs, back up services, and physical elements involved in a produc-tion, such as equipment, transportation, and operations personnel, including the cameraperson, soundperson, and technical director. However, in the cryptic world of the film industry, these are not all fixed costs. The rates of director of photography, composer, editor, production designer, and other HOD's (heads of departments) are generally negotiated.

Budgets are also divided into a summary, top sheet, and then many pages of details that break down every element of the top sheet. Budget forms are available from many sources, including equipment rental houses. Budgets can range from a very sparse million dollars to the Hollywood heavyweights of around $200 million, with the average Hollywood movie budget running around $104 million, including prints and advertising. The range of the budget depends on the scope of the project, from talent cost, length of production, complexity, number of locations, set ups, stunts, grip and electrical requirements, action/adventure versus drama, stunts, and obviously visual/special effects.

Of course, there are those movies that do more with much less. Robert Rodriguez of *Spy Kids* fame made his first big splash in the talent pool with his movie *El Mariachi*, a very entertaining movie that was produced for $7,000. Such a small figure is hard to believe, since this is near the average budget for catering tea and crumpets on most Hollywood productions!

Here is a sample top sheet for an **$18,731,642.83** medium budget movie:

B. PRODUCTIONS Inc. Presents
"MOVIE TITLE"

Producers: Screenplay:
Director: Script Version: Writer's Third Draft
Schedule: 57 Days Principal Photography   Budgeted for: Canada
Unions Budgeted: WGA, Canadian ACTRA, Canadian I.A.T.S.E.
Assumptions: 20 Days Location; 37 Stage
British Director, Cameraman and 3 Crew

Budget Dated: 00/00/2000
Budget Prepared by: Claude Lawrence **Initial Pass Budget**

Acct#	Category Title	Page	Total
11–00	story & scenario	1	$711,838
12–00	producers unit	2	$877,815
13–00	direction	2	$634,391
14–00	cast	3	$3,370,505
15–00	a/b/l travel & living	5	$562,357
TOTAL ABOVE-THE-LINE			**$6,156,906**
20–00	production staff	7	$1,017,218
21–00	atmosphere (extras)	10	$225,275
22–00	art direction	12	$313,032
23–00	set construction	13	$910,402
24–00	set operations	18	$318,744
25–00	special effects	19	$215,848
26–00	set dressing	21	$303,844
27–00	property	24	$153,222
28–00	animals & picture vehicle	24	$108,373
28–50	animatronics & puppets	25	$55,350
29–00	wardrobe	25	$284,248
30–00	makeup & hairdressing	28	$211,80
32–00	lighting	29	$374,364
33–00	camera	30	$571,503
34–00	production sound	32	$94,036
35–00	transportation	33	$517,301
36–00	location	37	$517,082
37–00	stages & facilities	39	$407,160
38–00	film (production)	40	$387,762
41–00	second unit	41	$32,500
Production Period Total			**$7,019,243**
45–00	editorial	41	$496,958
46–00	music	42	$423,609
47–00	post production sound	42	$264,050

48–00	post-film & lab	43	$111,240
49–00	titles & optical	44	$67,000
50–00	computer generated images	44	$2,331,254
51–00	green screen	47	$130,000
52–00	miniatures	47	$217,750
	Total Post Production		**$4,041,861**
65–00	publicity	47	$47,050
66–00	legal & accounting	47	$190,250
67–00	insurance	48	$228,488
68–00	general expense	48	$502,263
	Total Other Costs		**$968,051**
70–00	Finance Fees & Marketing Allowance	49	$0
	Finance/Marketing Fees And Costs		**$0**
	Contingency: 0.00%		$0
	Completion Bond: 3%		$545,581.83
	Finance interest & points not budgeted: 0.00%		$0
	TOTAL ABOVE-THE-LINE		$6,156,906
	TOTAL BELOW-THE-LINE		$12,574,736.83
	TOTAL ABOVE & BELOW-THE-LINE		$18,731642.83
	GRAND TOTAL		**$18,731642.83**

Often, the producer uses the 3–4–5% formula: 3% of budget for story unit, 4% for Directors unit, 5% for Producers unit. This varies a great deal but is a reasonable standard.

Here is how a detail of one account in your top sheet might look:

_____

_____

Project:_____

Date Prepared:_____

Acct. Description	Rate	Total	Totals	Totals
20 / Costumes & Make-Up				
A. Wardrobe Dept.				
1. Wardrobe Designer	1,400/wk 5 wks	7,000.00		
2. 1st Wardrobe Person	2 wks	1,788.0		
3. 2nd Wardrobe Person	16 days	2,063.00		
4. Tailor				
5. Seamstress	500.00			
6. Extra Help				
			Subtotal	
			11,351.00	
B. Make-Up & Hairdressing				
1. Head Make-Up Person	1,200/wk 5 wks	6,000.00		
2. 2nd Make-Up Person				
3. Head Hairdresser	1,000/week 4 wks	4,000.00		
4. Body Make-Up Person				
5. Extra Help				
			Subtotal 10,000.00	
			Total $21,351.00	

Most accounts on your budget will be broken down into even greater detail than "Costumes & Make-Up." Many costs will be negotiable, or can be lowered through substitution.

At the same time you prepare your budget, you will prepare a production timetable. Your master production timetable will be an overview of the entire production and help you to establish the deadlines that will keep your production on course. You will also want to prepare detailed timetables relating to each element in your production, such as personnel. Here is a sample of a master production timetable:

Master Production Timetable

Task_____ Month_____

_____1 / 2 / 3/ 4/ 5/ 6/ 7/ 8/ 9/ 10/ 11 / 12_____

Scripting ___ xxxxxxxxxxxxxxxxxxxxxxxx_____

Staffing_____ xx   xxx   xxxxxxxx xx   xx_____

Preproduction xxxxxxxxxxxxxxxxxxxxxxxxxxx _____

Production_____xxxxxx_____

Postproduction _____ xxxxxxxxxxxxxx

Distribution or Broadcast_____   _____ xxxxx

SUCCESS, STEP 5: STORYBOARD AND PLAN YOUR PRODUCTION

Many experienced directors don't bother with storyboards except for the action sequences, which often require a storyboard to get the action right. Some create "animatics" or simple computer animated storyboards to better conceptualize their movies, and some use "animatics" instead of storyboards.

Even so, every first time director should storyboard his movie, and many of the great directors always use storyboards. The producer may require a storyboard so he knows where the director is going.

Preparing a storyboard is essential to helping you, your director, and your producer picture exactly how you want each shot to look and to flow together. When I brought in the Christian theological advisors to help advise on *The Prince of Egypt*, many of the walls of the DreamWorks animation facility were covered floor to ceiling with storyboards. Extensive storyboarding makes the actual shooting of the movie much easier. Preparing your storyboards will help you to make many of the artistic decisions beforehand, so that your movie just has to be shot and edited together.

Storyboards help you and the director think visually about your story. You do not need to use realistic drawings in your storyboards. Stick figures for the people are fine as long as your storyboard gives you an idea of how each shot will look.

As you prepare your storyboard, think about:

Composition—the positioning of people and things in each shot.

Lighting—from above, below, or from the side.

Point of view or POV—From whose point of view—the hero? A third person?

You can find many examples of storyboards on the internet, even some from famous movies. The completed storyboard below is from a James Bond movie:

Figure 15

So that you can accurately plan your production, turn your script into a rough storyboard that you will want to revise and perfect as you proceed. The following three images are examples of blank storyboards.

Figure 16: Storyboard Form 1

STORY BOARD FORM

Figure 17: Storyboard Form 2

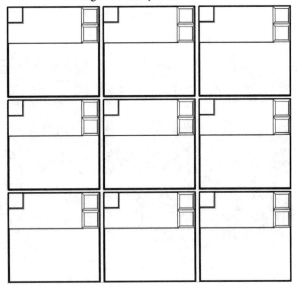

Figure 18: Storyboard Form 3

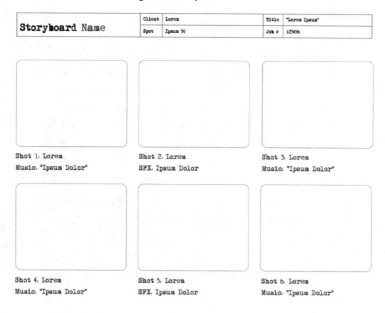

Storyboard Name	Client	Lorem	Title	"Lorem Ipsum"
	Spot	Ipsum 30	Job #	123456

Shot 1: Lorem
Music: "Ipsum Dolor"

Shot 2: Lorem
SFX: Ipsum Dolor

Shot 3: Lorem
Music: "Ipsum Dolor"

Shot 4: Lorem
Music: "Ipsum Dolor"

Shot 5: Lorem
SFX: Ipsum Dolor

Shot 6: Lorem
Music: "Ipsum Dolor"

Page 1

You may want to use your storyboard to sketch important scenes and difficult shots from different angles to show required camera treatment.

Another approach, used by Robert Rodriguez, is to scout the location with a video camera and use stand-ins to approximate scene blocking. That way, when the crew arrives the key folks already know exactly where to place equipment.

Study your script, storyboard and sketches. From discussions with your key talent, determine how you are going to produce every aspect of your production. Remember to consider:

1. Cast, including costume and make-up requirements.
2. Pre-production publicity.
3. Sets and staging designs, including sketches showing

lighting, directions, action, and camera shots. Make sure you have enough studio or location space for: shots, moves, cable routing, and equipment, such as booms. Therefore, you must predetermine the facilities, both studio and location, which you will use and what permissions and arrangements are needed.

4. All "on camera" props and other set dressing.
5. Photography, filming, stock shots, and all material that needs special arrangements, clearances, fees, permissions, permits, insurance, scheduling, and extra staffing.
6. All music and sound needs, including sound effects.
7. Special effects, graphics and titles, including artwork, maps, charts, models, and displays.
8. Equipment.
9. All other necessary and special equipment including teleprompter, telecine, slide chain, film chain, monitors, and cuing facilities (most of these are for television).
10. Lighting and atmosphere, making sure that shots will match. Analyze any special lighting that is needed in terms of cost, manpower, equipment, and feasibility.
11. Film, videotape, and audiotape.
12. Editing needs.
13. Publicity.
14. Distribution.

Keep in mind throughout your production that every effect (including a camera move, special effects, insert, action, and a technical move, such as a wipe, fade and dissolve) acts as a blinking neon light to attract the attention of the viewer. Too many effects, like a busy neon sign, are annoying. Too few and you may lose your audience.

Every effect and action must flow organically from the story and not intrude on the story, unless there is a compelling artistic reason to do so. The technical effects should affect the viewer, but at no time should he or she be aware of any specific effect, unless you are engaging the viewer as an active character in the action of the story, or you are exposing the mechanism of the story for stylistic reasons.

SUCCESS, STEP 6: BRING YOUR KEY ABOVE-THE-LINE TALENT ON BOARD

Besides making your story bankable, the above-the-line talent will affect: your budget, because of the size of their fees and percentages; your story, because most of them will want a voice in the final script, or you will want to adapt the final script to fit them; and, your production, which they will help you plan and interpret. Be open to their input and their genius. You will probably pay them a great deal of money, unless they are giving you their time for charitable reasons, so get as much out of them as possible. They can help your production succeed.

There are many qualified Christians in Hollywood, and there are many qualified Christians in the Christian movie world. They may make a better fit with your project than someone who is not a believer, although great movies with strong Christian themes—such as *Chariots of Fire*—have been made by unbelievers. Make sure that you hire the right person for the right job. One production hired a top-notch cameraperson to be the producer, something he was incapable of handling. Furthermore, avoid using your friends just because they are your friends or they invested money in your production.

As you team up with these entertainment industry notables, please remember:

> **The Producer** is the most important person who is chief executive and operating officer. He is in charge of the production and the production personnel. He controls the budget and is ultimately responsible for the success or failure of the production.

An Executive Producer is either responsible for financing the production or for interfacing with the network or studio, or both. He may assume the role of chief executive officer, but he will delegate budget responsibility to the Producer or an Associate Producer. The Executive Producer credit given in most long form television is the equivalent of a Producer credit on a film. The Executive Producer in TV is directly involved with the creative and physical production. The Executive Producer in film is generally only concerned with the financing of the project.

The Director is responsible for directing the actors and crew. He stages the production. He is responsible for the visual and audio treatment of the production. He became the auteur of the production in the 1960s as a result of the French New Wave movement. Before that, and even now in many instances, he was the conductor for hire, but not the auteur—that is, he was and is part of a collaborative team, not the sole author of the movie.

The director is usually responsible for the entire production up to a completed movie. He defines his vision for the movie and helps to determine the schedule and create the storyboards. The director often selects the locations or must approve them if you have a location scout. He helps plan the shots with the cinematographer and works with the editor to edit the movie.

The Assistant Directors are responsible for organizing, scheduling, and managing the daily set operations. The ADs are the ones responsible for the schedule and tracking the daily production report that translates into a daily hot cost for the studio or financier. Often there are three A.D.s.

A Director of Photography (D.P.) helps the director set the visual treatment of the film. Thus, the creative aspect of the shot is set with the Director, and the D.P. supervises the crew elements to achieve that shot, freeing the Director to direct the actors, crew, and stage action.

SUCCESS, STEP 7:
FINALIZE SCRIPT AND ORGANIZE PRODUCTION

With the input from your key talent, finalize your script. Then working from your final script, obtain or arrange for graphics, photography, film, stock shots, film clips, properties, and everything that needs to be in your production.

SUCCESS, STEP 8: CAST AND STAFF

Casting is critical. Be selective. Be careful. Cast the right person for the role, someone who can play him or herself, at least.

Movies are a larger-than-life medium that lend themselves to spectacle and close-ups. Make sure that your cast will emote naturally in a close-up. Your characters become the cast; therefore, make sure that the actors you choose are truly your characters. Television is a smaller window on the world. In movies you can have a cast of thousands, in television a small group will suggest a large crowd. The actors should work closely with the director to find out how their characters can best be played. They must go beyond just memorizing lines to think about how their character would really say his lines. This is best accomplished by paying attention to what that character wants in the scene. The actors should work with the director to determine their character's goals, desires, or needs.

Here is another important document: the Actor Day Out of Days. This document tells the producer and casting director exactly how many days during the production an actor will be working, which is instrumental in determining what an actor will cost you.

DAY OUT OF DAYS

TITLE: IT'S A WONDERFUL LIFE

PROD. NUMBER   PRODUCER: Date:

DIRECTOR: UPM/ASST. Dir:
_____

S - Start   W - Work;   F - Finish;   H - Hold,   T - Travel   D - Drop;   P - Pickup;   R - Rehearse

Start Date: Report created Mon, May 24, 2004

Month: July

	Day of Week →	Mon	Tue	Wed	Thur	Fri	Sat	Sun	Mon	Tue	Wed	Thur	Fri	Sat	Sun	Mon	Tue	Wed	Thur	Fri	Sat	Sun
	Day of Month					0	1	2	3	4	5	6	7	8	9	0	1	2	3	4	5	6
	Shoot Days								1	2	3	4	5									
ID	Character																					
1	George								W													
2	Mary									W												
3	Harry									W												
4	Uncle Billy									W												
5	Mr. Potter											W D										
6	Mr. Gower								W D													
7	Ernie								W													
8	Bert								W D													
9	Joe										W F											

Day Out of Days schedule

ID	Character	Mon	Tue	Wed	Thur	Fri	Sat	Sun	Mon	Tue	Wed	Thur	Fri	Sat	Sun	Mon	Tue	Wed	Thur	Fri	Sat	Sun
	Day of Month:					0	1	2	3	4	5	6	7	8	9	0	1	2	3	4	5	6
	Shoot Days:												0			1	2	3	4	5		
10	Clarence																					
11	Violet	W																				
12	Ma Bailey			W																		
13	Mrs. Hatch																					
14	Mr. Martini																					
15	Cousin Tilly											W	D									
16	Annie					W D																
17	Peter Bailey					W						W	D									
18	Cousin Eustace											W	D									
19	Ruth												W									
20	Peter																					
21	Goon				W D																	
22	Carter																					
23	Mary									W D												
24	Sam Wainwright									W D												
25	Maria Martini																					
26	Ed																					

ID	Character	Mon	Tue	Wed	Thur	Fri	Sat	Sun	Mon	Tue	Wed	Thur	Fri	Sat	Sun	Mon	Tue	Wed	Thur	Fri	Sat	Sun
Day of Month:						0	1	2	3	4	5	6	7	8	9	0	1	2	3	4	5	6
Day of Week:		Mon	Tue	Wed	Thur	Fri	Sat	Sun	Mon	Tue	Wed	Thur	Fri	Sat	Sun	Mon	Tue	Wed	Thur	Fri	Sat	Sun
Shoot Days:						0										1	2	3	4	5		
27	Freddie									W F												
28	Nick																					
29	Tommy Bailey																					
30	Janie Bailey																					
31	Charlie																					
32	Tom																					
33	Zuzu Bailey																					
34	Dr. Campbell				W							D										
35	Mr. Carter																					
36	Principal									W D												
37	Grumpy Old Man	W	F																			
38	Jane																					
39	Toll Keeper																					
40	Mickey																					
41	Lawyer				W F																	
42	Real Estate Salesman				W F																	
43	Insurance Agent				W F																	
44	Suitor #1																			W F		
	Total Actors on Set																					

TITLE: IT'S A WONDERFUL LIFE

Start Date: Report created Mon, May 24, 2004

Month: July

Day of Month:	7	8	9	0	1			1	2	3	4	5			0
Day of Week:	Mon	Tue	Wed	Thur	Fri	Sat	Sun	Mon	Tue	Wed	Thur	Fri	Sat	Sun	Mon
Shoot Days:	6	7	8	9	0			1	2	3	4	5			6
ID **Character**															
1 George															
2 Mary															
3 Harry															
4 Uncle Billy		D													
5 Mr. Potter										D					
6 Mr. Gower															
7 Ernie									D						
8 Bert															
9 Joe															
10 Clarence															

Day of Month:		7	8	9	0	1			1	2	3	4	5			0
Day of Week:		Mon	Tue	Wed	Thur	Fri	Sat	Sun	Mon	Tue	Wed	Thur	Fri	Sat	Sun	Mon
Shoot Days:		6	7	8	9	0			1	2	3	4	5			6
ID	Character															
11	Violet															
12	Ma Bailey		D													
13	Mrs. Hatch		D										D			
14	Mr. Martini				W											W D
15	Cousin Tilly		W													
16	Annie															
17	Peter Bailey															
18	Cousin Eustace		W													
19	Ruth		F													
20	Peter															
21	Goon															
22	Carter															
23	Mary															
24	Sam Wainwright												W			W F
25	Maria Martini															
26	Ed									W D						
27	Freddie															
28	Nick															
29	Tommy Bailey															
30	Janie Bailey									W D						
31	Charlie									W D						

Day of Month:	7	8	9	0	1			1	2	3	4	5			0
Day of Week:	Mon	Tue	Wed	Thur	Fri	Sat	Sun	Mon	Tue	Wed	Thur	Fri	Sat	Sun	Mon
Shoot Days:	6	7	8	9	0			1	2	3	4	5			6

ID	Character	Mon	Tue	Wed	Thur	Fri	Sat	Sun	Mon	Tue	Wed	Thur	Fri	Sat	Sun	Mon
32	Tom									W D						
33	Zuzu Bailey															
34	Dr. Campbell															
35	Mr. Carter															
36	Principal															
37	Grumpy Old Man															
38	Jane															
39	Toll Keeper															
40	Mickey															
41	Lawyer															
42	Real Estate Salesman															
43	Insurance Agent															
44	Suitor #1															
	Total Actors on Set															

TITLE: IT'S A WONDERFUL LIFE

Start Date: <u>Report created Mon, May 24, 2004</u>

Month: <u>August</u>

Day of Month:		1	2	3	4	5	6	7	8	9	0	1	2	3	4	5	6	7	8
Day of Week:		Tues	Wed	Thur	Fri	Sat	Sun	Mon	Tue	Wed	Thur	Fri	Sat	Sun	Mon	Tue	Wed	Thur	Fri
Shoot Days:		7	8	9	0			1	2	3	4	5			6	7	8	9	0
ID	Character																		
1	George																		
2	Mary																		
3	Harry																		
4	Uncle Billy																		
5	Mr. Potter			W															
6	Mr. Gower																		
7	Ernie										W								
8	Bert																		
9	Joe																		
10	Clarence							W											

Day of Month:	1	2	3	4	5	6	7	8	9	0	1	2	3	4	5	6	7	8
Day of Week:	Tues	Wed	Thur	Fri	Sat	Sun	Mon	Tue	Wed	Thur	Fri	Sat	Sun	Mon	Tue	Wed	Thur	Fri
Shoot Days:	7	8	9	0			1	2	3	4	5			6	7	8	9	0
ID **Character**																		
11 Violet																		
12 Ma Bailey																		
13 Mrs. Hatch																		
14 Mr. Martini																		
15 Cousin Tilly			W															
16 Annie																		
17 Peter Bailey										W								
18 Cousin Eustace																		
19 Ruth							W											
20 Peter																		
21 Goon			W															
22 Carter																		
23 Marty																		

Day of Month:	1	2	3	4	5	6	7	8	9	0	1	2	3	4	5	6	7	8
Day of Week:	Tues	Wed	Thur	Fri	Sat	Sun	Mon	Tue	Wed	Thur	Fri	Sat	Sun	Mon	Tue	Wed	Thur	Fri
Shoot Days:	7	8	9	0			1	2	3	4	5			6	7	8	9	0

ID	Character	1	2	3	4	5	6	7	8	9	0	1	2	3	4	5	6	7	8
24	Sam Wainwright																		
25	Maria Martini																		
26	Ed																		W F
27	Freddie																		
28	Nick																		
29	Tommy Bailey																		
30	Janie Bailey																		
31	Charlie																	W	
32	Tom																	W	
33	Zuzu Bailey																		
34	Dr. Campbell																		
35	Mr. Carter																		
36	Principal																		

Day of Month:	1	2	3	4	5	6	7	8	9	0	1	2	3	4	5	6	7	8
Day of Week:	Tues	Wed	Thur	Fri	Sat	Sun	Mon	Tue	Wed	Thur	Fri	Sat	Sun	Mon	Tue	Wed	Thur	Fri
Shoot Days:	7	8	9	0			1	2	3	4	5			6	7	8	9	0
ID / **Character**																		
37 Grumpy																		
38 Jane Wainwright	D																	
39 Toll Keeper																		
40 Mickey																		
41 Lawyer																		
42 Real Estate Salesman																		
43 Insurance Agent																		
44 Suitor #1																		
Total Actors on Set																		

TITLE: IT'S A WONDERFUL LIFE

Start Date: Report created Mon, May 24, 2004

Month: August

Day of Month:	9	0	1	1	2	3	4	5	6	7	8	9	0	1	2	3	4	5
Day of Week:	Sat	Sun	Mon	Tue	Wed	Thurs	Fri	Sat	Sun	Mon	Tue	Wed	Thurs	Fri	Sat	Sun	Mon	Tue
Shoot Days:			1	2	3	4	5			6	7	8	9	0			1	2

ID	Character																		
1	George																		
2	Mary												D						
3	Harry					W													
4	Uncle Billy				W														
5	Mr. Potter																		
6	Mr. Gower					W													
7	Ernie																		
8	Bert																		
9	Joe																		
10	Clarence													F					

Day of Month:		9	0	1	2	3	4	5	6	7	8	9	0	1	2	3	4	5	6
Day of Week:		Sat	Sun	Mon	Tue	Wed	Thurs	Fri	Sat	Sun	Mon	Tue	Wed	Thurs	Fri	Sat	Sun	Mon	Tue
Shoot Days:				1	2	3	4	5			6	7	8	9	0			1	2
ID	**Character**																		
11	Violet																		
12	Ma Bailey																		
13	Mrs. Hatch					W F													
14	Mr. Martini					W	F												
15	Cousin Tilly																		
16	Annie					F													
17	Peter Bailey																		
18	Cousin Eustace																		
19	Ruth												F						
20	Peter			W															
21	Goon																		
22	Carter			W		D													
23	Marty																		

Day of Month:		9	0	1										0	1	2	3	4	5
Day of Week:		Sat	Sun	Mon	Tue	Wed	Thurs	Fri	Sat	Sun	Mon	Tue	Wed	Thurs	Fri	Sat	Sun	Mon	Tue
Shoot Days:				1	2	3	4	5			6	7	8	9	0			1	2
ID	Character																		
24	Sam Wainwright																		
25	Maria Martini																		
26	Ed																		
27	Freddie																		
28	Nick						W	F											
29	Tommy Bailey			W									F						
30	Janie Bailey			W									F						
31	Charlie					F													
32	Tom					F													
33	Zuzu Bailey					W												F	
34	Dr. Campbell					W F													
35	Mr. Carter					W D													
36	Principal					W F													

Day of Month:		9	0	1										0	1	2	3	4	5
ID	**Character** / Day of Week:	Sat	Sun	Mon	Tue	Wed	Thurs	Fri	Sat	Sun	Mon	Tue	Wed	Thurs	Fri	Sat	Sun	Mon	Tue
	Shoot Days:	7	8	9	0		4	5		3	4	5	8	9	0		8	9	0
37	Grumpy																		
38	Jane Wainwright					W F													
39	Toll Keeper													W F					
40	Mickey																		
41	Lawyer																		
42	Real Estate Salesman																		
43	Insurance Agent																		
44	Suitor #1																		
	Total Actors on Set																		

TITLE: IT'S A WONDERFUL LIFE

Start Date: Report created Mon, May 24, 2004

Month: September

		6	7	8	9	0	1	2	3	4	5	6	7	8	9	0	1	2	3
	Day of Month:	6	7	8	9	0	1	2	3	4	5	6	7	8	9	0	1	2	3
	Day of Week:	Wed	Thurs	Fri	Sat	Sun	Mon	Tue	Wed	Thurs	Fri	Sat	Sun	Mon	Tues	Wed	Thurs	Fri	Sat
	Shoot Days:	3	4	5			6	7	8	9	0			1	2	3	4	5	
ID	Character																		
1	George																	F	
2	Mary							W											
3	Harry																		
4	Uncle Billy																		
5	Mr. Potter																		
6	Mr. Gower										F								
7	Ernie																		
8	Bert									F									
9	Joe																		
10	Clarence																		

	Day of Month:	6	7	8	9	0	1	2	3	4	5	6	7	8	9	0	1	2	3
	Day of Week:	Wed	Thurs	Fri	Sat	Sun	Mon	Tue	Wed	Thurs	Fri	Sat	Sun	Mon	Tue	Wed	Thurs	Fri	Sat
	Shoot Days:	3	4	5			6	7	8	9	0			1	2	3	4	5	
ID	**Character**																		
11	Violet							F											
12	Ma Bailey																		
13	Mrs. Hatch																		
14	Mr. Martini																		
15	Cousin Tilly																		
16	Annie																		
17	Peter Bailey						F												
18	Cousin Eustace																		
19	Ruth																		
20	Peter																		
21	Goon															W F			
22	Carter														J			W F	
23	Marty																		

Day of Month:

ID	Character	6	7	8	9	0	1	2	3	4	5	6	7	8	9	0	1	2	3
	Day of Week:	Wed	Thurs	Fri	Sat	Sun	Mon	Tue	Wed	Thurs	Fri	Sat	Sun	Mon	Tues	Wed	Thurs	Fri	Sat
	Shoot Days:	3	4	5			6	7	8	9	0			1	2	3	4	5	
24	Sam Wainwright																		
25	Maria Martini																		
26	Ed																		
27	Freddie																		
28	Nick																		
29	Tommy Bailey																		
30	Janie Bailey																		
31	Charlie																		
32	Tom																		
33	Zuzu Bailey																		
34	Dr. Campbell																		
35	Mr. Carter		W				F												
36	Principal																		

ID	Character	Day of Month:	6	7	8	9	0	1	2	3	4	5	6	7	8	9	0	1	2	3	4	5
		Day of Week:	Wed	Thurs	Fri	Sat	Sun	Mon	Tue	Wed	Thurs	Fri	Sat	Sun	Mon	Tues	Wed	Thurs	Fri	Sat	Sun	Mon
		Shoot Days:	3	4	5			6	7	8	9	0			1	2	3	4	5			6
37	Grumpy																					
38	Jane Wainwright																					
39	Toll Keeper																					
40	Mickey																					
41	Lawyer																					
42	Real Estate Salesman																					
43	Insurance Agent																					
44	Suitor #1																					
	Total Actors on Set																					

TITLE: IT'S A WONDERFUL LIFE

Start Date: Report created Mon, May 24, 2004

Month: October

		Day of Month: 6	7	7	Travel	Work	Hold	Holiday	Start	Finish	Total
		Day of Week: Sun	Mon	Tue							
		Shoot Days:	6	7							
ID	Character										
1	George				F	4			7/6	10/7	7
2	Mary					6	0		7/7	10/2	6
3	Harry		F	F		1	9		7/7	10/5	0
4	Uncle Billy			F		9	9		7/7	10/6	8
5	Mr. Potter			F		1	9		7/9	10/6	0
6	Mr. Gower						6		7/13	10/2	4
7	Ernie								7/6	9/15	1
8	Bert						5		7/6	10/1	4
9	Joe								7/15	7/15	
10	Clarence						0		8/17	9/10	9w

| | | Day of Month: | 6 | 7 | | | | | | | | |
| | | Day of Week: | Sun | Mon | Tue | | | | | | | |
		Shoot Days:		6	7	Travel	Work	Hold	Holiday	Start	Finish	Total
ID	Character											
11	Violet							4		7/16	9/29	3
12	Ma Bailey							1		7/10	10/5	9
13	Mrs. Hatch									7/30	9/2	
14	Mr. Martini									8/10	9/3	
15	Cousin Tilly				F		0	3		7/16	10/6	3
16	Annie							0		7/10	9/2	
17	Peter Bailey							5		7/10	9/28	1
18	Cousin Eustace				F		0	3		7/16	10/6	3
19	Ruth									7/17	7/28	
20	Peter									8/31	9/30	
21	Goon				F		0	0		7/9	10/6	0
22	Carter									8/31	9/30	
23	Marry									7/14	10/2	
24	Sam Wainwright									7/4	10/2	2
25	Maria Martini									8/10	8/10	

Day of Month:		6	7		Travel	Work	Hold	Holiday	Start	Finish	Total
Day of Week:		Sun	Mon	Tue							
Shoot Days:			6	7							
ID	Character										
26	Ed								8/4	8/27	
27	Freddie								7/14	7/27	
28	Nick								9/3	9/4	
29	Tommy Bailey								8/31	9/9	
30	Janie Bailey								8/31	9/9	
31	Charlie								8/4	9/2	
32	Tom								8/4	9/2	
33	Zuzu Bailey								9/2	9/14	
34	Dr. Campbell								7/9	9/2	
35	Mr. Carter								9/2	9/21	
36	Principal								7/14	9/2	
37	Grumpy Old Man								7/6	7/7	
38	Jane Wainwright								8/10	9/2	
39	Toll Keeper								8/26	9/10	
40	Mickey								7/14	7/14	

ID	Character	Day of Month: 6	7		Travel	Work	Hold	Holiday	Start	Finish	Total
		Day of Week: Sun	Mon	Tue							
		Shoot Days:	6	7							
41	Lawyer								7/9	7/9	
42	Real								7/9	7/9	
43	Esatate Salesman								7/9	7/9	
44	Suitor #1								7/24	7/24	
	Total of Numbers on set										

PRODUCTION STAFF DESCRIPTION:

Line Producer/Unit Production Manager—keeps track of the budget.

Assistant Director—lines up all the elements of the production for the Director and manages the daily running of the set. The first A.D. runs all the extras on big Hollywood films.

Production Assistant, Continuity, or script person—checks the production against the script and keeps track of time.

Set Designer—designs the sets and works with the art director.

Production Designer—determines the look of the production by designing and preparing all graphics and visuals.

Art Director—works under the Production Designer. The art director also works with the set director to convey the essence of the story for each scene. The set can be a pre-existing place, like a church, or a place that is constructed to look like a church. The art director helps to design the set and looks at every single scene on the shooting schedule to figure out how to make each scene look just the way you want it.

Make-Up Artist, Hair Stylist, The *Costume Designer, Gaffer/ Chief Lighting Technician*—The more you know about movies and television, the more you will realize how important and difficult lighting is. Achieving the right level of lighting on camera is difficult, even if it is a low light camera. Achieving good, attractive, atmospheric, uniform lighting for multiple television cameras is an art.

Post Production Sound Mixer—controls audio quality and mixes the sound. Good sound quality demands great care, and marks the difference between a poor production and a good one.

Camera Operator and *Camera Assistants*—operate the camera(s) with the help of the camera crew.

Soundperson—operates the sound booms, microphones and audio equipment (can also be a team of sound people).

Grips—responsible for changing the camera positions by building platforms, operating dollies, rigging camera mounts, building stands, and securing lights or mounting the camera equipment and personnel in unimaginable places.

Gaffer and Electricians—are responsible for all electrical wiring and for rigging lights and measuring light in order to expose the film properly. Never use a first time gaffer who does not have a well-established mentor available as a lifeline by phone.

Special Effects Person—creates and produces all special effects.

Production Assistant—goes for this and that.

Visual Effects Supervisor—helps determine and execute the necessary digital and optical visual effects, 2-D and 3-D animation, etc. (This is different from Special Effects, which is all practical.)

Location Manager—initiates all conversations and negotiates with property owners as well as files location permits.

Property Manager—secures and props and places.

With the new lightweight, compact equipment, some documentary producers have cut the number of personnel down to just themselves and their camcorder. However, to be sure you get your shot, the minimum staff needed for a small production is:

Producer/Director

Assistant Director

Production Assistant

Cameraperson

Soundperson

Lighting

Talent

Writer

SUCCESS, STEP 9: ORGANIZING ARTISTIC/ TECHNICAL SERVICES AND FACILITIES

1. Reserve all facilities, studios, and locations.
2. Prepare for the rental and purchase of all equipment. Each department develops a list and initiates conversations with vendors. The Unit Production Manager/Line Producer finalizes the deals. The Production Coordinator organizes the pick up and delivery of the equipment according to the schedule prepared by the A.D.s.
3. Prepare for all artistic services and technical services so that everything is ready and available when you need it.
4. Prepare all artwork, graphics, special effects, audio effects, music, costumes, and props.
5. Prepare for all location filming. The Location Manager initiates all conversations and negotiates with property owners as well as files location permits. Once upon a time, my wife was serving as a Location Manager for an Italian production company filming in New York City. They kept changing their minds about locations and started filming a shootout in a new location. Needless to say, the New York City Police were not amused.
6. Begin the construction of all sets and scenery.
7. Reserve all facilities, studios, and locations.

The chain of command and delegation are crucial to the success of any shoot, so there is a specific person attached to each of these tasks. Thus, a movie production is similar to a complex military campaign in its need for organization, command, and delegation.

PRODUCERS ARE COACHES

Worldwide audiences have been thrilled by the stunning, memorable family movies entitled, *Who Framed Roger Rabbit, Hunchback of Notre Dame*, and *Beauty and the Beast*. These movies boasted several "firsts" in the areas of animation technology advances, digital enhancements, and colorization. The producer of these movies, as well as other beloved classics such as *Lion King, Emperor's New Groove*, and *Atlantis,* is the talented Don Hahn, of the Walt Disney Company.

THE SECOND GOLDEN AGE OF ANIMATION

—AN INTERVIEW WITH DON HAHN

ART CAN INSPIRE

Don attended Cal State Northridge as a music major and art minor. "I never studied film. I studied opera, musical theatre, and orchestras, and I was always interested in storytelling, drawing, painting, and color theory. I saw the art side of movies as more of an inspiration than the story side. I think movies can be too self-referential sometimes . . . too insular. I get inspiration from life, nature, other characters, and people. I think there are more interesting ways to make films . . . films inspired by reality."

PRODUCERS ARE COACHES

Don feels that his job most closely resembles that of a coach on a football team. "I'm not calling plays or passing the ball, but in every way I'm responsible for pulling a team together, creating the project, creating the idea, and encouraging the gifts and talents that help the team work together. I'm coaching them to get the best work out of them. I get to work with amazing people. They're the best musicians, artists, and technical people in the world. We all work much better together than separately; no one could make a movie alone. Joint collaboration makes a movie great. I especially appreciate my core team—the storyteller and songwriter of each project. If we understand each other, it's powerful. I feel lucky to have them in my life."

FAVORITES PROJECT VS. BEST EXPERIENCE

When asked what his favorite project has been, Don responds with, "Oh, that's hard. That's like asking 'Who's your favorite child?' I guess if I were pushed I'd have to say *Beauty and the Beast*. I had a great team, the response was so great, it won Best Picture nomination, and it had fantastic direction and lots of innovations. It was an interesting time back in '91."

Don feels that it's less about favorites, though, and more about quality of experience. "With *Roger Rabbit, Lion King,* and *The Haunted Mansion*, I learned so much. I worked with different teams and very different stories. Each project had different stories that surrounded it, and each gave me great life experiences that I drew from on subsequent projects. I've been fortunate to have the opportunity to produce films that involve both live action and animation, and I know it's rare that I've gotten to work with both. *Mary Poppins* was both, and that always inspired me. I produced *Roger Rabbit*, and *Pete's Dragon*, which were both the combination deal. It was a lot of fun."

IT'S ALL ABOUT TALENT

When asked about the potential for people of faith to get involved in Hollywood, Don responded with, "There's an open door for people of talent. There are no barriers beyond that, honestly. There are many people of many varieties of faith—Christian, Muslim, and Jewish, who are all very successful, but it has little or nothing to do with their faith. Hollywood's all about talent. A person who has an interesting idea or perspective, has done his homework, and learned the craft of filmmaking, that's what it's about. It's all about the talent and ability to deliver something fresh and entertaining."

FIND A LIKE-MINDED ENVIRONMENT, IF POSSIBLE

According to Don, Disney is naturally a family medium, in keeping with his faith and values. "It's not often that moral dilemmas come up in my environment. It's the reason I work at Disney. I could have worked and still can work anywhere else, but there's a great spirit in this company, and the kinds of movies they promote make it a great place for people with strong values to function well."

"*Pirates of the Caribbean, Finding Nemo,* and *Miracle* are all examples of fun, cool-to-watch, incredibly successful films financially. They're also spiritually connected, positive family movies about overcoming obstacles. Our movies are always obstacle-related, not faith-related or religion-related. Though like any other company, there's plenty of great water-cooler talk about politics and religion, that's not what our work is about. Sure we're humans who read the paper, watch TV, and like to gossip. But if you want to know the truth, most of us who work here are stuck in a state of perpetual adolescence. We're kids, so we tell stories and make movies about pigs and lions and little lost fish. We dream in 'cartoon' at night."

EXCELLENCE RULES

Don Hahn believes that producing animation and live action movies takes a combination of talent, skill, and luck. "Luck is being in the right place and right time. You have to understand the industry enough so that you're not stunned. It's a business, and it depends on excellence and quality to make money. Make yourself excellent. Hire the job candidate who is most excellent— the one with the best qualities, instincts, and knowledge. Don't skip the knowledge part just because it's not fun. Don't be like the piano player who doesn't want to practice his scales. Spend time learning, drawing, understanding the craft, seeking out mentors, and immersing yourself in the industry."

NEVER GIVE UP!

In order to make it in the industry, believes Don, one must find his natural talents and gain knowledge of his craft. It takes persistence—and patience—he says, so most don't stick it out. "They give up. But that's part of the talent, is persisting. I've had to persist through a lot of seemingly closed doors in my day, and there's always a level of frustration in every endeavor, but I'm fortunate to have known the people I've known and that I've made it long enough to have done the things I've done. Persistence is definitely the key."

BE RELEVANT

The common thread in great movies, says Don, is relevance. "So often movies and stories are told that are unrelateable to mainstream audiences. They're distant and abstract. The audience has to relate to the characters on the screen, whether it's an animated elephant or a live pirate character. In good movies audiences have some feelings about the protagonist's dilemma. If they can't understand the characters, or they're unredeemable jerks, audiences will feel squeamish, frustrated, even let down. If they're not real enough, they're not relatable, and you've got a bad movie."

TRANSCEND TARGETING

When asked what the major target audience is for his films, Don says, "I never try to have a conversation about target audience. A good movie, or a satisfying movie, transcends the idea of a target audience. For instance, no one liked *Lizzie McGuire* more than me. Good movies don't punish parents; they're as entertaining for the parents as the kids. Yes, we do have generalities of targets, but the most successful movies are relatable to audiences from 6 to 85. For example, in *Lord of the Rings* one can't point to the film and say, 'This was our target audience.' It was for all of us. Just like the majority of the movies Disney produces."

NO BAD DREAMS

The goal of a good Disney film is to excite and entertain, but not truly scare, it would seem, to at least one of its producers. "Intense movies really bother me," admits Don. "It's a personal thing. For instance, *Braveheart* was a work of powerful filmmaking, but the graphic images stayed with me for a long time. I just don't think people need that gratuitous violence in their gray matter."

IT'S NOT CALLED "SHOW FRIENDS!"

Producer Hahn reminds us Hollywood wannabes that the entertainment industry is, indeed, a business. "Movies have to, for the most part, be profitable. That's the goal. Sure, there are some rare exceptions, like the movies made simply for the art, but the entertainment industry has to have profitability at its heart. Financiers want to know, 'Is this movie relevant? Excellent in quality?' People don't want to pay $10 and feel ripped off. They want to come away saying, 'I loved those characters.' Where quality and entertainment meet in a movie, the money will follow."

Most animated movies are made for between $15 and $100 million dollars, says Don.

"One of lowest, most restricted budgets I had was with *Beauty and the Beast*. We had to do so much corner cutting, put in overtime . . . It was a pressured financial situation. We had to make something fantastic for a low price. As the producer, I had to be responsible to that, to understand the business of it all."

IT'S BIG BUCKS, FOLKS

When asked about the expenses on an animated film, Don tells us "Big money goes to the labor pool of animators, and the voice cast would be a more minimal cost. We're paying people to sit at a drawing board and painstakingly draw out each scene. For instance, there were close to six hundred animators per major movie about years ago, but now the movies require less due to the impact and efficiency of computerized animation advances. Other crew needed for an animated picture include musicians, sound effects guys, or "Foley artists." In *The Hunchback of Notre Dame*, we used thirty animators and one hundred clean up people, or the folks who draw in the details after the initial rough drawings."

IN-HOUSE DEVELOPMENT WORKS

Don and his team don't get many scripts sent to them, they say, mainly because they don't solicit from outside sources. Don develops projects himself with writers, and mostly does movies based on favorite kids' books. *Atlantis* was an original, but *Hunchback of Notre Dame, Lion King*, and *Roger Rabbit* were novels. "You never know where the stories are coming from. We rarely read anything from the outside. We're more likely to find good ideas and hire writers to carry them through. Actually, the writer on *Hunchback* was a first-time screenwriter. He had been an intern and Disney, then a staff writer. Then, we just trusted him with a big one. Obviously, he did a great job."

And just as obviously, Don Hahn does a great job as he continues to entertain the world with his colorful, well-produced Disney animated classics. More, more, more!

* * *

Lights, Camera, Action

STEPS TO SUCCESS:
10–17, PRODUCTION

Production is where all your planning pays off. This is where you get to finally tell your story through the medium of film or television. Before getting to the step-by-step instructions, let's look for inspiration to expert producer Ralph Winter . . .

> Two mutants come to a private academy whose resident superhero team must oppose a powerful mutant terrorist organization.
>
> To save Earth from an alien probe, Kirk and his crew go back in time to retrieve the only beings that can communicate with it—humpback whales.

Such are the loglines of movies produced, co-produced, or executive produced by Ralph Winter. Ralph has been involved in the making of *X-Men I*, *II*, and *III*, *Star Trek II*, *IV*, *V*, and *VI*, *Mighty*

Joe Young, and the *Fantastic Four,* after the famous comic book. Its logline reads, "A group of astronauts gain superpowers after a cosmic radiation exposure and must use those powers to oppose the plans of their enemy, Doctor Victor Von Doom." No way!

What's in the mind of one who would produce such wild and incredible sci-fi movies? Actually, audiences might be surprised to find a very normal guy—with an extraordinary outlook.

Think Outside the Box
—an interview with Ralph Winter

From School . . . to the Store. . . to TV . . . to Film

Ralph Winter was a history major at the University of California at Berkeley. Upon graduation, he began creating industrial videos for department stores. After winning some national awards for his videos, he moved into Paramount Studios, working in a post-production role for television programs. This experience whet his appetite to produce movies, so after three years at Paramount as the co-head of his group, he ventured out to co-produce some of the *Star Trek* movies. "It was a great experience, and I've been fortunate since then to be able to leverage my skills as an executive producer or producer on a variety of features and TV shows at various studios."

Faithful in Little . . . Entrusted with Much

Ralph considers each phase of his education and work history to be valuable stepping-stones to his current projects. During this interview, Ralph was hard at work on *Fantastic Four* with Twentieth Century Fox. The crew was shooting in Vancouver, British Columbia. "Part of my job is to revitalize this forty-year-old comic book and make the material accessible even to those unaware of its cultural significance."

The movie was filmed in live action, rather than animation, and will highlight the four superheroes of the Marvel world. "Gamma radiation hits, and these guys get superhero abilities. The movie is about how they get their powers, then how they work together and live—taking care of the bad guys with a lot of live action." The plan is the same as it was on the *X-Men* movies. "We'll make this first one for a price, and if the story and characters are enthralling, we'll be making more."

Cultivate Faith, Integrity, and Relationships

Ralph grew up in the church, becoming a Christian at the age of twelve. "I was very involved trying to walk the walk of faith and see what it means to follow Christ. The biggest way it informs me now is in the kinds of materials I choose, the people I work with, and the goal of just trying to do excellent work with integrity." Ralph believes that the way people are treated is just as important as the product being produced. "I have fun making important, compelling, and inspiring works, but God has impressed me to build relationships and cultivate them with the same or greater zeal as making each movie."

Stay Accountable

Through the years, a number of pastors have come alongside Ralph, teaching him and acting as sounding boards for various issues. "Bill Tibert of Colorado Springs, a guy who used to be in the Navy, was a youth leader at my church. He mentored me after my conversion to Christ. Also, there's a friend H. Spees, who was running for the Mayor of Fresno, but now the pastor of a large church in Fresno. He's done the same thing." Ralph believes that it's all about the journey, not necessarily the destination. "These relationships can be very helpful, and very useful. I'm in business with others, in partnership with other Christian filmmakers right now, and I get mentored as much or more as I ever give them."

Excellence and Integrity First

Ralph Winter is more focused on doing excellent work with integrity than on evangelizing Hollywood. "I'm not interested in necessarily producing overt, evangelical, heavy agenda films, but rather in telling inspiring stories about how people get through life and negotiate issues. I have worked on the clearly Christian movies like *Left Behind*, which was fun and a bit more overt than some of the others, but pronounced evangelism is not my first intention in selecting projects. I like to stay more in the mainstream sector of the industry, and if people have questions along the way, I'm delighted to share the good news of what Christ has done for me, rather than preaching it through the material. I do want everyone to have what I have, and I hope that through the excellence of good storytelling my projects stir up those questions and cravings in my audiences."

Ralph has seen through the years that people don't want to be preached at. "Movies aren't good at that. Audiences can smell that a mile away. It must be subtle, if a message is to be sent at all. Actually, even *The Passion of the Christ* is not as overt as you'd think. It's a great movie, but it's portrayed as a love poem. Everybody knows the story. It's a question of seeing it as a work of art. It's fantastic. It's a powerful story of sacrifice and what Jesus went through in giving that sacrifice, but it raises lots of questions about, 'Who is that person? Why would he do this? Who is that baby?' It stirs cravings and opens the door for believers to answer questions. Churches and Christians can fill a unique role right now to answer the questions sparked by this movie."

Bring Excellent Crossover Material to the Studios

It's an open playing field in Hollywood for people of faith if they can create commercial material that will connect them to an audience, believes Ralph. "For instance, we made, distributed, put in theatres, and now in video stores a movie called *Hangman's Curse*. We made this Frank Peretti adaptation for $2 million, brought it to a studio, and they recognized, well in advance of *The Passion*, that they wanted to be involved. We brought them a fully financed movie, from an author who is basically a rock star in the Christian fiction world, and we presented a way to get it into that market, and sell the product for a profit. Twentieth Century Fox was more than happy to buy the product, distribute it, and get it to the market."

Many Christians are interested in preaching and having an agenda, but studios don't find that to be marketable, says Ralph. He tells rising Christian artists that studios don't want heavy-handed, obvious preachy-ness, or movies that lack production value. "*The Passion* had top, top production value. It had a big movie star, Mel Gibson, to conceptualize and bring it to the market, it had a fabulous actor, Jim Caviezel, it had a huge budget, and it was very, very well made by an Academy Award-winning director. Christians want quality, too. Their desire for entertainment is no different than the secular world."

Another movie that impressed Ralph was Tom Shadiak's *Bruce Almighty*. "This movie showed an A-list actor, Jim Carey, basically praying the sinner's prayer—laying it out there. But, it wasn't preachy. It was totally entertaining and captivating. Other long time Christian filmmakers couldn't have done as well, though I must say I wish I had come up with the idea."

As for more biblical epics on the heels of *The Passion*, Ralph isn't sure. "There's room for the biblical epics like *Ben-Hur*, but I'm not seeing that coming out [of] the studio's mind right now. I could be wrong."

In a Multitude of Counselors Is Wisdom

As to discerning talent, Ralph suggests examining whether or not others are recognizing it and finding it inspiring and page turning. Many young Christians want him to read their material, but he tells them he's not the benchmark to determine whether they're a good writer or not, that they've got to test it inside and outside the community. "At Glendale Presbyterian Church, where I'm still attending, I did videos for mission trips and stewardship campaigns to try out my skills. I had to ask, 'Are people motivated to help because of the video? I had to track very specific, targeted programs and measurements. I had to assess the encouragement level of others, too. Were they saying, 'We want to see more?' That's a sure way to discern your gift early on. Unfortunately, Christians aren't taking advantage of that. They're not offering and testing out their talents in church—a market that's very forgiving, by the way."

Ralph points out that the New Testament tells believers how to understand their giftings and places in the body of Christ, and any good pastor can also help an artist discern their talents and gifts.

Serve in Humble Jobs First

Everyone wants to write or direct in Hollywood, but many do not have a proven track record, states Ralph. "Equipment is cheap. If you really want to do this, get some equipment and help your pastor tell a story through video. Then see if your work is compelling. Does it set fires under people and really makes them think? If you can't do it in a 3-minute format, what makes you think you can do it in 2-hour format?"

One of the biggest roadblocks Ralph sees for people of faith is the lack of good material and the often-unethical environment of the industry. "With the level of competition in the industry, it's easy to step on people, to steal projects, and to do unethical things to push your agenda ahead. There's a daily temptation and pressure to do that." Ralph tries to resist taking the easy way out, but rather works hard to develop each project with excellence and a focus on honoring others through fostering trusted relationships.

Think Outside the Box

Ralph encourages those interested in Hollywood to consider alternate avenues as well. "There are a lot of opportunities out there in the movie business and television, but there are other venues in many cities such as video and film work for universities, corporate videos, churches, etc. Everyone uses media in some way. It's admirable that people want to be in the movie business, but you've got to play college ball first before you play in the NBA. There are very few walk-ons in the NBA. There are lots of opportunities to be involved in the media. You just have to connect the dots and find out what's going to make it all work for you."

Not only does this producer think outside the Hollywood box with his focus on relationship building, integrity, and evoking audience questions through good story-telling, he's obviously unafraid to shoot straight to those with ears to hear. Best to you, Ralph Winter!

* * *

With Ralph's insights in mind, let's get back to our step-by-step recipe for a movie.

SUCCESS, STEP 10: REHEARSALS

This step applies mostly to television, although top movie producers have said that there should be more rehearsing going on in film production.

At this point, if you are producing for television, you will start rehearsing your cast and crew. Run through your script to begin the process of blocking out all movements of cast, cameras, sound equipment, and crew. Have your performers practice their lines, actions, and performances. Make sure that the timing is what you want.

The sequence of "recorded live" TV rehearsals may include:

1. A walkthrough or dry run
2. A stagger through to coordinate technical services
3. A pre-dress run through to polish
4. A dress rehearsal
5. Production

For many movies, there may not be a rehearsal. Often there is just a walkthrough, because time is money on a film production. Stars are paid big bucks, so the producer will want to film them and dismiss them as fast as possible. However, many top producers have said it is ideal to rehearse on a film set, to potentially save time and money.

Here is a possible order for movie production:

1. A walkthrough or dry run for technical people
2. A rehearsal, which often means that the actors go off the set and work on the scene
3. Production

Note that you will want to rehearse each type many times to achieve a quality production run.

SUCCESS, STEP 11:
CAMERA AND OTHER SCRIPTS

In Chapter 9, we looked at a shooting schedule. Using your shooting schedule, you may want to prepare a "shot list" showing what the camera is doing when and how, especially if you are producing a television movie.

It is important to lock a script prior to shooting. Locking the script means confirming a final version—this is the script you are filming. Even under the best of circumstances, there may still be some changes to a locked script. These changes would be inserted in the script as pink, yellow, red, or other colored pages in place of the white pages being replaced.

In television, you will want to prepare scripts for each and every member of your team who needs to know what they are doing when and how.

TV MOVIE CAMERA SHOT LIST

Camera:_____

Shot	Position	Lens Angle	Scene
1	B	13	Restaurant CU Painting
2	A	35	PULL BACK to LS of Telly in front of painting
6	C	20	MCU of Telly at table

As you plan your shot list, keep in mind the distance a camera needs for a shot and what camera angles give you or your director an ECU (extra close-up), CU (close-up), an MCU (medium close-up), a BCU (big close-up), a 2-S (two shot), a 3-S (three shot), an MS (medium shot), or an LS (long shot).

You may want to familiarize yourself with the working of the respective equipment and with standard abbreviations to prepare these scripts. Books on production will take you only so far. You must have some working knowledge of basic equipment and what it can do to adequately prepare your production, even when you have hired the best talent.

SUCCESS, STEP 12:
PREPARE SOUND STAGES AND LOCATIONS

Most movies are filmed on rented sound stages (unless you own a major studio). In the rush to the sound stage to produce the program, the producer and director often find that the studio is not prepared to do the type of production work that is required.

You, your producer, and your director should meet with the sound stage to confirm the availability of everything that is essential to your production, including: the space, the equipment, the back-up facilities, the crew, the storage space, the time to set up, the technical equipment, the electrical facilities, the dressing rooms, the green room, and anything else specifically relevant to your production.

Every production process is different. In movie production, many sound stages rent the special equipment they will need for each production from an equipment house. (Unlike movie sound stages, most television studios have equipment, but you still have to rent each piece of gear separately.)

You need to prepare the sound stage to have everything you need available: on line, in the system, before the big day of the production, when you will be spending money by the minute on cast and crew.

Before the day of production, know your way around your studio: know the key personnel, know the equipment, and be prepared for emergencies. Also, be sure you have insurance to cover your losses, should any occur. Make sure you have filed the proper work orders, forms or requisitions depending on the facility, and prepare contracts for everything. You know what you need at the studio and on location—spell it out in writing, for the record.

As your production becomes more complex, you will add more equipment. The grip is responsible for the adjustment and maintenance of production equipment on the set. Typical duties include laying dolly tracks and erecting scaffolding. Be aware of how any new equipment works and how it interfaces with the equipment you already have.

Line up transportation for your staff and cast. Also line up catering so that you have the food and beverages in the studio or on location that will keep your personnel happy.

Check with your property manager to make sure all necessary props are accounted for. Props include all the items on a set that will be used during production. Props help the audience understand what is happening in the movie by defining different aspects of the scene or character.

SUCCESS, STEP 13: CAMERA BLOCKING AND EQUIPMENT PREPARATION

Before your production starts, you need to know: (1) What you want your camera, sound equipment, and other equipment to do, (2) When you will need each piece of equipment, and how it will be used. Since the camera is a critical piece of equipment, you should be personally familiar with operating a camera and know the different ways that video and film cameras are used to tell a story.

Camera Basics

There are three key people on the camera staff:

> The *Cinematographer* or *Director of Photography* is in charge of the camera staff, lighting the set, and making all the important decisions.
> The *Camera Operator* films the scene.
> The *Gaffer* or *Chief Electrician* works with the cinematographer to light the set.

There are three basic camera positions:

> A *stationary* camera in the same place for an entire shot, although it may swivel, usually mounted on a tripod to keep it steady.

> A *hand-held* camera is held by a cameraman and moves with him. Often, the image looks shaky.

> A *moving* camera is moving during the shoot. This term can apply to either a camera on a dolly or a hand-held camera.

There are three basic camera moves:

> *Pan*—where the camera moves from side to side.
>
> *Tilt*—where the camera moves up and down.
>
> *Zoom*—where the camera moves in from a wider shot to a closer shot or out.

Whenever the camera moves, remember that the camera is shaking even more than it looks like through the viewfinder. Always shoot each scene several times and in several ways. This thorough method of shooting is known as "coverage," and is aptly named— those extra shots provide coverage for mistakes during editing.

WITH RESPECT TO THE CAMERA:

Your cameraperson has to compose a good picture. He or she must keep in mind the subject and the lights at all times. Help him or her by planning your shots.

Here are four of the *most common shots*:

> **Long shot (LS)**—where you see the person at a distance, small in comparison to the surroundings.
>
> **Medium shot (MS)**—where you see the person from the waist up.
>
> **Close-up (CU)**—where you see details only, such as a face, etc.
>
> **Extreme Close-up (ECU)**—where you see extreme detail, such as an earring.
>
> Plan your shot so that:

> - It shows what you want it to show and no more.
> - It accomplishes your purpose.

- Every camera move has an effect on your audience. You should know what those effects are and use them to tell your story.
- It emphasizes what you want it to emphasize.
- Simplify the elements in a picture. Note that with a zoom there is no parallactic movement, there is only compression or stretching of perspective. It is not a natural movement. When we move through a space, such as down a city block, there is parallactic movement so that the parallel lines of the buildings increase in size as we approach them and then decrease as we pass them by. A dolly is better to convey the feeling of parallactic movement because it actually moves through a scene. The movie 2001: A Space Odyssey was applauded in contrast to many earlier films because the dollying through the star field created a feeling of actual movement. Zooms in and out on a flat star field, while cheaper, do not create the feeling of movement. However, zooms have the advantage of creating other emotional reactions. So, the best rule at first is to use zooms sparingly and where appropriate.
- It is neither too close nor too distant.

Attention is focused and not diffused or distracted by extraneous objects or lines in the shot.

You can focus attention by:

- Exclusion
- A visual or audio clue
- Color
- Camera angle
- Composition

- Contrast
- Movement
- Performance

Vertical or horizontal lines in the scenery or background should never divide a scene or the subject in two halves. A change in camera position will solve this problem.

The main subject is framed properly. This is easier said than done. Do not compose your picture for perfect symmetry because symmetry will take away from visual interest. Shoot for an interesting perspective, from a slight angle.

You know when action will enter and leave the shot. Movements away and toward a camera are more dramatic than lateral movements across the field of vision.

The shot establishes the effect you want by revealing, concealing, misleading, or focusing on the central subject. Low shots, shooting up, make subjects look stronger. High shots, looking down, make subjects look weaker. Normal viewpoint is chest high.

The camera avoids lateral reversal effects that occur because the human eye tends to wander toward frame right. Frame left can support more people, more weight and more darkness without looking shut in or crowded.

You will use unusual angles or moves only where appropriate.

The camera will not intrude on your story.
Your picture has: unity, variety, harmony, balance, rhythm, pacing, proportion, and continuity with everything before and after.

In my classes, each student videotapes a scene to demonstrate how the medium affects communication. Reviewing those scenes, many evidence a lateral reversal effect, which the student producer didn't expect and which distorted what they wanted to communicate. Lateral reversal effects are perceptual tricks played by our eyes and minds which cause subjects to look heavier on screen right, diagonals to suggest up or down depending on the direction of their slope, and pictures to look static composed one way and dynamic the other way. Such effects can often change the meaning of a scene by affecting audience perception.

With regard to diagonals and slope, the following illustration is instructive:

Figure 19: Perceptual Orientation

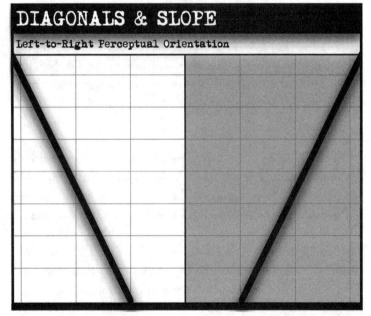

Both these lines are the same in every respect except the direction of their slope. Our left to right perceptual orientation causes us to perceive the line on the left as having a downward slope and the line on the right as having an upward slope. In fact, neither line goes up or down.

Every environment is made up of lines. Filming or videotaping an environment without regard for the lateral reversal effects lurking in the background can cause interesting perceptual consequences that will, to some degree, alter the meaning of your shot.

Consider the following guidelines in choosing your composition, but remember, ultimately it's what you want it to be. Rectangular or square compositions can be boring, and are best avoided. Triangular compositions are pleasing. The right angle suggests opposition and contrast. An S curve is slow and restful. A Z curve is fast and exciting. A cross expresses a merging of interests. A circle represents continuity.

The color choice is also appropriate. Green backgrounds have been shown to upset an audience. Blue backgrounds are pleasing. Pink backgrounds establish warmth and love. Be aware of how colors affect people and how to use them properly. In Japan, they tend to use more yellow tints in their pictures; in Hollywood, they tend to use more blue; and in New York, photographers tend to use more gray and green.

Captain of Composition

If the movie looks great, it may be because the Director of Photography/Cinematographer is the highly experienced, faith-filled J. Michael (Jim) Muro. Jim has worked on a number of music videos and independent films, including his own, as well as grand epics like *Open Range* with Kevin Costner and *Titanic*, with James Cameron. Jim jokingly points out that it wasn't just Titanic's captain that went down with the ship—it was also he and his Arriflex camera!

In order to be given such responsibility on these films whose budgets sometimes exceeded $200 million dollars, Jim has had to prove himself capable of delivering the goods. This experience has come over the past two decades—in formal schooling at The School of Visual Arts in New York City, and maybe more importantly, the School of Hard knocks—with classes held everywhere. During this journey, Jim has seen the industry go through some major changes. And according to this busy, sought-after D.P., things are changing now . . . for the better!

The Ship is Turning

—an interview with J. Michael Muro

They're Getting It!

Jim was excited about Mel Gibson's blockbuster movie, *The Passion of the Christ*. "Finally, a major, established player in Hollywood has stepped out for Christ," says Jim. "He's put out a statement of faith and said, 'Here it is; watch it, or don't!' And people are watching!" (As of the writing of this article, *The Passion* had garnered $430 million at the worldwide box office.) "I was already feeling the ship start to turn when *Lord of the Rings* did so well. For Hollywood to embrace Tolkien's work is a serious step in the right direction. The trilogy is not a silly, trite, selfish, stupid story at its core, which is what Hollywood usually delivers. People in this country are asking for more depth and meaning, so more opportunities will arise for people of faith, understanding, and depth to do similar projects."

As cinematographer, Jim is trying to pick and choose the projects that will touch the soul. "*Crash* is being filmed now [as of this writing], which is an awareness piece on the state of racism. . . . It's well written, but doesn't attract a lot of funding. Current industry people are looking for big shows and big dollars of yesteryear, but they're few and far between. People are more willing now to work for real content, Christian content. It does pose a quandary, though: Do we work on this (lower-paying, Christian) stuff? We have to feed our families. On the other hand, it's a ministry. There's a mission field wherever you go . . . right next door, not just Serbia."

It's a Circus

Jim believes that his work is a gift from God, and that there is definitely more room for people of faith in the industry. "With digital video a reality, there's more room for these folks. On the surface, it appears to be a member's only club, but new opportunities are now arising with the doors that *Lord of the Rings* and *The Passion* opened."

Jim describes the entertainment industry as a bit of a circus. "If you're a fat lady, and that's what they're looking for, you'll get hired. If you happen to be bald and standing around, you're grabbed, and you're suddenly Vin Diesel's stand in. There's a certain amount of seemingly random destiny." Jim also points out that television programming is a wide-open, circus-type forum. "The guy in the hotel next door to me can access an assortment of spiritual material on TV and choose to become a member of the KKK, or whatever they're happening to sell at the time. We need to saturate the Internet and the movies with something more spiritually challenging that will stand compellingly above the rest of the deceptive choices."

People Want God's Universal Truths

Jim feels that audiences want authenticity, relevancy, and truth in the movies they watch. "For instance, in old, period pieces, filmmakers portray church as old Christians drudgingly singing in pews. That's not the truth. We worship a living, breathing God who interacts with us. People need to discover this God through the truths they see in films. In *The Passion*, the nonbeliever sees that evil exists. Even more subtly, people who believe in ghosts are attracted to something bigger, more powerful than themselves. In *Lord of the Rings*, they're captivated by the war between good vs. evil because they know it really exists, not just in movies. Our faith, presented in the subtle or overt art form of film is a luring thing to people. It evokes curiosity and stirs the spirit."

007 for God

"The Christian in Hollywood," says Jim, "should be a 007 for God. I'm a fan of saying, 'We're going to make movies, and we can't call them Christian.' I really believe that God doesn't just want that. Sometimes I pretend I'm making *The Omen*, to scare people. In *Lord of the Rings*, for instance, there are great, but subtle, lessons to see, like when Frodo puts his society and his people before himself.

If Christians had made the movie, they might have gone overboard, instead of being cautious. My motto is 'be modest, cautious, and careful about reaching people. We make movies people will want to see. We want to slip in the truth while they're laughing. I also think it's important to be sensitive to the fact that the country is polarized. There are other people besides Christians."

Remember Your Roots

After eight years of Lutheran school, young Jim Muro vowed not to stray from his spiritual foundation. Years later, however, the vows were forgotten, and in film school, he found himself directing the X-rated *Street Trash*. "I'd fallen a long way from my roots. The movie I was making still had heart and soul at its core, and now, in 2004, it wouldn't be that offensive, but it was in the '80s. . . . It was made to make people angry. And, it pulled me down, spiritually."

God didn't let Jim stay down forever, though, and He began surrounding him with people of faith—including a great wife!

Find a Good Spouse

Jim has seen that the movie industry breeds spiritual warfare, which one cannot handle alone. "I met my wife when we were both working on *Dances with Wolves*. . . . We had the time of our lives. . . . She did hair. I'm glad we didn't meet on *Freddy vs. Jason*," Jim laughs. The couple married and moved to Ventura, California, where they attended the Vineyard and received some intense discipling. "We had some spiritual work to do, trying to break the generational wall of sin from our pasts. We both had divorce in our families. We decided to pick some rules. We said, 'How about the Bible as our basis? Let's create a contract, or a covenant, and stick by it.' And, we did. In our world, divorce is not an option."

It's all About Relationships

During this time, Jim picked up the Steadicam and became friends with its inventor, soliciting jobs from others in New York City.

He began working for James Cameron, and the two have since worked together on every movie he's made. "I'm his collaborator with the camera."

Jim also worked for ten years with Oliver Stone and Michael Mann, both of whom seasoned everything Jim does today. "Oliver called me 'Jimmy the Christian.' I love the guy immensely. He's a brilliant filmmaker."

It's important to Jim to develop and cultivate relationships with both believers and non-believers, for the purposes of serving them and sharing God's life with them. "Many Christians are segregated from film industry, believing it's totally of the devil. That's not true. Our country is polarized at an interesting time in the industry. My wife and I feel it is God's certain calling on our lives to be salt and light in this industry, and we seek prayer support earnestly. People are watching me wherever I go. I often think to myself, 'Everyone is looking at you . . . one hundred people want your job.' It can be a pastoral position sometimes. It's good for people to see you living the life, walking the walk. . . . We often travel as a family, going on from movie to movie, then finally going home—kind of like a rock and roll tour. It's important for people to see our lives, that we live the real deal."

Jim believes that in the movie industry, it's not just the content that speaks to people, but one's behavior in the industry. "It's growing," says Jim. "It used to be that there was one other believer on the set; now there's five. People are reaching out to each other. There are still many camps here, and it can be polarized, like anywhere else, but I'm seeing a change."

Artist or Businessman?

The Director of Photography is often known as the "unsung film-maker." He must partner with the director to champion how the film will look, how the lighting should look, and how to tell the story with the camera. "It's a struggle to keep production costs as the foremost consideration when we're making important decisions about the lighting, preparation, and shooting, though there's a lot of money at stake," Jim adds. "The director and the D.P. go from place to place and choose each setting, working closely with the production designer and art director to choose colors, settings, and tone. We now do two days of work in one day to stay within the parameters of the budget. You have to know when you say, 'We have it in the (film) can.' We can't nitpick. It's the old angst between the artist and the businessman . . . art versus economy. Either way, the movie will be made; it's a roll of the dice. We just have to ask, 'Is this thing blessed?' When the movie's wrapped, we'll definitely see in the court of public opinion."

Historical Epics and Adaptations Do Well

Jim believes that about one in five scripts is going to do very well, and many of those he's been associated with are epics or adaptations. "Even on *JFK*," he says, "people took big chances." On *Crash*, the director said, 'If you're not going home sleepless, you're not doing it right.' When I read *Dances with Wolves*, my first reaction was 'Subtitles? Indians? Three hours? You're kidding?' But, it paid off. It was the same with Jim Cameron on *Titanic*. On that one, though, some bad press started happening, which he had to fight by being kind. He won over the historians by being humble and saying, 'You teach us.'"

Pray About Everything

When Jim shot *Open Range* in beautiful Alberta, Canada, he an a fellow believer—the lighting director, or "gaffer,"—prayed every day for an hour on the way to the set. "We prayed that the film would speak to the individual and touch hearts. God really gave us a blessing of beauty, too. We couldn't believe how gorgeous the scenery was. Our jaws were hitting floor. There was one time I said, 'That scene tonight will be beautiful, though it's foggy now.' And, it was. It was breathtaking. Everyone felt that God was with us on that. The movie set had a nice, family, spiritual, vibe."

Just Do It!

For the young person wanting to get involved in movies, Jim Muro says, "Just do it! And then people will start referring to you as the guy who does that thing." Jim believes it's all in the attitude. "When you keep things light, and you're happy, that's your opportunity to say I'm blessed by God. You can share. Some are placed in the industry just as intercessory prayer warriors; others are doing technical skills. No matter where you're called, you can make a difference and share your life with these folks."

According to Jim, there are two schools of thought on becoming a Director of Photography: (1) Go to film school. "I did it, and you can go far this way, but it can be depressing, expensive, and a lot of work." (2) Start working. "Knock on someone's door and just start helping them. Both can work. . . ."

Be an Apprentice

A lot of young filmmakers want to get right into directing, but they don't have enough time in the apprenticeship stage, believes Jim. He suggests that wannabes find some job—any job—and prove themselves from the bottom up. "The free, 'get me coffee' jobs are everywhere. Hopefully, you'll be faithful with these jobs and hook up with someone who'll help you move up. If somebody spots you and you have a good attitude and want to help, you'll go far. There are people forced upon me sometimes, but if they're collaborative and good, I'll bring them along. They'll start out getting coffee, then move to holding the camera, then who knows? They'll do more work, then, word of mouth will bring them higher. There's no 'hiring hall' around here. If you're a good person who likes your craft, you'll probably make it. But, don't worry, the director will take credit for everything anyway," Jim laughs.

Look for the Adventure in Everything

During the shooting of *Titanic* in Mexico, the crew got food poisoning, some believing that there was LSD in the shellfish. "There

I was, sitting in the hospital with James Cameron and Bill Paxon, moaning and laughing. What a time! I really get into each location, especially when on the set of *Titanic*. I remember studying the bell in the crow's nest. I walked around the decks and asked myself, 'Why didn't the guy launch this boat first? Oh, these wires were blocking it.' I remember being in the captain's wheelhouse, alone with my camera and captain when he died . . . sinking into water with the captain. I thought, 'This is the biggest and best script I've ever read. It's probably going to win an Oscar." And, win it did!

Be Thankful

Throughout the interview, Jim continued to say phrases like, "God has blessed my life . . . I just want to share how God can bless people." Regarding his career, Jim says, "I'm definitely at a blessed place, though it took fifteen years to get here. I'm still not earning a lot of money, but hopefully these adventures will pay off in the end."

If past history is, indeed, the best indicator of future performance, we have high hopes for the adventures of J. Michael Muro to pay off in a big way as the S.S. Hollywood ship continues to turn toward the shores of faith and values.

* * *

WITH RESPECT TO THE LIGHTING:

The gaffer is the chief lighting electrician. The gaffer is in charge of all the electrical wiring and equipment.

Plan your lighting to help establish mood and atmosphere as well as focus attention. Lighting influences your audience by changing their perception of a scene. Lighting can be realistic or atmospheric. Lighting may: reveal, hide, enhance, texture, shade, modify, and enlighten. Soft, broad light illuminates without casting shadows. Hard light focuses attention, creates modeling, and casts shadows.

Often you will have a *direct fill light* to light your subject, with a *back light* to cut down on modeling and harsh shadows, and a *key light* within ten to twenty degrees of a person's nose to give form to your subject. Note that your fill light will reduce wrinkles and unwanted features, and your key light will enhance desirable features.

Plan Your Lighting:

- Have the subject of your key light look toward the light.
- Avoid steep lighting. A steep backlight will spill over onto the face of your subject. A steep front light will cause harsh modeling, give black eyes, long nose, and neck shadows and a haggard appearance. It will also emphasize baldness.
- Avoid shallow lighting. A shallow backlight will flare into the picture. A shallow front light will make the subject look flat.
- Avoid lighting that is too far off the camera axis. Such lighting will create hot spots and strange shadows.
- By careful balance of back and front lighting you will give your subject the appropriate three-dimensional look.
- You can create realism by imitation or simulation. For example, if you wanted to create the look of a church by imitation, you could shine a light at an angle through a stained glass window on the set. If you wanted to create the same look by simulation, you could use several lights with gels,[107] or use a slide. You can also use stencils, flicker wheels, and patterns to create atmospheric effects.
- Your lighting must be planned with the type of camera you will use in mind. Every camera has different light sensitivity for which your lighting has to adjust.
- Analyze your subject to see what features you want to minimize and what features you want to emphasize.

- Make sure that any graphics are evenly lit.
- Determine how movement will affect your lighting.

WITH RESPECT TO GRAPHICS

In traditional television, plan your graphics so that they will compose properly within the future proof 16x9 while being safe for the standard 4:3 proportions of television. Always provide an adequate border. Make sure that there are no wrinkles or imperfections, because television will magnify any imperfection. Plan your colors and tones to be pleasing, or to achieve the effect that you want. Clear tonal and color separation is advisable if you want your graphics to be clear. Keep detail to a minimum and simplify structural forms. Maps should have no more than the essential blocks necessary to indicate the main features. One graphic is better than a succession of graphics; therefore, simplify and combine information.

WITH RESPECT TO AUDIO

The audio may control the picture's impact, or the picture may control the audio's impact, or the impact may be the cumulative effect of both. Plan the relationship between the audio and the visual.

Plan Your Audio

Contrast. A loud sound in the midst of a peaceful picture.

Uniqueness. Your sound can establish that the same picture has a different meaning than it had before. Examples include:

- Suspense
- Humor
- Emphasis
- Repetition
- Surrealism
- Comparison

- Foreshadowing
- Revelation
- Incongruity
- Remember to check the microphone boom and all the microphones so that there is no sign of them in the picture. Make sure that there are no unwanted shadows and cables in the shot.
- Microphones are designed with different "listening" or pickup patters, and with different ways of mounting. The audio person chooses the right microphone and puts it as close as possible to the source of sound in order to get the most audio and the least unwanted noise.
- Note that in very low budget productions, the video camera-mounted microphone is usually too far from the source, and the voice recording has too much sound pollution. The camera microphone is still good for recording ambient or "natural" sounds of crowds, traffic, rustling leaves, etc.
- Try to record ambient or natural sound for each location. In editing, the natural sound mixed with program audio will help create smooth audio transitions.
- Audio is just as important as the picture; therefore, always test your sound equipment before you use it.

SUCCESS, STEP 14: RUN THROUGH
AND FINAL REHEARSAL

In television production, you will want to run through your script to remove any kinks and timing problems. The last run through is sometimes called a giggle through because it gives the performers and the personnel a chance to let out any unwanted emotions or feelings prior to production. It would be nice to have one uninterrupted rehearsal prior to production, but this rarely happens!

PAY CLOSE ATTENTION TO CONTINUITY

The director will make sure that the performers know who they are in terms of the script, props are being used properly, and the performers hit their marks. The director will not let one performer cover another, and won't let them be too far apart. On camera the performers will look further apart than they are, so the director will bring them in closer than you would normally imagine. He will make sure that one performer does not up stage another. The director will think in terms of shots and how the shot will look. You may want to use a viewfinder, if it helps you to think in terms of shots.

The director will make sure that the performers are framed properly and that the audience can see who they are supposed to see. He will get rid of excess detail. With the help of the D.P., he will make sure that your camera is not shooting off set, and that there are no unwanted subjects in the shot.

Check the Boom and Microphones.

There should be no sign of audio technology in the picture. Keep an eye out for unwanted shadows and cables in the shot. Make sure that everything is straight, level, and the way you want it to look. Check for any distracting set elements, blemishes, or inconsistencies.

The first A.D. Will Check Costumes.

The director may have the cast stay away from satins or any reflective materials, unless he intends that effect. Light tones make people look bigger and formless. Dark tones minimize size, but also decrease modeling. In television, colors that are too strong will saturate the picture. Noisy patterns can cause a strobe, flicker, or moire effect that can be very annoying for your audience. Noisy costumes and jewelry can create sound problems. Stay away from colors that will look like skin tones, giving your performers a naked appearance.

The Make-Up Artist Will Help Your Performers to Look Natural Under the Lights.

Less is more. He or she will choose a base that is slightly lighter than the skin tone of the performer and use powder to prevent shine. They will not choose colors that will read blue or orange on camera unless that is your intent. Highlights and shading will correct for facial faults and define features. Encourage the director to check the make-up on camera to make sure that it works. Costumes, makeup, and hair styling help tell your story by giving the audience visual details about the characters. The hair, makeup, and costume people *visually* transform the actors into the characters they are playing. They help the actor look the part while he acts the part. The makeup artist should write down the cosmetics used for each and every actor and, if possible, should take photos of the actor to help continuity between scenes and shoots.

Plan your production so that your story is told and none of the technical aspects of the production intrude on and detract from the visual dramatic telling of the story. If you have decided to pursue a symbolist approach to your material by revealing the technical aspects of your production to your audience, do so; however, make sure that such revelation is part of the fabric of your program and not an obstacle to the audience's enjoyment of your film. The French playwright, Maeterlinck, the Father of symbolist theater, revealed the stage to his audience by making them a part of the play, not by having effects intrude on the perceptions of his audience.

Please remember the cardinal rule of production: "Do not break the suspension of disbelief."

SUCCESS, STEP 15: LOCATION PRODUCTION

If you have planned carefully for shooting on location, things should go well. Beware of extraneous noise, weather, crowds, and traffic. Bring everything you need. Double check all connections, lighting, sound equipment, video equipment, and continuity to make sure that you get what you want. Continuity can be a large problem when you are shooting on location:

- Make sure that color, brightness, contrast, tones, light direction, shots, perspective, and picture quality are consistent from shot to shot.
- Make sure that weather conditions match from shot to shot.
- Don't let your camera cross the line of axis on reverse shots.
- Make sure that costumes match makeup and hair. These are all continuity issues.
- Make sure that performances match.
- Make sure that action matches.
- Make sure that props match and time passes uniformly. Don't jump from a half full glass to a full one.
- Make sure that sound matches.

SUCCESS, STEP 16: SOUND STAGE PRODUCTION

Come in as early as possible. If you can, set up your sets the day before or even before that. Check and double check all equipment to make sure it works the way you want it to work. Warm up all equipment. Test every part of your equipment. Clear out all unnecessary cables and all obstacles. Make sure that all equipment is clean. Check quality. Relax. Pray. Enjoy yourself; you are paying for this production. Shoot.

SUCCESS, STEP 17: CAST PARTY

Establish a good rapport with your cast. Plan to work together again. Be supportive.

11

Cut

STEPS TO SUCCESS: 18–22, POST-PRODUCTION AND BEYOND

No matter how well everything went in production, the post-production brings it all together in a way that will not only make sense, but also captivate your audience. Post-production is the key to making a good movie great.

As of the time of this writing, Pixar is the only movie company in history that has hit a home run with every one of their movies, *Toy Story*, *Toy Story 2*, *A Bug's Life*, *Monsters, Inc.*, *Finding Nemo*, *The Incredibles*, *Cars*, *Ratatouille*, *WALL-E*, *Up*, *Toy Story 3*, etc. Each one of their movies has been a blockbuster because they cared enough to strive for excellence. I was asked to screen *Toy Story* a few months before it opened. Then, I was asked to screen it again about a month before it opened, and I was surprised to see that significant changes had been made. Finally, I screened it just before it opened and even more changes had been made in editing, music, and sound. The same thing happened with *Finding*

Nemo. Talking with the producers, director, and other key people at Pixar, I found that they wanted excellence and were not satisfied until they achieved it.

SUCCESS, STEP 18: MUSIC AND SOUND

Music and sound effects will make or break a movie or television production. The right music and the right sound can propel a movie into fame and fortune. Sound helps set a mood. With animated movies, sound is even more important in capturing the audience and making them believe. Walt Disney used to screen his famous animated movies without dialogue and then add only the dialogue that was absolutely necessary to tell the story. The silent section in the Pixar movie *Up* is in effect an ode to Walt Disney.

The *Post Production Sound Mixer* figures out what kind of sound effects and/or music can be used to enhance the movie. He often creates those sound effects. He is in charge of making sure the overall sound of the movie is correct, including the dialogue. Sound effects and sweetening are crucial for filling out a production's sound design, setting mood and atmosphere. Good sound effects (SFX for short) not only make a movie a lot more interesting, they help tell the story as well. The sound of footsteps off screen will set up suspense or foreshadow mood. Great sound and music stir the audience's imagination. When you use music, be aware of the impact of music and SFX on your movie. Choose your music and sound carefully to reflect the feeling and pace of your shoot. There are different types of music, such as an original score and licensed songs. A score can come from library music or may be composed specifically for the production.

How important is music? Watch the same scene from a movie with and without sound. It is essential for creating tension, suspense, and many of the other emotional flavors necessary for an effective production.

The Poseidon Adventure was a hit to a large degree because of its great Academy Award winning music. Here Al Kasha gives us an insight into music and wanting to be in pictures.

Hope, Not Hype

—an interview with Al Kasha

"The Morning After" [selected lyrics]

There's got to be a morning after
If we can hold on through the night
We have a chance to find the sunshine,
Let's keep on looking for the light.

There's got to be a morning after
We're moving closer to the shore
I know we'll be there by tomorrow
And we'll escape the darkness,
We won't be searching anymore.

Years later, the two-time Oscar winning composer, songwriter, and producer who penned these famous lyrics that Maureen McGovern sang so plaintively for *Poseidon Adventure*, would indeed find what he was searching for. And not only would he find the elusive hope, he'd also become a servant-leader in Hollywood, teaching others for the past twenty-five years through an in-depth Bible study, as well as songwriting and producing seminars, the amazing truths he's discovered along his journey with the Lord.

Find Your Bent Early

Originally from New York, the Jewish-born Al Kasha had been writing songs since he was seventeen. He started with black artist Jackie Wilson, writing such tunes as "My Empty Arms," "I'm Comin' on Back to You," "Talk That Talk," and "Forever and a

Day." From there, he went to Columbia Records, "The first record contract I had was with Aretha Franklin, a rhythm and blues hits album called 'Operation Heartbreak.' I produced 'Go Away, Little Girl' with Steve Lawrence, came to Columbia in '60, and left four years later to go into business for myself."

Know When the Winds are Changing

Al then came out to L.A. in 1968 to work for Clive Davis in the music publishing industry. Clive was president of the record and publishing end of CBS's Cinema Center Films and wanted Al to write songs for the movies. Al got started and quickly wrote several great songs for *April Fools* and *The Grasshopper*. He stayed with CBS for a year, then moved on to become president of the music division of National General Corporation, distributors of films for CBS. The company went belly-up within a few years, but it was a blessing for Al in that it got him out of the business rat race and back to his first love—song writing.

Rewards Make the Journey Worth It

After leaving the company in late 1971, in 1972, Al wrote "The Morning After." A year later, he and Joel Hirschhorn were delighted to be nominated, and then win, the Academy Award for this haunting, soulful, "hope-amidst-the-darkness song." Sung by Maureen McGovern and heard around the world, "Morning After" was number one on the charts. How did this Jewish boy from New York come to write such spiritually powerful lyrics?

Early Seeds Planted in the Soul

During the Clive Davis years, Al had lunch with a lighting man while shooting his song, "Morning After." The man said, "You're a believer, right?' To which Al replied, "I do believe in God, but I'm Jewish." The lighting technician said, "The song you wrote is a song of hope. . . . It's very Christian." Those words would stick in Al's mind for years to come.

In the meantime, he continued writing many other songs of hope and inspiration. "Oscar Hammerstein was my role model. He, too, had hope-filled songs like, 'I'm Stuck Like a Dope on This Thing Called Hope' from the song, 'Cock-Eyed Optimist' in the famous musical *South Pacific*. Oscar also wrote "Walk On, Walk On with Hope in Your Heart"—from *Carousel*. Oscar's mother inspired him to write like that—'Promise me you'll write songs about hope,' his mother pled on her deathbed.'"

Face Your Demons

Al Kasha is a self-described perfectionist, workaholic, and striver at heart. Like Mr. Hammerstein, he also wrote about hope, he says, because that's what he longed for. In 1975, Al realized that he was working himself to death. He felt empty despite his many successes, which now included his second Academy-Award-winning song, "We May Never Love Like This Again"—the theme song for *The Towering Inferno*, again sung by Maureen McGovern.

"I was pushing myself terribly," admits Al. "My father had continued to be an abusive alcoholic who hit my mother and my brother. My parents were Jews from Russia and Poland, and they were never satisfied with what I did. I remember my mother saying, 'Someday when you win a Tony on Broadway, then I'll be proud.' Two Academy Awards weren't enough, Mom? I was always striving for her and for my family. I actually supported them, but I had no peace in my life. I had everything and yet nothing because I had no god but work. This business fosters that performance mentality, too. People will ask you all the time, 'What are you doing now?' Yesterday's accolades don't matter tomorrow. . . . It breeds emptiness. As Pastor Tim Timmons says, you become 'a human doing, rather than a human being.'"

Faith Over Fear

Al wrote the adaptation for *Seven Brides For Seven Brothers* from his home studio. During this time he became agoraphobic—

afraid of leaving his house. "I felt isolated in my own home. I had tremendous fears. I was never perfect enough. My relationships, and particularly my marriage, suffered terribly. My problem wasn't easy on Ceil. She was prisoner in her own home, too. She and I eventually separated."

When he had been separated from his wife for a month, he was in his new apartment watching a Reverend Robert Schuller replay at three in the morning. Schuller said, "God's perfect love casts out fear." (1 John 4:18–19 NIV). "In my mind," said Al, "I immediately turned that around. I said, 'Fear casts out love. My fear is casting out God's love.' That night I had an experience with Lord. I felt the presence of God in that room. On October 7, 1978, I accepted Jesus. The next day, I went home, though my wife and I were not communicating. I stopped the drugs—the uppers and the downers, and I received the real deal: the peace of God."

Get Into the Word

Shortly thereafter, a young girl, Pat Hollis, came by and asked Al if he would listen to her demo. "In the past, that would have been the furthest thing from my mind to listen to Christian students, but I did. She said, 'Would you want to go to church with me?' 'Sure,' I said. My wife was so shocked she spun around like the girl in *The Exorcist*. She had been a Catholic who converted to Judaism and was now shocked that I was agreeing to go, and especially that this might involve her. We drove from Beverly Hills, over the hill, which was tough for an agoraphobic and made it to the church. There, Ceil and I officially and publicly accepted Christ together, and three days later went to a Bible Study in Beverly Hills."

For many years, Al and his wife hosted a large Bible study from their home, attended by many stars and Hollywood heavyweights. "It's all about growing in God," he says. "I tell people, 'Don't hand me scripts here, and don't make me the pursuer of your entire career. There are places and times for these pursuits.'"

Be Realistic

Al encourages Hollywood wannabes to ask some trusted people whether they've got the talent and "what it takes" to make it in entertainment. "Just because you sit next to stars such as Charlize Theron, that doesn't mean you're her. You can't perform like that. Or Mel Gibson . . . you're not him. You must be discerning about where you're good and where you're not. You must be discerning and honest with yourself about where you're good and where you're not."

Stay in Your Field of Passion

Al is quick to advise newcomers: "Don't come to Hollywood wanting to be an actor and then work as a waiter or personal trainer. Be a mail person right in your industry. Work at night as [a] personal trainer if you must, but during the day, stay in your industry. This'll show others that you're an obedient servant. Like the comedian Rodney Dangerfield says, 'Italians build; Jews get estimates.' In other words, check out the land—who you're working for, their values, etc. You must get in and stay on the inside, somehow. Work as an intern and get a letter of recommendation for the next higher place. Make money on your weekends, but work your industry during the week. I used to go to NYU in the morning, and work at Howard Johnson's Restaurant in the afternoon. I wrote songs in between. You just have to do that sometimes."

If You're Really Good, Go West!

Al says he feels blessed to have been born in New York. "You can't make movies from Idaho. Forget about it. It's not going to happen. You've got to be where the power is. If you've got real, confirmed talent, you go out there, and if you're a songwriter, you join the Songwriter's Guild, ASCAP, and get to know your industry community. Join the organizations that relate to your profession. You must belong to them. I used to be involved in 'Act One,' and Dennis Quaid used to come down and teach us. You don't have to work for a Christian. You be the Christian. If you're that weak in character and are going to fall away, you'll fall away anywhere you are. You just stay involved, love, and serve, and let them ask, 'Why are you different?'"

Make a Plan

Throughout his career, Al worked at selling sheet music, making demos, and doing anything he was asked to do. "I feel like it made me well rounded in my career. Actor Clint Eastwood used to watch what others (non-actors) did; he'd talk to the director. He knew he'd be too old some day to be star, so he made a plan. Psalm 51 says that God has the real plans for our lives, but we've got to have something on paper. He can change it if he wants."

Express Your Gratitude

To people of faith Al says, "Don't be boastful. Don't shout hallelujah. Just be a Christian, loving and serving people. Don't hurt people. Thank them. Always thank them. I write thank you notes for my thank you notes. Recognize who took care of you, and tell them. Validate them. Jesus always used the right words for the right situation and encouraged people."

Get Mentored

After Al and Ceil became believers, they attended a Bible Study in Gabri Ferer's home, formerly Rosemary Clooney's (his mother's) home. Gabri prayed for the couple, and they absorbed everything, taking notes on it all. Within the first month of walking in their newfound faith, Clark Mathias, of Wheaton College, lost his job and asked if he could move in with the Kasha's. Ceil joked with Al, "We became Christians, and now we have people moving in with us?" Clark stayed with them eleven months, taking the couple through the Bible from Genesis to Revelation. "He really discipled me," smiles Al.

Four months later, Gabri Ferer married Debbie Boone, and the couple moved away. Al and Ceil were living on Roxbury Drive in

Beverly Hills at the time, and they felt it would be a great, central, alternate location. So the study was moved to the Kasha's. Coleman Luck and Ken Gullickson taught the study, and Donna Summer and Bob Dylan were among several stars that attended. "I think people were comfortable here, knowing I had worldly success already . . . That I wasn't looking to Christ just to help me succeed. I really wanted to know Him."

Grow in Discernment

Al became embroiled in his faith. Four years later, he became an ordained minister. Yet, he kept on writing music. "I kept at it, but now that I was a believer, I started having more discernment about the pictures I made. For the first two years, I was afraid to speak up, but then I began softly, but surely, to talk about Jesus. Being Jewish, I could explain Jesus. He was the lamb that was put up on Friday, as a sacrifice to God. He's a human lamb. Jews understand this. Also, Jews talk in opposites . . . 'Faithful in little, faithful in much,' and 'If you lose your life, you'll gain it.' This is Jewish language, and I use it."

Pray Hard and Work Out

Today, Al gives seminars to guide newcomers in Hollywood. He often tells this story: "Many years ago, I was friends with Floyd Patterson, the heavyweight champ of the world. At a certain fight in Montreal, his opponent, a fella with green and white trunks, prayed before the fight. Well, Floyd knocked him out in four rounds. I was concerned. I said, 'Floyd, did you see that guy? He was Irish. He prayed!' Floyd turned to me and said, 'Did you notice how I knocked him out? It was a punch to the stomach. He might have prayed, but he never did any sit-ups.' So many artists come out here without having studied their art form. Study, study, study! You have to know what you're doing. Prayer is vital, but so is research. Know what pictures are making it and why. You've gotta know your craft."

The Secret Is Adaptations

Norman Brokaw, co-chair of The William Morris Agency, says, "The fastest way to Hollywood is through New York." "It's true," says Al. So many winning movies are adaptations of books or famous plays. *Chariots of Fire, Gone with the Wind,* and *Godfather* were Oscar winners, and all adaptations of books. *Beauty and the Beast, The Full Monty*—so many of them are made from books or musicals. They're tried and true stories. For instance John Grisham' books make great movies. Also the classics are great."

According to Al, artists have so much leverage when they go to the studios with their idea and say, 'Well, it was a hit book.' Just like in the motion picture *The Player,* you say 'It's a combination of (blank) and (blank).' Then they can pitch it to their investors with a certain degree of surety. Producers and investors say, 'Tell me a reason I should do this? Why will people come?'"

Richard Zanuck followed in his father, Darryl's steps (Darryl was President of Twentieth Century Fox Pictures). They both did great adaptations of books and plays including Darryl's *Gentlemen's Agreement, Oklahoma,* and *Carousel.* Richard did *Jaws, The Sound of Music,* and *The Road to Perdition*—all adaptations of books or plays. "One third of movie audiences go to a movie based on its title. Studios typically spend as much money promoting a film as they do making it, and each print runs about $10,000. For example, *The Passion of the Christ* had to produce over 4,600 prints, so just that cost would be $46 million. Most movies are title-driven or star-driven. Write your version, your adaptation of something fascinating."

Current Issues with Redemptive Endings

Al believes that moviemakers should produce movies about the issues of the day, but with redemptive endings. "Marshall McLuan says, 'Movies must be larger than life.' Make the character bigger than he really was. Make the action grander, everything magnified. You've only got two hours."

Don't Say it; Live it

If a person walks in and says, "I'm a Christian," it's the worst thing they can say, believes Al. "It's more important to show your talent by just being a great writer . . . or producer. Just live it. Fundamentalists have no *fun*, are *mental* cases, and have *lists* on everybody. Make your work so good that people will say, 'Oh my God, this person must have been a Christian.' Don't use Christian terms like 'share.' Use words that relate to the people you're talking to."

Al recommends a large dose of sensitivity, too. "When you're around industry folks think 'This one can't take the hard stuff.' One time a doctor asked me, 'Can your mother take bad news?' 'No,' I said. That was very sensitive. Be a good hearer . . . discerning. Write a letter to writers and producers when they've done a good picture. Even if they're not Christians. Constantly write encouraging letters to people. Don't bang people over the head with your faith. They get the message."

Al suggests that Christians pray, ask advice, and work within their communities, or with people that are on same page. "Also work on people not on the same page," he encourages. "Show your good works with your faith. It's not just grace without works. That's why they call it 'A labor of love.' Show perseverance. The famous theologian Charles Spurgeon said, 'Even the snail made it onto Noah's Ark.' Christians can be seen as mad at the world. In John 3:17, Jesus said He came not to judge the world, but to save it. Christians need to not be so judgmental, but encouraging. Always be constructive. You do your work, and make sure it's good. We need to be disciplined and obedient, thinking 'I'll write my best, and God's spirit will touch their hearts.'"

Pull Out the Power of Passion

Al believes in the power of music to profoundly affect the soul. "In *Les Miserables*, there was a song of salvation, and people stood up. The power of music is incredible. Vangelis' music absolutely made *Chariots of Fire*. The right music can make a good picture great. I've worked for TBN, CBN, and lots of Christian companies, and on one project a producer said (of my musicians), 'Are all the people Christians?' I said no, but when I talked to the guys, I said, 'I don't know where you all are spiritually, but I want you to play as if you were playing for God. Play with great passion. You're getting paid anyway, so please give it your best.' And they did."

By the way, as of this writing, *7 Brides . . .* is running for an entire year throughout Spain, and running through a separate company in Italy and England, as well as all over the United States. It's the eleventh most performed musical in entire world. "It goes to show that people still want family musicals."

Final Thoughts

Al Kasha truly believes in research and development. "Study, study, study the best. You can be the best by studying the best. Pray for favor, strength, and grace to direct your steps. Have a servant's heart. That's what people really respect deep down."

"Passion is everything; winning is not," says Al.

Yet, there is no doubt that audiences will enjoy a whole new decade of hope-filled songs from the man who certainly has both.

* * *

SUCCESS, STEP 19: EDITING

Some of the best directors, such as Alfred Hitchcock, teamed up with great editors throughout their career. Some of the most talented directors fall short of greatness because they cannot cut out surplusage, which, as they say, vitiates. The editor takes all the raw film or video and sound that is shot for a movie and shapes it into a finished movie. The editor, working with the director, decides:(1) Which shots to use; (2) How to put the shots together; and (3) How long to hold each shot before cutting to the next one.

Good editing involves selecting shots and combining them to

convey the director's vision. Poor editing makes the movie seem labored and boring. Before you edit, you will want to spend a great deal of time off line[108] reviewing your production. Plan your cuts precisely, so that you will save as much money as possible during on line editing. Keep track of all your edit points so that you can go on line and make your edits without searching for your edit points. Avoid mismatched cutting. Watch for continuity and make sure your transitions are so smooth that they are invisible, unless your story demands otherwise.

Add titles, music, audio effects, graphics, film clips, and whatever you need to make your production work. Take your time. Be free to improve on what you have filmed even if the improvements lead you away from the strict letter of your script. An editor can make or destroy a production. Good editing requires as much creativity as a good script. Good editing potentially alters the structure of the movie. The ending might become the beginning; the beginning could become the end. You might want to add a voice-over narration, write entirely new lines of dialogue to explain unclear plot points, play scenes in slow motion or fast motion or backwards or whatever might seem appropriate. Ironically, the simplest, least complex form of storytelling is generally the way to go, but sometimes an editor will have to use every trick in the book to make the best possible film.

Think in visual terms. Advancing your story through pictures is more important than advancing it through words, although both must be there in harmony to fully tell a story through movies and television. A movie is like a puzzle with individual scenes, music, sound effects, and perhaps some visual effects. All these elements need to be put together to make a complete movie. The audience often does not notice good editing, but the story moves along quickly with plenty of surprises. When the editing is poor, the movie tends to be boring or confusing.

The final cut is the finished movie.

- When editors create a scene, they often talk about it as 'building" a scene because they are building it by adding layers of picture, natural sound, music, and special effects.
- There are different types of edits, which is simply a change from one shot to another.
- A cut is when you go immediately from one shot to another.
- A fade is when a scene slowly goes black for a moment, before another scene comes up.
- A dissolve is where one scene fades in while another is fading out.
- Review everything that has been said up to this point to make sure you are on target and you have used the medium to its maximum effectiveness.
- Pray.

SUCCESS, STEP 20: REVIEW

Does your program work? Re-edit if necessary.

SUCCESS, STEP 21: DISTRIBUTION/SALES

After completing Steps 1–20 with your production, your work is ready to be distributed. Whether it will show in movie theaters or air on network television (other avenues of distribution, such as PBS, foreign television, or cable). Be ambitious—remember smaller avenues of distribution, such as: PBS, cable channels, or foreign television. Keep track of where your program is going. Make copies, distribute, and keep records.

Your movie or program may have a long life if you keep on top of the distribution. Every new sale brings in revenue—financing for your next production!

THE LIFE OF A MOVIE

Here is a chart of the life of a theatrical motion picture. Walt Disney established the golden cycle where he re-released a movie every five years or so, to a new generation of children. Most movies, however, will not stand up to re-release. Television movies generally do not have the life span of theatrical films, but yours could always be the exception:

The Life of a Movie

	1	2	3	4	5	6	7	8	9	10	11	12	13	14
Year	1	2	3	4	5	6	7	8	9	10	11	12	13	14
Theaters	x													
Pay-per-view Cable	x													
Pay Cable & STV	xx	xx	x											
Network TV	x	x	x											
Independent TV	xx	xx	xx	xx	xx	x								
Home Video	xxxxxxxxxxxxxxxxxx													
Foreign	xxxxxxxxxxxxxxxxxxxxxxxxxxxxxxxxxxxxxxxx													

Now, that you have come this far in your production, you should be aware that the real "work" has not yet even begun. Distribution is such a time consuming and convoluted process that major movie stars and moguls have given up on it. The success of *The Passion of the Christ* offers great hope, but regrettably, the distributor and Mel Gibson's company collected far fewer box office receipts than they should have.

For many years, people have come to me to discuss distribution, and I have introduced them to some of the best on both sides on the equation: the distributors and the theater companies. One group wanted to distribute a well-made movie with strong Christian values, so I introduced them to one of the biggest theater companies. The person in charge spent an hour talking about all the different ways producers lose money in theaters, from the local theater that hides ticket sales to delayed payment for independents who have no clout. In brief, the theaters need to be monitored continually.

In the beginning, Woody Allen hired a New York accountant (a friend of mine) who hired young men and women to monitor each theater where Woody's movie played, so he could contest the box office receipts if there were any discrepancies. The Christian producer mentioned above tried to do the same thing and was overwhelmed by the extent of the coordination and work involved.

Even if the theater gives a real accounting of box office, they often delay payments to independent distributors because those distributors have so few movies coming down the pipeline. Without an in-demand movie, the independent has no clout to demand payment backed by the threat that they won't give the theater their next big movie if the theater does not pay promptly. Major distributors, on the other hand, get paid and often squeeze the theaters, because they do have the clout.

To find out more about the arcane world of theatrical release and distribution read *Fatal Subtraction* by Pierce O'Donnell and Dennis McDougal, about Art Buchwald's 1988 lawsuit against Paramount Pictures. The authors expose the questionable accounting practices that have enabled the major studios to deprive creative talent of millions of dollars in royalties by claiming that top-grossing films earned zero net profits. The book details Hollywood's net-profits clause, allowing a studio to deduct its overall losses from the earnings hit movies, so that through creative accounting, small-time creators are denied rewards despite a film's massive returns.

The entire process of distribution is tough as nails. A *Los Angeles Times* article on March 3, 2002 entitled "The Mild-Mannered Superman of Disney" by Claudia Eller, details a battle between Disney and two of the largest theater chains. In 1989, Disney took on two of the country's most powerful theater chains: United Artists and Cineplex Odeon. To increase Disney's percentage of box office receipts, Disney said that it:

. . . abandoned the customary practice of negotiating 'the split' with exhibitors across the country. [Disney] told them they had to bid against each other to show Disney films. UA and Cineplex, feeling squeezed, retaliated. They refused to screen Disney movies in any of their theaters, including those in 20 cities where one or the other had a lock on the market. But [Disney] struck back. In those cities where Disney was shut out, [they] made deals to play the company's new releases in high school auditoriums, community halls, churches, and at Rotary Clubs. 'In a couple of towns, we exhibited films on bedsheets,' [Disney's representative] said. In Baton Rouge, La., [Disney] rented the civic auditorium for an entire summer. 'We never did more business in that city, before or since.' According to [Disney], the battle continued for about a year, until UA and Cineplex relented.

One of the greatest distributors of all time is Barry Reardon, the former President of Distribution for Warner Bros. Most people over about thirty will likely remember the thrill and amazement of sitting in the theatre in 1981 and watching *Chariots of Fire;* a beautifully produced, directed, and acted film that clearly showed an admirable protagonist living his life to glorify God through his skills and talents. "When I run, I feel God's pleasure. . . ." Had Hollywood really produced such a God-honoring, inspirational movie for secular audiences? And what about the film that followed closely behind it, *The Mission?* Who could forget the opening scene of a missionary strapped to a cross, cascading over a waterfall?

Fans may not realize that these inspiring productions, which opened the door to modern faith-based movies, were almost not released. Believing that their market was too limited, major studios passed on *Chariots*, but the foresight and vision one distributor— Barry Reardon—rescued the film from its demise. Here, Barry shares some of his journey in the world of movie making and gives insight into a process that involves divine appointments, seizing opportunities, and persistence through challenges.

If You Believe in it, Take a Chance on it
—an interview with Barry Reardon

Watch for Divine Appointments

After graduating from college and doing intelligence work in Europe, Barry went to graduate school in business, and then worked for United Technologies and Litton Industries for several years. One day as he was flying from California to the East Coast, he sat next to Charles Bluthorn, Chairman of the Board of Gulf and Western Industries. Charles mentioned that he was interested in buying Paramount Studios, and six or seven months later Barry read that he had, indeed, bought the company. Charles contacted Barry and asked him if he wanted to work for Paramount. Barry was delighted, joining the company in 1967 and working there until 1975.

Barry first worked on the financial end of the business, using his business major to help clean up the company. "Paramount was an old-line company that had gone through tough times and had not moved along as expected. We were desperate to make it work. In the old days, when we did a movie that made $250K/week, we were happy. Finally, we did *Barefoot in the Park* and *Love Story*, which helped profits tremendously, and then we put out *Godfather*, *Chinatown*, etc. If not for this good string of success, we could have gone bankrupt. Now, they were hiring me to close down some operations, open others, and streamline some business practices. We finally brought the company into the twentieth century, and the rest is history."

What if he hadn't been on that plane?

Be Open to New Opportunities

After the company was stabilized in many of its business practices, again Charles Bluthorn came to Barry, revealing that the company was weak in the marketing and sales of movies, and asking Barry for some help. In 1970, he went to work in that area, doing financial planning and running the operations of the selling and marketing of movies. Soon, he became the Executive Vice President of Paramount, and remained such until 1975. He was then recruited to run General Cinema out of Boston, and did so until 1978. That year, Warner Bros. recruited him to go to California, and there he became president of Warner Bros. Distribution, where he served until 1999 when he retired.

Be Very Flexible

Barry's retirement was short-lived—within three months, Warner Bros. called him back to help solve a crisis. At the time, Warner and Paramount had a joint venture with a theatre chain that went bankrupt, and the company's name was on the lease and thus obligated financially. Warner-Paramount decided to buy back the company out of bankruptcy, and Barry was there to straighten it out, modernize the theatres, and balance the books on the deal. He finished this task in May of 2000, and retired once again. Now he lives in Florida and serves on the Board of Directors of several companies, stating emphatically that he is most definitely and truly retired this time.

The Spiritual Climate is Improving

According to Barry, the industry has changed dramatically over the last few decades. "Twenty years ago, I would have questioned whether 'faith and values' people could get into the industry, but things have changed over the last two decades, and are continuing to change. There's a good opportunity for them now."

Barry had a faith-based education, attending Catholic schools and continuing his religious studies in college. "That background of faith always permeated my life and directed how I lived my life. Even in a secular industry, people respect you for your business acumen and your faith, if you show it."

For Christians desiring to enter the field, Barry notes that entertainment is a very diverse industry, still open to people of talent and persistence. "You can get involved in acting, producing, directing, business, or marketing. There are a lot of areas that could be addressed, based on skills, desires, and passions. It's certainly not saturated. There are great opportunities for talented young people. If you have great ideas, you can move ahead fast in the entertainment industry. They're always looking for the next great idea."

Take a Chance

The key to Barry's success through the years was seeing an opportunity and taking it, he says. "I believe everyone has one or two chances to make a big success of themselves. I really feel I got lucky in my career. When I got to Warner Bros., we had a movie that nobody wanted called *Chariots of Fire*. We didn't make it, but eventually Twentieth Century Fox made it, financially partnering with Dodi Fayed's family. The movie was made in England and produced by David Putnam. Fox went to see [the] movie after it was finished, thought it had no chance in America, so they passed on it. David Putnam called Alan Ladd, and we bought movie, though we had no idea how well it would do."

Chariots of Fire was released in September of 1981, and it made $68,907 dollars its first weekend. Not a lot of money relative to some, but it had only opened in three cities—New York, L.A., and Toronto. "Everyone knew I loved it at WB. They called it 'Barry's movie.' After its first weekend, it got wonderful reviews. In our Monday morning marketing meeting they said, 'Well, Barry, what are you going to do with your movie now?' I told them, 'Same thing. Wait and see. This thing is going to grow.' And sure enough, the next weekend was better. Obviously, you know the rest of the story. The movie made $54 million dollars and won the Academy Award for Best Picture. And we were up against some stiff competition, too, like *On Golden Pond*. It was a very satisfying experience."

Strike While the Iron's Hot

The success of Chariots of Fire opened the door for a lot of other great films. Barry distributed *The Mission* a few years later. "Even today, I hear that music played all the time. They called it 'Barry's movie' again. There was a tremendous faith theme in it, and I actually went around to see Jerry Falwell, the Bakers, Pat Robertson, and others, trying to enlist their support. I went on their shows and had many good philosophical discussions with people like Bill Bright of Campus Crusade for Christ. Bill did endorse the movie, as did Ted Baehr and Movieguide. The movie did well, but it never reached the potential we'd hoped for. You just don't know sometimes. Even to today, though, this stands out as one of my all time favorites."

In addition to these secular movies with spiritual themes, Barry and his team distributed overtly Christian movies along the way, such as the 1979 WB release of *Jesus*, made by John Heyman. "This was the first time in modern movie-making that any major studio did a religious movie. We played off regionally, in the south, and then in the Midwest, mid-central America. We didn't release it nationally all at one time. We did a huge group sales effort and kind of broke the ice for religious movies to be broadcast on the big screen."

It was very satisfying for Barry to know that he was instrumental in pioneering a new paradigm for faith-based films. "I am thrilled to have been part of the equation for opening the door, but a lot of others helped along the way. I'm glad I could actually do something to advance the knowledge of God through entertainment . . . I'm honored."

Find Your Own Path

According to Barry, there is not a straight-line road to Hollywood. "I didn't plan my life this way, but I always followed the path, or opportunity I saw just ahead. I'd always loved the movies, and I liked the entertainment field, and as certain opportunities presented themselves, I began to see that being in this industry would afford me access into a lot of areas that could affect people's lives. I became one of the first Christians that worked in the distribution of movies, basically. There's a lot now. Chuck Viane, whom you've also interviewed, worked for me at General Cinema. He and several other believers are making a big difference in the industry."

Check Your Character

Barry encourages Hollywood newcomers to always be true to their ideals. "Always tell the truth," he says. "Understand that it's a complex industry that uses a lot of hyperbole in advertising to boost their dollars, but that's just part of the industry. Realize that and wade through it, always maintaining truth and integrity in yourself."

Scripts are Subjective

As to what makes a good script, Barry believes that there is no easy answer. "That's a difficult question in that it's very subjective. I've had scripts I didn't like but that others have liked, and they've been very successful. I've also had scripts I've loved a lot, and they haven't been successful. It's not how successful a script is itself; it's the interpretation by the directors and actors. We had a script at WB that sat around for close to ten years. Nobody did much about it. Everyone said, 'It's OK.' But we never could find just the right people to put in it. All of the sudden, fall of '92, we had an opening in our production schedule for this movie, *The Fugitive*. Harrison Ford said, 'I like this. Let's do it.' So we shot it, and it was done in four months."

A Great Movie Can Change the Rules

The team finished *The Fugitive* in March and released it in the summer. Usually in those times, Memorial Day weekend and the Fourth of July were big targets for opening movies. "At that time, the Fourth of July was the end of summer in the movie business, but we couldn't get it ready until the end of July. It opened on August 6, 1993. Because of the ill-timing, people said, 'This must not be a very good movie.' It did $190 million at the box office. After that people started saying, 'Gee, August is a really good time to open a movie.'"

The rules now are that any time is a good time to open a movie—as long as you market it correctly, says Barry. "The key is distribution and marketing. If you don't do that right, you won't get a second chance."

Start Slowly, End Hugely

Barry and his team had a marketing strategy that was somewhat unusual for its day. The best marketing job he ever did, he believes, was with *Chariots of Fire*. They started with three markets, or three cities, and then let the positive buzz create the demand for additional markets in subsequent weekends. "Movies need two things," says Barry. "Reviews, and what I call 'positive word of mouth.' People see it, tell their friends, tell more friends, and become successful. If a movie doesn't have this, it's very difficult to make the movie a success. And if you don't believe in it, you don't stand a chance. If I hadn't believed in *Chariots* and *The Mission*, it wouldn't have worked. You won't do a good job in marketing and selling it without fully believing in it. You've gotta have that positive attitude going. You say, 'This movie will work, and here's how we're going to do it,' and others will catch on quickly."

Another one of the great movies that sat on a shelf for a while was *Driving Miss Daisy*. Apparently no one really seemed to want to make it. Finally, a girl at WB, who really had great faith in the project, finally got WB to agree to make it, but only if it could be made for under $12 million. "The Zanucks, who were the producers, got creative, hired Morgan Freeman plus some other fine actors, shot it in the south, and worked deals like trading off premieres to use a factory, etc. It was released in December of '89, only opened in four theatres, but got great word of mouth reviews. It was a huge success, though it took a whole year to get the movie rolling. A year into it, it was still playing in theatres, just reaching the small towns."

Moviemaking Is Staggeringly Expensive

Over the years, it has cost more and more money to produce and market films. According to Barry, the world of financing and distribution has changed dramatically. "In 1975 movies would open in fifty to a hundred theatres, at the most two hundred. Now they often open in 3,000 theatres. This is a very dramatic change. The number of dollars spent is huge. There are massive television buys, which used to be cheap. Now, if you run an ad on *Friends*, it'll cost you $100K. If you run it around the Super Bowl, it'll be $2 million. We've changed our marketing strategy over the years, but television still has the biggest impact and reaches the most people. It's still the best way to go, though it's expensive."

Another area costing moviemakers great deals of money involves unions. "Hollywood has a real problem that no one wants to address, and that's the problem of unions. The guy who drives the truck from the studio to the set has about six to eight hours where he does nothing, but you're still paying him $40-$50/hour. I'm not anti-union, but the rules need to be changed, and things need to become reasonable. A lot of productions do move off shore or film in other countries to get non-union crews. Now Vancouver, Toronto, and Montreal are used a lot, with Montreal often doubling for New York. In Canada the dollar goes farther, so it's appealing to filmmakers. This is a very complex subject, though, and not an easy thing to change overnight."

Tough, But Worth It

In conclusion, Barry encourages anyone who wants to get in to move forward and forge ahead in the film industry, despite its challenges and old mindsets. "It's a very tough road, but it can be done. On the business side, especially, it's a great opportunity for young people to show their talents and make a difference."

Millions of fans are grateful that, through the foresight and determination of one inspired distributor, quality, God-honoring movies were made, and a formerly closed door was opened for people of faith to influence an often dark industry. May many more Barry Reardon's be raised up to make a difference in this generation!

***

SUCCESS, STEP 22: FOLLOW UP

Check the ratings, promotion, and advertising for your production frequently. Stay on top of any payments and billings due. Artists will receive payments every time your program plays. Know when and what you have to pay. You will receive money according to the distribution deals you set up. Keep all your paperwork. Know when and how you are to be paid. Trust God and not man.

Survey the reaction to your production.

Learn from your mistakes, so you can do better next time.

To produce a movie or a television program, you have to be creative, self-disciplined, organized, unstructured, persistent, flexible, imaginative, and practical. As a rule of thumb, fifty percent of your energy will be expended doing the work of producing your movie (or show); another fifty percent will be expended fighting for your production. If this seems overwhelming to you, trust that God will help you succeed in producing a powerful program—telling the story He has given you to tell.

If you are embarking on producing a video for your church, review the steps and select those principles and techniques that are relevant to your production. By familiarizing yourself with the most complex form of production, you will excel in simpler productions, including productions in other audio-visual media. An excellent exercise is to assemble a group from your church and produce a movie in miniature with amateur equipment. If you take care to follow all the appropriate steps, you will be proud of your production. If not, you will quickly see the glaring flaws in your final product. These flaws will help you learn what to do better next time. Practice; try out what you've learned. Have fun and apply yourself to achieving excellence, in His service.

· 12 ·

Snapshots

THE DIRECTOR AND THE ACTORS

The Director

The director is the storyteller. He turns the story into a film. He decides where and how the images are filmed and edited, how the actors portray their characters, and what the audience experiences. The director's vision for the story determines how the audience feels about the story: sad, amused, bored, scared, or humble. The director translates the story into a movie by using the techniques of filmmaking, such as character development, camera angles, and editing.

The director has to deal with the time limitations of a movie, such as actors, locations, weather, and of course, money. Being prepared for all eventualities is one of the most important keys to success for a director. The director should try to anticipate all of the things that could go wrong on any individual shoot and have a backup plan. Below is some advice—on backups, and everything in between—from award-winning director of *Gettysburg* and *Gods and Generals* Ron Maxwell.

Realness, Role-Models, & Relationships

—an interview with Ron Maxwell

On September 11, 2001, Ron Maxwell's whole crew was out filming the Battle of Antietam for the movie *Gods and Generals*. When they heard about the terrorist attacks, they stopped their work, gathered together, and prayed for the country. On that set in the Shenandoah Valley, actors, producers, lighting and electrical technicians, makeup and wardrobe specialists, directors and stuntmen from all walks of life dropped not only their equipment, but also their religious differences and came together to beseech God for help and mercy. "That day, we were in church—under the great big canopy of sky," says producer/writer Ron Maxwell. While filming *Gods and Generals*, which follows the rise and fall of legendary war hero Stonewall Jackson, not only were souls united in prayer for our country; the faith of the civil war characters left an indelible mark on the hearts of all involved. Below, this producer shares some of his background and insights for others seeking to make films of historical, inspirational significance.

Watch for Early Signs

Ron Maxwell was writing, producing, directing, and acting in plays long before he had any notions that this would become his career. By the time he was in junior high, he had already formed his own theatre company and was writing plays in blank verse and iambic pentameter. "By then I was already seeing Shakespearean plays, writing historical plays, and producing, directing, and acting in them." In the ninth grade he did Charles I, and wrote, directed, and produced Henry III—also in blank verse and iambic pentameter. In his junior year of high school he formed the Garden State players, actually selling stock in the theatre company to teachers and friends and raising a few thousand dollars on the deal.

Keep Fine-Tuning the Passion

Upon graduation from Clifton High School in New Jersey, Ron enrolled as a theatre major at New York University College of Arts and Sciences where he was a member of the Hall of Fame Players and the Green Room Honor Society. At NYU, Ron acted in plays and musicals, including the title role in *Hamlet*. His work in NYU's theatre program earned him an invitation and scholarship to attend the New York University Graduate School of the Arts, Institute of Film and Television. In 1970, Ron completed his graduate film thesis, writing and directing an adaptation of Albert Camus' *The Guest*. Upon graduation, he worked in Spain as Charlton Heston's personal assistant in Heston's directorial debut, *Antony and Cleopatra*.

Ron married and had two children—Olivia and Jonathan, both born in the early 1970s. From 1974–1978, Ron worked with Jac Venza at WNET-13, NYC, as an associate producer and subsequently producer for the Emmy and Peabody Award-winning series *Theatre in America*. "This was a very exciting environment. We were doing about forty hours of programming that captured the burgeoning national theatre in America, bringing many fabulous stage productions to television. I worked there four years—as an Associate Producer, producer, and director. It was an incredible experience."

At WNET, he produced and co-directed *Seamarks*, starring George Hearn and Veronica Castang. In 1978, he produced and directed *Verna: USO Girl*, starring Sissy Spacek, Bill Hurt, Sally Kellerman, and Howard DaSilva, for which Ron was nominated for a Best Director Emmy.

"I had read the book, *Killer Angels*, and before I was finished reading it, I knew it was on my heart to make the movie *Gettysburg*. Little did I know it would start a fifteen-year saga to get it made. I acquired the rights in '78, had a script by '81, and by '84 realized that the only way I could make it into a movie was to clear the decks and concentrate full time on it. This was a big, conscious life decision. I did do other films in the interim, but I was really bent on making *Gettysburg*. That was where my passion was." Ron did team up with Ted Turner, and the movie was finally filmed in 1992 and released theatrically in the fall of 1993. In the summer of 1994, it was broadcast over two nights on TNT where it established the all-time highest rating for a dramatic film on cable television. The video and DVD have sold millions of copies. *Time* magazine heralded it as "that rarest of cinema, an intelligent epic."

Keep a Good Thing Rolling

In keeping with his love and talent for historical epics, Ron has since produced, written, and directed the film *Gods and Generals*, the prequel to *Gettysburg*. It was released in February 2003, and the DVD/VHS was released on July 15, 2003 as the #1 selling video in America, with over 600,000 sales in its first week. Currently, Ron is in pre-production on *Joan of Arc: Virgin Warrior* and in long-range pre-production on *Last Full Measure*, the final part of his Civil War trilogy.

"*Joan of Arc* will empower young people, especially young girls, to become all they're supposed to be in life. This is not like some of the other movies about her life, which were really filled with awful, pernicious lies and gross misrepresentations, but this is the story of the real Joan."

Keep Faith Alive

Regarding Ron's current passion—the *Joan of Arc* movie, one of the aspects of this movie that intrigues him is that Joan of Arc had to explore her own personal faith and the whole mystery of her calling. "I realized that, like her, I was called at an early age, in a way I didn't even comprehend; I only understood it after the fact. This whole film explores that mystery. There's no more striking example of someone who is called, accepts their calling, and receives the grace to carry it out, than Joan of Arc."

Assess the Cost

Ron believes that everyone is called to do something, and that if you heed the call, there's always a price to pay. "I had to surrender a lucrative income to do *Gettysburg*, mortgaging my house and borrowing money from friends—at age forty, to add injury to insult, to make this movie. I had to live through that in order to understand Joan. Joan was asked to dedicate her life for what she was called to do." Ron believes that whether a person is called to be a teacher, a fireman, or a businessman, if you're willing to pay the price, it's Aristotelian happiness. "If you're operating in your calling, you can't wait to get up in the morning, to do your job. The whole thing is joyous, no matter what the circumstances."

Ron reminds believers in Hollywood that there is always a price to pay for doing great exploits for God's kingdom, and many will have doubts and even quit after realizing the price tag. "Even our lord in the Garden of Gethsemane showed His human fears and doubts. And when Joan of Arc realized the price she'd have to pay—being away from her parents, her home, and her village, not having the opportunity to meet a man, marry, or become a mother, this price was enormous. But she knew it was her calling and her sacrifice."

Check Your Motives

Ron has also seen that it is wise to analyze one's motives in a given endeavor. "If someone tells you that you have to do another job— for money-making purposes, or prestige, and you do something that you're not supposed to be doing, you're asking for misery, frustration, disappointment, and alienation. This is the mystery of the calling. You might be called to simple things, not grandiose projects. You might wake up and say, "I'm making money in the legal practice, but I really need to be teaching in a grammar school. There's a little voice inside that says 'this is what you're to do.' Whether it's carpentry, working as an executive, teaching, directing—whatever—you know it in your heart. Nobody else can tell you, or measure it for you."

It's Natural to Doubt

Despite Ron's fame and success, he has often wrestled with career doubts. "Yes, I've lived the life I wanted to live, but so often I've questioned my calling. I've asked, 'Who am I kidding? Am I worthy? Am I good enough? But after all the self-doubt, I always come out with renewed conviction." In order to find the quiet voice of conviction, Ron believes you have to get quiet. "Turn off the television and radio, and shut down the world that's bombarding you with their sales pitch. Get quiet and pray. If not, you won't hear it."

Seek Confirmation

Others will confirm the high calling in one's life, Ron believes. "With Joan of Arc, powerful men and women endorsed her. People examined and interrogated her, realized her mission was real, gave her the armor and authority she needed, and publicly confirmed her calling. By the time she was captured, she had developed a strong inner strength."

One of the ways Ron suggests that artists in the industry judge their work is to think about what they'd like others to say when they're gone. "What I've learned as film watcher, now in my fifties, is that the faith of characters, spirituality, comes through in a well-made film. As the old saying goes, 'Sometimes actions speak louder than words.' If you look at *Gods and Generals*, *Gettysburg*, and *Joan of Arc*, you will meet people grappling with issues of faith. That, to me, when I'm gone, in the twinkling of eye, will be what mattered in my career. Years from now I want people to say of me, 'Look what questions his movies asked! All his movies addressed issues of faith in honest and provocative ways, engaging people in a powerful, spiritual way.'"

Let Your Work Evoke Questions

Ron believes firmly in the 'Show it, don't say it' principle of film-making. "I don't want my works to be preachy or heavy. I'm not interested in answering every question, or in proselytizing. I'm interested in raising questions and exploring mysteries. These are the films worth exploring, those that un-churched people can't help but wonder about. I want to raise their curiosity about people of faith. I want them to come away from *Gods and Generals* asking, 'What makes Stonewall Jackson tick?'"

People over Product

Ron hopes that artists of faith will create projects that add joy to the world and foster strong relationships in the process. "This is easier said than done, but even the process is important. Make the best movie you can make. The making should be memorable and worthwhile, and the process joyous. "When we made *Gods and Generals*, we were outside in the cold weather, and it was not always fun, but we always had a sense of joy in the process." Ron adds that the most important part of the process is how you work with others, and the mutual respect shared on a project. These are components as important, or more important, than the actual product.

After studying his works, interviewing Ron, and especially interviewing others like actor Donzaleigh Abernathy, who raved about working alongside Ron, it is clear that Ron does value relationships above all, and that he is intentional and equally at ease with sharing his vision—both to large audiences and one-on-one to friends and film associates. If past history is, indeed, the best indicator of future performance, we should see more historically accurate, inspirational movies that will evoke profound questions of faith in audiences worldwide.

* * *

THE ACTOR

There are several approaches to acting. The classical approach to acting, and the oldest approach—held that the actor's job was to become the character and leave his or her own emotions behind. The classical approach believed that you learned your lines, showed up prepared, and acted the way you and the director thought that the character would act.

In the Twentieth Century, "the Method" came into vogue. I studied at the renowned Lee Strasberg Studio, which is now known as Lee Strasberg Theater Institute, while Lee was still teaching. Lee brought the Method developed by the Russian Constantin Sergeyevich Stanislavsky to the United States. Born in Moscow in 1863, Stanislavsky asserted that if the theater was going to be meaningful it needed to move beyond the external representation that acting had primarily been. Over forty years he created an approach that was the forefront of the psychological and emotional aspects of acting. The Stanislavsky System, or "the Method," as it has become known, held that an actor's main responsibility was to be believed (rather than recognized or understood).

To reach this "believable truth," Stanislavsky first employed methods such as "emotional memory." To prepare for a role that involves fear, the actor must remember something frightening and attempt to act the part in the emotional space of that fear they once felt. Stanislavsky believed that an actor needed to take his or her own personality onto the stage when they began to play a character. This was a clear break from previous modes of acting.

To understand acting, you should ask yourself how often you have "said your piece," stated your argument, given detailed instructions, or tried to communicate an intensely felt emotion, only to find that your audience did not understand what you were communicating. All of us who have communicated to an audience have experienced that sinking moment when we find out that our audience did not understand the most basic point of our communication. What we communicate is frequently not what we want to communicate.

Performing a scene in an acting class is an excellent way to discover communication problems. Our clothes, our posture, our grooming, our state of mind, our self-control, our objectivity, and our environment interact to determine what we are communicating. Knowing our lines, knowing what we want to communicate, is only the first step toward communicating exactly what we want to communicate. For an actor or actress, the other steps involve getting in touch with his or her feelings, being relaxed, putting on makeup, getting into costume, going on stage, pacing his or her delivery, reading the audience, and physically expressing the appropriate feelings within the context of the role. For other communicators, the other steps involve applying the answers to the pertinent ascertainment questions and constructing a logical communication with reference to the medium of choice.

When Richard Burton performed in his first movie scene with Liz Taylor in *Cleopatra*, he thought that she couldn't act because she was so low-key. However, when the film rushes came back from the laboratory that night, he noted that her acting was very powerful while his acting was too exaggerated and unnatural. Watching the rushes, he realized that he was accustomed to theatrical acting where he had to project his emotions to the back of the theater, but the film medium magnified everything he did. Underplaying the part, as Liz was doing, was what was necessary to achieve a natural yet powerful effect on screen.

Translating a communication from one medium to another can drastically alter the message. In her review of the BBC television program, *The Jewel in the Crown*, adapted from the novel by Paul Scott, Ms. Martha Bayles notes:

> The trouble is, the obsessive reconstruction of events which occurs in Mr. Scott's fiction is hard to bring off in the relatively literal medium of film. When we see something happen on film, we assume it really happened that way. Granted, this is a pretty obtuse

reaction, but filmmakers usually have to respect it. There is no real cinematic equivalent to the novelist's device of having characters ruminate in different voices about an event they can neither fathom nor forget.[109]

Not only does the medium affect our message, our delivery can make a difference in the way the audience perceives our communication. Even a slight mispronunciation can make the difference between life and death—as in the Old Testament Book of Judges, where the revengeful Gileadites slaughtered the fugitive Ephraimites because they could not pronounce the password, "shibboleth."[110]

Most professional actors spend many years studying acting by taking classes, studying movies, plays and television programs, and reading a lot of books. An actor should read and re-read the script, meditate on the character's history and daily activities, and ask:

> Who is my character?
> What does my character want and why?
> What motivates my character?
> What does he think?
> What does he feel—is he happy?
> What does he do in his spare time?
> What kind of mass media or entertainment does he use?

Acting is doing and reacting. Actors react to what other actors do, using body language as much as dialogue. Here are some enlightening reflections by some wonderful actors.

FAITH-FILLED, FUNNY, AND FAMILY-FRIENDLY
—AN INTERVIEW WITH JOHN RATZENBERGER

We all know him as Cliff in the television show, *Cheers* . . . and also as the voice of the Fish School in *Finding Nemo* . . . and maybe the voice of the Abominable Snowman in *Monsters, Inc.*. . . or how about P.T. Flea in *A Bug's Life*? But, how many fans realize that this talented guy has acted in about fifty films, thirty television shows, written and directed plays and TV shows, and lived in England for a decade before he ever sat down at that famous bar stool? John Ratzenberger has lived a life of adventure, disappointment, fame, family, and faith. Below he shares just a bit of his decades of wisdom for those, like him, whom the acting bug has bitten.

Doors Open in Unusual Ways

"I was in college," says John. "The last thing on my mind was to be an actor, but I had a crush on a cute girl in the drama department, so the best thing for me to do was audition, help out, do carpentry, whatever it took to get me on that project. Much to my surprise, I got the understudy for Tennessee Williams' *Summer and Smoke*. I hung around and had a blast, knowing that the odds I'd really need to act were slim. Much to my chagrin, however, the lead quit the night before the show was to open. Unfortunately, I hadn't paid enough attention during rehearsals, so I ended up improvising a lot of the lines in the second half of the play. I just didn't know lines. Funny thing, though, it worked! All the other actors hated me because they didn't get their cues, but the audience loved it. They didn't realize it wasn't a farce. From the very first laugh at my desperation with the lines, I enjoyed it . . . I was hooked."

You Don't Have to Train in Hollywood

After that, John joined an improvisation troupe, then after college, he spent some time in North Vermont as a blacksmith's apprentice. From there, he went to London, where he co-founded *Sal's Meat Market*, a two-man improvisational group in which he co-wrote, directed, and starred. During those years, John became a master at integrating mime, dance, song, and improv in over six hundred performances. The show grew, and most of the time John and his buddies performed in standing-room-only houses. The *Sal's Meat Market* show in London was the only American group to have received a grant from the British Arts Council. "It was 80% improvised," says John. "We just planned a beginning, middle, and end. We had tons of props in the back and would duck back in with a character no one had seen before. It really got the adrenaline going. We had so much fun in those days. As a matter of fact, two of our students, Steve Stein and Jim Sweeny, helped start the popular show *Whose Line Is It, Anyway?*"

John then toured Europe for six years, writing comedies for BBC, Granada TV, and acting in major motion pictures over there, where many American companies were making films because of the positive exchange rates. "I always played a soldier, sailor, or policemen. I was privileged to act in *Gandhi*, *Yanks*, *A Bridge Too Far*, and *The Empire Strikes Back*. I worked with top directors like John Schlesinger and Richard Attenborough, some of the best directors in the world. I'd never been to acting school, so I never thought I'd get this far."

Humor Is Universal

Although John has performed extensively in Europe and America, he truly believes there's no real difference in the humor. "People are people," says John. "They laugh at the same things. Take Laurel and Hardy, or Charlie Chaplin . . . Everyone thinks it's funny when a guy leans down to get water, stands back up, and knocks over an ironing board. A farce, or slapstick humor, does well universally. The people who get in trouble go over to Europe and think they don't have to write something unique for the English. They'll talk about the New York Yankees in their script, but no one can relate to the Yankees in London. You've got to write for your audience. If the writer had done his homework, he'd have researched that the Manchester United football team would fit nicely in that spot."

Be Faithful and Be Entrusted with More

"I also got to work in *Ragtime*, James Cagney's last film. Also with Pat O'Brien. What incredible men! I was soon hired to write with Ruby Wax (of *Absolutely Fabulous*), a late night comedy for CBS back in the States. Someone I knew said, 'You're from New England, aren't you? There's a show for Paramount that takes place in a Boston bar. I'll get you in.' I'd never auditioned before that time, but again I thought, 'Why not?'"

Learn the Drill!

The jump from British acting to American acting turned out to be funny, embarrassing, and finally very lucrative. "In England, the casting director's job is to make sure you're a professional," John explains. "Everyone sits in a room and chats, everyone assuming that we're all professionals. In L.A., though, people get off busses calling themselves actors, so many are really not professionals. The process here is that everyone sits in a room and reads lines to a less-than-enthusiastic casting assistant, who's usually not that committed to the script. So, not knowing this, I went in there, fully expecting to sit and chat."

Sitting, chatting, and sipping tea, however, were apparently not priorities for the team of American casting agents. "When I got in, I looked around for the chair, which seemed to surprise the casting team. 'You're not here to chat,' they said. 'This is an audition. Please read.' 'Ohhhh,' I thought. Now these two pages of a script they'd handed me were starting to make sense. I was supposed to have practiced it! I thought that it was just a basis of what the show was generally about. Embarrassed, I headed for the door; ready to go back to London.

Seize the Day!

As he was walking out door, though, John had a thought . . . a good one. "Suddenly I turned around and asked, 'Do you have a bar know it all?' Their expressions said back to me, 'Are you still here?'

But one man, Glen Charles, said, 'What do you mean?' That's all I needed to hear. I started improvising the Cliff character, based on someone I grew up with. Really, I was just trying to regain my dignity and get off their carpet. They chuckled, said thanks, and goodbye. Two days later I got a call that they wanted to try out the character for seven episodes. Eleven years and 22 Emmys later, Cliff was still sitting at that bar."

Whatcha Doin' Now?

The big question is Hollywood is always, "What have you done lately?" These days, John is enjoying doing voice-overs for Pixar Animation. As a matter of fact, he's the only actor to have performed in all the Pixar movies. "I think my favorite was *A Bug's Life*, playing P.T. Flea. I also liked Ham the Pig in *Toy Story*."

In addition to his continual work with Pixar, John is a prominent humanitarian, serving as chairman of the world's largest internet venture connecting diabetes information and research. The web site, (www.childrenwithdiabetes.com) receives an average of 3 million hits per month. John has raised over $100 million for diabetes, the sixth leading cause of death in the U.S. In his "spare" time, John enjoys sailing, fishing, billiards, fencing, karate, and playing his drum in a bagpipe band!

Staying active with a constantly expanding resume of buzzing activities is certainly a priority and a recommendation from Mr. Ratzenberger, and likely a determining factor in his being sought out in so many arenas.

Lose the Lazy Language

As a person of faith and conviction, John has tried to either steer away from, or at least challenge, those who feel compelled to use foul language to get a laugh. "There are times over different projects when I've asked the writers why people are swearing for no good reason. I tell them that it would be funnier if there weren't these swear words. 'Even make up a word!' I say. And sometimes they've done that. I've turned down projects based on raunchiness before. Once, I even got into an argument with a producer with a big L.A. company. They wanted me to play the father in a sitcom. After they sent me the script, I said, 'I have to tell you as a parent I'd turn this show off at page four. The young man is swearing at his mother in front of his father. There's no way that this kid would get away with this, and there's no consequences, either. You're doing it just for laughs.'

'Are you a prude?' they asked me. 'No, I'm a dad.' In fact, my son learned his first swear word from *E.T.* at age five. The way I look at it, *E.T.* stole a bit of my son's childhood."

"Anyway, this producer really got her hackles up. 'Oh, so this offends you?' 'Yes,' I said, 'but more importantly, it'll offend families in Omaha, Tallahassee, and Chicago, those people who invite you into their living rooms every week. Don't insult your hosts. You're not there to shock or convince them of your 'hipper than thou' philosophy or to politicize; you're there to make them laugh.'"

John tells actors to "Reach up! Don't pander! Don't go below the belt. It's so easy to get a laugh by mentioning body parts or playing dirty. But in *Cheers*, *Seinfeld*, and some of the others, they don't play dirty. There's not a lot of lazy language. Sure, the comedians who swear or use scatological humor can get laughs, but they're uncomfortable laughs. I want to go for a good, hearty, belly laugh that's based on real, well-thought-out humor. Some of the current generation of writers grew up watching TV, but last generation grew up reading books. Read books, read everything you can, and you'll increase your vocabulary and do better as an actor and comedian."

Get a Respectful Agent

To get an agent, one must have a good resume of performances, says John. But to get a good resume, you've got to have an agent who will get you work. "It's a Catch 22 . . . When I got to the United States, I couldn't get an agent because they didn't believe me—or all the work I'd done in England. One agent had his feet on his desk when I walked in. I said, 'You'll need to get your feet off that desk . . . or I'll knock them off.' The guy sat up straight and started laughing. 'No one's ever said that to me before.' It's all about dignity . . . respect."

Develop Thick Skin

John believes that television and movie actors must be thick-skinned, taking all the criticism with a grain of salt. "After all, at end of the day, when you're breathing your last, it's not your producer, director, or cast mates by your bedside; it's your children. Keep that in mind."

Buy an Alarm Clock

According to John, showing up on time is so important. "I tell young actors, especially in L.A., give themselves an extra hour. Show up early and get the lay of the land. The last thing you want to do is rush into a room and use four of your seven audition minutes on excuses. I direct as well, and actors have sauntered in to my auditions forty-five minutes late, not thinking anything of it. I say, 'If you're forty-five minutes late for the audition, how can I trust you to be on time to the set? Life is too short for me to hold everything up for one late person who doesn't care.' One guy who was perfect for a certain role didn't get the job because he couldn't get places on time."

Find Like-Minded People

John suggests that actors seek out others in the industry with the same faith and values as their own. "Find them, and keep them close; you'll need their support. You'll be tested every single day. You'll run up against someone in authority telling you your outlook is wrong, and you'll see this in his or her attitudes, deeds, and scripts. Get into a position of power and change the system. But you can't do it alone; you have to stay interconnected with others of faith. It's good to know someone who's already there, someone from

your same school, your old neighborhood, a friend of a friend. . . .
Whoever you can find. When you come to L.A., get an apartment
near a church you want to belong to. Find people who share your
values, and you'll conquer the world together."

Be Courageous

John believes that it's not in trying to fit in that one succeeds—it's
in making an unusual mark, based on what you believe in. "Hollywood has lost touch with their audience a long time ago. Mel
Gibson's film *The Passion of the Christ)* is proof of this."

Some Practical Hints

In order to find out if an actor is ready for Hollywood, he must
determine whether he can make an audience laugh or cry, says
John. "So many people aren't ready for Hollywood—professionally
or practically. You've got to make sure you have a lot of gas money.
You'll need a car that runs. So many actors have sheer guts, will,
and determination; they just need some preparation. When that
opportunity arises, meet it, without excuses. I don't want to hear
that you couldn't find your socks. Finally, relax, and have fun."

Walk in Wisdom

According to John, there are some genuinely good people in show
biz, but there are also some really unscrupulous folks. "It's just like
any other small village; there's the whole gamut of characters. I've
actually gotten really screwed, monetarily . . . conned out of money
by professing Christians—nice, church-going, family folks. There
have been points in my career where I've said, 'Lord, just give me
the industry folks!' As the saying goes, 'A friend in Hollywood stabs
you in the chest' . . . up front. When you're trying to swim your
way to the top, many will try to prevent you from getting there and
lead you down bad paths. But, you also meet really nice people.
You've got to watch the trappings—and stay wise."

Keep a Level Head

One of the toughest things to do in Hollywood is to keep a level head amidst great fame. When asked how he handles the accolades, John tells us, "I come from Bridgeport, Connecticut and have friends I grew up with there. As a matter of fact, my daughter's godfather is someone I was in third grade with. On my visits back home, if they saw that I was getting a big head, they'd let me know right away. That's actually the basis of a program I did called *Made in America*. I interviewed people like John Deere combine harvesters. I went around and profiled companies that make things here in America. It highlighted the Judeo Christian ethic of honoring people that keep civilization together. In show biz, you've gotta surround yourself with real, down-home people. They'll keep you straight."

After talking with John for just an hour, it is clear that his down-home, Connecticut friends have certainly done their jobs in the life of this warm, witty actor who occupies some dear space in all our hearts and minds—and now in our children's, too!

* * *

LIVE WITH NO REGRETS

—AN INTERVIEW WITH MORGAN BRITTANY

Remember that 80s show about the captivating, backstabbing machinations of Dallas oil magnate J.R. Ewing and his family? *Dallas* (1978–1991) chronicled the exploits of wealthy Texas oil millionaires, and many of its plots revolved around shady business dealings and dysfunctional family dynamics. However, acting amidst all this on-screen corruption and greed was a star with a true heart for God. Beginning her career as a successful child actor, the beautiful Morgan Brittany actually played the evil, snobby Katherine Wentworth on the show for five years. Her own heart, however, had a much more lovely and captivating story than her character's. After all, reality is often more fascinating than fiction.

It's Never Too Early to Get In . . . Or Is It?

Morgan Brittany has been in show business her entire life. She started when her parents and her grandmother made the decision to put her into the business at age five. She was thinking about dancing lessons, singing lessons, auditions, and callbacks when the other children in the neighborhood were thinking about school busses and sandboxes. It was all she knew. "I had a hit and miss education because of the many interviews, working on productions, and going to school at the studios." And work she did. Morgan performed in many television programs and movies such as *Twilight Zone, Sea Hunt, The Birds*—with Alfred Hitchcock, *Gypsy*—with Natalie Wood, and many other films. It was a very successful career as a child actress. As with many other great things in life, however, there's always a down side.

"It's great when successful, but kid actors are put in a little category. You're only sellable and marketable when you're cute and little. In the teen years, everything slows down. Work isn't there like it used to be." At this time, Morgan found herself floundering, desperately trying to find direction. "I didn't feel like I was a viable human being anymore. Most child actors go through that. Unless you can transition into an adult star, your career is over. Most kids turn to drug addiction, alcoholism, and even suicide. It's very tragic. Child actors have a lot of tragedy."

At age fifteen, Morgan was searching for who she was, and what she wanted to do with her life. "I really wanted to be in the entertainment industry, but I felt there was no place for me. I went to school, but I didn't really fit in there, either. I kind of felt like an adult in a kid's world." Indeed, at age fifteen, Morgan had already made money, established—and seemingly lost—a full career, and had already been successful in an adult world. "I found myself having no direction, and no support system at all. I was basically only of use to the family when I was making money. I didn't quite know what to do."

You've Got to Go Down to Go Up

Morgan got to her lowest point at sixteen as she concluded that she was a hopeless failure who didn't fit in. "I remember a turning point happening in my life. . . . My family was not very religious; they weren't church people, but I had a strong faith from an early age because I'd always go with my instinct and deep feelings. I had always asked, 'What choice shall I make? In what direction should I go?' I'd put myself in God's hands, and I'd get an answer. Now, at sixteen, I wasn't hearing. I was very desperate and very depressed, feeling like there was no reason to go on. One night in my room, I said, 'God, I have to have an answer. If I don't have an answer by tomorrow, I'm not going to make it. I can't go on like this.' I just laid it all out. I left it up to God and went to bed. The next day, I had such an inner peace and strength within me. I looked in the mirror and said, 'You're going to make it. You're going to start over. You have the courage and the strength, through God, to keep going. My life turned around, I changed my attitude, took one step at a time, and headed in the right direction."

Christianity Is Not Trouble Free

After that, Morgan went to school, focused, and though she knew that maybe it would take awhile, she did want to make it in acting. She assumed that her spiritual turnaround would give her some relief from life's troubles, and though she did have a new peace, tribulation was often at hand. "There was a lot more rejection, and a lot of cruelty. It was even brutal sometimes. Unless you've been in it, you don't know," says Morgan. "Everything is a rejection of you, not your product, or your script, or a cosmetic. It's you. You put yourself on the line as a performer, and when people reject you, it's a personal rejection. Especially as a teen what you're hearing is, 'I don't like you. You don't measure up.'"

Tap into Your Inner Strength

Morgan believes that actors must have an inner spiritual strength, or they will slip into various crutches like alcohol or drugs. "People grasp whatever they can to deal with the rejection. That's why there are so many wounded people in the business with addictions. You can be an Academy Award Winner, but you've still got to put yourself out there. And they'll continue to question you. Unless you have a faith that says 'This doesn't matter so much, and this doesn't constitute my identity,' you'll be clobbered emotionally. You have to say, 'If it happens, great, but in the big picture, it doesn't matter that much.' The more I had that attitude, the more success I realized."

With Success Comes Temptation

As Morgan began to learn how to center herself in God and in the truth, her career began to take off once again. She did very well as an actor in New York and in Japan. When she came back to Hollywood, she performed in various television movies of the week and became more and more successful. All of a sudden, temptations were thrown her way. Producers would say, 'OK, we want you to do this movie. Sure, there's nudity, or graphic excesses. But this will really boost your career.' It's so tempting, and you have to make those tough choices. I lost agents and managers because I turned down big movies that were smutty. I didn't want to compromise my values, or my morals as a Christian. There are certain things I will and will not do. I'm not going to change. That's the way I am. There were those who told me I was destroying my career . . . that someone else would take the part, and she'd be a big star. Well she did, and she was. But I have nothing to regret. I have two children who can see everything I've every done, and they have nothing to be ashamed of or hide from their friends. They don't have to say, 'My mom did *Playboy*, or this sleazy movie.' In my twenties these things were all thrown at me. I had no kids, no husband, but I looked into the future and said, 'If I make this choice, the consequences will never go away. This will always, always, be there. What if I do have kids some day? Would I really want them to see this?'"

"God said, 'You don't need this. You'll be successful anyway.' It was the same with drugs. They were all around me, but I made the choice to not do them. I was looked at as weird, odd, not fitting in with the Hollywood crowd. But I didn't care. In 1981, a famous manager wanted to manage me, and we had a meeting. I'll never forget this. I wore a cross that day, and the first thing he did was walk over to me and say, 'You're going to have to lose that.' 'Excuse me?' I asked. 'You'll never work in this town with that. If there's anything Hollywood doesn't accept it's: Republicans and Christians.' I was shocked. I told him that this relationship wouldn't work out. The man said, 'Why don't you just go home, get married and have kids? This business is never going to work for you.' Well, I don't know where he is today, but I'm here and very OK with who I am as a person."

Morgan attests to the fact that these scenarios are what children have to deal with in Hollywood today. "It's very difficult for Christians, and conservatives. But it can work. I'm proof of that, and I have friends who are proof of that. But you have to be strong, and you have to have the faith to go forward without being a sellout. That's the road I've taken. I'm at a point where I work when I want to work, do the things I want to do . . . I'm trying to present myself in a positive way."

Find Redemptive Roles

Morgan's goal is to be a positive role model. However, that doesn't mean she has ruled out all negative characters. "I've played killers, crazies, and really bad people. But, every single time I play those, that bad character loses out. I'm either dead, or miserable, or clearly a bad example. Kids don't want to be that character. Once on *Dallas*, they were going to have my character win, or triumph over the good. I said, 'Guys, you can't do that. Let J.R. Ewing be the bad guy who seems to do well in the short term. Not my character. You don't want to make her a role model.' They said, 'That's true. We have good, and we have evil, and you're the evil.' My character did end up dead," Morgan chuckles.

A lot of the scripts Morgan gets glorify evil. "I say, 'You're preaching that evil gets rewarded?' I feel bad about a lot of the movies I see that teach kids that if they do bad, they'll win. Hollywood has an obligation to watch what they put out there. Kids do imitate what they see—good or bad. The irresponsibility in the music and film industry is outrageous. I spent years trying to counteract what my kids saw. I had to go in and say, 'Wait! Don't you see how this is wrong?' A lot of parents don't take the time to do that. The entertainment business has got to get a grip and realize that they're responsible."

Find a Like-Minded Spouse

Morgan has been married for over twenty-years. Her husband, Jack, does action adventure movies as a stunt coordinator. "He does a lot of films, but he turns down graphically violent films and does a lot of comedies. Even though there's less money, he feels better about it. We do think the same way, but it's tougher for him in the industry because he's surrounded by very, very liberal people. He has to keep quieter about what he thinks, and how he believes. I'm a little more out there, vocal about it."

Industry Kids Need Loving and Firm Limits

At the time of this interview, Morgan and her husband have two children: an eighteen-year-old daughter and a sixteen-year-old son. When asked if the children would follow in their parents' footsteps, Morgan hesitated to think. "Well, our children do know what this industry is about, but they have a good grip on who they are. Our daughter is doing modeling and some commercials, but some of the pilots and TV shows are very sexual, very much against what she is. She's a very conservative girl. Even as an actress, she won't do the raunchy stuff. She won't even go to the auditions. It would waste her time and theirs. She makes enough money as a model for various products. Our son wants to be like his dad and learn precision driving. He's also into tennis, and very athletic. So, who knows what they'll choose."

Morgan proudly attests to the fact that both of her children have strong value systems. "It's tough on them because many of their friends don't understand why my two kids are so strong in morals and values. I recently had a big discussion with one of my son's friends. He is sixteen-years-old and was using a string of profanities in our home. I said, 'Excuse me. I don't know whether Cody told you the rules of the house, but we don't talk like that. We don't use that kind of language.' The kid looked at me like I was out of my mind. But from that moment on, he didn't say another curse word. Now if he slips, he quickly apologizes. Kids do need limits. They do need us to say, 'Hey, you're out of line. This is the way it is.' I've learned a lot about teenagers. I put a lot of limits on my kids, and they're actually OK with it. Sometimes you've got to be the bad guy, but I think it's worth it."

Sometimes Dreams Come True

Morgan's favorite movie is *Gone with the Wind*. When she was twenty-two, she got the opportunity to play Vivian Lee in a miniseries where Vivian is discovered by a producer and they hire her to play Scarlett O'Hara. "Playing that role and living out a dream of mine was really one of the coolest things I've ever done. Garson Keenan and Ruth Gordon were on the set. One day at 3:00 in morning, Ruth said to me, 'I feel like I'm standing with Vivian. You look and act just like her.' For me, that was wonderful. I loved it; it was a dream."

Sometimes Glamour Is Hectic

"*Dallas* was the most hectic time in my life," says Morgan. "I truly didn't have any down time. When I was working on *Dallas*, I worked five days a week, and then flew all around the country for speaking engagements and fund-raisers for the March of Dimes. I visited hospitals, ministered to children and just traveled all over. There was no time for myself. It was wonderful in many ways, but it was very hectic. Once *Dallas* was over, other things started falling in line. It was quite a few years of non-stop career. I remember I had my daughter in the midst of all that commotion. She went with me everywhere. I look back on that time as a whirlwind of publicity, magazines, and frenzied life. How in the world did I get through that?"

People Are Always Watching

Morgan feels that it was great fun to be successful and known all over the world, but she is sobered by the incredible influence of American television. "If Jack and I went to the Far East, people would know who I was. They knew me in Europe, South Africa, everywhere. You don't realize the impact that a prime time American show like that has. It was pretty amazing."

Die to "Rich and Famous"

Actors need to go into the entertainment business with open eyes, believes Morgan. "Don't be blinded by the star light—the glamour, the money, and the fame. The kids on *American Idol* seem to teach that you can be famous and rich. Well yes, possibly, if you get the breaks and have the perseverance to take what the industry dishes out. Be careful what you wish for, though; you just might get it. You have to work in this business on your own terms. Don't sell out for money, fame, or notoriety. Once you sell yourself, it's over. You've got nothing left. You've got to hang on to who you are, what you are. Don't let anyone take it from you. Say 'I'm going in on my own terms. There are things I will and will not do, and I won't vary from this.' A lot of women have no problem with nudity and sex scenes. If they're OK with that and can live with that, I won't condemn them. But if you're not OK with that, don't let anyone convince you to go against what you believe."

"It's the same with anything else," says Morgan. "Drugs won't enhance your performance. That's a lie. They'll mess you up. Hollywood people want to build you up and make you famous only to knock you off you're the pedestal they built for you. The minute you get to an elevated level, they're looking to hit you and bring you down. You've got to have your faith; you can do it. It's harder and tougher than anything else you'll do, but anything worth getting is worth working hard for. You'll value it more when you do get it. I can meet any producer in Hollywood and look them in the eye, knowing I didn't sleep with them, or do drugs with them. I can go up to anybody from my past and say hello. I've always wanted that. I have nothing to be ashamed of. But so many people do. So many actors do. They say, 'I can't believe I was so young and stupid.' They regret their choices, especially after they've had kids. They think, 'My kids are going to see this, and how can I tell them not to do something that I obviously did?' You just have to think before you do things."

Help the Christian Projects

Morgan did two films in 70s and 80s for Billy Graham, one of which was *The Prodigal*. "I was working on *Dallas* at the time. My agent called and said, 'There's a little film they want you for, but it's not a lot of money, and it's a religious theme. Not too many want to go in on it. I said, 'Absolutely!' And it was great! I loved it! To this day, people still buy, rent, and order that movie. In 1980, I acted in [the movie] *In Search of the Historical Jesus*. I played Mary, the mother of Jesus. It was a wonderful project as well. . . a family film. It was done on a low budget, but we all had such a wonderful time doing it. These were not widely known films, but now, with Mel Gibson's movie, maybe people will start thinking differently and valuing these films with spiritual truths at their core. Hollywood has underestimated the public. Hollywood thinks that the world thinks as they do. It's not true. People are hungry for messages of hope and life. Dr. Baehr talks about it all the time.

The highest grossing films have great, moral messages—not dirty, base themes, so we're trying to get producers to make more of the uplifting movies. I'm hoping things will turn around."

* * *

Next time we all watch our favorite *Twilight Zone,* Hitchcock movie, *Dallas* or *Melrose Place* reruns, we'll be able to look beyond the beautiful face of Morgan Brittany and remember the path heaven took her on to produce such a powerful example of God's transformation and faithfulness to a child of a scary and volatile industry.

* * *

Everything's Changed!

—an interview with superstar Jane Russell

Be Open to Opportunities

When Jane was modeling with the Tom Kelly Agency in the early 1940s, an agent came by the photo studio and swiped her headshot. Kelly quickly grabbed it back, saying, "Never mind, Mr. 'Silverwolf.' She's a nice girl from the valley." Not to be dissuaded, the agent showed it to the movie studios, and Jane was soon pulled in to test for an upcoming movie that needed a half Irish/half Mexican gal. In a large basement-looking factory, a director named Howard Hawks screen-tested ten people, five guys and five gals. Hawks would simply point to the various couple combinations and say, "You and you do the part . . . now you two." He didn't even know the actor's names. He figured out the name of newcomer Jane Russell pretty quickly, though, and soon he was calling to award her the leading role in *The Outlaw.*

How life was quickly to change from model to movie star!

Learn Flexibility

Jane was ecstatic to land the leading role in *The Outlaw,* alongside the handsome Jack Beutel. Though Howard Hughes was supposed to be making the film, no one ever saw him. Hughes called Hawks every night, wanting to change things, and finally—when the frustrated Hawks dropped out of the deal—Hughes showed up and directed the picture. Hughes was not a very good director, according to Jane; he was much better at dealing with mechanical things than people. The cast had to do many, many takes on each scene, over and over again—without mistakes—for about nine months of filming. Howard Hughes had to have many choices.

Finally, after a huge three-year publicity campaign that touted the movie (and Jane, in particular) as, "Sensation Too Startling to Describe," *The Outlaw* made it to the silver screen. The movie had a limited release at first because it was hard for it to pass the censorship board. Finally, the film gained general release in 1946 and was a smash at the box-office. "The movie was supposed to be naughty," says Ms. Russell, "but it wasn't. Today, it's rated PG."

Advertising Matters

After more thought, Jane adds, "I have always wondered if the publicity for *The Outlaw* (which I objected to) was responsible for the lowering of decency standards in Hollywood. When Howard Hughes made *French Line*, the same thing started again. Howard promised me it would never happen again, though, and it didn't." On the subject of decency, Jane recalls her distaste for the times that actors sacrificed their brains to flaunt their bodies. "I remember standing and talking to a lady star about a serious subject, and the moment she saw a photographer she threw out her bust and posed provocatively, then sat down, and we finished the conversation. It was really sad."

Remember Your Roots

Though Jane Russell was known for her tall, shapely, sexy figure, she would have never compromised her Christian morals to please a studio. "In those days, you didn't have to worry, though. There was a decency code that kept us safe." Jane speaks fondly of how her mother was an actress and a fabulous Bible teacher, and had come to Christ after her first baby boy had died. She had wanted to know where he was going and whether or not there really was a heaven, so she'd studied the Bible until she found out. "Mom made the Word come alive," remembers Jane. "That stayed with me forever."

There Will Be a Few Lemons in the Bunch

After the successful *Outlaw,* Jane made a movie called *Young Widow.* She shakes her head as she remembers how poorly it did at the box office. "I'll never forget a critic commenting, 'If that woman had only died when her husband did, the movie would never have been made.' And she was right," laughs Jane. "It was terrible . . . But you move on, you know?"

Look for Ministry Opportunities

Jane went on to star in a string of popular movies, having the joy of working with Bob Hope, Marilyn Monroe, Clark Gable, Robert Mitchum, and others. One of her most famous films was *Gentlemen Prefer Blondes.* She also starred in *Paleface* with Bob Hope, then, during World War II spent time touring air bases and army camps with Bob, entertaining the soldiers and refreshing them with hope and light-hearted humor. "It was wonderful to work with Bob," Jane comments wistfully, "and we felt such a sense of privilege about our work with the troops."

Family Matters

Jane got married during these war years, staying with her first husband for twenty-three years and adopting three children. Her second husband died three months after their marriage, and eventually she married John Peoples, to whom she stayed married for twenty-five years until his death in 1999. Between the two of them, Jane remarks in amazement, they had eight children, fifteen grandchildren, and seven grandchildren.

Children remained vitally important in Jane's career, though she had none of her own biologically. With her first husband, Bob Waterfield, she adopted a baby girl, Tracy, in 1952, then a British boy, Tommy, that same year. Finally, she adopted Buck in 1956. Through her own organization, World Adoption International Fund (WAIF), she placed about 51,000 children with adoptive families. Jane also championed the passage of the Federal Orphan Adoption Amendment of 1953, which allowed children of American servicemen born overseas to be placed for adoption in the United States.

According to some critics, Jane devoted much greater energy to WAIF than to maintaining her movie stardom. At various points in her career, she took years off of movies to attend to family and ministry matters. Her priorities were clear, and often very public.

Where's the Breen Office?

In the olden days of Hollywood, says Jane, studios had control of everything. "You did what they wanted you to do, or you didn't get paid. The studios also had a 'Hays Office,' supported by the church 'Breen Office,' where they checked everything about the morality of the movies. There were to be no nudity scenes, bad language, or excessive violence. We felt protected and happy with that covering."

At one point, a studio wanted Jane to wear bikini, but Jane immediately protested. "Only naughty girls in France wear those!" she insisted. She adamantly refused and left the set, but the studio scrambled and quickly came up with a good one-piece alternative. Jane felt vindicated and protected. "Now, studios have nothing to say about these things. Outside people just rent the areas, and it's all independent. There's no Breen Office, no guarding . . . It's a terrible time today. If I had to start all over today I'd have to go home to the ranch!"

The Olden Days Were Golden Days

Jane believes there was a certain innocence and a morality among the industry leaders, in the 40s and 50s. "People were patriotic. They loved the army and navy. The studio heads were mostly Republican, and if someone was a Democrat, he really stood out in the crowd. There was the Decency Code and the Protestant Film Office. I don't understand the kids in Hollywood today. Everything's changed . . . There's no accountability."

Practice Makes Perfect

In the earlier decades of filmmaking, recalls Jane, the studios paid for dance lessons, voice lessons, and acting lessons. Actors didn't need the enormous amounts of money they do today. Today the actor has to be very self-motivated, says Jane. She's not going to be pampered along with everything being taken care of. She's got to just get out there and learn how to do it all. "Just get up and do it!" encourages the star.

"Be in school plays, in theatre, wherever you can act. Just get the experience. Do a great play and get everybody to come. The studio sent us to Florence Enright. She taught us our lines and our business: how to naturally pick up the coffee pot and fiddle with the coffee while delivering a powerful line."

Jane also took drama classes with the famed Russian actress Maria Ouspenskaya. In her 1985 autobiography, *Jane Russell: My Path And My Detours*, the star recalls, "Years later Ouspenskaya was watching me at a television rehearsal. When I came off the stage to say hello, she said to me in her marvelous Russian accent, 'You know, Jen, you could be a very good acktress, but you haff no henergy.' No energy. It's true. I've watched myself too often on the screen, and I seem to be moving in slow motion."

Two-dozen movies, however, seem to attest to the fact that audiences certainly didn't mind Ms. Russell's pace.

Find Good Resources

According to Jane, agents are a must in the entertainment business. "Agents are running everything today. You've got to get an agent. My agent was a friend who started at a small agency, then moved to MCA, then retired. When I first began, though, my friend's mom worked at Warner Bros. and knew Charlie Feldman, and she took me to his office before I signed the Hughes deal. She told him she thought I needed an agent. Charlie mentioned that he didn't take unknowns, only the already working folks. He discouraged me about the odds of really making it in Hollywood and mentioned that Howard Hughes, for instance, wanted to find someone to do a picture. 'That'll be a one in a million chance,' Charlie snorted . . . I saw Charlie a few months later, after I'd signed with Howard, sitting at a table in a restaurant. From across the room he put his hand up and ran his finger under his chin, as if to admit he'd cut his own throat . . . So funny!"

Establish Your Credibility, Then Preach Your Message

As to sharing her faith, Jane has seen that taking a stand for Christ can create some enemies. "The trouble today in Hollywood is that the kids that try to share their faith overtly just don't get work, unless they're already a big star. Even then, it's hard. Mel Gibson's having a horrible time with the press over *The Passion of the Christ.*"

Having recently attended a seminar in Los Angeles, Jane comments sadly, "This Hollywood is not the place I was in. I wouldn't fit in these days with my beliefs. When people question me I just tell them I'm a mean-spirited, narrow-minded, conservative Christian bigot—not about race, but about those idiots trying to take the Ten Commandments off the wall, the Bible out of schools, and prayer even out of football games. I'm against kicking prayer and God out of the country. I don't like the ACLU and the liberal judges that threaten our religious freedoms. So label away!"

Jane laughs apologetically. "I've become practical, with my feet on the ground, instead of charming. Today they're doing crazy things . . . I'd simply go home to the ranch. I just wouldn't have made it today."

Others think perhaps she would. Many would love to see more fiery beauties like Jane Russell in Hollywood these days, passionate about faith, family, and freedom.

* * *

· 13 ·

Movers and Shakers

Every movie and television production involves a constellation of talents. There are key roles that need to be addressed, such as the studio executives, important variations on roles, which provide different insights—such as an animation or television producer, and the little known, but crucial role of the film buyer for the theater company. In this chapter, you get to hear from some of these behind-the-scenes people in the world of entertainment.

Major Movie Studio CEOs

COLLEAGUES, CREATIVITY, AND CHARACTER
—AN INTERVIEW WITH DICK COOK

During his Oscar acceptance speech, Pixar's Andrew Stanton genuinely thanked Dick Cook, the former head of the Disney Studios, for making movies like *Finding Nemo* possible. In an article for the April 2004 issue of *Business 2.0*, Betsey Steisand notes,

. . . the nod to Cook was noticed in Hollywood—
and Disney shareholders should have been clapping
loudest. For while the world has been absorbed with
Disney's boardroom melodrama and a Comcast take-
over bid, Cook in early March confirmed the largest
worldwide corporate box-office gross in history—a
cool $3 billion last year. Throw in DVD and home
video sales, and Cook's unit contributed 36 percent of Disney's $1.3 billion operating profit in the
most recent quarter—and nearly 80 percent of the
growth. 'Dick Cook has done a very good job,' says
independent analyst and former UBS media research
chief Christopher Dixon, in a most un-Hollywood
understatement. The question is, where do they go
from here?

How did the easy-going, mild-mannered Dick Cook become the
head of a major studio, and what principals and philosophies guide
the leader of this multi-billion dollar enterprise that has been a
household name for more than half a century?

"Makes No Difference Who You are . . . "
Dick Cook's career is reminiscent of the famous Disney song,
"When You Wish Upon a Star." His rise was meteoric, from the
Disney equivalent of the mailroom to the President's office.

He started with the Disney Company in 1970 as a monorail
driver at Disneyland. Says Mr. Cook, "I did start out in the industry
in one of the more unusual ways. I didn't major in film like a lot of
my peers, but I was fortunate that a lot of wonderful things happened along the journey. I worked at Disney as a ride operator,
having no idea I'd end up working my entire career for Disney."

"Anything Your Heart Desires Will Come to You . . . "
In 1976, Dick moved over to the studio side, wanting to participate

in the new video revolution. One thing led to another, and he soon found himself being groomed in the company's distribution, marketing, and production divisions. At the time of this interview, Dick was the head of the studio at age fifty-three and had worked with Disney for thirty-four-years. "We joke about the fact that I was their last choice. They had to give it to me because I've worked here the longest . . . I was the only one left! Seriously, it's been a wonderful opportunity to learn about the business and what makes it work from every level."

Pray for Great Bosses

Over the course of those thirty-four-years, Dick was mentored by a number of different bosses who were instrumental in teaching him the ways of the industry. "I had a lot of good bosses. So much of what I am today is due to the fact that I've been surrounded by a quality team of co-workers and an esteemed group of mentors. I think this is absolutely essential for advancing in Hollywood."

Early in his career, the man most responsible for mentoring Dick was Milt Albright. "Milt was a legend in his own right—and he was the first Disneyland employee. He was just a fantastic person with enormous integrity, creativity, and understanding of the business. He gave me many crucial insights along the way." Another of Mr. Cook's mentors was Irving Ludwig. "Irving, along with Chuck Good, was a patriarch of motion picture distribution. I learned so much from these men." Dick also makes reference to Jeffrey Katzenberg and Joe Roth—"very gracious people"—who also helped him learn the business.

Seek Out and Learn From Great Colleagues

Dick Cook explains that another key to his success has been working with great colleagues. "I know that everyone probably labels the time they've worked in Hollywood as the Golden Age of Hollywood, but for me it's really true. It's been a fantastic opportunity to work with wonderful people during this golden time, and I continue to meet, work with, and be challenged by those in the industry. There are so many quality people of brilliance and integrity out here—both in my company and outside it." Dick likes to quote Milt Albright who said, "Always hire people better than you." "It's true," he says. "They'll push you up and keep you motivated and challenged. Right now, the entertainment industry has some of the best and brightest people of all time in key positions. It's a privilege to work with them."

Hire Character

Through the years, as Mr. Cook has had the opportunity to hire newcomers for various positions in various departments, he has continually sought out those with great character qualities. "I want to see great, varied life experiences, high integrity, compelling ideas, good communication skills, and the ability to bring things from the idea stage to the project stage. I ask, 'Can he or she actually push things through and make things happen—whether it be in marketing, distribution, or production?' I want to see new ideas and innovations."

Speaking of innovations, Dick made his own mark at Disney as a distribution and marketing expert. He's credited with transforming Disney's home video division and staging grand premiers like the *Pearl Harbor* debut on a U.S. Navy carrier.

Enjoy the Process; Love It All

Many people come to Hollywood expecting instant stardom, not recognizing the significant value of enjoying each experience and making the most of each opportunity as it comes, even if it's not yet the "big thing" they are gunning for. It's actually taken Dick Cook thirty years to learn every aspect of the Disney Company, and he has used every bit of what he learned along the way. When asked about which was his favorite division or job at Disney before this, his answer says a lot about the reasons he was in the driver's seat for so long.

"Whatever I'm doing at that moment is my favorite part of the job. I grew up in Bakersfield, and my favorite sport was whatever sport was in season. So it is now. If I'm working in marketing, that's my favorite part. If I'm in production, I'm having a blast. The bottom line is that I love movies! I love how they communicate. All the great movies somehow move us, and they all have an emotional undertow that pulls us along. Honestly, I do get excited about coming to work every day.

Keep Creative at the Center

Dick's greatest priority at Disney was keeping the people in the studio energized, excited, and enthused about the great creative flow. "Creative always drives the business. When all else is said and done, it's what's on the silver screen that counts. You get involved in finances, creative, and the physical part of making movies, and that's all truly fun. But it's the creative process that draws us all there, and that is what I try to foster as my foremost priority."

Hollywood Is for the Faith Filled

According to Dick, there is an open playing field for believers in Hollywood. "Faith and values play a big part in all our lives out here, even in those who don't necessarily profess to be Christians. The people I work with have many different ways of believing, but there's a similar value system we were brought up with in America, that points us in certain directions on important decisions . . . People of faith, values, and integrity will always have a place in this industry."

Though there are many people in Hollywood who profess great faith and who exhibit high moral character, Dick is quick to point out that the industry is ultimately built on one foundation: talent. "If you feel you have the talent and want to pursue the field of entertainment, don't let anything get in your way. But you must persevere; there's a lot of rejection. But keep following that dream. Never give up on that dream."

Hollywood Is Not for Those Averse to Change

On a typical day in Dick Cook's life, he touches every aspect of the business including distribution, marketing, production, legal, business affairs, physical production, home entertainment, television, publicity, and advertising. "Many times during the day or week I'll touch all these aspects, and they're all interesting and fun, and always changing. I'm very energized by change. If you stand still for very long, even on the right track, a train will run over you. Show business is built on innovation and creativity, and it's constantly changing."

Keep Work in Perspective

Despite the frenetic pace at the office, a piece of Dick's heart was always at home. Dick has a wife, Bonnie, to whom he's been married for over thirty years, and two daughters. "I have to make sure there's a balance in my work that allows me to spend time with them. No matter how well someone is doing in his career, it is so important to make sure you're there for your family. I've been very blessed to have a supportive and loving wife and a couple of great girls who will love me when I come through that door. They don't really care what kind of day I had or what deals I made; they just want to spend time together. That's what keeps me going."

The American Dream Is Fully Alive

Just like many of the stories Disney has produced over the years, The Dick Cook story demonstrates yet again that our country is still the land of opportunity. Talented, hard-working, and enthusiastic people can still move up from the mailroom to the boardroom—from humble beginnings to positions of great power and influence. As Dick continues to move mountains in arguably the most fascinating industry in the world, we rightly anticipate many more decades of great stories from a man with a zest for work, family, and the movies he creates.

* * *

CAN YOU DEFINE SUCCESS?

—AN INTERVIEW WITH FRANK YABLANS

Who was the president of Paramount Pictures of the 1970s era, often known as "The Golden Age of Paramount?" Who green-lit *The Godfather, Chinatown, The Great Gatsby,* and *Paper Moon?* Remember *Silver Streak*—with Gene Wilder and Richard Pryor—the movie that made us all want to take a trip on a sleeper train? How about the creepy *Mommie Dearest* with Faye Dunaway playing the fascinating Joan Crawford? Perhaps the more recent films like *Star Chamber, Congo,* or *A Dog of Flanders?* Who produced these memorable blockbusters, and what is he doing now?

The answer is Frank Yablans, former president of Paramount Pictures, also former Chairman MGM/UA. Who is this Frank Yablans . . . and what did his journey through the maze of show business look like?

Childhood Dreams

Frank was born into a poor family in New York City during the Great Depression. His father was a truck driver and taxi driver, and Frank received "the classic education on the streets of Brooklyn." He knew early on—he says, by age seven, that he'd like to be president of a company some day . . . any company.

Don't Despise Small Beginnings

Frank's movie career started with a training program for Warner Bros. in New York City. It was 1956, and the studio was hiring Korean vets (of which he was one) to work as trainees, responsible for booking newsreels in theatres. It was here with Warner Bros. that Frank decided the entertainment industry was the path for him. In 1958, he joined Disney and the newly formed Buena Vista, where he worked in the Midwest until 1966.

Never Quit Reaching

From 1966–69, Frank had his own independent foreign distribution company in New York City, and in 1969, the owner of Paramount, Gulf and Western Company, recruited Frank to join them as Assistant General Sales Manager. This began his meteoric rise, culminating in the presidency in 1970. In 1975, Paramount was nominated for thirty Academy Awards, including three Best Pictures. Frank left Paramount in 1976 to begin his independent producing career with Twentieth Century Fox and Paramount Pictures. In 1983, he became the chairman of MGM/UA. Two years later, in 1985, Frank returned to independent producing and split his time between Europe and the United States.

Make Family Your Priority

Frank has been married twice, and both marriages lasted over twenty years. With his first wife he had three children, Robert, Sharon, and Edward, to whom he is very close. He also boasts four grandchildren. His son, Edward, followed in his father's steps and went into the entertainment business. Ed is a senior agent at ICM in Hollywood. Frank obviously adores his family and loves, above all, the time he spends with his grandkids.

"Family values, faith, integrity, and the pursuit of what is good, honest, and right are the essential elements in what I produce, on and off the screen," says Frank. "I've tried not to veer from that even in the heady years as head of a major studio. I lived in the suburbs and commuted to Manhattan. Unless I was traveling, I was home for dinner, giving my children my most important time. I learned this by example from my parents, and I sought to teach by my example."

According to Frank, there's no business accolade that can compare to getting honored by one of your children. "My son, Edward, was highlighted in the Hollywood Reporter as an up-and-coming executive. He had to write a paper on who his idol was." (Frank chokes up a bit.) "He said his idol was his father . . . 'What did you learn from him?' they asked. He answered, 'integrity.' There's my reward for this life . . . forget the movies."

Tribulations Will Come

"Did I have *trials?*" asks Frank Yablans, incredulously. "The only one that had it worse than me was Job, but Job did much better than I did. I don't think I passed the test like him. Look, it's a big struggle to keep your sense about you, to keep your standards high. I lived through the unrest of the '60s, the disco fever of the 70's, the 'me-generation' '80s, the drug years, and the Clinton years, which were often one in the same, I might add. I was a Republican surrounded by liberal Democrats. It was tough to keep my bearings and not be enticed into all the world was selling."

Asked about the basis of his moral compass, Frank recalls that his grandmother had a big influence on his life. "She believed I could do anything, and she encouraged me to do it well, and faithfully. 'If you lock the door,' she said of me, 'he'll come through the key-hole.' She was Romanian—a very persistent, remarkable woman."

Talent's the Key

Frank Yablans believes that the door isn't closed to people of faith, but it's not exactly wide open. "Talent will always win in the end. If you're true to yourself and your talent, you'll thrive. I can't say you won't pay a price. There'll be snickers behind your back, and even derision. That's the price of believing in your faith. You'll succeed if you don't compromise. It's actually more of a problem being conservative than Christian out here, though they lump the two together."

Don't Buy Hollywood's Definition of Success

Asked about the keys to his success, Frank asks how one defines success. "Are you talking about keeping a job? Doing memorable projects? Or raising a wonderful family? It's the latter that defines success for me, and those successes are few and far between in this town. Some are doing it well, like Sherry Lansing, [former] Chair of Paramount, and Amy Pascal. I think women are better at keeping integrity than the men I know. Sherry has such integrity . . . a really decent woman."

Frank's definition of success includes not only integrity, but also faith. "Success is found in your faith. You cannot let go of your faith, no matter what adversity you face. Even when you become successful, finally, the only thing you can fall back on is your faith."

Find a Mentor

"One of the great joys in life is to mentor," says Frank. "Some I torment, and others I just mentor. I like to be available to share insights and experiences with young people. They need that kind of support system to help them find their way. You can't follow in anyone's footsteps; you've got to find your own groove."

Frank suggests that students of the industry adopt the good and honest qualities they see in their mentors and apply it to their own lives, recognizing and avoiding their foibles, just incorporating the good."

Emphasize Emotion

"Great movies all have emotion," says Frank. "There's a connection between the image on the screen and the audience. There's an emotional investment with hero or anti-hero. You've got to have this, or the movie won't make it. I was a studio president who green-lighted many films, and if I had an emotional connection, that's the film I wanted to make."

Start With a Great Screenplay

Frank Yablans believes the underlying screenplay makes the movie. "Take *The Godfather*, or *Chinatown*. If it's not between the pages, it's never going to be on the screen. Make that screenplay perfect before you ever turn on a camera."

Birthing an Elephant

"Producing a movie is akin to giving birth to a baby elephant," laughs Frank. "It begins with idea, perhaps adapting a book or musical and turning it into a screenplay. Then, there's the arduous, painfully long trek of arranging financing, finding a distributor, casting, shooting, post-production, marketing, interviews, etc., etc. It's a long, arduous path. Some of my movies took nine years to get made. Who's got that kind of patience? That's what it takes, though no one wants to hear that up front."

According to Frank, making a movie requires tremendous faith in what you're doing. "Only three or four hundred films are made each year from thousands and thousands of scripts submitted. And you don't get an actor unless you have financing . . . The studio's word is as good as an escrow account." "The good thing about labor pains is that you eventually do give birth," Frank assures us.

Get Distribution in Place!

Distribution is the most critical element to the end product, believes Frank. "Which is why I've stayed close to marketing. Distribution is getting a particular film in a particular theatre. Marketing is how you reach them to get them to come into the theatre. Independent producers make the mistake of beginning the process and the investment without distribution. Get it in place, or it's a prescription for financial disaster."

Buck Up Under Rejection

"Rejection is part of show business," says Frank. "If you can't live with it, you'll never make a living. We're in a business that celebrates failure. Only one of five movies will be successful, so the other four are rooting against you. Your success only points out their failures more dramatically."

Frank's advice is to really believe in yourself and your project. "Anybody who rejects you is insane. Believe in yourself, and if you're a person of faith, God will help you. Don't look at the rejecting atmosphere as a negative. One of the reasons that faith is so rare in this town is that it's the antithesis of rejection. If you have faith, you can't be rejected. It's very difficult to feel the rejection of failure, but the true test of character comes with success . . . how well you handle that. The Bible says that a man is tested according to the praise given him."

* * *

And no doubt the praises will continue to flow for the next series of great Frank Yablans movies!

* * *

FORMER TV NETWORK OWNER

"PARABLES, NOT PREACHING"

—AN INTERVIEW WITH BUD PAXSON

Surrender

It is January 1, 1987. A distinguished-looking businessman stumbles over to his bed in a hotel room, collapsing in emotional exhaustion. A flood of despairing pictures passes through the screen of his tormented mind . . . yelling . . . accusations . . . his wife angrily stuffing Christmas gifts and clothing into suitcases . . . the door slamming . . . depression and hopeless entering through the same swinging door she had exited. But wait, one last picture is coming to mind. . . . It's his mother praying on her knees . . . for him.

On that memorable New Year's Day, Lowell "Bud" Paxson found himself mechanically reaching for the Gideon Bible on the nightstand. Through tears, he began reading, having no idea that he had just picked up the mightiest weapon in the universe, a sword of God's love and truth that would change his life forever. God met Bud Paxson on New Year's Day and gloriously saved him at the lowest point of his life.

Study

Bud was delighted to be a new believer and doggedly set about giving himself a crash course in Christianity. Perhaps then, he prayed, God would help him get his wife back. For seven months, Bud spent his every possible waking hour studying, reading, discussing, and absorbing Christianity and the meaning of Bible. He became deeply rooted in his faith, gaining a timely peace from God as he went through the divorce he couldn't seem to prevent.

Soul Ties

Some time after his divorce, Bud started dating again. He laughs as he admits he went out with a new lady every week. And every week, he asked his new date the same question: "What do you think of Jesus Christ?" To his immense disappointment, he got thirty-seven wrong answers—but finally—on his thirty-eighth date, the lovely woman responded, "I've known Him all my life." "Really?" asked Bud. "What are you doing next Friday?" Soon he had changed his question to "What are you doing the rest of your life?" "God chose my wife," says Bud. "You just can't have a marriage without God in it."

Radio and Television

Prior to this spiritual, emotional, and romantic drama, Bud Paxson had been busy in the exciting world of radio and TV. After spending his early years as a radio announcer at a small station, Bud purchased radio station WACK in Newark, New York, in 1956. In 1977, he began selling merchandise on a Florida AM radio station. Out of that experience grew the concept of the Home Shopping Network, which Bud Paxson founded in 1982. By 1986, the company had gone public—and national, and Bud created the Silver King Communications group of broadcast television stations, growing the group to twelve stations; eight of which are in the top ten U.S. markets. In 1990, Bud sold his interest in The Home Shopping Network and started a new company, Paxson Communications.

PAX TV

After a number of high-dollar business dealings, including mergers, acquisitions, and a move to the American Stock Exchange, Bud Paxson created PAX TV: the nation's seventh and newest broadcast television network at the time of its launch, in 1998. With its nationwide broadcast television and cable distribution system (including the nation's largest group of owned and operated television stations) PAX TV quickly became known as *the* national family entertainment network.

Worship

Amidst the great business successes he was experiencing, Bud Paxson remembered his own desperate search for God—alone in a hotel room—and he longed to meet the spiritual needs of other troubled television viewers. So, together with Christian Network, Inc., he created The Worship Network, a soothing montage of breath-taking nature scenes, scripture, and praise music, carried at night in thirty-four countries. "If you have problems, you can't sleep," says Paxson. "99.9% of people who discover The Worship Network are searching for answers to their problems. We thank God they find them here."

Parables, Not Preaching

When questioned about advice he would give believers desiring to enter the entertainment industry, Bud is clear. "Jesus gave one sermon: The Sermon on the Mount. The rest of the time He told stories and parables about the Father. I believe God wants us to be story and parable tellers. There are great preachers and bad preachers. Storytellers can reach the heart." Paxson comments that movies such as *Oh God* with George Burns did a lot for God's kingdom by moving audiences toward a greater awareness of the Lord."

Churches, Not Couches

Bud Paxson is clear about his views on people making TV their church. He encourages all who are physically able to get into church and not rely on the mass media for their spiritual sustenance. "TV is not a great media to get personal ministry, which is important. Relying on Christian TV to save America won't work, but we're glad to be here, and we always want to be a light in the darkness, even though we're just a pinpoint."

Seeking Out Excellence

Mr. Paxson also encourages industry newcomers to strive for creativity and excellence in everything they do. A prime-time example of this combination, he says, is seen in the hit show, *American Idol*. Bud recalls, "Ed McMahon's *Star Search* did not do well in the ratings, leaving a vacuum for this kind of entertainment. Suddenly, *American Idol* came onto the scene, and Simon stole the show. It's the creative thing that fills the need of American television today. Who knows what the rage will be tomorrow? I do know that America values excellence. . . ."

Hiring the Best

On the issue of excellence, Paxson recommends a "hire the best" strategy. PAX TV had a policy of not just hiring Christians because they're Christians—they had to be good. As a matter of fact, Bud sought out good scriptwriters, even if they've written scripts for (morally) bad shows. "Maybe they had something great in a desk drawer that fit with our style of programming. We just used the best people for the need at hand. Our number one shows were *Doc* and *Sue Thomas, F.B.Eye*. The stars of these shows, Billy Ray Cyrus and Deanne Bray, were terrific actors, who both happened to be great Christians."

Being True to God and Self

Another of Mr. Paxson's words of wisdom and caution is to remain true to who you are. Regarding his super-clean, family-friendly programming, Bud chuckles. "A lot of people think I'm crazy. They say, 'If you'd become more mainstream, you'd make more money. I can't. . . . I'd have to quit. I feel like God doesn't watch TV, but I sure wouldn't want to put anything on that he couldn't watch."

Bud believes that there are just as many Christians in film and television as there are in other industries, but there's often an attempt at compartmentalization. "If a person is Christian, you can't separate his private life and professional life; his faith will affect both his business and private life. It must. People are afraid to stand up for their beliefs in this industry, as political correctness mandates that they not offend. You know—no politics, sex, or religion. I admire the way President Bush challenged this rule and wore his faith on his sleeve."

Perfect Truth in Perfect Love

As to witnessing, Bud says that God helps him with discernment in industry circles. "I can't deny my God. I know that He selects us, according to Romans 28, and He foreknows and chooses His own, but when He does choose, I feel privileged to be able to share my beliefs and testimony in the process. If someone doesn't want me to share, I won't. Am I tolerant? Absolutely. I want to love them. . . ."

* **

ANIMATION STUDIO HEAD

PASSION AND PERSEVERANCE

—AN INTERVIEW WITH PHIL ROMAN

Animation Magazine touted Phil Roman as one of "The Most Influential People in North America Over 15 Years." Roman's animation studio produced many popular television programs such as *Charlie Brown, The Simpsons, King of the Hill, The Tom and Jerry Movie,* and *Garfield*—to name only a few. With a heart to entertain and a gift for building talented creative teams, Phil understood and unwaveringly pursued his calling from youth.

Keep Faith Alive

When Phil was eleven-years-old picking grapes with his Mexican born, Catholic-Christian parents during The Great Depression, he saw Walt Disney's *Bambi* and decided that all he ever wanted to do was draw. Because his family's focus was sheer survival at the time, Phil had high doubts that his dream would come true. His parents encouraged him, however, and as Phil spent time as an altar boy at his Catholic school, he kept his dream close to his heart and ever in his prayers.

Phil thought about how viewing *Bambi* had excited him as he saw the moving, colorful images that so evoked emotion. It was tremendously impressive to the young boy that someone had *drawn* this movie. From then on, he picked up any scrap sheet of paper he could find. He found blackboards to draw on, or sketched on the sidewalks in his spare time. He practiced copying the look of *Bambi*, checked out books on drawing from the library, and eventually taught himself to become an animation artist. Phil had his own comic strip in high school, and when he graduated in 1949, he took his whole bank account of $60 and went to art school in Hollywood. Working at a theatre at night, and attending school by day, Phil was privileged to come under the tutelage of a Disney animator.

Despise No Small Beginnings

After some time in the Air Force, Phil went to Art School on the GI bill. Soon he heard that Disney was hiring, so he brought in his portfolio and was hired within a week. At a salary of 99 cents per hour, Phil dug in and began his professional career. Soon he was on the permanent staff, at $1.25 per hour! Here he worked for three years with the giants of the business—many influential animators, and found it very fulfilling to know them and be considered their peer.

Risk Equals Reward

In 1984, at age fifty-three, Phil was an animator and director, but didn't have his own studio, which had always been his secondary dream. After directing *Charlie Brown* specials, he hung out his own shingle, thinking, "If I don't try, I'll always regret it. I'd rather fail, knowing I tried, than not even tried."

The first job he got was a *Garfield* special, which came in on budget and on time—and won an Emmy. He picked up the rights to do *Garfield* and began producing quite a few shows, including *Bobby's Rules, The Simpsons, King of the Hill,* and *Felix the Cat.* His animation was accepted all over the world, and some very exciting and heady times were at hand as accolades came forth both nationally and internationally.

Don't Fear the Industry

According to Phil Roman, Christians seem to read a lot of the negatives about Hollywood, but the fact is that people in this industry are just like people in any other. "There are great families who go to church, care for their children, and constantly try to do the right thing. There are great clubs and devotional groups for Christians, and there are good churches in Hollywood where entertainment business and studio people are seen every week. We just see the negative role models, but it's really an open industry to people of faith. As believers, we're creating stories to entertain, works we can be proud of and not embarrassed of. I ask myself on these projects, 'Can my parents be proud of this?' I never wanted to embarrass my parents. As a matter of fact, I choose projects based on my values as a Christian. Some are too over the line, and I turn them down. I've actually gone to work for other places for less money to be part of a better team with more uplifting projects."

Understand the Process

The animation process begins by turning a script into storyboard, says Phil. "You work for visual continuity, record voices, and animate to the sound track. As the director, I determine close ups, long shots, pans, and establishing shots—all on paper. The storyboard is the bible for the show. If I make a storyboard change, everyone gets a copy. I direct the actors to get good voice performances. My animators then create character expressions based on the actors' voice inflections. If we have a good budget, we'll videotape the actor's voice-over recordings. Most animators like to use their imaginations, though, in determining a character's expressions and attitudes. As a matter of fact, our animators keep a little mirror in front of them at the drawing board so they can see their own facial expressions and draw from there."

A Good Team Is the Key

A good creative team is important, Phil believes. "This business is not a one-man job. I've got to choose people I can work with, who will do the best job. The producer, director, and the animators are all part of our team. Hundreds of people are involved, here and in other countries." Phil's job is to maintain tight creative control over the look, the actions, and the movements of an animated piece.

"I have to know budgets, schedules, and deliver on time. I get the right-brained people to keep things moving . . . When I became a producer, I had to move from artist to businessman. I learned financing, contracts, and the art of putting projects together. I was working with editors, artists, and lab technicians. Though I went to art school, not business school, I learned it all by putting good right and left-brained teams together. It's all about paying attention and having the right people in the right spots that can handle their end of the load. You have to rely on them. If it works, everyone succeeds."

It's Talent, Not Toys

When asked about his use of the latest, hottest computer animation programs, Phil is clear, "It's just another fancy pencil. You still have imagination and put your drawings on paper. You get your ideas onto paper, then onto the screen. It's hard and fun as we do our brainstorming and drawings, and there is some stress as we try to meet the deadlines, but everyone enjoys it and does their best possible job with the talents they've been given." Phil chuckles as he adds "The Emmy makes it worth it all."

Comparison Breeds Inferiority

As to the trials of growing up in a poor family, having to learn two languages in a new culture, and having to teach himself and fund his own dream, Phil has an infectious attitude: "You just accept each hurdle, one at a time, like going to school. It's where I came from. I knew I had to fend for myself but I had no basis of comparison to know any different. I think that's good; it kept me moving forward instead of being paralyzed by seeing what road others were taking."

Phil is clear that his advancement came from determination more than skill. "I never considered myself having a lot of talent—just perseverance. Of course I had enough talent to compete in the industry, but when I see others' work, they blow me away sometimes. You've got to be secure in who you are and what your part of the team is to be, or it could be intimidating to see all the brilliant masters of the craft around you. I just try to work hard, focus, set a goal, and not get distracted. If I do get rejected or beat out by a competitor, I just accept it and move on, knowing something else will soon surface for me."

Show Your Passion

In the world of animation, Phil believes that artists must have a love for what they do; they must stay focused, and show their energy and passion for the game. "When I'm hiring kids, interns, I always look at enthusiasm, energy, and their love and passion for this career. I can teach a kid to draw, but not to be in love with the business. If I see the passion, I know they'll be successful. And they've never let me down."

Phil encourages animation wannabes to practice their drawing and not give up easily. "Focus and keep practicing away. Keep calling, there will always be an opening. People are always hiring. Stay competitive, and have a positive attitude. No one wants to work with [a] negative complainer. Smile. Show you enjoy what you're doing. Maybe that's what they saw in me. I'd do anything to work here."

Follow Your Values

Becoming a Disney animator was an easy choice for the Christian-raised, family-values Phil Roman. "To me, Disney was the epitome of good values, great storytelling, fun people, and high energy. I had the privilege of working on *Sleeping Beauty, The Wonderful World of Disney,* and *The Mickey Mouse Club.* I think we've lost the sweetness of these classics through the years as people are putting out "shock" materials. I think back on how MGM and Warner Bros. put out such good, solid shows like *Charlie Brown* by Charles Schultz, a fine Christian man who quoted the Bible in some of his filmstrips. He was a very positive influence. We're desensitized now, though, as shock value seems to be more and more prevalent."

Enjoy the Ride

One of the most exciting parts of Phil's career has been traveling abroad as a producer of animation. It's truly exciting to meet foreign animation executives and hear them say, "Oh yes, we know your work. We have your programs in our library." Phil never tires of the delight he feels from seeing his cartoons in so many other languages as he travels the world. His cartoons have aired in: France, Spain, Italy, Germany, India, and many Asian countries.

Those who know Phil Roman's work—and especially his humble heart—are confident that he'll continue to enjoy the thrill of such acclaim.

* * *

MAJOR MOVIE STUDIO DISTRIBUTOR

TALENT AND TEAMWORK

—AN INTERVIEW WITH CHUCK VIANE

Chuck Viane is the president of Disney's Buena Vista Film Distribution Group. Chuck joined the Disney group after serving as the senior vice president and head film buyer for General Cinema Theatres. During these years Chuck had fallen in love with the world of moviemaking. He loved watching good movies and buying great films for the public, but he really wanted a deeper involvement in the industry. Then, when Disney went through its big restructuring in the 80s, Dick Cook offered Chuck the opportunity to become part of his group, and he jumped at the chance. Through hard teamwork and perseverance, Chuck eventually became the president of Buena Vista Pictures, handling the distribution for Touchstone Films, Hollywood Pictures, Jerry Bruckheimer Films, Pixar Animations, and others.

Align Career Choices with Personal Values

About the time Dick Cook offered Chuck the position at Disney, several other offers were coming down the pipe line. The major reason Chuck chose to work with Disney was because the company praised family values and markedly avoided the seedier projects many of its competitors were producing. "Disney literally stood out among the group because of its family values. Disney thrives on family products, and I'm on board with the types of movies they release. It makes it so enjoyable when I walk into an auditorium and see entire families gathered together, enjoying themselves with good, clean quality entertainment. Makes me proud of what we're doing. I couldn't have gone with some of the others."

Focus on Open Doors, Not Obstacles

According to Chuck Viane, there are no obstacles for people of faith and values in the entertainment industry. "I have never seen a wall put up regarding those with religious beliefs. The opportunities still abound in Hollywood, and it's an open playing field for those with real talent. It's truly talent-based out here; that's the bottom line."

By taking the job with Disney, Chuck had to move his family from Boston to Los Angeles, though the company graciously gave the family some time to allow his son to finish high school. He and his wife were raising their high school and middle school age children in a solid community with a strong foundation in church. They were concerned because they had heard all the usual rumors about L.A. having looser family units and slippery values. "We found it was just the opposite, though. There were great families like us who loved their children, had them in church, were involved in sports *and* tied to the entertainment industry. California is no different from other places . . . but the weather's nicer," laughs Chuck.

Push In Instead of Pulling Back

Chuck advises Christians to move forward and become part of the solution in Hollywood instead of shrinking away in defeat. "People of faith often tend to read things or hear things, get upset, and naturally pull back in fear. Instead, they should become part of the process and help steer the industry in the right direction. There's often an obvious and workable answer, but it's the old problem of not seeing the forest for the trees . . . You just have to decide to be part of the solution."

Chuck encourages believers to enter the industry with the understanding that Hollywood's problems are common to man. "People of faith and values need to understand that the entertainment industry is like any other industry, with the same problems and opportunities. The only difference is that we're so visible . . . much more visible than a pharmaceutical or manufacturing company.

We're always right out there in front of the public, so we have to be extra aware of our product and our image . . . which is good."

It's All About the Team

Throughout his career, Chuck watched as some of his friends in the industry jumped around from job to job, always looking for the next big break that would advance their personal careers. Conversely, Chuck's philosophy was to fully engage the talents of those around him, forming solid teams that would move forward together. "I try to build fabulous teams. No matter what the size and level of a business, it's the people who surround you that make you who you are. It's how I use their talents, not how brightly my talents will shine, or how quickly I'll get personal advancement. It's kind of like the tortoise and the hare. You wait for the opportunities to develop and gently allow your skill set to find its way into important roles. In my case, I quietly watched and listened, understood problems as they developed, and stepped in and helped, with the expertise of my team discovering appropriate solutions. That's how I rose to the top of both organizations."

Part of teamwork, Chuck explains, is loyalty. "I'm loyal to the people I work with. Loyalty is big to me, and I try to form lasting relationships with my teams and my business associates. When there's a problem, I try to find ways to say yes, to look beyond the obvious no and see if a compromise can be struck and the deal can move forward. Because I value loyalty and teamwork, I try not to take the easy way out."

Stay True to Your Dream

Understanding a dream and sticking to it are big values in Chuck's life. "I always wanted to lead," he says. "I moved from assistant general sales manager to sales manager to president. It took some time, but I held onto my dream of becoming president, and I wouldn't be deterred by the temptation of jumping around to other jobs just to gain a few extra dollars. I realize that there are times, for your family, that you should change jobs, earn more money, help more people, but I just stayed, and it paid off. I love what I'm doing."

Part of staying true to a dream is taking the risk to trust those around you, says Chuck. "Have faith in the people around you, that they'll reward commitment, loyalty, and expertise; that they'll put you where your talents will best be served. I started on the operations side of exhibition and moved to auditing, management, human resources, and then the film department. There, I finally found the thing I loved . . . seeing movies and putting them in their proper places, finding the areas where a movie could be most successful. Others saw that this was my gift, and they encouraged me in this direction. I truly believe in the mentoring system, finding a mentor in a company who can help you. Listen to him. Ask him questions. Good mentors can speak into your life by saying, 'Wait on that; you're not ready for that job.' Or, 'You're underestimating yourself; broaden your horizons and go for it!'"

Model Commitment, Quality, and Consistency

As a person of faith and a leader in his industry, Chuck feels strongly that he should model what he believes. "The keys to success are commitment, quality, and consistency," says Chuck. "You have to be committed to what you do, you must deliver a quality product— whether you're filming a motion picture, creating a distribution plan, or negotiating a movie sale, and you must be consistent in your beliefs and management style. That's what you're judged on. People around you need to know you and understand when they've crossed a line—professionally or ethically. If they see that you're consistent in your beliefs, they'll judge themselves by your rules and adjust their own behavior accordingly. You've got to be true to yourself, to your beliefs—or you definitely won't be happy."

Understand the Process

In the world of distribution, there are many steps that require great patience and foresight.

"The process begins," Chuck shares, "with script approval. Then the production team begins casting it, producing it, and bringing the project to life. When the movie is totally shot and tweaked through research screenings, then the distribution arm—my team, comes in. We see it, try to understand its upside potential, and find the appropriate time of year in which to place the film. We look for opportunities like holiday weekends, Christmas, Easter, summer vacation, whatever seems best for that particular movie. We try to make it the most available to that particular audience at any one time. For instance *Miracle* was placed one week prior to a four-day holiday. That way the word-of-mouth buzz would give its second weekend a great chance for big sales. It just takes some understanding and foresight with each movie."

Understand the Factors

Chuck advises Hollywood newcomers to study the marketing factors that determine how well a movie will do at the box office. "Word of mouth is so important in this industry," explains Chuck about marketing. "We hope that people will volunteer positive feedback on a movie to their friends . . . as opposed to 'reactive' endorsements, or simply answering friends' questions on a film. We're hoping that people will say, 'Kirk Russell is unbelievable in *Miracle*.' The public becomes your best friend those first weeks of a movie's release. But no one can clearly define all the factors of a movie's success. Marketing is a big key for us. We have great materials for television, radio, and outdoor advertising. Trailers are great for starting movies, but the length of a movie's run is determined by word of mouth endorsements. It's hard to predict, though. For instance, who would have thought that *My Big Fat Greek Wedding* would have caught on so hugely and run seven or eight months? If a movie runs eight weeks it's a huge hit. We have to make out best guess about how well a movie will do, and based on that, we'll place it in 900 theatres, or 2,600, or 3,000."

"Every theatre has limited seating capacity based on auditoriums. It's equivalent to having shelf space in a grocery store. We're just like Coca-cola, fighting for the most shelf space and getting the best exposure to our product."

Discern the Avenues

To those interested in the industry, Chuck offers some helpful tips: "Find a good agent," he advises. "Agents are the keys to getting a successful script read. And don't give up. Though *Miracle* was read and loved by Disney, others probably passed it on earlier. Rejection happens every day, but you can't give up. If it's good, the right door will open."

He's also in favor of going the film festival route. "I think film festivals are a great way to showcase a good movie. Our production people go there all the time to see talent levels. An acquisitions person might say, 'I love it! I have to have it!'" Chuck concludes, "In general, I'd say that with great talent, a good agent, and a spirit of teamwork, people of faith have a high chance of making it—and making a difference—in this exciting and challenging industry."

***

MAJOR CORPORATE ADVERTISING EXECUTIVE

INSPIRING KIDS' IMAGINATIONS

—AND INTERVIEW WITH ROB HUDNUT

Rob is the Executive Producer for Mattel Toys, overseeing the creation of all of Mattel's movies, television series, and videos (Barbie, Hot Wheels, Rescue Heroes, Little People, etc.). His work has been seen by over a billion children and has been translated into over thirty-five languages. The movie *Barbie in the Nutcrakcer*, which he co-wrote, has generated over $100,000,000 in video and DVD sales and won Best Animated Feature at the Video Premiere Awards. His works have also won Emmy, Parent's Choice, American Library Association and other awards.

"I'm proud to be part of a company that has as its mission inspiring kids' imaginations. We believe that doing the right thing for kids is doing the right thing for your business. As the head of storytelling for the company, I work to ensure that our stories are built on an ethical foundation. I'm proud to bring kids stories under-pinned by Judeo-Christian values that help them make the right choices in the world."

God's Plan Is Clear in Hindsight

After graduating from Princeton with a degree in Politics, Rob started as an Assistant Account Executive at the Benton & Bowles advertising agency in New York working for clients like Procter & Gamble and Nabisco. From there, having never been to California, he decided to move to the Los Angeles office of the ad agency Foote, Cone & Belding. He began work on the Mattel business, and three years later, Mattel asked him to join the company as Marketing Director. "The marketing training I received in the advertising business and at Mattel has been invaluable," Rob says. "I learned the importance of understanding the needs of your 'target audience' and then rigorously determining if, and how, your product or idea is uniquely suited to meeting those needs."

Advice from A Mentor

After two years in marketing at Mattel, Rob felt that he was being called in a new direction. He needed career advice, and sought it from his grandmother (a minister's wife; Rob's father, grandfather and great-grandfather were all Presbyterian ministers).

"It was Easter of '92, and I was visiting my grandmother in Phoenix. It was just the two of us. I was trying to decide whether to go to seminary or not. 'How do you know?' I asked her, the woman with the strongest faith of anyone I know in the world. 'How do you know God's call for you? God only wants good for us, so if I can figure out what He wants from me I'll do it.' She thought for a moment and said: 'The key is to devote your life to that area in which you can make the greatest contribution. With your unique gifts and experiences, where can you make the biggest difference in the world?' A week later, back in L.A., I wound up with a friend at a breakfast with two executives from Word publishing, and it hit me for the first time that faith and business need not be mutually exclusive. I realized that my call was not to seminary but to creating stories for children that can help them learn how to be strong, brave, morally-centered people. I quit my marketing job a week later."

Rob's plan was to write children's books, but his call took him in a different direction. "Once you commit yourself to doing God's work, your decisiveness has its own power in it, and doors will open that you never knew existed." For example, without looking for an agent, he wound up with one. "On the patio after church, a friend introduced me to a friend of hers who had just become an agent at an agency called Triad Artists. I told her that I was going to create morally-positive stories for children. She called a couple of days later to say she wanted me as a client, which I thought was pretty silly since I hadn't done anything yet and because I didn't think I needed an agent. A few weeks later I met her and two of her associates in the spacious Triad conference room, told them my vision and, after they offered, agreed to become their client. That afternoon, William Morris bought Triad and I found myself—a guy with a vision who hadn't done anything yet—represented by an agent at William Morris."

The doors continued to open. "The first meeting my new agent set up for me was with Phil Roman," Rob says. "I was pitching a TV series called *Mighty Max* based on a toyline I had helped greenlight when I was at Mattel. Phil liked the idea, liked the toys and, I believe, liked my vision of an action series for boys where the hero is eleven-years old and never uses a gun. It was only later that we realized we were both Christians and our families have been friends ever since. I am forever grateful to Phil for the break he gave me." In the first episode of *Mighty Max*, Rob had Virgil, the mentor character, tell Max that "every person has a gift, and in that gift lies their destiny"—the very lesson Rob's grandmother had taught him ten months before. Phil and Rob produced forty episodes of *Mighty Max* that performed well around the world.

So You Want to Be in Show Business?

Rob says, "You need to closely examine your motivation for getting into the entertainment business. If it's for selfish reasons—fame, money, [and] power—then you will fail. Either you'll fail outright, or even if you 'succeed' you will have failed: you'll climb the ladder only to find it's leaning against the wrong wall."

Rob says that, as in life, and as in God's relationship to us, the right decisions start in love. "If you love your audience, and care passionately about helping them make the right choices, you will have a greater chance of doing God's will and therefore of success."

In addition, you have to ask yourself how much job insecurity you can live with, since the entertainment business has a lot, especially when you're starting out. "I suggest that your ability to tolerate uncertainty will be directly proportional to your belief in your mission. If you're married, it's important that your spouse feels as strongly about your mission as you do."

It Starts with Story

If you do choose to be in the storytelling business—whether as a writer, director, cinematographer, storyboard artist, production designer, editor, or composer—Rob says you must know the basics of the storytelling craft. "As in architecture," he says, "[T]here are general principles that increase the odds that you will build something elegant and effective. You need to know the rules." The books Rob suggests are *Story* by Robert McKee, *The Writer's Journey* by Christopher Vogler, and (for craft and not content) Francois Truffaut's interviews with Alfred Hitchcock. He also recommends *The Artist's Way* by Julia Cameron for general creative inspiration.

Rob says, "The best production designer I know, and with whom I'm privileged to work, always starts with me in talking about the ideas that drive the story and then we construct the production design around those ideas."

Know Your Customer

Once you've decided to be in the business, you have to get people to pay you to be creative. Rob's advice is to be sure of two things: "You have to be passionate. Passion and enthusiasm [he notes that the Greek root for "enthusiasm" is "God within"] are infectious, and people want enthusiastic people around them. 'I always hire passionate people'" Rob says. "Their quality bar will be higher."

The second key is to know your customer. "As an agent once told me, 'It's not show art it's show business.' You have to understand your customer's business (the person who's paying you) and how you can help him or her meet his or her needs."

A story that illustrates this principle is Rob's work with the Fisher-Price brand Rescue Heroes. "It was 1998, and I had just come back to Mattel (Fisher-Price is part of Mattel) to head up the entertainment division. The Fisher-Price team had launched the *Rescue Heroes* brand that year and had created a twenty-five-minute animated video featuring the characters Billy Blazes, Wendy Waters, Jake Justice, and Ariel Flyer. However, the brand was dying. I knew that CBS had pared its children's block to three hours on Saturday morning, and that all of that time had to be committed to educational programming in order to meet FCC requirements. As a result, CBS' kids ratings, especially their boy ratings, were plummeting. I knew Brian O'Neil at CBS, and caught up with him at MIP-TV (the international television convention that happens twice yearly in Cannes). I suggested to him that *Rescue Heroes* was a perfect fit for CBS because it was pro-social and educational, but also an action show that appeals to boys. Brian and his CBS team bought the series. The Rescue Heroes brand not only stopped its decline but went on to become the biggest boys brand in the country by the Fall of 2002. The series teaches kids lessons of teamwork, safety and honesty. The Fisher-Price team and I could proudly say that the world was better because of our efforts."

Ask For God's Help

Rob's advice is that "when you get stuck, professionally or creatively, pray. God hears all prayers and answers all prayers, though sometimes not in the ways that you expect. Others have noted that God either says 'Yes,' 'Yes, but not now,' or 'No, I have something better in store for you.' Keep praying and keep listening."

Rob says one of your greatest assets will be a strong moral foundation. "It will set you apart from many in the business. Honesty is extremely effective." In addition, he says, "Just as we reveal character in stories by forcing our protagonists to make moral choices under pressure, so will your character be revealed as you make hard choices in the entertainment business." Fortunately, he says, you already have the best "How to Succeed in Entertainment" book in your possession. "It's the Bible," Rob says. "Keep it close."

***

TELEVISION EXECUTIVE AND PRODUCER

QUALITY AND COMMUNITY

—AN INTERVIEW WITH PETER ENGEL

For those who got to enjoy the 2003 TV series *Last Comic Standing*, or great television shows of the past decade like *All About Us*; *One World*; *Malibu, CA*; *City Guys*; *USA High*; *Hang Time*, or the famous *Saved by the Bell*, perhaps the more discerning could spot a common thread woven by the talents of producer Peter Engel. Engel's productions are entertaining, witty, often directed toward teenagers and pre-teenagers, and always safe for the family. Below, Peter shares some of his wit and wisdom for those pursuing the entertainment industry as determinedly as he's done over the past three decades.

Seize the Day!

The old saying, "If you want something done, give it to a busy person" appears to be true when it comes to Hollywood producers. They even start out busy, it seems. Peter Engel went to NYU Film School and worked at night at NBC on the famous NBC page staff. "The NBC pages were famous. Not the ABC or CBS guys . . . You wanted to get on with NBC," recalls Peter. When he graduated from college, he started a local sports show and worked for a company out of Philadelphia that moved him to California around 1970. Then, he worked for Metromedia Productions and ended up as Vice President in charge of television programming. He then took a position with Universal Studios as an executive producer for a couple of years, and then became president of First Artists Television—a company in which Barabara Striesand, Paul Newman, Steve McQueen, Dustin Hoffman, and Sydney Portier owned controlling stock. Peter then began his association with CBN and the Family Channel.

In keeping with his busy beginnings, Peter still wears many hats. In 1996 he formed his own company within NBC called Peter Engel productions, where he produced 816 half-hour shows.

Establish Your Niche

Peter Engel is often credited as the inventor of teen television with his world-famous thirty minute shows like *Saved by the Bell*;*California Dreams*; *Hang Times*; *USA High*; *City Guys*; *All About Us*; *One World*; and *Malibu, CA*. Though they weren't spin-offs, they all started with *Saved by the Bell,* the story of six high school students and their misadventures at Bayside High. The show featured Zack Morris the cool trouble maker; A.C. Slater the kind-hearted jock; Screech Powers the smart and funny nerd; Kelly

Kapowski the teen dream (who is Zack Morris's obsession); Lisa Turtle the gossiping fashion lover; and Jessie Spano the feminine straight-A student. Many of the actors who played these characters went on to star in other Peter Engel shows, as well as other television shows and movies. *Saved by the Bell* reruns still air throughout the nation—even in that getting-ready-for-school morning slot to which parents are most attentive, content-wise.

Follow the Lord's Leading

Peter's own faith has affected his career path very definitively. "It was hard enough getting prime time programming on the air to begin with, but I also had a vision of doing shows my children could grow up with and watch—which often meant going against the current culture trends. The Lord gave me the idea for *Saved by the Bell*, and all my decisions from then on were based on my "family values" faith and on heeding God's direction."

Peter believes that it's tough to get into show business, no matter what you believe. "The entry-level jobs are full because everyone wants to be in film and TV . . . everyone. If you're good, you're good, and if you're very good, there will be a place for you. It's tough, though . . . very, very difficult. However, the playing field for Christians may be a bit wider because of *The Passion of the Christ*, and we'll begin to see others like that because Hollywood does try to replicate what's selling. You see this in TV more than motion pictures. We'll see more biblically based things coming from mainstream Hollywood, and some will be successful, whereas others won't. *The Passion* showed that there's been a wake up call for those interested in portrayals of faith-based issues, so there will be some more opportunities during this window of acceptance."

Learn from the Politicians

Though Peter expects a good round of faith-based movies to emerge, he knows that their success is completely dependent on how good they are and how well they market the films on a grassroots level. "Hollywood is suddenly interested in putting out 'spiritual films,' and if they're enjoyable and highly entertaining, audiences will accept less (biblical) accuracy than they should; it all depends on how it's treated and who is making the films, "Mel got great support from the evangelical community. He was smart in that a) he brought the movie to Christian leaders, and b) He had done his homework. The movie was probably 98% accurate. He took some creative license, but everyone knows it's a movie—subject, of course, to some personal interpretation, so it was well received by the Christian community. The key, I believe, was the grassroots support from people of faith."

You Must Have Passion!

Peter is clear that people must have passion to make it in movies and television. "There must be an inner desire, and a love for the process you want to write, produce, direct, or act. You have to love it. You have to have a need. You should be saying, 'I must do this! You can't say, 'Well, I'll just try this.' It must be a deep, deep desire. The second way in is through writing. Everyone is looking for that terrific, next new writer. I tell my students to write full scripts, not treatments or outlines. Writers must write . . . that's the best way in."

Mentor and Be Mentored

In order to navigate the entertainment industry and its challenges, Peter is an advocate of mentoring. "I had a few people who I felt were kind of mentors, and there were a couple who affected me more than others. I was a mentor at UCLA, which had a great mentoring program. They can draw on so many in that community. I'd meet with a student once or twice a month and just help them with whatever challenges they were facing. The best mentors are in the work place—a supervisor, a boss, or the president of the company. You want someone who will contribute positively. The success of mentoring depends on who you listen to, though. Make sure you're listening to the right people."

Emotion Equates to Excellence

Peter's advice for those in the industry is to make value-based films that are better than anyone else's. "You can't say, 'It's good enough.' Shows like *7th Heaven* were successful because they were done well and they were entertaining. You've got to create quality programs or movies that evoke emotion, whether it's through adventure, comedy, science fiction, or history. Your audience has to laugh, cry, be excited, or even scared. Your program must have emotion attached to it, or it won't work."

Be Persistent and Decisive

Peter believes that the key to his success was that he never gave up. "I was like a mosquito. I kept buzzing, and never gave up until I got what I wanted. Once a production began, I'd never say, 'OK, that's good enough.' We would do major, major preparation before shooting . . . major organization. We cultivated an environment that was a fruitful one for the creative process, and I personally made decisive moves very quickly. If I were wrong, I would never defend myself. I'd say, 'I made a mistake. Let's go do this or that to fix it.'"

It's All About the Team

Good teams are a huge factor in creating a successful television show or movie, says Peter:

> Teamwork is the whole thing. We did 816 shows in fifteen years . . . Everyone in the top positions had moved up through the ranks with the help of the others. Our biggest success was that we were family— everyone on the set knew our systems, ways, and values, even if they didn't share those values. They knew the issues we'd take on and what we were trying to accomplish. We'd move people up through ranks, show to show, all as a family. When we started off the

season of a new show, we'd have a kick off party, and the producer and cast would come to my home . . . The next day we'd be working together. Most of them didn't know each other prior to that. Many times I'd say, 'Let's have a dinner, a producer's dinner—with the producers, key staff, and cast. Here, they'd get to know each other through swimming, tennis, and eating barbeque together. Sometime during the night, I'd explain to everyone what was going to happen in the coming days and weeks. The director would talk, and the line producer would talk. I figured that everyone has wrap parties, but I also wanted parties at the beginning. I've always valued relationship, unity, chemistry, and creating a family feeling from day one."

Go West!

On the subject of cultivating relationships, Peter believes that people can write from afar, but it's much better to be on site—in New York or L.A. "There are people who have done it, though, and made great strides from mid-America. It obviously helps to be where the action is, though, with your hand on the pulse of what's going on. If someone wants to see you, or to meet you, it's difficult to be very far away."

Show Me the Money!

Financing is the hardest thing there is to do, Peter says. "It's hardest to sell a show, and the second hardest thing is to keep it on the air. In features, it's very hard to get financing because the results can be so varied. Investors could lose everything; you can't guarantee an investor that he'll get a return . . . otherwise everyone would be doing it. It's not like any other business. Quite frankly, there are businesses where you can make a product and know that if everything goes wrong, this or that will happen, and there are ways to recoup. It's not very clear or definitive in the entertainment industry; it's very subjective and very risky. And you have to get a distributor—right away. I know of great films that never get distributed because they never got to the right people. If people are going to go wrong, they usually do it by obtaining financing when there's no distribution in place. You could have the best picture that no one ever sees. Distribution is the key to moving forward."

Understand Your Market

The other major problem Peter sees is people not understanding their potential marketplace. "In a perfect world, you could say 'I'd love to do this; it must be done like that.' But when you're working with others' money, you must know your market and your potential. Sometimes it's difficult to face that you don't have any market for your project."

Peter is also aware that markets and their values can change. He has worked in the arena of teen pictures for decades and is disappointed that they've become so sexually oriented. "If you want to do a clean teen picture, you'll have a much more difficult time in connecting with that audience because of what they've been bombarded with in the media. It's very discouraging, but you cannot compromise or stoop to conquer . . . You just have to be smarter, more clever at what you do."

Studios and TV networks, especially, must understand their audiences, says Peter, who is amazed that most studios gear their movies toward teenage boys. "seventeen-year-old boys are important, but teenage girls are just as important, if not more important. Many of them will see drama/romance pictures like *Titanic* three, four, and five times. Because everything is so advanced in the area of overt sexual dialog and depictions, *Saved by the Bell* wouldn't do equally as well today, though it was a giant in eighty-five countries throughout the world. It's too clean-cut."

Peter believes it's a different time and place now. "The tween/

teen audience has been bombarded by a different culture since *Saved by the Bell*, which went eleven years. It's harder to capture the older end of the teen audience of which we were so dominant. The WB Network changed all the tone of teen shows over the last few years. We created romance, and they expanded on what we had done. They were all about teenage sex. As they grew, our audiences—and all Saturday morning shows, for that matter, started to diminish around 2001, because they were losing the higher end of their audience. It's romance vs. sex. Unfortunately, we couldn't compete with sex. We were telling morality tales and good stories, but they were appealing to the hormones. You can't compete with that."

Find Your Audience and Go to Them

The broader the audience, the more difficult it is to understand it. "Your audience is harder to reach if they're all over the place. If you go broader, it's more expensive, more costly on many fronts. In *Saved by the Bell*, we found out that we had targeted a very, very under-served audience of 12–17. We were huge with teen girls. Once we knew who they were, we knew where to find them and market to them. We found that our audiences were listening to top 40 radio, on the phone, in the mall, and reading teen magazines. You have to find out where they are, go get them, and bring them to your show or movie. You find out how to reach them. We bought cable spots, top 40 radio spots, teen magazine advertisements, and mall tours. If you know who they are, and where they are, you can figure out how to get them."

Live Your Dream

Peter's final advice to those with stars in their eyes is, "Don't let anyone steal your dream. If it's inspired, go for it!"

The next time we're laughing with *The Last Comic Standing* or watching a *Saved by the Bell* rerun as we're munching our Cheerios before school, we'll do well to remember Peter Engel—a man of quality and community who went for his dream and continues to inspire generations of households toward positive, uplifting family entertainment.

* * *

TELEVISION PRODUCER

You're doing it Backwards!

—AN INTERVIEW WITH BRENDA HAMPTON

One of America's top television programs was the family-friendly *7th Heaven*. The one-hour prime time program was created, written and produced by Brenda Hampton, who also wrote such fun and memorable shows as *Mad About You*, *Blossom*, and *Lenny*. Originally from Atlanta, Georgia, this busy, talented writer/producer lives with her multi-cultural family in Los Angeles, and is still milling out one great *7th Heaven* after another. Below, Brenda shares a glimpse into her life and gives Christians some great food for thought on how to make inroads into a largely secular arena.

Look for the Next Opportunity

Brenda lived in New York City and started writing jokes for comedians. She also had a corporate writing job. Soon an opportunity arose for her to write a book on cancer for Bantam in California. Shortly after moving to California, she joined a friend from New York, William C. Kenney, to pursue television writing. Together, they wrote a spec script, got an agent, and got a job a month later to write for a television program called *Sister Kate*. "From that point on, I've continually worked," says Brenda. They continued to *Bagdad Café* and *Blossom*, where Hampton began writing on her own. She worked on *Blossom* for five seasons before co-creating a show for Dudley Moore called *Daddy's Girls*. She was Supervising

Producer on *Mad About You* when she sold the pilot of *7th Heaven*, which has lasted eight seasons so far. Brenda is the show's creator, Executive Producer, and show runner.

Variety Is the Spice of Life

In the second year of *7th Heaven*, Brenda adopted a ten-year-old girl, Zoë, from Vietnam. It wasn't until she arrived that Brenda discovered the little girl had never been to school, so Brenda's plans for sending her to a private school with an interpreter went out the window. Now she needed someone to home school the girl, so she hired a man named Tim Bui to catch her up. During that first year of home schooling, however, Brenda and Tim fell in love and got married. Now, the couple is trying to adopt again.

"Our family is very multi-racial and multi-cultural," explains Brenda. "Zoë is Buddhist, Tim's Catholic, and I'm Protestant, I go to the First A.M.E. We have a multi-cultural, multi-religious belief system. On the show, what we share are moral values with people of all religions. Many think *7th Heaven* is about a religion, but it was actually more about religious tolerance. We featured people of all faiths on the show."

As for the show, Brenda tells us there was no agenda for *7th Heaven*. "We gave no specific message. The show was first entertaining, and then a bit of a morality play, like *Leave it to Beaver*, *Donna Reed*, and *Father Knows Best*—only in a one-hour format. We tried to remain harmless, rather than trying to help people with a specific, religious message."

Write Well, and Write Fast

Brenda wrote about half the scripts for *7th Heaven*. They started every season with six scripts, with Brenda usually writing the first three to start off the season. "We sat down in January and plan the theme, and the characters' arcs. Then we break that down into episodes. By the end of March, when we go on hiatus, the first six scripts are being written."

Be On Time, On Budget

Brenda's team was very organized. "We were always on time and under budget," she says. "We had to be. If you make last minute changes and the crew has to make changes or actors have to be rescheduled, costs go up. Fortunately, this show didn't solicit a lot of network notes, which was great because last-minute notes can be costly."

You've Gotta Go with the Dollars

"If I could, I'd do nothing but family TV," says Brenda. "But there aren't enough buyers. I've had six projects for new family shows in development, but it's difficult to sell these properties. Networks continue to turn down family programming, which I think has a universal appeal. We had a large audience for *7th Heaven* because audiences from five to ninety-five, Christian or not, could watch it."

Be Able to Wear Many Hats

Brenda oversaw all aspects of *7th Heaven*: scripts, casting, wardrobe, sets, crew, and directors. "But I also had the good sense to step back and let people do their jobs. If I happened to see something that bumps me with a wardrobe selection or a set design, I'd call the department. But there was a lot of creative freedom here. The writers write, the producers produce, the director directs, the actors act, and the crew does all hard stuff! Before each script was filmed, the producers, the director, and the line producer went through the script with me. If anyone saw a way to save money, we'd do it. We were very efficient."

Each episode of *7th Heaven* took seven-and a-half days to film. "We filmed on the stage about 5 ½ days, and we were out on location two days. . . . The director had a few days to give me a cut of the show, and I cut it down to time. It then goes back for sound effects, music, and color timing. It took 8 days for the director and crew to prep, seven and a half days to shoot, about a week to edit, and a week for all post-production. It could be done more quickly, though, if we were rushed."

Give and Make a Difference

Brenda says that her faith comes into play in her daily life as she tries to make generous and thoughtful choices about how to appropriate her income. "For example, I wanted to do a show about the Lost Boys of Sudan. Once I made contact with the woman who's their mentor, I invited her to bring two of these young men, Jacob and Nicodemus, to my house for lunch so we could all get to know them. When they came to L.A. to shoot the episode, I had Nicodemus and Jacob stay in my home, and my husband and I surprised them by flying in four friends they hadn't seen since they left the refugee camp in Kenya."

From this relationship, Brenda and her husband decided to also sponsor several of the family members of the Lost Boys left behind in Kenya, who want to go to school in Nairobi. "These guys try to send money back to their family members. Only $450 sends one child to school for a year and that includes housing, education, and food. I feel strongly about putting my faith into such tangible humanitarian efforts. Once the crew heard what we were doing, many of them also volunteered to help other Lost Boys by sponsoring other families. It's true that I enjoy a nice home, a nice car, and some travel, but I also try to share my resources with those in need."

Persevere, Unafraid of Change

Brenda believes that her number one key to success is perseverance. "Hollywood's a difficult environment," affirms Brenda. "You must be strong, and you can't take things personally. You have to work at writing." Brenda's first love is writing, with producing second to that. "I've always been a writer, and I knew I wanted to be a writer since 3rd grade. I've just always written." Brenda graduated from the University of Georgia's Grady School of Journalism. Her first job was for the U.S. Navy in the Bahamas as a technical writer.

From there, she did some substitute teaching at an Atlanta high school, teaching reading. She then got a job as a technical writer for Krystal Hamburgers in Chattanooga, Tennessee. "I wrote manuals on everything from opening a can of tomato juice to frying a hamburger. Did you know there are seventeen steps to frying a Krystal?" Brenda laughs.

Brenda also worked for the Tennessee Valley Authority, writing a corporate magazine for a power plant, and giving tours. One day, she realized that she was bored with life in Chattanooga, and wanted to go to New York or Boston. So she did! The rest is history. Through perseverance, and a fearless approach to life, she says she has succeeded far beyond her wildest dreams.

No Agendas

Brenda reminds Christians not to 'preach to the choir.' "Now, when I look at Christian broadcasters, frankly I just wince and wish they could do a better job. Clearly, they have an agenda—to get Christian teaching on TV, and they're doing that. But it's almost as if Christ only talked to His disciples and no one else; the messages are only for those that are already Christians. I'd like to see Christians create a mainstream program and make it palpable to the general public. And there's no reason, by the way, that you can't do that. You could develop and produce *7th Heaven* and *Touched by an Angel*—things of this caliber and content—for mainstream audiences. . . ."

"So many Christian programs could be better produced. Again, if your only agenda is giving Christian teachings to Christian audiences, you're certainly doing that. But you need to raise the bar. I think Dr. Baehr gets it, and I think he could run a studio that produces a show where the response won't immediately be, 'Ohhh, I see. The Christians are trying to feed us their agenda? Until you get there, you'll only stay on cable.'"

Brenda recently wrote a pilot with Fannie Flagg based on Ms. Flagg's best selling novel *Standing in the Rainbow*. It is about a time in history when everyone loved America. "It's a sweet family show, but all three networks passed on it, saying it was too soft. However, I know I could get my *7th Heaven* audiences to watch it. I mean, getting Fannie Flagg as a TV writer is like getting Mark Twain to come to TV. She's a great American novelist. Adapting her book, she and I created the kind of show that Christians should buy, produce, and support—a good, safe, entertaining show for families. Christians have been good at rewarding good shows and supporting good shows, and they're more than capable of creating those shows and getting them on the networks, but something has to shift. Take a nice family show with no agenda beyond family entertainment, and you can be successful."

Surround Yourself with the Best

When Brenda moved from half-hour sitcoms to full hour programming with *7th Heaven*, Aaron Spelling's partner, E. Duke Vincent, saw to it that she had the best production people by her side. "They totally protected me, and as I got to know more about process, I brought in others to make improvements. The show had terrific production quality. Our Director of Photography, Ronnie High, gave it a great look. Also, our line producer, Lin Parsons, and our coordinating producer, Pam Cotton, made a great contribution to improving the production and creating a terrific family atmosphere on our set. We had a lot of hardworking and lovely people working in production."

Take Criticism and Rewrite!

According to Brenda, it's difficult to discern if you're a good writer, and even more difficult to get good advice. "I pass the first draft of what I write to people around here. I trust them to say, 'What, are you crazy?' if they don't like it. But it's hard to find good people like that. The most important thing about writing is rewriting. Rewrite until you feel your script can't possibly be better, then let go. Brandon Tartikoff said something along the lines of, 'Throw out the worst of what people say and the best of what they say, and the truth will be somewhere in between.' That's a good rule of thumb for taking criticism."

We'll use that rule, Brenda!

* * *

MARKETING MAVEN

Study and Serve the "Faith and Family" Market

—an interview with Paul Lauer

It's certainly the movie of the year for 2004, and possibly will be the movie of the decade in many people's estimation. Surrounded by controversy and accusations of anti-Semitism, *The Passion of the Christ* gripped the hearts, rocked the charts, and blew the minds of an amazed and bewildered movie industry. Talk shows featured theologians and scholars pontificating on the merits and cautions of such a film. Newscasts covered its opening, unafraid to show footage of puffy-eyed audiences streaming from theatres holding well-worn tissues. Websites sprang up, capturing the testimonies of those whose hearts and minds had been enthralled by the love story of the century.

How did such a movie, which couldn't find distribution from any of the majors, find its way to the Number One position on the movie charts, raking in hundreds of millions of dollars from mainstream America, and more importantly, grip the hearts of the world? The answer is that one company with vision and foresight took a risk on the man and the mission of Mel Gibson. Below, Paul Lauer of Icon Pictures, director of marketing for *The Passion of the Christ,* shares some of his history and philosophy in hopes of guiding others with such a desire to risk it all on inspiring, life-changing movies.

Keep Narrowing Your Focus

Paul spent twenty years creating, distributing, and marketing products to the "faith and family" market. He started first by focusing on teens, publishing *You* magazine, which was distributed all over world in six languages. His work with *You* birthed various youth-oriented projects in media and entertainment. From here, Paul migrated upward to begin serving the whole family and not just the youth culture. "I realized that I must not just reach the kids, but I also had to deal with their parents." While doing some consulting for a variety of companies (mostly developing marketing plans and helping launch projects), Paul got a call to work on a film. "This was a film with some very interesting potential. I turned it down at first, too busy to add another project to my plate, but something told me I needed to do this thing."

Prior to coming on board with Icon Pictures, Paul had spent some time working on a large film project for IMAX Films, the company that produces bigger-than-life mostly-documentaries for the giant screen. "This type of movie-making is a very different world for the Hollywood community." So although he had the bug to work in film, it took a while before he got the call to work on a "normal" feature. "I combined my IMAX knowledge with my marketing knowledge, and I took my skills to the faith and family market. I started working on marketing films. That was around early 2002."

Study the Market and Become the Solution

Paul worked on independent and studio projects as a consultant, helping them market and position the film to the faith and family market. He found that, whether it was an independent or studio film, the same distribution dilemma existed: There is a lack of quality material with faith-based content. Independent films were below the quality of what most moviegoers had come to expect. Studio films were rarely catering in content to faith and values community. "I found a content dilemma on one side, and an exploding demand and starvation on the part of the faith and family market on the other. Families were longing for wholesome content that wouldn't offend their religious and moral sensibilities." Paul knew that his calling was to solve that dilemma by serving such a niche.

He began by looking at the two realities and examining possible avenues that might have the effect of meeting both the content dilemma and the exploding demand from faith-based moviegoers. "The best way to have an effect on content is to deliver this hungry market to quality moviemakers. Hungry consumers, once they're being fed, will keep coming back, generating high dollars for studios, which will in turn be motivated to continue creating quality content for them. I had to figure out a way to generate the business necessary to support higher quality and volume on the content side. That was the trick."

Four months later, Paul emerged with a business plan for a company, the goal of which was to build the channel of marketing and distribution for quality products aimed at the faith and family market. Others could utilize those same principles to serve any niche market. "It's actually an oxymoron to call the 'faith and values sector' a niche. It's just so huge. It's like saying 'jumbo shrimp.' I think that the studios are now grasping the size and depth and even buying power of this sector."

What is the "Faith and Values" Niche?

According to Paul, the "faith and values" sector of moviegoers has representatives from all across the religious spectrum. "The faith community has high standards in terms of content and their acceptability of content, but their values are all over the board. We can see broad generalizations in that most of this group respects the person of Jesus Christ and adheres to basic biblical doctrines, but beyond that, it's very segmented by denomination, region, age, and other factors. We even study the habits of young Christians versus senior Christians."

Flowing, Not Forcing

The ebbs and flows of the movie industry stem from the desires of the movie going public, not any mandates from the industry, Paul believes. "We must figure out what the market wants, and then respond to their needs and interests, letting the content adapt accordingly. Instead of creating content and hoisting it on the market, saying this is what you're getting, you'd better love it, we just get good at analyzing what the market is asking for and then providing it to them on a silver platter."

Get the Product Out There!

Though Paul was clearly able to discern both the lack of content dilemma and the demand side of the equation, he eventually chose to go spend his efforts on the market side, not the content side of the problem. "So many people choose to deal on the content side of equation, fixing that by making films, especially independent films, and trying to get the studios to make better films. I think all of that is worthwhile, but my call was to the market side. If I can deliver to the market, the market will support the hunger, and the interest in the market will produce the revenue and capital necessary to mature the content."

Indeed, audiences worldwide are grateful that Paul and his associates at Icon not only took a risk on such an incredibly spiritually impacting movie as *The Passion of the Christ*, but also that the time Paul spent in years of analysis of the "faith and values" market allowed for the creation of such a powerful marketing plan that others will undoubtedly utilize for upcoming world-changing movies.

* * *

SCRIPT DOCTOR

Creative, Collaborative, Comforting, and Clear

—an interview with Linda Seger

What in the world happens when a movie is in production and suddenly the producers realize there is something wrong with the story—a problem no one can quite put a finger on? The answer is: They don't panic; they call Dr. Linda Seger, Hollywood's foremost script consultant. When Linda gets on the case, papers fly, story lines are restructured, characters are dissected and recreated into living color, and a compelling, well-flowing screenplay starts materializing. Possibly the most amazing part is that, though her proverbial "red pen and scissors" are flying, her comforting countenance reassures and encourages even the frailest of egos and keeps the creative process flowing.

What is a script consultant, and how did this Wisconsin girl become a household word among screenwriters and movie producers—as well as a prolific writer and international speaker?

Step One: Get Your Comeuppance!

Linda had been teaching college at the University of La Verne near Los Angeles when the drama department was over-developed and almost everyone lost their jobs. She decided to stay in the area and try to find a job in television or film. "I assumed that the industry folks would fall all over themselves to hire me when they found out I had a drama background," she recalls, laughing. "It was very difficult at first. I'd call people and write letter and try to get interviews. Although some people would meet with me, I got no jobs. Finally, there was someone from La Verne who knew someone at NBC, who agreed to meet with me for ten minutes. He saw my strengths and agreed to let me do story analyses for him on three scripts—with no pay. I could then take my three samples and get a 'real' job. It was the only offer I had, so I agreed. Then, with my newfound experience and resume, I knocked on doors and actually started getting a little work."

Learn to Pinch Pennies

By keeping her rent really low—two hundred dollars a month—Linda scraped by as a story analyst, where she reviewed scripts for production companies, and recommended them for production if she felt they were commercially viable. She then landed some temp work at Norman Lear's Tandem/TAT as the assistant to the Assistant of the Director of Development. "I worked there for six months, and ordinarily, one would move up in the ranks, perhaps becoming a development executive, however, the writer's strike hit at that exact time, and all the temps were let go. . . . It was a major blow."

Remarkably, shortly thereafter Linda found a job at EMI Films as a Resident Story Analyst. "I made $1,000 a month and had to cover twenty five scripts—or over six a week. As meager as that sounds now, it was the first time I had something stable going on. My stability was short-lived, though, because six months later, the company fell apart, and I felt like I was back at Square One. It was sobering to realize that I only had a toe in the door to this industry, not a foot. I had to come up with a game plan."

Someone Will Pay for Your Unique Knowledge

As part of Linda's doctoral dissertation, she developed a method for analyzing what works and what doesn't work in scripts. She began analyzing scripts for friends. "People were delighted by my work, and I remember one writer saying, 'This is amazing. I've spent three years not knowing what was wrong with my story, and in one hour, you put your finger on it.' It was very confirming to hear such things, and I knew I was in the right field. I just had to find a way to turn it into an official career."

Market Yourself—Even on a Budget

In 1981, Linda put an ad in the *Hollywood Reporter* as a "Script Consultant." Her hairdresser had helped her coin the term. "Before that, the job just didn't exist," Linda recalls. "Some people, such as Syd Field, were teaching classes and analyzing scripts for writers, but I envisioned this job differently. I saw the job as an independent entrepreneur, focusing specifically on analyzing scripts for writers, producers, directors, production companies, and maybe studios as well. At that time, no one wanted to admit they needed or went to a script consultant. Those that could did hire me, however, and liked my work, so I kept thinking that maybe the studios would start coming to me. But after awhile, I realized I liked being an entrepreneur. I put an ad in the *Hollywood Reporter*, got a client, got $70, and put another ad in. It cost me $18.50 for each ad, and back then it was really hard to get that money together. Thankfully I slowly got some clients. I'd get one script one week, or maybe one or two a month. It was inconsistent, but I was grateful for the work."

Consultants are Crucial

To make this career viable, Linda needed more clients. In March of 1983, she met a career consultant. "I told her that I wished I could make this a full time business, but I'd have to get more clients. She really helped me understand what success is and how to get it. She suggested that I do a free script consultation for producers in the industry, so I did one for Tony Bill, Al Burton, and Jay Weston, and then got their advice. I said to them, 'you tell me what I should charge, and if I have a service that's worthwhile.' Tony said $500, so I started getting people at a higher level. In 1983, I got three jobs in one day."

Then, Linda started going to other consultants for help. She went to one consultant to learn how to make cold calls and do a 10–15 minute presentation. She also solicited advice from a media consultant, a clothes consultant, a seminar consultant, and a public speaking consultant. Finally, by March 1984, Linda was doing well. After living on the financial edge for fourteen years, doing part time jobs, discovering creative ways to market herself, restructuring her business plan, updating her pricing structure, and hiring shrewd consultants, Linda Seger made a career as a Script Consultant. In 1987, she wrote her first book and married her wonderful husband, Peter.

Expand Your Horizons

In Linda's first book, she taught script structure, which naturally led to speaking at seminars, including lectures for ABC, CBS, and the Television Academy. Her career consultant, Judith, helped her evaluate the seminar work. "Do more seminars," Judith told Linda, "and you'll get more consulting work." So she did. Soon, she found that women began hiring or recommending her from the group "Women in Film." Linda began producing seminars that analyzed the Academy Award nominees, having fun but barely breaking even. She went to the Director's Guild and suggested that she do a seminar for them. "At first they said, 'We only have Director's Guild members teach here,' but I persisted, and they relented. I did that seminar for fifteen years," says Linda, smiling.

Why Not Go International?

At about this time, the University of Wisconsin at Milwaukee's Department of Continuing Education hired Linda to do seminars around the U.S. on script structure and storytelling. Linda did many seminars in Milwaukee, Chicago, Florida, and Atlanta. She did a great deal of traveling, including training the story analysts for Turner Network Television in Atlanta and Los Angeles. During this time, she got clients in Europe and brought the seminars to them. "I met a guy at one of them who said, 'You should come to Australia and do a seminar for us.' I told him I'd like to, but that someone needed to invite me. Peter and I decided to go to New Zealand for a vacation, so I hired a woman—yes, another consultant—to figure out who could sponsor us. She found the Australian Film & TV Radio School, who was happy to do so in Melbourne and Sydney. I had a blast, and almost broke even on the trip!"

Linda was invited back to New Zealand, where Peter Jackson and Fran Walsh attended her next seminar. Peter then hired Linda to work on his script, *Brain Dead*—released around the world, but not in the U.S. (*Heavenly Creatures* brought him recognition over here.) In 1993, Linda spoke at a conference in Spain where people from all over Europe gathered. Danes, Germans, Swedes, and Spaniards got to know her and invited her back to their countries. For the rest of that decade, she went everywhere, teaching others and building her own business through consulting. "I've taught in 21 countries," reports Linda, "and I have clients from six continents. However, no one has called me from Antarctica . . . yet."

Never Give Up!

The little girl who paid $18 for an ad and got a $70 job has now written over eight books—over seven on screenwriting and one on "web thinking," another subject Linda is passionate about.

"No one does it alone. My friends laugh at all the consultants I've gone to, but it meant everything to my career. I didn't know anyone; I didn't have a mentor. I had to depend on others. When I moved my thinking from competitive to collaborative, or team thinking, I was successful within a year. I started thinking about what kind of team I could get around me. Besides the career consultant, I hired a publicity person, a media consultant, and a speech consultant. The speech consultant gave me good tips about my seminar speaking like, 'You're not breathing . . . Slow your speaking, which makes you better. You'll be more articulate . . . Don't be afraid to be funny. Give people time to laugh.' These little adjustments made a huge difference."

Linda also believes that screenwriters who are in screenwriting groups and industry organizations do better than their peers. "The whole thing about being connected is really important."

You Lead the Discussions

As Linda looks back on her career, she now realizes that she missed some good opportunities by taking too passive a role in her career. One year, as Linda recalls, she interviewed for job at Twentieth Century Fox. "I was extremely well-qualified for the position, but the interviewer didn't ask me the right questions. She simply didn't know enough to lead the interview or pull the goods out of me. I was so upset when they called me to say they had hired someone else for the job, someone with a fraction of my education and experience. I hung up the phone and said to myself, 'My happiness won't be dependent on Twentieth Century Fox. And, I need to take my career into my own hands.' I didn't want to feel victimized anymore, by waiting for others to find me."

Pray a Radical Prayer

During some of the early career years, Linda says she truly felt like Job. She prayed, "God, I can't figure out why you don't let anything work for me. I'm talented, educated, and nice. Why won't you help me? Whatever is between success and me, I'm willing to deal with it. I'll even go to a therapist if that's what's needed (although she added, 'Hopefully it will be a cheap therapist since I have very little money.'), and if I have something in me that is afraid of success, I'm willing to look at that. I'm willing to do whatever it takes to get rid of these obstacles." Soon, things began to work.

Linda believes that it takes a real leap of faith to start a consulting business. "You've got to know, though, when it's faith and when it's stupidity. I did a lot of praying to know it was a leap of faith and it would be fine." After a while, she recognized, "This job really suits me . . . I had studied drama for years, directed plays, and had both practical and academic training. I understood group process and psychology, and I knew how to be nurturing and talk 'issues,' not problems. I'd created a business that suited exactly who I was. There's a place where you say, I'm living what God made me to be; I'm on the right path. I'm working in all my strengths and none of my weaknesses. That realization brought me a lot of joy and happiness."

Become All Things to All People

At first, no one in Hollywood knew that Linda was a person of faith. "I wasn't very connected with Christians in the industry, but people soon began to learn that I was a Quaker and a Christian. Perhaps because Quakers are known to be very tolerant, many of my clients who were "spiritual," but not necessarily Christian, presumed I was spiritual the same way they were. So many would say, 'I know you're spiritual, so I know you can help me. . . ' I did. I just helped them tell their story—with their own voice, not mine." I discovered I was accepted by many different kinds of people, whether religious or not."

Regarding her faith, Linda found it necessary to lay out some boundaries in the industry. "People need to know I don't do porn scripts, or bestiality. Yes, I actually got one of those and quickly gave them their money back. But, I am open to doing work on various spiritual planes. I have a lot of clients who are Jewish, New Age, lots of paths . . . I honestly don't think I could be in my business without being broad-minded. In fact, I think it's difficult for anyone to be in Hollywood unless they're broad-minded. The truth is, you honestly don't know around here. Is the professing Christian really a Christian? I try not to make judgments. Christians who come to me presume that I'm like them, whether they're fundamentalists, liberals, Catholics, or Charismatics. I understand, and I speak their language, but I don't compromise my own values. My job is to help them pull their own values from their script."

Linda has had many friends and acquaintances in the film industry who have often shared stories about bad experiences with Christians. "One friend told me that when she grew up, as a Jew, that children called her 'Christ killer.' This has obviously scarred her. Others have told me that instead of seeing a vision of a loving, merciful, kind and accessible God, they have met so many Christians who seem rigid, and show a God who is judgmental and inaccessible. I have tried to change some of these perceptions, through my own behavior, but also by introducing my non-Christian friends to my Christian friends. On the other hand, I have had the fortune of meeting Christians, and non-Christians, who are kind, loving, caring people. I'm consistently surprised by how many different people consistently break my stereotypes of them and I've long felt that part of my mission is to be a bridge between Christians and non-Christians."

Ask Good Questions

Not only is Linda a bridge regarding spiritual matters in script writing, she is also one who awakens writers to both the overt and subtle messages in their screenplays. Linda teaches her clients to become very good at making their story themes conscious. "For example," she says, "I asked one client if he really wanted to say that violence is the best method for resolving problems. He had written from the perspective of the IRA, and truly believed that sometimes you do have to revert to violence. 'But is that the message you really want to give audiences?' I asked him. 'Have you thought through the possible consequences of such a theme? Let's find the value in what happened in your story.' After much thought and discussion, the writer gave his story a redemptive ending. At the end, the character walks away, instead of fighting."

Show It; Don't Say It!

Linda teaches her students that drama should communicate values and theological ideas without getting preachy. In the six or so Billy Graham movies on which she has consulted, she has convinced the writers to cross out the extra, preachy verbiage in many cases. "If you play your images and characters right, you've said it. If you have to preach, do it in two lines or less. On the script consulting for the epic, *Luther*, I kept paring down the preaching. When there are sermons, they have great emotional content, terrific movement, and strong, clear themes. It's emotional, rather than a 'let me pound you in the head' feeling."

Keep it Positive

On *Luther*, Linda's first script report was forty-five single spaced pages. She worked on the film through four to six drafts, including meeting with the producers, writer, and director. "I loved this script. Yes, there were many problems to resolve, but I always believed this would make an excellent film. I thought it was fabulous, beautiful writing. It just needed structure. It was unfocused in some places. I filled my analysis with praises, rightly telling both writers that they did a good job. By the way, writing by committee is really hard on a writer. The writer, one producer, and I stayed in a hotel room for two days, taking notes and reconstructing the script. When we were finished, we told the reconstructed story to the other producers, and they clapped."

Get Educated

For those who want to follow in Linda Seger's steps, Linda suggests a strong education in drama—at least a B.A., if not an M.A. "You learn so much by analyzing dramatic literature. The other area to know is psychology. The people in the film industry have fragile egos, and you can't demoralize them or act angry or pushy . . . That gets around. You're there to serve the writer, to serve what the writer wants from their script . . . to shape the work, to make it work. I'm not there to recreate a new story. I'm there to help the writer get the most out of his or her script; I get them to the best place they can. Maybe they'll get a job out of it, who knows? Only the talent of the writer will determine that. If you want to be a script consultant, you don't want to say, 'What I would do is this. . . ' You help the writer get what *they* want, not what *you* want."

Linda reminds Hollywood wannabes that it really takes a while to break in. "Don't give up until after five years," she tells friends.

"Give it the five-year college try, and then re-evaluate. There are people who conduct their business haphazardly, but if you're really trying and you really love it, stick with it, and it will pay off."

Resist Greed

Another snag that Linda has hit is that a lot of script consultants don't understand how to charge for their services. "You have to have a lot of clientele to keep up business, so you can't analyze one script a month. And you can't overcharge. You have to start low enough, because at the beginning, you're going to get the writers who can't afford very much. Part of my success is that I was always able to match my rate with my clientele. My rate never got higher until I saw that I could get the higher-rate clients. On the other hand, if you're not losing 10% of your business because your price is too high, your price is not high enough. You have to have a few people say, 'I can't afford you.' Most script consultants are priced too high. If you can't get enough work at $250/script, you're priced too high. My base price is now between $1,000 and $1,500. I'm not dependent on higher end work, like the occasional $7,500 job. My $1,000 price has stayed the same for years, especially in light of the recent economy."

Focus on Serving

As Linda built her business, she had to learn not to think of the money, and focus on how to serve her clients. "In the beginning, I had too much ego. There was a point where the ego and money thing got out of hand. In the '80s, people said I was the goddess of screenwriting, and sometimes I believed them and got off track. I saw that this was just ego, and I changed. Now, I do a lot of saying, 'I have to stay centered in this.' I've seen plenty of people fall because of pride. I made a choice to walk in humility and kindness. I made a decision in the '80s never to talk negatively about colleagues, and I believe I've kept that policy. I'm nurturing to my colleagues and writers. I'm very careful that people know that my world is a safe place, that their work will be confidential, that I'll not talk badly about them."

Send a Message to Heaven

"Years ago," says Linda, "I made a determination that I will work every day, whether I have work or not. It kind of sends a message to God, that I'm here. If I don't have work, I'll still sit down and analyze a film. I'll make phone calls. I'll do a script for free. But I will have a working day. This sends the message that 'I am here, and I'm serious. God, you're my employer.' I pray with open hands sometimes, just to show my willing heart. I say, 'Lord, I will not look down on any work you send me, but I will thank you for it. God, I don't care what you send me. I'll be thankful and give it my best.' Last month, when work was down, I sent such a message to God. The art critic for a local newspaper had written a play, a farce, and a friend had directed it. They needed a rewrite, and I said, 'I'll do it for free. I'm lonesome for my work, and I enjoy a good farce.' Plus, I really believed in these people. I did the $1,000 job for free. We had a very good meeting, the clients were flabbergasted, and it was an adorable play. After that, my work picked up. I have to believe there's a correlation."

Diversify

In this industry, there will be times when work is low, so Linda believes in having diversified income sources. She writes books, holds seminars, does consulting, and serves as an expert witness for legal cases—four different income sources. Generally, when one thing isn't going well, another income source is doing all right.

Linda also tries not to get stressed out when her workload is down. "Oh," she says, "I'm supposed to write an article. God has opened up two days for me! I've moved from a more fear-based, anxiety-based mindset to a faith-based position." Over the years, she's also developed a better sense of God's timing. "Creative time is not regular time."

Listen to God's Still, Small Voice

After a recent letdown regarding a book that was rejected, Linda had a heart-to-heart talk with God. "What's this about?" she asked. "I don't get it. This isn't working. What do you want me to do? That still, small voice of God seemed to say, 'Linda, you are standing in the middle of a bridge. Christians are on one side and "spiritual people" are on the other. You're trying too hard to be everything to both camps, and it won't work. I want you to get over to Christian side, because that's who you are. Share what you have to say, and the others will hear you and follow as you make a clear stand.'"

"I do think I have a unique gift for speaking to the spirit within people, and I always want to remain accessible to all. I think it's important as Christians to have that voice."

For those who know and love Linda, and have benefited from her wisdom and grace, there is no doubt that her clear, uncompromising voice will, indeed, continue to speak volumes to her industry associates, and her work will continue to yield incredible, well-structured, inspiring movie scripts for years to come.

* * *

· 14 ·

Conclusion

FURTHER IN AND FURTHER UP

Whoever listens to you listens to Me. Whoever rejects you rejects Me. And whoever rejects Me rejects the One who sent Me.

—Luke 10:16

WHAT DOES GOD WANT ME TO COMMUNICATE THROUGH THE ENTERTAINMENT INDUSTRY?

Knowing God, knowing His presence and power, standing face-to-face in awe of Him—if only for an instant—fills us with the need and the desire to communicate what He wants us to communicate. For that experience of Him through faith, through His Word written, through His Holy Spirit, makes us His ambassadors destined to communicate Him in word and deed. From the moment when we accept His salvation and His Lordship over our lives through the indwelling of His Spirit, we are his ambassadors, His official messengers, communicators of the highest rank sent to officially represent His truth to all the kingdoms of the world. As Jesus said before His ascension:

> You will receive power when the Holy Spirit has come upon you, and you will be My witnesses in Jerusalem, in all Judea and Samaria, and to the ends of the earth.
>
> —Acts 1:8

That we will be His witnesses is a fact—a necessary consequence of our being His people filled with His power by His Holy Spirit. Like all witnesses, we attest to a fact and an event of which we have personal knowledge, the great news of the resurrection and Lordship of Jesus Christ. According to Jesus, testifying to Him—communicating His gospel—is not a choice, an alternative, or a probability. Instead, communicating Him is a joyous aspect of our enthusiastic love for Him, exceeding in intensity all other loves: our children, our beloved spouse, our friend, or our favorite sport or pastime. There is no alternative; you and I will be His witnesses. Believing and being united with Him, we want the world to believe and share in His blessings.

What is the message?

To what or whom are we to testify?

What does God want us to communicate through the mass media of entertainment?

He wants us to communicate Him:

> God, Father, Son and Holy Spirit, His Lordship, His Salvation—His Son, Jesus the Christ:

> For this reason God also highly exalted Him and gave Him the name that is above every name, so that at the name of Jesus every knee should bow—of those who are in heaven

and on earth and under the earth—and every tongue should confess that Jesus Christ is Lord, to the glory of God the Father.

—Philippians 2:9–11 NIV

The simple, straightforward reason for history, for our creation in His image, for our salvation in Christ, and for our communication of His gospel, is to glorify God: "If anyone speaks, [his speech should be] like the oracles of God; if anyone serves, [his service should be] from the strength God provides, so that in everything God may be glorified through Jesus Christ. To Him belong the glory and the power forever and ever. Amen" (1 Peter 4:11).

His plan for our lives and His reason for rescuing us from righteous judgment, death, and eternal damnation derives from His pleasure and purpose which is simply to be with us, walk with us, communicate with us, and give us life eternal so that He may be praised and glorified:

Blessed be the God and Father of our Lord Jesus Christ, who has blessed us with every spiritual blessing in the heavens, in Christ; for He chose us in Him, before the foundation of the world, to be holy and blameless in His sight. In love, He predestined us to be adopted through Jesus Christ for Himself, according to His favor and will, to the praise of His glorious grace that He favored us with in the Beloved. In Him, we have redemption through His blood, the forgiveness of our trespasses, according to the riches of His grace that He lavished on us with all wisdom and understanding.

He made known to us the mystery of His will, according to His good pleasure that He planned in Him for the administration of the days of fulfillment—to bring everything together in the Messiah, both things

in heaven and things on earth in Him. In Him, we were
also made His inheritance, predestined according to the
purpose of the One who works out everything in agreement with the decision of His will, so that we who had
already put our hope in the Messiah might bring praise
to His glory. In Him, you also, when you heard the word
of truth, the gospel of your salvation—in Him, when you
believed—were sealed with the promised Holy Spirit. He
is the down payment of our inheritance, for the redemption of the possession, to the praise of His glory.

—Ephesians 1:3–15

Sometimes it is hard for us to completely appreciate the fact that
the gospel is God-centered, not self-centered. Often, we first look
at "what God can do for me" as an individual.

First, we look for God to "get me out of the mess I am in," or
to improve my life: by redeeming me, blessing me, and providing
for me—all of which God promises and gives me in Christ, for He
is the answer. Then, when it becomes clear that there is a larger
problem—the fallen state of our world—we look for God to change
others, so that our lives will improve and we will be able to live
together in His kingdom here and now.

Finally, as He sanctifies and glorifies us, we realize:

. . . that the focal point of the good news is God Himself;

. . . that the problem is not sin, just estrangement from our
Creator with whom we were created to be in community;

. . . and that turning our attention to Him, by the power
of His grace, brings life eternal.

Rearing children illustrates this process of spiritual maturation.
At first, when he was very little, our eldest son (of three sons and
one daughter) would condescend to say "please" when it was made

perfectly clear to him by his parents that he was not going to get what he wanted until he said "please" and showed some consideration for the giver, rather than demand what he desired. Then, our son moved on to using "please" to manipulate, reasoning that "please" would cause his parents to change their response, and often it did. This "please," and the subsequent "thank you," sounded nicer than the previous condescension, but still fell far short of respect for the rights of the giver, since this "please" manifested the unmistakable tone of manipulative self-interest. Finally, "please" and "thank you" started to become expressions of appreciation and love; this love transforms his character from selfishness to gracefulness. Our will for him was that he would become what he had the potential to become: a loving, caring and giving person—and he did. After graduating with honors from Wheaton, he is now in Tasmania establishing a Christian retreat. His maturation glorifies us as parents and blesses him by making him a blessing to others.

Just as my wife and I asked our son to say "please" and "thank you," God calls us to glorify and appreciate Him. "Rejoice always! Pray constantly. Give thanks in everything, for this is God's will for you in Christ Jesus" (1 Thessalonians 5:16–18). In the process of thanking, praising, and glorifying Him, we ourselves are transformed into what He meant for us to be, co-heirs of His kingdom, in communion with Him, expressing love toward Him and our neighbors, worthy communicators of His truth.

When we communicate, by thanking and praising Him, we are called to be transparent, so clearly focused on Him by the power of His Spirit that those around us see Him in us. In this way, we become truly ourselves, truly what He meant for us to be, His heirs. As we love, respect, and appreciate the Lord as giver, we grow by leaps and bounds. When we focus on His gift of new life and our rights as heirs, we stop growing spiritually.

The appropriate word here is "agape," one of the four words for love in Greek. "Agape" is selfless, giving, love so oriented toward others that the lover takes no thought for his or her self. The example of "agape" is Jesus' death on the cross to save you and me—and even His worst enemies—from the wrath of judgment.

To communicate what God wants us to communicate (Jesus and His salvation), we must allow Him to reconstruct us in His image. When a building is being rebuilt and improved, there are times when the dust, the materials, and the exposed guts of what needs to be replaced look worse than before the reconstruction started. At those moments, when decay is being stripped away, it may appear better to tear the building down and start from scratch. However, when the reconstruction is finished, it becomes clear that the temporary state of disrepair was absolutely necessary and worthwhile.

The same holds true for our lives. While God is stripping away the rotten materials, we often question the process, but when we perceive the new person that He is making each of us, we rejoice in His grace. As we glimpse the new self, we see that the cost to us is temporary, while the cost to God was the life of His Son, who He raised to new life in order to reconstruct us. In the same way, the cost to a child of being brought up well is temporary moments of discipline, in the midst of having all his or her needs met. The cost to the parents is hard work and selfless giving, in preparing the child to leave home as an independent person.

Because of our new life in Him, we joyously communicate Christ and His salvation. Because God is reconstructing us in His image, we will communicate Him in both word and deed. He is the Lord of our life and we are His ambassadors—we must strive to communicate Him and His gospel more effectively. It is as His ambassadors, under His Lordship, that we are called to excellence in our communications. As Paul said, each of us must strive:

> Not that I have already reached [the goal] or am already fully mature, but I make every effort to take hold of it because I also have been taken hold of by Christ Jesus. Brothers, I do not consider myself to have taken hold of it. But one thing I do: forgetting

what is behind and reaching forward to what is ahead,
I pursue as my goal the prize promised by God's heavenly call in Christ Jesus (Philippians 3:12–14).

Quality in our communication of the Lord and His truth means
that we dedicate ourselves to running to the finish line and that
we avoid short cuts. Years ago, a runner in the New York City
Marathon slipped from the pack and took the subway to the station
nearest the finish. At first, it appeared that she had won in record
time. Then someone recognized her as having been on the subway.
How often we deceive ourselves into thinking that we can take a
short cut only to be caught and lose the prize.

Our communications, no matter what genre or medium, must
be as carefully executed as the best non-religious communication.
Because He is our standard of excellence, our communications
through the industry of entertainment should reflect the highest
quality of creative work; Christian or otherwise. Yet, how often do
we look at Christian films, television, and other communications and
wince at the lack of quality, or get bored, but excuse the mediocre
communication because it adheres to our theological perspective?

Do we think that we can step out of the pack and ride the
Holy Spirit to the finish? In a way, we can, but not by impatiently
jumping the gun or by cutting corners. To win the prize, we must
follow the rules and run the race, and by the very act of doing so,
we "shall run, and not be weary" (Isaiah 40:31 ASV) because His
Spirit will empower us.

The very first step in running the race is for us to wait upon
the Lord for the gun to sound. Not only should we wait, going
over the course in our minds, counting the cost and reviewing our
strategy, like any good runner; we also wait for God to give us the
opportunity, the message and the boldness to communicate, as Paul
notes in his Letter to the Ephesians, 6:19–20. In the very process
of waiting, the Lord shall renew our strength by filling us with His
Spirit, so when He gives us the signal to run, we "shall mount up

with wings as eagles," (Isaiah 40:31 ASV) soar ahead of the pack, and ride the power of the Holy Spirit to the finish.

Waiting on the Lord is an active process, where we allow Him, by faith, to rebuild and spiritually circumcise us; cutting away the excess spiritual flesh around our hearts so that we are personally and privately marked as His people, capable of communicating His Truth. This spiritual circumcision is not our doing, but His doing, as Paul writes, "In Him you were also circumcised with a circumcision not done with hands, by putting off the body of flesh, in the circumcision of the Messiah." This circumcision of our hearts: "Is the work of God's Spirit, not of the written code . . . [So that we may receive] praise from God, not from man" (Colossians 2:11, Romans 2:29 NIV).

We can be the best communicators in the world, but until we allow His Spirit to work in our hearts, cutting away our sinful selves and filling us with Him, our communications will be empty, hollow, and spiritually dead (Revelation 3:1). This process of allowing God to operate on us involves pain, but ends in glory:

> Now the God of all grace, who called you to His eternal glory in Christ Jesus, will personally restore, establish, strengthen, and support you after you have suffered a little.
> —1 Peter 5:10

Therefore, we rejoice that He shapes us and disciplines us, "For the Lord disciplines the one He loves, just as a father, the son he delights in" (Proverbs 3:12).

> He comforts us in all our affliction, so that we may be able to comfort those who are in any kind of affliction, through the comfort we ourselves receive from God. For as the sufferings of Christ overflow to us, so our comfort overflows through Christ.
> —2 Corinthians 1:4–5

Waiting on God does not mean that we ignore His mandate to communicate the gospel, informing our fellow Christians that we are under construction and can't witness until the gun goes off. The gun sounds—the instant we are filled by faith with His Spirit and are presented with the opportunity to communicate Him to someone who does not know Him. Just as we must not jump the gun, so we must not miss the gun by lingering at the starting line. We must always be on watch, actively aware of the opportunities He gives us: "Don't you say, 'There are still four more months, then comes the harvest'? Listen [to what] I'm telling you: Open your eyes and look at the fields, for they are ready for harvest" (John 4:35).

Some of these opportunities demand only that we gossip the gospel, telling others in conversation about our faith and experience of His presence. Other opportunities arise because we are actively involved following Him, praying and seeking His opportunities to communicate through the appropriate medium and genre. As Paul tells us, we should be "making the most of the time, because the days are evil. So don't be foolish, but understand what the Lord's will is" (Ephesians 5:16–17).

Let Us Go Forward as God Permits!

Sometimes we do not even linger at the starting line. Worse, we hide in the parish hall amongst our friends.

> We have a great deal to say about this, and it's difficult to explain, since you have become slow to understand. For though by this time you ought to be teachers, you need someone to teach you again the basic principles of God's revelation. You need milk, not solid food.
> —Hebrews 5:11–12

The problem with hanging around the parish hall with our Christian friends is that God just might kick us out. After Jesus told His followers to go to Judea, Samaria, and the ends of the earth once they were filled with power by the Holy Spirit (Acts 1:8 NIV), they were filled with power on Pentecost, but they did not go to Judea and Samaria, rather they stayed in Jerusalem and went daily to the Temple (Acts 2:43 NIV ff). Then, Stephen was stoned: "On that day a severe persecution broke out against the church in Jerusalem, and all except the apostles were scattered throughout the land of Judea and Samaria" (Acts 8:1 NIV).

Soon thereafter, Saul was miraculously converted on his way to Damascus to persecute believers. Saul's conversion is a dramatic act of God, but why didn't God convert Saul before Stephen was stoned? Or before the persecution of the believers began?

If Saul had been converted sooner, he might have been able to stop the persecution, the stoning, and the scattering of the believers. However, if he had stopped the persecution, would the believers have left the Temple—which was defunct because the believers were now the Temple of God's Holy Spirit? (2 Corinthians 6:16) Or would the believers have lingered in Jerusalem, ignoring the command Jesus gave them?

Of course, this line of reasoning is pure speculation. Jesus had told the believers to testify first in Jerusalem, and they were doing His work when the persecution broke out. Furthermore, God disciplines us, but He is not the author of the evil desires which tempt us to sin (James 1:13–14), although God can and will bring good out of our disobedience, to bring about His will (Romans 8:28). Being forced out of Jerusalem, the believers fulfilled God's call to testify in Judea, Samaria, and to the ends of the earth. However, God may decide not to bring faithfulness out of our disobedience, rather He may make us take another lap around Sinai, or we may find ourselves wrestling with Him until our hip is thrown out of joint and we limp away, living testimonies to His power.

In any event, God calls to us, whether we are hiding in the fellowship hall or in our garden: "You who dwell in the gardens . . . let me hear you!" (Song 8:13).

He wants to hear our voice outside of our own gardens. He calls to us to speak up. He calls us out of hiding to the starting line, where he fires the gun and we are off running to win the prize of eternal life with Him, in His garden, in His kingdom.

This is not to say that we do not need fellowship—we do. God has called us: "into fellowship with His Son, Jesus Christ our Lord" (1 Corinthians 1:9).

We are called to be the church of God: "to those who are sanctified in Christ Jesus and called as saints, with all those in every place who call on the name of Jesus Christ our Lord—theirs and ours" (1 Corinthians 1:2).

We are as one body, the Body of Christ, and cannot function apart from the body, which is defined as all the believers (1 Corinthians 12:12ff). It is in the body—the church—that we are nourished, supported, and sustained during the grueling race He calls us to run. Not only does the local church provide essential fellowship, but also professional groups, bible studies, and other groups to nourish and sustain Christian communicators.

For example, in Los Angeles there are over one hundred fellowship groups that give Christians in the entertainment industry a refuge and support. Actors and actresses, dancers, singers, writers, artists, producers, executives, and others in Hollywood can discuss the problems they face, vent frustrations, confess failings, and work through the decisions confronting them, with other believers who are sensitive to the unique forces in their professions and committed to a biblical faith. Quite often, the local parish can't relate to the problems facing these professions, whereas the fellowship of believers can. Furthermore, these groups have proved to be a vehicle for evangelism, strengthening the faith of the members and giving them courage to witness to the people with whom they work. There are many other fellowship groups around the country that have a similar purpose and ministry.

The fellowship of His church provides us with rest stops along the route of the race and, between laps for Jesus, continues to send us out into the world to testify to Him just as He sent the twelve, the seventy-two, and all the believers (John 17:20ff) with the words:

> All authority has been given to Me in heaven and on earth. Go, therefore, and make disciples of all nations, baptizing them in the name of the Father and of the Son and of the Holy Spirit, teaching them to observe everything I have commanded you. And remember, I am with you always, to the end of the age.
>
> —Matthew 28:18–20

Of course, as part of His body, we never leave the fellowship of the church—even as we are in the farthest mission field—for He is with us. Throughout the *Book of Acts*, God is uprooting believers, scattering churches, and even splitting up teams of itinerant evangelists (Acts 15:36ff), so that His Word can be proclaimed to the ends of the earth. Often, three years is the maximum time for an evangelist in the *Book of Acts* to stay in one particular local church. We should not be surprised if God calls us to be uprooted from the comforts of our communities.

Furthermore, we need to learn and obey the rules of the race that can be found in His Bible. If we submit to Him, He will write these rules on our hearts by the power of His Spirit. As God told the prophet Jeremiah: "I will place My law within them and write it on their hearts. I will be their God, and they will be My people" (Jeremiah 31:33).

Submission to His authority is the key to running the race successfully. As James tells us, "Therefore, submit to God. But resist the Devil, and he will flee from you. Draw near to God, and He will draw near to you, 'Humble yourselves before the Lord, and He will exalt you'" (James 4:7–8, 10). Running the race is often exhilarating. When we do well, we can be overcome with pride in our accomplishments, and end up running toward the wrong goal. It is at these moments when we must "beware the yeast of the Pharisees" (Matthew 16:5), those false doctrines which cause us to put our faith in ourselves. When our communications are well received, when we are being courted by politicians and when we are prospering as communicators of His truth, we must humble ourselves and give credit to Him before we are swept along by the crowd and turned from proclaiming Him to selling a watered down version of His gospel for our own self-aggrandizement. As Peter says, "In their greed, they will exploit you with deceptive words. Their condemnation, [pronounced] long ago, is not idle, and their destruction does not sleep" (2 Peter 2:3).

The problem is the strong appeal of recognition and approval:

> Be careful that no one takes you captive through philosophy and empty deceit based on human tradition, based on the elemental forces of the world, and not based on Christ, Do you not know that friendship with the world is hostility toward God?
>
> —Colossians 2:8; James 4:4

The longer we run the race, the more we understand how easy it is to fall into hypocrisy by taking too seriously the approval of the crowd. Often it is when the crowd is least enamored of our work for His sake that we are succeeding in proclaiming His Word. As Jesus says:

> If the world hates you, understand that it hated Me before it hated you. If you were of the world, the world would love [you as] its own. However, because you are not of the world, but I have chosen you out of it, the world hates you.
>
> —John 15:18–19

If we are not careful to keep Him in focus, our striving for excellence can turn us from our goal of proclaiming God, but if we love Him, He will keep us on course. For example, several years ago our company produced a nationwide teleconference on aging that was satellite-cast to over thousands of people at fifty-nine locations around the United States. We worked very hard to make sure that the quality of the communication was excellent. With our client, we asked the right ascertainment questions and applied the answers and the correct principles of the genre and medium to the communication. We produced the teleconference at the most modern video production studio in New York City. The teleconference was scheduled so that one-hour of satellite casting the views of local experts on our topic would alternate with one hour of local discussion, for a total period of six hours. We were in production and on the satellite for a total of three hours, with local discussion bracketing the on-air time.

After the first hour of telecasting, the engineers and the studio personnel praised the high quality of the production. I was proud because it was beautiful. However, as I was basking in self-satisfaction, a Christian friend of mine in television production said that she loved beautiful productions, but asked, "Where is the heart, Jesus, since this production is for the church?"

I was convicted. Stepping to the side, I prayed to God to stop the production if it was not honoring Him (thinking while I prayed that the production was for a church agency, $120,000 was being spent and there was no way the production would stop).

Immediately, the power went off in the control room—although the power in the studio stayed on, so the circuits were ok. Con Edison was still in service, but with the power in the control room, the brain, went off. All the computers—which had taken hours to program—were out. All the camera control units were dead. No power, no explanation. The engineers were desperate. The second airtime was fast approaching. I took our production team aside and prayed, "God, forgive me for that impertinent prayer. This is your production. Glorify your Name. Amen."

Ten minutes had passed. Suddenly, the power came back on. Only thirty seconds of satellite time were actually lost. Color was perfect. Miraculously, the computer programs were intact. The next speaker preached Jesus and His gospel. We thank Him, for communicating so clearly to us on that day.

As we run, the good news we are called to preach to those along the way is that Jesus is Lord and Savior, and His good news of "repentance and the forgiveness of sins" (Luke 24:47). It is the great news—that the drug addict who has been told that he is trapped—can turn from drugs to Christ through the power of His spirit; the good news that the malcontent can turn from a life of unhappiness, to a new life in Christ; and the news that even the most self-centered among us can enter into a relationship of love and giving with the Son of God. This is good news, that we who stand condemned by our disobedience are set free by the judge, if we accept His Love. Jesus' first message is: "Repent, because the kingdom of heaven has come near!" (Matt. 4:17).

Repentance and forgiveness are good news because they offer us a new opportunity to be who God created us to be, but we often preach repentance as if it were bad news and we—not God—stand in judgment. Paul puts it bluntly, "Or do you despise the riches of His kindness, restraint, and patience, not recognizing that God's kindness is intended to lead you to repentance?" (Rom. 2:4)

Preaching repentance as bad news often predisposes us to combative relationships that undermine the effectiveness of our communications. To be able to turn from a life of alcoholism, a life of fear, or a life of greed which can only lead to eternal damnation, to a life of freedom from the bonds of sin and self is great news which offers help to the helpless and hope to the hopeless. Unlike Jonah, we should long for the joyful repentance of the lost, tell them the good news and pray for God's patience and forgiveness for even the worst of our acquaintances, which just may be ourselves (Romans 2:1–4).

As Jesus tells us:

"I tell you, in the same way, there will be more joy in heaven over one sinner who repents than over 99 righteous people who don't need repentance."

—Luke 15:7

One evening, as I was discussing the gospel with a few followers of a Tibetan Buddhist monk, they informed me that according to their teacher, life was a cesspool, and the best thing to do was to give up and drown in the filth to reach a state of non-being. As a Christian, I agreed that we lived in a fallen, sinful world, but the Good news is that Jesus is offering us His hand to pull us out of the cesspool into a new world of light and life. There is no need to drown in hopelessness, for we have the opportunity to live in hope. The call to repentance is simply a call to turn around from looking at the filth, so that we can see His outstretched hand and grab hold of His offer of life eternal.

As we run the race, we exercise our commission to communicate Him and thereby develop our spiritual stamina and strength that is our ability to trust in Him. The more we trust in Him the more courage we have to tell others about Him, and the more we have to tell others. As Paul says:

God in his mercy has given us this work to do, and so we do not become discouraged. We put aside all secret and shameful deeds; we do not act with deceit, nor do we falsify the word of God.

For it is not ourselves we preach; we preach Jesus Christ as lord, and ourselves as servants for Jesus' sake.

We are often troubled, but not crushed; sometimes in doubt, but never in despair; there are many enemies, but we are never without a friend; and though badly hurt at times, we are not destroyed. At all times, we carry in our mortal bodies the death of Jesus, so that his life may also be seen in our bodies.

The scripture says, "I spoke because I believed." In the same spirit of faith we also speak because we believe. We know that God who raised up the Lord Jesus to life, will also raise us up with Jesus and take us, together with you, into his presence.

For this reason we never become discouraged. Even though our physical being is gradually decaying, yet our spiritual being is being renewed every day.

—2 Corinthians 4:1–2, 5, 8–10, 13–14, 16 GNT

With every step we take in faith, we find that God is faithful, our faith grows and we become better communicators of His gospel. Not only does our growing strength, which is a gift from Him, help us to deal with the blows of the Adversary and forgive the sins of others against us (Matthew 18:21–22), but it also gives us the ability to repeat and refine our presentation of the gospel. Robert Price, a political communicator commenting on how he would run New York City Mayor Koch's re-election campaign many years ago, noted: "I would promote that theme by repetition. I've always gone on the theory that only after you repeat it a hundred times will the public first begin to hear the message."[111]

Paul concurs:

"Finally, my brothers, rejoice in the Lord. To write to you again about this is no trouble for me and is a protection for you."

— Philippians 3:1

However, no matter how well we communicate the gospel, nor how many times we repeat it, it is His Holy Spirit who converts—not us. Christianity is not like Islam, where the believer has to convert the non-believer in any way possible, including bribery, and if unsuccessful, death to the non-believer. As Christians, we are blessed that the Holy Spirit teaches us what to say (John 14:26), convicts the world of sin (John 16:8), converts (John 3:5–8), and baptizes (1 Corinthians 12:13). But, we also must testify (John 15:27), for we are His fellow workers (1 Corinthians 3:9).

Running the race to fulfill His call does not always mean to take off around the world looking for opportunities to proclaim the gospel; rather, as we have discussed, He often calls us to witness where we are and tells us to:

> "Occupy till I come."
> — Luke 19:13 KJV

In fact, we are called to occupy all areas of life, all professions and all nations, and to make disciples of Him everywhere. We are not to abandon the lost nor the institutions of the world to the Adversary. Instead, we are to occupy and help Him to redeem all of mankind.

We are not the only people with a mission. Many excellent communicators are proclaiming many false gods, including sex, money and even the forces of darkness.

We have a mission to proclaim the Author of all creation who entered His creation to give us the gift of eternal life in fellowship with Him through the death and resurrection of His only begotten Son, Jesus the Christ. We should make movies and other communications at least as successful as, if not better than, those of communicators who follow false gods.

We must wait upon Him; pray for His guidance; and seek the message He has for us to deliver to the audience of His choice; and, when He sounds the gun to start, we must run the race to the finish line, victoriously communicating and celebrating with shouts of thanksgiving His victory over death.

We are His communicators. Let us glorify His Holy Name.

> "For everyone who calls on the name of the Lord will
> be saved. But how can they call on Him in whom they

have not believed? And how can they believe without hearing about Him? And how can they hear without a preacher? And how can they preach unless they are sent? As it is written: How welcome are the feet of those who announce the gospel of good things! But all did not obey the gospel. For Isaiah says, Lord, who has believed our message? So faith comes from what is heard, and what is heard comes through the message about Christ." Amen.

—Romans 10:13–17

NO OTHER GODS

Trendy dilettantes have the gall to say that movies and the other mass media product are art, so anything in the name of art is acceptable. Art, they say, is truth, and so all art is worthy of some audience.

The movie industry is more than a billion-dollar-a-year business that appeals to people's visceral emotions to separate them from their hard-earned dollars. Much of that money comes from mass media products with a heavy dose of perverse sex and violence, what some in the entertainment industry call "horny boy" movies because they are targeted at the hormones of teenage boys who drag their dates along so they can be desensitized to promiscuous sex and physical violence.

All of the mass media of entertainment employ some artistic elements and some communicative elements, but these are employed only to enhance the money making value of the product. Art per se is not truth. It is a product of man's creativity or, as Aristotle said, "Art is contrary to nature."

Art is sometimes truthful, sometimes lies, and often does neither. Not only should we avoid setting art 'set apart' as some holy object to be venerated, we must stop setting the entertainment industry apart from God's Law as if it were beyond good and evil. Ignoring God's Law in the name of art, speech, or entertainment is the heresy of antinomianism (anti-law), which is abhorrent to God. Those who condone such lawlessness in the name of art are condoning the moral decay of our society.

Christians must resist the temptations of the world—the flesh and the devil—and stand up for what they believe. United we can influence the media elite by impacting the box office and the cash register.

GOD IS STILL IN CONTROL

Too many moral Americans believe we are facing overwhelming odds and unassailable power.

Paul Klein, former vice president of NBC, said, "Television is the most powerful force in the world today." Not even close. Television, nuclear power, Communism, capitalism, the United States, sin, Satan, man, and all other powers combined, pale in importance and potency to shadowy insignificance when compared to the power of God:

> "Through Him all things were made; without Him nothing was made that has been made."
>
> —John 1:3 NIV

Do not despair. God is in control. Trust in Him at all times.

The Answer

Jesus, of course, is the answer. He alone can deliver us from sin and death. Only the Sword of His Spirit, His written Word, can give us victory over the evil influences of this age.

Jesus was the master of communications. His dramatic parable word pictures are as pertinent today as they were 2,000 years ago. He understood the power of communications and how ideas shape civilizations. His Word toppled one of the most powerful civilizations in history, the Roman Empire, and continues to transform the world today.

We must care enough for Him and for our neighbor to communicate His gospel with power and love throughout the world and to take every thought captive for Him. We must learn the principles of powerful communication so that we can communicate the gospel through the mass media of entertainment to reach every man, woman, and child with the His Truth.

Furthermore, we must redeem the mass media of communications so that the good, the true, and the beautiful—not the vain, false, and evil imaginations are proclaimed through the mass media of entertainment throughout the world.

In obedience to His Word written, Christians need to reclaim the media for Christ by advancing on several fronts:

- We need to raise the consciousness of Christians to impact the industry.
- We need to lobby the television and motion picture companies to observe a code of decency so they can be inclusive, not exclusive, of the Christian audience.
- We need to witness to and disciple those in the mass media.
- We need to produce quality programming and motion pictures.

Help Stop Christophobia

One reason that there is so little evangelism and so much ignorance about the biblical worldview is the rampant growth of Christophobia in our society. Christophobia is a term coined here to refer to those who have an irrational fear of and hostility toward Jesus Christ and anything Christian.

The symptoms are quite simple and insidious. Some of the symptoms of this aberrant phobia include:

- An unhealthy fear of using the name of Jesus as anything but a profanity in public.
- A dread of discussing biblical principles in public.

- A horror that someone, including politicians and government officials, would expose or discuss his or her Christianity in public, much less put Christian principles into action.
- An aversion to using biblical standards to make decisions and to determine right and wrong in any given situation.
- A perverse fear of the Bible.

There are many more symptoms of this dysfunctional condition, and many other situations where Christophobia rears its ugly head in our society.

Christophobia rears its ugly bias all too frequently in our schools, media, and government institutions. For example:

- Christmas is now called Winter Holidays.
- Easter vacation is avoided by school systems, even if it means skewing school calendars to create unbalanced terms.
- Newspapers, radio stations, and television executives ask Christians to edit out any biblical references, while those who do are mocked and humiliated in print and on the public airwaves.
- Courts refuse to consider the biblical point-of-view.

This destructive phobia has spread throughout our culture to the extent that Christians are often the most Christophobic members of our society. These Christophobic Christians get livid when someone brings up a biblical perspective; apologize when the Name of Jesus is used in reverence; complain when Christians stand together; and worry that some Christians may be wearing their Christianity on their sleeves.

Often these fearful, Christophobic Christians fret about using biblical standards to determine right and wrong. They are horrified that these standards might be applied to common "problems" such as murder, adultery, lying, sodomy, homosexuality, and the other evils condemned by the Word of God.

If this phobia continues at its current pace, it will become the most debilitating psychological aberration of our age. Christophobia causes many to hide their Christianity, others to deny it, and still others to lash out at Christians. It may even inaugurate a widespread persecution of Christians and a denial of the Christian roots of our society. History will be revised to blame Christians for all the problems in the world. And the immorality condemned by the Bible will be acclaimed as the solution to our problems.

This abnormal psychological condition must be routed out of our national psyche before it is too late. Christians must help others understand the dysfunctional aspects of this disease. We must deliver those who suffer from it by introducing them to Jesus Christ and instructing them in the wholesome benefits of the biblical worldview.

Deliverance

There is a war raging around us, but not the one on the news. Rather, the war is a spiritual war being fought for the hearts and souls of each human being. The victory in this war is only to be found in Jesus Christ. In Christ, protection from powerful negative spirits begins with the awareness of the subtle effect that other individuals, groups and even the media often exert on us. Following such awareness, we need to recognize that He wants to, and will, deliver us from the demons of our age.

In addition, if we discover compromise in our lives, we need to repent, turn away from it, and seek the Lord with all our hearts. We also need to break off any associations not of God and renounce any ungodly spirits. Then we must avoid any further spiritual oppression by staying in the Word of God daily, walking in the Spirit of God and using the spiritual armor God has given us through Jesus Christ. Thus we can enjoy the provision Christ has made for us to walk in Him and not give way to the evil that surrounds us, for "greater is he that is in you than he that is in the world" (1 John 4:4 ASV).

Delivered from the judgment they deserve, those who know His salvation cannot keep on sinning, for "No one who continues to sin has either seen him or known him" (1 John 3:6 NIV).

Cast Your Vote

Once we are saved, redeemed and delivered, we need to exercise discernment in order to know the difference between good and evil. Discernment comes from seeking knowledge of God and understanding of God's Word, the Bible. However, there is more than discernment. As one young caller said to me on a radio program, "I have discernment, that's why I can see these vile movies." Therefore, the next step after discernment is wisdom, which means choosing the good and rejecting the bad.

This choice at the box office is known as patron sovereignty. Patron sovereignty has traditionally been commended by Hollywood as the right of movie patrons to determine what they want to see, or avoid, by their activity at the box office. In our free society we can again exercise our freedom to influence the motion picture industry to produce moral, uplifting movies. Despite widespread preferences that favor sex, violence and anti-Christian messages, the producers in Hollywood are ultimately concerned about the bottom line—how much money they can make at the box office. If Christians attend good films and avoid immoral films, our impact will be quickly felt in Hollywood.

The Adversary often convinces us that we are powerless—that there is not much we can do except complain, escape or avoid. The truth is that we have great power. We can change the nature of television and films.

TOOLS

Movieguide

We publish *Movieguide: A Biblical Guide to Movies and Entertainment* constantly on the Internet at www.movieguide.org. *Movieguide* gives you a detailed review of each movie so you can choose the movies to see and those to avoid. Each review provides a biblical perspective, enabling you to decide whether to go based on your biblical worldview.

Movieguide also equips you to confront ungodly communications and take every thought captive for Jesus Christ.

While some Christians choose not to watch any movies, more than two-thirds of the born-again, evangelical, and/or charismatic Christians watch what non-Christians watch. And many parents have written us saying they had no idea what their sons and daughters were watching until they consulted *Movieguide*. Now they talk about movies with their teenagers and discuss why they should not watch specific movies and videos. Other people thank us for making them aware of things they missed in a movie or video, which helped them be more discerning.

Movieguide is available on the Internet and World Wide Web at www.movieguide.org for those who want immediate information on movies and videotapes. It is reprinted in many Christian publications and is broadcast over the USA Radio Network. In addition, the Movieguide television program is telecast by many television stations, networks, and cable/satellite systems throughout the United States and in many countries.

Many teenagers tell us they did not notice the evil, bad, or abhorrent in many movies until they started reading *Movieguide*. Many say they turned from those films toward the Bible. Others say they gave up movies entirely.

Movieguide exists in five formats:

1. Movieguide **TV Program**—Featured on many net-

works and TV stations, *MOVIEGUIDE*® is broadcast all around the world and in the 50 states.

2. Movieguide **Online—www.movieguide.org** is available on the Internet.

3. Movieguide *Radio Program*—The program features capsule summaries and critiques of the latest movies and occasionally news and notes. It is available in two and five-minute versions. The program is produced every two weeks and delivered to participating radio stations free of charge. It is also available online.

4. Movieguide **Early Edition for Publishers**—Allows other publications to reprint its reviews in exchange for running a *Movieguide* advertisement, or paying a fee based on the size of readership. This version is produced every two weeks and is now available on the Internet. Those who do not have Internet access can still receive a printed version of our publisher's edition.

Books on Movies

The *Culture-wise Family* and *The Media-Wise Family* books teach you how movies, television, and other entertainment media influence your children. It helps you understand the way your children learn and what is appropriate viewing at different age levels. It also gives you skills, tools, and fun exercises you can do as a family to evaluate what you view and to help you use discernment in your media choices.

Beverly LaHaye notes, "Practical ways for parents to protect their children from inappropriate entertainment. . . . One of the best resources a parent can own."

"A Godsend to parents," adds Cal Thomas, nationally syndicated columnist.

Dean Jones says, "Required reading for anyone negotiating the mind fields of today's movies and television. . . an encouraging revelation. . . Four Stars!"

FRODO & HARRY: Understanding Visual Media and Its Impact On Our Lives, a comparison of *The Lord of the Rings* with *Harry Potter*, contrasts the fictional "real world" in *The Lord of the Rings* with the occult world of *Harry Potter* and gives guidelines on protecting your children against negative influences.

Good News

Good News Communications, Inc. and the Christian Film & Television Commission ministry have undertaken to re-establish the church's presence in Hollywood, and by God's grace, we are making a difference. In fact, we have seen great breakthroughs visible in the movies being released at the box office. Undergirded by the grace of God, the reasons we have had such success in Hollywood are five-fold:

1. We have been able to demonstrate through our extensive research to Hollywood executives that family films and clean mature-audience films do better at the box office.
2. As the audience gets older, which it will continue to do until the year 2012, it will move to more family fare in movies and television programs.
3. Many of the Hollywood executives and talent now have families and want to produce movies and programs their families can watch.
4. Many Hollywood executives and talent are now involved in their own causes and find it difficult to deny the influence of the media with regard to violence and sexual mores when they claim it influences people politically or environmentally.
5. Many Hollywood executives and talent are coming to know Jesus Christ as Lord and Savior and are going or returning to the Church.

Some of the Signs of Success as of 2010 Include:

- The number of movies with Christian, redemptive content reflecting a Christian biblical worldview has increased from 10.38% of the major movies released by Hollywood and the entertainment industry in 1991 to 54.51% in 2009, up from 47.8% in 2007.
- The number of movies with Christian, redemptive content has increased 425% since 1991.
- The number of movies with Christian, redemptive content has increased 20% in the last five years.
- The number of family-friendly movies has shown similar increases since Movieguide and its Annual Faith & Values Awards Gala and Report to the Entertainment Industry began in 1985 and 1992–93, respectively.
- Movies with very strong Christian and redemptive worldviews averaged $65.3 million per movie in North America from 2005 through 2009, but movies with very strong negative or anti-Christian worldviews only averaged $23 million during that time.
- The average earnings of movies with very strong Christian and redemptive worldviews have increased from only $21.14 million per movie for movies released in 1995 to $80.03 million per movie for those released in 2009.
- Movies with very strong Christian and redemptive worldviews averaged $73.56 million for movies released in 2008 but climbed to $80.03 million for movies released in 2009.
- R-rated movies among the Top 25 at the Box Office in North America have decreased from 12 in 1996 to only two in 2009.
- Movies with a strong or very strong moral worldviews or very strong Christian worldviews in the Top 25 have

increased from only three movies in 1996 to 18 movies in 2009, a 500% increase!

- Movies marketed to teens have shown a steady decrease in the amount of foul language, from 35 obscenities per movie in the 1980s to 25 in the 1990s to 16 from 2000 through 2009.
- Movies with little or no foul language (0–9 obscenities and/or profanities) have increased from 21% of the market in 1996 to 34.60% of the market in 2009.
- Movies with no depicted sex have increased from 58.57% of the market in 1996 to 63.18% of the market in 2009.
- Movies with no explicit sexual nudity have increased from 61.43% in 1996 to 73.29% in 2009.
- Since Movieguide began awarding the $200,000 Epiphany Prizes for Inspiring Movies & TV in 1996 at the Annual Faith & Values Awards Gala and Report to the Entertainment Industry, movies with very strong Christian and redemptive worldviews make the most amount of money by far at the box office, by 2.5 times to more than 7 times more money than movies with very strong negative content.
- The most family-friendly movies also make the most money by far when compared to the least family-friendly movies (see Movieguide's recent Annual Reports to the Entertainment Industry).
- Overseas, year in and year out, about 80% of the Top 25 Movies at the Box Office have either strong or very strong Christian, biblical, moral, and/or redemptive content.
- On home video, year in and year out, 70% to 90% of the Top 10 and Top 20 Home Video Sales have either strong or very strong Christian, biblical, moral, and/or redemptive content. And, the majority of them tend to be Movieguide Award winners as well as family movies marketed to children and/or teenagers.

- The number of unique monthly visitors to the Movieguide website, www.movieguide.org, has increased from an average of about 40,000 unique visitors to more than 360,000 such visitors in the last year! Our articles and reviews are also distributed to more than 10 million visitors on other websites.

Many top executives and producers met with us to learn more about broad audience movies and programs. To help encourage more godly movies and television programs, the late philanthropist Sir John Templeton appointed Movieguide and the Christian Film & Television Commission to present a cash Epiphany Prize for the "Most Inspiring Movie" and the "Most Inspiring Television Program." Doors to the most important offices in Hollywood have been opened and evidence mounts that a powerful sea of change is occurring in the entertainment industry at the very highest levels. Though pessimistic voices say the golden age of Christianity is over and suggest the Christian faith is being replaced by Islam and other beliefs, Christianity is the world's fastest growing religion. It is growing faster than the world's population.

The Lausanne Statistics Task Force reports the ratio of non-Christians to Bible-believing Christians now stands 6.8 to one, the lowest ratio in history. The evangelical movement, worldwide, is growing three times faster than the world's population.

While the mass media of entertainment tries to associate Christians with rednecks and rubes, the Barna Research Group says church attendance increases with education.

What Will Happen?

We will continue to make an impact on the entertainment industry, encouraging production of positive, morally uplifting films and television programs. We will continue to help the heads of the entertainment companies understand the issues involved. And, we will help more Christians develop discernment.

Despite those who rail against biblical values, the work of Movieguide and the Christian Film & Television Commission ministry will have a lasting effect on the mass media of entertainment. It has already caused many of those who fashion the popular culture to shift their perspective and reevaluate their relationships.

The bottom line is that, through this proven strategy, the United States of America may truly become a kinder, gentler nation.

Communicate with Power

Another key to winning the culture war is to equip Christians to produce successful mass media products. Throughout history, the church used drama to communicate the gospel. We need to reclaim the power of dramatic communications by producing quality television programs, films, and radio programs. To do so we need to learn and apply the principles of powerful communication.

To produce these good movies and television programs, Christians are going to have to take up scriptwriting and learn that craft much better than the hacks in Hollywood. That means not only learning the principles of powerful communication but also refining the craft, paying one's dues, and going the extra mile.

Christians often want to short circuit the process of learning how to communicate with power by appealing to their friends with money on the basis of shared ideological goals. The result is a mediocre, embarrassing movie—because the scriptwriter, director, or producer has cut short the refinement process necessary to perfecting a script— or they aim the movie at their backers instead of the audience.

Be Approved

The greatest communicators of the gospel of our age have learned the principles of powerful communication. You can do the same if not better. However, it takes work. You must master the principles of powerful communication. God is more concerned with our character than our accomplishments. He will patiently work on us until we are ready to fulfill the mission He has given us.

The great missionary/explorer Dr. Livingstone left England for Africa at a young age to bring the gospel to the Dark Continent and to deliver the people of Africa from the slave trade. He preached every day for years with little success. He suffered malaria attacks more than sixty times and lost the use of one of his arms to a lion while rescuing a black friend. Then he disappeared into the uncharted jungle.

A brash reporter named Stanley was sent to find Dr. Livingstone. After one year, by the grace of God, he found Livingstone being cared for by the slave traders he had come to destroy. While on his deathbed, Livingstone introduced the reporter to Jesus Christ. Stanley's articles opened up Africa to the missionaries and within three years, the King of Portugal signed an edict abolishing the slave trade. All Livingstone had set out to do was accomplished, but first he had to become the humble man of character who could serve as a vessel for the pure gospel of Jesus Christ. In a similar manner, you must first submit to Him before you can reach the world with the good news of His salvation.

ARE YOU ON GOD'S SIDE?

In the midst of the worst fighting of the Civil War, Abraham Lincoln was approached by a minister who said, "Mr. President, I hope that the Lord is on your side."

Lincoln replied, "I hope not."

The minister was shocked.

Lincoln explained, "I pray that I am on the Lord's side."

Let us all pray that we are on God's side and that He does His will in and through us to the honor and glory of His Holy Name.

WHAT YOU CAN DO

Become informed about what is happening in Hollywood and the media by subscribing to Movieguide and other publications that give you information from a biblical perspective.

Spend your entertainment dollars wisely. Every time you buy a movie ticket, it is a vote to the producer to make more of the same. Cast an informed vote.

Voice your concerns to those responsible. Write to producers, distributors, and sponsors. The only way they will know your objections is if you tell them. (Movieguide gives you those names and addresses.)

Become a member of the Christian Film & Television Commission ministry by sending us your name, address, and email, so that we can increase our clout in Hollywood and the mass media.

For more information, call or email:
Movieguide
Christian Film & Television Commission
2510–G Las Posas Road, Suite 502
Camarillo, CA 93010
(805) 383–2000
ted@movieguide.org

Epilogue

So whoever believes the word of God has this testimony in his own heart; but whosoever does not
believe God, has made a liar of him, because he has
not believed what God has said about his Son. The
testimony is this: God has given us eternal life, and
this life has its source in his Son. Whoever has the Son
has life; whoever does not have the Son of God does
not have life; whoever does not have the Son of God
does not have life.

—1 John 5:10–12

GLOSSARY

Ambient sound: background sounds

Audio: any kind of sound in a film or video

Base light: the existing amount of light in a room

Cast: the actors in a film

Close-tip (CU): a very close shot of something—usually a person's face or some other object

Composition: the positioning of people and objects in the frame

Continuity: the art of maintaining consistency from shot-to-shot and scene-to-scene, or shooting in sequence

Coverage: a shot used by the editor to break up the action

Crew: the technical people working on a movie

Cutaway: an abrupt cut away from the scene to something else or to a new scene

Dailies/Rushes: the film shot during one day of shooting

Dialogue: a conversation between actors

Dissolve: when the end of one shot fades into the next one

Edit: to assemble a film by cutting and repositioning the shots

Establishing shot: shows the audience a wide shot of the setting

Extreme close-up (XCU): a really close shot

Extreme long shot: taken from a great distance

Eye–level angle shot: shot at eye level

Fade: when the end of a shot darkens into a black screen and then fades up

Final cut: the final edited film

High angle shot: higher than subject

High contrast: when the tones of color, or black and white, are more extreme

Hook: an enticing beginning of a movie that sets the tone

Illumination: the amount and quality of light on a subject

Lamp: a special light used for photography or cinematography

Lighting: the method of illuminating a shot

Long shot: taken from a longer distance, giving slightly more details than the extreme

Low-angle shot: subject is above the camera

Lyricists: people who write the words (the lyrics) to songs

Medium close-up: a shot of a person from the waist up

Montage: editing many images rapidly together

Narration: the off–screen voice of the observer-commentator

Object: things in a shot that are not people

Pan: moving the camera from side-to-side

Pick-up shot/scene: a shot that is added after the editing phase

Props: objects in a scene that decorate the set or objects that an actor uses

Real time: a shot or scene filmed in actual time

Score: adding music to the movie

Sequence: number of scenes taken together

Set: the place, created or pre-existing, where a scene is shot

Set up: each time the camera position is changed

SFX/Sound effects: sounds created to mimic objects or subjects in a film

Shot: the smallest unit of film taken in one uninterrupted process of the camera

Sound glitch: unwanted sound on the film footage

Storyboard: a shot-by-shot layout drawn before shooting or editing the scene

Subject: a person in a shot

Superimposition: when two images are shown one on top of the other

Tilt: moving the camera up and down

Voice over: when the invisible narrator speaks

Zoom: moving in on an object from a wider shot to a closer one

NOTES

1 George Barna, "Americans Draw Theological Beliefs From Diverse Points of View," The Barna Group (October 2002): http://www. barna.org/barna-update/article/5-barna-update/82-americans-draw-theological-beliefs-from-diverse-points-of-view.

2 Ibid.

3 Richard H. Niebuhr, *Christ and Culture* (London: Faber and Faber, 1952).

4 The Coalition on Revival, Inc.

5 Noam Chomsky, *Language and Responsibility* (New York: Pantheon Books, 1979).

6 The Holy Bible New International Version (Zondervan), Acts 11:26, 26:28; and 1 Peter 4:16.

7 Ephesians 2:9.

8 Proverbs 6:6 and Romans 12:11.

9 1 Peter 4:11.

10 King James Bible, John 1:14.

11 Also note that each medium is composed of one or more tools from pencil and paper which compose a note to the sophisticated cameras, recorders, editing machines, satellites, and other hardware and software which are necessary to produce and broadcast a television program.

12 The Holy Bible New International Version (Zondervan), Matthew 5:9.

13 Luke 6:20.

14 Leviticus 25:23.

15 Years later, I found out that there was an excellent film at the Protestant Exhibit. But, at the time of the New York Fair, the existence of that film was hidden from some of the visitors by the solemn atmosphere of the primary room, which was the first room a visitor entered.

16 Including animators, architects, artists, audio engineers, builders, choirs, composers, computer programmers, contractors, directors, electrical contractors, exhibit designers, engineers, film producers, lighting designers, music producers, photographers, production assistants, sensory effect producers, sound producers, video producers, and writers.

17 The African Methodist Episcopal Church, The African Methodist Episcopal Zion Church, The Christian Church (Disciples of Christ), The Christian Methodist Episcopal Church, The Church of the Brethren, The Church of God, Cleveland, TN., The Church of God, Mountain Assembly, The Cumberland Presbyterian Church, The Episcopal Church, The Greek Orthodox Archdiocese of North and South America, The Lutheran Church in America, Presbyterian Church in the U.S., The Roman Catholic Church, The United Methodist Church, and The United Presbyterian Church.

18 Romans 10:14–15.

19 Matthew 4:19, 28:19; Luke 24:47; and Acts 1:8.

20 1 Corinthians 3:9.

21 John 14:26. Also see Chapter 13 for more information.

22 John 3:5–8.

23 Matthew 10:32-33; Revelation 3:1, 3:15–16.

24 The Public Broadcasting Service.

25 1 Corinthians 5–6.

26 2 Timothy 4:2 and Titus 2.

27 John 14:12–21; 2 Corinthians 9:6ff.

28 Matthew 5:42 and 10:8.

29 I was nominated for an Emmy Award for hosting a program on *War and Peace.*

30 In fact, PBS carries a great deal of religious programming, and Christians should use PBS more often. On the other hand, some member stations do not carry religious programming.

31 In telecommunications, radio, and television, the gatekeeper is the individual or corporation who controls access to the use of the channel or medium of communication.

32 John Donne, *Devotions.*

33 William Wordsworth, "My Heart Leaps Up."

34 David Puttnam, "Hard Cash: How to Finance Independent Films." (Los Angeles: Independent Feature Project, 1982).

35 Johannes Heinrichs, "Theory of Practical Communication: A

Christian Approach," *Journal of the World Association for Christian Communication*, vol. XXVIII (1981): 6.

36 Pasolini, a well known Italian film director and committed Communist, did not give an ideological interpretation of the life of Christ in this film, but adhered closely to the spirit and the facts of the gospel.

37 Abraham Harold Maslow, *Motivation and Personality* (New York: Harper, 1954).

38 William Shakespeare, *Hamlet*.

39 Lajos Egri, *The Art of Dramatic Writing* (New York: Simon & Schuster, 1960), 32.

40 Romans 13:1; 1 Corinthians 12; and Colossians 1:16.

41 In *Career Satisfaction and Success: A Guide to Job Freedom* by Bernard Haldane, one of the pioneers in career counseling, and *What Color Is Your Parachute?* By Richard Bolles, you can find some very simple, do-it-yourself guides, charts, and tools to help you discern your motivational talents. I highly recommend these books if you are interested in in-depth career counseling or self-discovery.

42 Richard Bolles, *What Color Is Your Parachute?* (Berkeley, CA: Ten Speed Press, 2003), 83.

43 Hal Lancaster, "Hey Fans! It Was Some Kinda Action, A Real Barnburner!" *The Wall Street Journal*, Vol. CCIV, No. 108 (December 3, 1984), 1, 24.

44 Kathryn Morton, "The Story-Telling Animal," *The New York Times Book Review* (December 23, 1984), 2.

45 Gary Smalley and John Trent, *The Language of Love*. (Pomona, CA: Focus on the Family, 1988), 20.

46 Stewart M. Hoover, "Television and Viewer Attitudes About Work." The Annenberg School of Communications (April 10, 1981).

47 Paul Johnson, *Modern Times: The World from the Twenties to the Nineties* (New York, NY: Harper Perennial, 1992), 130.

48 Gerhard Rempel, *Hitler's Children: The Hitler Youth and the SS* (Chapel Hill and London: The University of North Carolina Press, 1989), 76.

49 Egri, *The Art of Dramatic Writing*, 263.

50 Ibid., 6.

51 Northrop Frye, *Anatomy of Criticism* (New York: Atheneum, 1968).

52 George Gerbner, "Television As Religion," *Media & Values* (Fall, 1981).

53 Rene Wellek and Austin Warren, *Theory of Literature* (New York: Harcourt, Brace & World, 1956), 226–237.

54 Rudolf Flesch, *The Art of Readable Writing* (New York: Harper & Row, 1949), 46.

55 For commercials, a rough correlation between number of words in a script and length is: 10 second = about 25 words; 30 second = about 65 words; 1 minute = about 125 words. Of course, there may be fewer words in the script depending on music, visuals, and action content.

56 This commercial was produced for the Episcopal Church. The actual script is much longer.

57 V.O. indicates an unseen voice over the picture.

58 A great introduction to scripting for television is Robert L Hilliard's book, *Writing for Television and Radio* (New York: Hastings House, Publishers, 1976).

59 Directors Guild of America: The Artists Rights Foundation, *Making a Movie: A Guide for Young Filmmakers* (Los Angeles: DGA, 2001), 26.

60 "My Palikari," starring Telly Savalis and produced by The Center for Television in the Humanities, played on PBS, HBO, SHOWTIME, and The Disney Channel.

61 b.g. is an abbreviation for background.

62 Mario Vargas Llosa, "Is Fiction the Art of Lying?" *The New York Times Book Review* (October 7, 1984), 1, 40.

63 James Scott Bell is a writer and novelist in Los Angeles. This article originally ran as an op-ed piece in the *The Los Angeles Times* on October 19, 2002. It is reprinted with the permission of the author.

64 Ibid.

65 Jim Impoco, "TV's Frisky Family Values," *U.S. News & World Report* (April 15, 1996), 58–62.

66 Ibid.

67 Michael Medved, "Hollywood's 3 Big Lies," *Movieguide*, Vol. XI, No. 1.

68 *Movieguide,* Vol. IX, No. 3, 4.

69 See: Jean Piaget, *The Origins of Intelligence in Children* (W.W. Norton Co., 1963), and David Elkind *Children and Adolescents: Interpretive Essays on Jean Piaget* (Oxford University Press, 1970).

70 Which Piaget called the sensorimotor period.

71 Which Piaget called the preoperational period.

72 Barbara J. Wilson, Daniel Lynn, and Barbara Randall, "Applying Social Science Research to Film Ratings: A Shift from Offensiveness to Harmful Effects," *Journal of Broadcasting and Electronic Media*, 24, No. 4.

73 C. Hoffner and J. Cantor, "Developmental Differences in Responses to a Television Character's Appearance and Behavior," *Developmental Psychology* (1985), 21, 1065–1074.

74 P. Morison and H. Gardner, "Dragons and Dinosaurs: The Child's Capacity to Differentiate Fantasy from Reality," *Child Development* (1978), 49, 642–648.

75 G.G. Sparks, "Developmental Differences in Children's Reports of Fear Induced by Mass Media," *Child Study Journal* (1986), 16, 55–66.

76 W.A. Collins, "Interpretation and Inference in Children's Television Viewing," Children's Understanding of Television: Research on Attention and Comprehension (New York: Academic Press, 1983),125–150.

77 G. Comstock and H.J. Paik, *Television and Children: A Review of Recent Research*, Report No. XX, (Syracuse, N.Y.: Syracuse University, 1987).

78 Ibid.

79 A. Bandura, "Influence of Models' Reinforcement Contingencies on the Acquisition of Imitative Responses," 589–595.

80 Ibid.

81 Potter & Ware, 1987.

82 "Influence of Models' Reinforcement Contingencies on the Acquisition of Imitative Responses," 589-595.

83 W.A. Collins, "Interpretation and Inference in Children's Television Viewing," *Children's Understanding of Television: Research on Attention and Comprehension* (New York: Academic Press, 1983), 125–150.

84 C.K. Atkin, "Effects of Realistic TV Violence vs. Fictional Violence on Aggression," *Journalism Quarterly* (1983) 60, 615–621; S. Feshbach, "The Role of Fantasy in the Response to Television, *Journal of Social Issues* (1976) 32, 71–85.

85 A. Bandura, *Social Foundations of Thought and Action: A Social Cognitive Theory* (Englewood Cliffs, NJ: Prentice-Hall, 1986).

86 Ibid. citing Huesmann, L.R., Lagerspetz, K., and Eron, L.D., "Intervening Variables in the TV Violence-Aggression Relation: Evidence from Two Countries," *Developmental Psychology* (1984) 20, 746–775.

87 "Interpretation and Inference in Children's Television Viewing," 125–150.

88 Berkowtiz, L., "Some Aspects of Observed Aggression," *Journal of Personality and Social Psychology* (1965), Vol. 2, 359–369; T.P.

Meyer, "Effects of Viewing Justified and Unjustified Real Film Violence on Aggressive Behavior," *Journal of Personality and Social Pscyhology* (1972), 23, 21–29.

89 Liss, M.A., Reinhardt, L.C., Fredrickesen, S., "TV Heroes: The Impact of Rhetoric and Deeds," *Journal of Applied Developmental Psychology* (1983), 175–187.

90 Ibid.

91 Bandura, A., *Social Foundations of Thought and Action: A Social Cognitive Theory* (Englewood Cliffs, NJ: Prentice-Hall, 1986).

92 Ibid.

93 Ibid.

94 Cline, V.B., Croft, R.G. & Courrier, S., "Desensitization of Children to Television Violence," *Journal of Personality and Social Psychology* (1973).

95 William J. Bennett, "Quantifying America's Decline," *Wall Street Journal*, March 15, 1993.

96 *Movieguide*, Volume VII, No. 3.

97 According to a 1994 UCLA Center for Communication Policy/*U.S. News and World Report* survey mailed to 6,300 decision-makers in the entertainment industry, receiving a 13.76% response.

98 For more information, see Chapter 2.

99 *The New York Guardian*, Dec. 1993.

100 Movieguide Volume VII#10: 920522

101 John Grisham, "Unnatural Killers," *Movieguide*, Vol XI, No. 18.

102 Paul Tillich, *Christianity and the Encounter of the World Religions* (New York: Columbia University Press, 1963), Chapter 1.

103 J.M. Barrie, "Kate, in the Twelve-Pound Look," (1910).

104 1934 Communications Act.

105 Prior to my presidency.

106 Note that these rules of thumb are very rough guidelines which may vary a great deal from the actual rights and percentage of profits a producer gives up depending on track record, negotiating strength, the nature of the program, time, and the state of the television industry.

107 Gels are transparent colored sheets that go in front of your lights to adjust color temperature and create mood.

108 Off-line time is time reviewing the videotape on a less expensive VTR, and any time where you are not on the line of full production with its heavy expense.

109 Martha Bayles, "A Passage Through India," *The Wall Street Journal* (December 17, 1984), 32.

110 Judges 12:5–6.
111 Robert Price, "Running on the Record," *The New York Times* (February 17, 1985), 6E.

INDEX